Observing Development of the Young Child

Observing Development of the Young Child

Eighth Edition

JANICE J. BEATY

Professor Emerita, Elmira College

PEARSON

Boston   Columbus   Indianapolis   New York   San Francisco   Upper Saddle River
Amsterdam Cape Town   Dubai   London   Madrid   Milan   Munich   Paris   Montreal   Toronto
Delhi   Mexico City   São Paulo   Sydney   Hong Kong   Seoul   Singapore   Taipei   Tokyo

Vice President and Editorial Director: Jeffery W. Johnston
Senior Acquisitions Editor: Julie Peters
Editorial Assistant: Andrea Hall
Vice President, Director of Marketing: Margaret Waples
Marketing Manager: Christopher D. Barry
Senior Managing Editor: Pamela D. Bennett
Project Manager: Sheryl Langner
Production Manager: Laura Messerly

Senior Art Director: Jayne Conte
Cover Designer: Bruce Kenselaar
Cover Art: Missouri Association for Community Action, Inc.
Full-Service Project Management: Nitin Agarwal/Aptara®, Inc.
Composition: Aptara®, Inc.
Printer/Binder: LSC Communications, Inc.
Cover Printer: LSC Communications, Inc.
Text Font: Optima LT Std

Photo Credits: All photos by Janice J. Beaty.

Credits and acknowledgments for materials borrowed from other sources and reproduced, with permission, in this textbook appear on the appropriate page within the text.

Every effort has been made to provide accurate and current Internet information in this book. However, the Internet and information posted on it are constantly changing, so it is inevitable that some of the Internet addresses listed in this textbook will change.

Library of Congress Cataloging-in-Publication Data

Beaty, Janice J.
  Observing development of the young child / Janice J. Beaty, Professor
Emerita, Elmira College. —Eighth Edition.
    pages cm
  ISBN-13: 978-0-13-286756-6
  ISBN-10: 0-13-286756-7
  1. Child development.   2. Observation (Educational method)
3. Education, Preschool.   4. Preschool teachers—Training of.   I. Title.
  LB1115.B32 2014
  305.233—dc23

                    2012036305

ISBN 10:   0-13-286756-7
ISBN 13: 978-0-13-286756-6

20 2019

In memory of my mother and father

About the Author

Janice J. Beaty, professor emerita, Elmira College, Elmira, New York, is a full-time writer of early childhood college textbooks and a consultant in early childhood education from her home in Cape Coral, Florida. Her textbooks include *Skills for Preschool Teachers,* Ninth Edition; *50 Early Childhood Literacy Strategies*, Third Edition; *Early Literacy in Preschool and Kindergarten*, Third Edition with Linda Pratt, and *50 Early Childhood Guidance Strategies*. She is also engaged in a literacy mentoring program with the Foster Grandparents Program in Columbia, Missouri.

Preface

*O*bserving Development of the Young Child* presents a unique system for observing and recording development of children ages 3 to 5 in early childhood classroom settings. It is based on a progression of children's skill development in six major domains. The text is designed for use by college students preparing to be teachers in prekindergarten programs, child care centers, Head Start classes, and preschools. The book can also be used in such programs by the teachers and assistant teachers who want to learn more about children in order to make individual learning plans, as well as for making assessments of individual children for program development. Staff members preparing for Child Development Associate (CDA) Assessment will also find this text helpful with its suggestions for classroom activities that are developmentally appropriate for young children. The text not only teaches readers how to observe, record, and interpret development of children 3 through 5 years of age, but also discusses what these children are like and how to support them in their development with exciting hands-on activities.

The text focuses on six major domains of child development—emotional, social, physical, cognitive, language, and creative—that are readily observable. It divides each of these aspects further into specific areas: self-esteem; emotional competence; social competence; physical development; cognitive development; spoken language; emergent writing and reading skills; art, music, and dance skills; and dramatic play skills. The principal observation tool to be used is the Child Development Checklist. Other observation methods and tools include anecdotal records, running records, samplings, rating scales, rubrics, audio and visual documentation, and document panels.

Finally, teachers learn to share their observational data with children's families. The text serves college students as a guide for observing and recording development of young children in their student teaching and coursework. The text is especially well suited as a supplementary text for child development courses. It also can help in-service teachers and assistants who are upgrading their skills in observing children, as well as those who are learning to plan for individuals based on their developmental needs.

Unique aspects of *Observing Development of the Young Child* include discussions of how to *observe* young children, how to *interpret* the data recorded, and how to *plan* for individuals based on the observations. Important topics include children's emotional development, how young children make friends, how to deal with bullying, how to help second-language speakers learn English, how children use exploratory play to learn, how to help young children emerge into reading and writing, and how to develop children's creativity through art, music, and dramatic play.

✓ NEW TO THE EIGHTH EDITION

This edition has been reorganized to broaden the coverage of observation and to make it more concise and accessible. Among its key changes are the following:

- Chapters 1 and 2 were reorganized to deepen and expand the coverage of basic observation methods.
- The former edition's chapters on large-motor development and small-motor development were combined into a new streamlined chapter on physical development.
- New Learning Outcomes were added to each chapter.
- Many more boxed features help to clarify ideas.
- New sections in domain chapters explaining benefits of using particular observing and recording tools for a particular domain.
- Chapter by chapter changes include the following:

Chapter 1   Observing to Assess Children's Development
Revised Child Development Checklist
Standardized tests as tools for assessment
Developmental screening
NAEYC program criteria
Portfolios for assessment
How to become an observer

Chapter 2   Recording and Collecting Observational Data
Using rubrics
Using Learning Prescriptions

Chapter 3   Self-Esteem
Playing without fear of bullying
Books about bullying

Chapter 4   Emotional Competence
Building emotional competence
Emotional literacy
Affective joy; cognitive joy

Chapter 5   Social Competence
Play and neuroscience research

Brain scan evidence
Strategies for gaining access to group play

Chapter 6   Physical Development

Combination of previous chapters on large-motor development and small-motor development
More vigorous playground exercise
Large-motor skills rating scale
Running skills rating scale

Chapter 7   Cognitive Development

Brain imagining; brain development
Making thinking visible
Using document panels
Recording dramatic play scenarios

Chapter 8   Spoken Language

Dual language learners
Books to promote speaking aloud
Telephone conversations
Documenting conversations

Chapter 9   Emergent Writing and Reading Skills

Dual language learners; readers
Writing Skills Checklist; Reading Skills Checklist
Name-Writing Rubric; Book-Handling Rubric
Books on CDs
Scaffolded readings

Chapter 10   Art, Music, and Dance Skills

Observation of creativity
Drawing Skills Checklist
Music and disabilities
Singing and literacy
Developing dance skills; checklist

Chapter 11   Dramatic Play Skills

Children who do not know how to play
Scaffolding dramatic play
Culturally diverse props
Prosocial superheroes

Chapter 12 Sharing Observational Data with Families

Parent outcomes of shared observations

Collaborative portfolios

✓ CHECKLISTS FOR OBSERVING AND RECORDING

Child Development Checklist

Vigorous Playground Exercise

Large-Motor Skills Rating Scale

Running Skills Rating Scale

Large-Motor Checklist

Small-Motor Checklist

Writing Skills Checklist

Reading Skills Checklist

Drawing Skills Checklist

Music and Dance Skills Checklist

✓ USE AS A COMPANION TEXT

This eighth edition of *Observing Development of the Young Child* is designed to be used as a companion volume with the author's text *Skills for Preschool Teachers,* Ninth Edition (Pearson, 2012). While *Observing Development of the Young Child* is intended as a child development text, the companion volume—*Skills for Preschool Teachers*—is a teacher development text focusing on 13 areas of teacher competencies.

Like this text, *Skills for Preschool Teachers* is also based on an observational checklist, the Teacher Skills Checklist, which documents teacher competencies in the 13 Child Development Associate (CDA) "functional areas": safe, healthy, learning environment, physical, cognitive, communication, creative, self, social, guidance, families, program management, and professional.

Together, the two texts form a cohesive, complete training program for preservice teachers, beginning teachers, and in-service teachers preparing for the CDA credential. Preservice teachers can use these complementary texts as especially effective guidance in their student teaching field experiences. Both books focus on positive behaviors in children and teachers. Both the development of children and the training of teachers look at "areas of strength and confidence" and "areas needing strengthening" to set up individualized training plans.

✓ ACKNOWLEDGMENTS

My special thanks for the new edition of this text goes to the directors, teachers, parents, and children of Tiger Paws Head Start, Park Avenue Head Start, and Trinity Lutheran Child Learning Center in Columbia, Missouri, with thanks to its director, Gail Schuster. It is always inspiring for me to visit these fine programs and photograph the children as they work and play together, developing their own unique selves.

Ann Gilchrist, director of the Central Missouri Foster Grandparents Program, once again deserves my gratitude for setting up my observations in these centers and allowing me to participate with her grandparents who have given so much of themselves to the young children in these programs. My appreciation also goes to Elaine West, executive director of the Missouri Association for Community Action, Inc., for allowing me to use some of the exciting children's art created for the annual MACA calendar; to my editor, Julie Peters, for her guidance and encouragement; and finally to the following reviewers of the text: Mary L. Flyr, Riverside City College, and Amanda Quesenberry, Illinois State University.

Brief Contents

Contents

2 Recording and Collecting Observational Data   26

3 Self-Esteem   52

4 Emotional Competence   77

7 Cognitive Development   161

8 Spoken Language   197

9 Emergent Writing and Reading Skills   225

10 Art, Music, and Dance Skills   254

11 Dramatic Play Skills   284

12 Sharing Observational Data with Families   314

CHAPTER 1

Observing to Assess Children's Development

In this chapter you will learn to:

____ Explain why observation is the most useful and meaningful way to assess young children's development

____ Describe a specific standardized test and explain how it can be used in an assessment

____ Explain in detail how certain tests present problems as assessment instruments and how teachers can help overcome their limitations

____ Gather data for a child through alternative methods such as child interviews, visual documentation, document panels, or portfolios

____ Become an observer by following the steps in systematic observation

____ Demonstrate that you "see" a child using all your senses

Most teachers of young children love to watch the children in their classrooms as they work and play together or apart. Which ones are excited about the activities? Who has found a new buddy to play with? Which one stands around and watches? As the days progress, so do the children, growing taller, speaking clearer, showing sparks of creativity never before revealed. And you are witnessing it all with wonder.

1

Such observations of children are more than just pleasurable these days. They are more than just the way to get to know the children. They have become an important component of your teaching duties. Observing children in early childhood classrooms has taken top priority in programs across the nation in order to determine child progress, curriculum requirements, and program effectiveness. Such progress and effectiveness needs to be measured—assessed—in a careful, comprehensive manner. Children can be tested, interviewed, compared with others, or asked to perform. But the most useful and meaningful way to assess young children is through observation.

☑ ASSESSMENT THROUGH OBSERVATION

As early childhood professionals, we have found that in most instances the best method to determine a child's strengths is *for the teacher to observe the young child in the regular classroom based on a particular set of criteria*. Early childhood specialist Seefeldt (1998) agreed when she talked about how observations reveal much about children's growth and development, their perceptions of self and others, patterns of behavior, and their strengths and weaknesses, as well as the fact that they take place naturally and spontaneously (p. 316). This is known as **authentic assessment** because the children are behaving in a natural manner in a normal setting.

We have chosen observation of child development to determine children's progress. Wortham (2012) notes that one of the most valuable ways to become aware of the individual characteristics of young children is through observation. **Developmental indicators** in early childhood are more likely to be noted from children's behavior in natural circumstances than from a designed assessment or instrument.

Observation might not work so well with an older child, but it is eminently suited to a preschooler. Because young children are unable to express themselves

Knowing the development of a child helps teachers plan the curriculum.

Figure 1.1 How Child
Development Occurs

- Development is continuous.
- Development occurs in a certain order.
- Development occurs in stages or sequences.
- All children go through every stage.
- Each child's rate of development may differ.
- Each child's development depends on age, maturity, and experience.

fully with words, direct observations are the next best thing. Preschoolers reveal themselves through their behavior because, unlike older children, young children are really incapable of hiding their feelings.

Observing Child Development

Knowing the development of a young child helps a teacher to plan the curriculum, to set up activities for individuals, or to ask for special help when necessary. Wortham (2012) talks about development as a process of change in an individual over time.

We realize that all children grow and change. Some do it more rapidly than others. Some do it more slowly. This change is affected by the child's age, the child's rate of maturity, and the child's experiences. Thus children of the same age may not be at the same level of development. Their rate of **maturity** may be different. Their life experiences may be different. But their development, nevertheless, is continuous. It occurs in certain stages or sequences. All children everywhere go through these same stages and in the same order—but not at the same rate. Most important for us as child observers: *These stages can be observed.* We are able to tell where a child stands in his or her development by observing the stage or sequence the child is in. Then as teachers we are able to provide activities that will help the child progress. Figure 1.1 shows how child development occurs.

Once you know the stages or sequences of the various **domains** of child development, you will be able to make sense of the assessment of children that is currently required of us as teachers. What is the purpose for such child observation? A number of researchers have noted two principal ways for using the data obtained:

- For **curriculum planning**
- For **child assessment**

For Curriculum Planning

To make daily and long-term curriculum plans for the children, you will need to know how the child is progressing in the domains listed in Figure 1.2.

Although we treat these domains separately, young children's development occurs in all of them simultaneously. To set up activities in the various curriculum

Figure 1.2 Child
Development Domains

Child Development Domains
- Emotional development
- Social development
- Physical development
- Cognitive development
- Language development
- Creative development

centers of the classroom that will help children progress, you will need to know where a child stands in each of these developmental areas. How will you do it? The most appropriate method we have discovered is by observing each child in a regular, continuous, systematic manner. By observing each child, you will be able to gather the necessary data to help you plan your daily and long-range program.

For Child Assessment

Assessment is the process by which teachers collect information about a child's capabilities. Teachers look at children's skill levels, interests, strengths, and weaknesses. McAfee and Leong (2011) include tests, observations, interviews, reports from knowledgeable sources, and almost any form of measurement and appraisal of what children know and can do as being assessment. Here we focus on classroom assessment of children's development ages 3 through 5.

Other terms connected with classroom assessment include **formative assessment**, the gathering of information to help in the formation of an instructional program, and **summative assessment**, the evaluation done at the end of a period of time, for example, the school year. McAfee and Leong stress it is important that assessment be aligned with a program's curriculum and expected outcomes. Although tests may require children to perform on demand, assessment should be measuring what children have gained through a particular curriculum.

Assessment of preschool children is a current issue of great importance and concern for early childhood educators. Most programs are now required to provide data about children's outcomes. Programs for young children have always attempted to determine children's needs and to evaluate their accomplishments, sometimes successfully, sometimes not. The number of instruments currently available for assessing the learning, progress, and behavior of preschool children is mind-boggling. Literally hundreds of instruments and procedures have come into use in the past 20 years. Behavior rating scales, tests of visual perception, performance inventories, developmental profiles, portfolios, language batteries, self-concept screening devices, social competence scales, sociometric tests, personality inventories, pictorial intelligence tests, case studies, developmental screening tests, performance-based interviews, and video or audio recordings are only a few.

The Child Development Checklist

We have developed a tool called the Child Development Checklist for students of child development and teachers of young children ages 3 through 5 for informally observing and recording children's natural development. It is a recording tool that can help observers determine where each child stands in the six areas of emotional, social, physical, cognitive, language, and creative development. (See Table 1.1.)

All children go through an observable sequence of development. From large- to small-motor coordination, from simple ideas to complex thinking, from one-word utterances to lengthy sentences, from scribbles to **representational drawings**—all children everywhere seem to proceed through a step-by-step sequence of development that can be traced by an observer who knows what to look for. The observer then records these data and later interprets them to make appropriate plans for individual children.

The Child Development Checklist (Table 1.1) helps observers focus on each of the six major areas. These areas are in turn divided into nine topics of child development. Each topic focuses on at least six observable items of child behavior based on recognized developmental sequences or progressions. Rather than including every detail of development on the checklist, six representative items are discussed. This makes observations inclusive enough to be meaningful, but not so detailed to be cumbersome for the observer.

Table 1.1   Child Development Checklist

CHILD DEVELOPMENT CHECKLIST

Name _____   Observer _____

Program _____   Dates _____

Directions:

Put an **X** for items you see the child perform regularly. Put an **N** for items where there is no opportunity to observe. Leave all other items blank.

Item	Evidence	Dates
1. Self-Esteem		
_____ Separates from primary caregiver without difficulty		
_____ Develops a secure attachment with teacher		
_____ Completes a task successfully		
_____ Makes activity choices without teacher's help		

Table 1.1   (*Continued*)

Item	Evidence	Dates
_____ Stands up for own rights		
_____ Displays enthusiam about doing things for self		
2. Emotional Competence		
_____ Releases stressful feelings in appropriate manner		
_____ Expresses anger in words rather than negative actions		
_____ Can be calmed in frightening situations		
_____ Shows fondness, affection, love toward others		
_____ Shows interest, excitement in classroom activities		
_____ Smiles, seems happy much of the time		
3. Social Competence		
_____ Plays by self with own toys/materials		
_____ Plays parallel to others with similar toys/materials		
_____ Plays with others in group play		
_____ Gains access to ongoing play in positive manner		
_____ Makes friends with other children		
_____ Resolves play conflict in positive manner		
4. Physical Development		
_____ Runs with control over speed & directions		
_____ Climbs up, down, across climbing equipment		

Table 1.1   (*Continued*)

Item	Evidence	Dates
_____ Throws, catches, & kicks balls		
_____ Turns knobs, lids, eggbeaters		
_____ Picks up & inserts objects with dexterity		
_____ Uses tools (scissors, hammer) with control		
5. Cognitive Development		
_____ Classifies objects by shape, color, size		
_____ Places objects in a sequence or series		
_____ Recognizes, creates patterns		
_____ Counts by rote to 20		
_____ Displays 1-to-1 correspondence		
_____ Problem-solves with concrete objects		
_____ Makes thinking visible		
6. Spoken Language		
_____ Listens but does not speak		
_____ Gives single-word, short phrase responses		
_____ Takes part in conversations		
_____ Speaks in expanded sentences		
_____ Asks questions		
_____ Can tell a story		
7. Emergent Writing and Reading Skills		
_____ Pretends to write with drawings & scribbles		
_____ Makes horizontal lines of writing scribbles		
_____ Makes some letters, prints name or initial		

Table 1.1 (*Continued*)

Item	Evidence	Dates
_____ Holds book right side up; turns pages right to left		
_____ Pretends to read using pictures to tell story		
_____ Shows awareness that print in books tells story		
8. Art, Music, and Dance Skills _____ Makes basic scribble shapes		
_____ Draws person as sun-face with arms & legs		
_____ Makes pictorial drawings		
_____ Moves arms & hands in rhythm to beat		
_____ Plays rhythm instruments		
_____ Sings with group or by him/herself		
_____ Moves body to represent people, animals, feelings		
_____ Dances with others to music		
9. Dramatic Play Skills _____ Does pretend play by him/herself		
_____ Assigns roles or takes assigned roles		
_____ Needs particular props to do pretend play		
_____ Takes on characteristics & actions related to role		
_____ Uses language for creating & sustaining the plot		
_____ Enacts exciting, danger-packed themes		

In this text, for items the observer does not check as apparent when observing a child, a section of ideas following the item called *If You Have Not Checked This Item: Some Helpful Ideas* can be useful in planning for individual needs. The purposes for assessing children's development in this manner are twofold:

1. It allows students of child development to gain an in-depth understanding of real children and their sequences of growth.
2. It helps teachers of young children to become aware of each child's growth and to support individual development with appropriate activities and materials.

STANDARDIZED TESTS AS TOOLS FOR ASSESSMENT

Many teachers measure young children's growth and development using more formal tools called **standardized tests**. These tests have been designed by researchers to interpret a child's performance in comparison to the performance of other children with similar characteristics (Mindes, 2011). Some of these **formal assessment tools** and procedures use the observation of children; some do not. Some need to be administered by professional testers; others don't. Some assessment procedures place children in artificial rather than authentic situations. Many ask children to perform contrived activities. Although such tools and tasks may be helpful to researchers and professionals who are evaluating children for developmental problems, many are not appropriate for the nonspecialist teacher in the early childhood classroom. Table 1.2 lists several of the **standardized assessment instruments** using observation of children.

Table 1.2   Selected Preschool Assessment Instruments

Instrument	Age Range	Description
Battelle Developmental Inventory, 2nd Ed. (BDI)	Birth to 8 years	Measures social, communication, motor, cognitive; observation of child in natural setting; parent interview; structured items
Child Observation Record—Revised; (COR) HighScope	2½ to 6 years	Measures child's development of initiative, social, creative, music, language, literacy, math, science; teacher observations throughout year; training may be needed
Developmental Observation Checklist System (DOCS)	Birth to 6 years	Observation questionnaire; language, motor, social, cognitive
Early Learning Accomplishment Profile Diagnostic (LAP-D)	2½ to 6 years	Assessment in 5 areas of development: motor, social, self-help, language, cognition
Early School Inventory Developmental (ESI-D)	Prekindergarten	80-item observation checklist of child; performance ratings

Source: Based on McLean, Wolery, & Bailey, 2004; Meisels & Atkins-Burnett, 2005; Mindes, 2011, Wortham, 2012

Figure 1.3   COR Category: Initiative—A

Source: Information based on HighScope's Child Progress Assessment Tools, 2012; http://www.highscope.org

> **COR Category: Initiative—A. Making Choices and Plans**
> **Level 1:** Child indicates a choice by pointing or some other action.
> **Level 2:** Child expresses a choice in one or two words.
> **Level 3:** Child expresses a choice with a short sentence.
> **Level 4:** Child makes a plan with one or two details.
> **Level 5:** Child makes a plan with three or more details.

The COR test, for example, developed by HighScope, is an observation tool with six categories (initiative, social relations, creative representation, movement and music, language and literacy, math and science), plus 32 items. Each of the items describes five developmental levels from simple to complex. Teachers spend a few minutes each day writing brief notes that describe significant episodes of each young child's behavior. They record the notes on printed forms or computer files. Then they classify and rate them according to COR categories, items, and levels. Figure 1.3 is a sample of the five levels for the category "Initiative—A. Making Choices and Plans." The teacher/observer lists notes she or he has taken about the child's behavior under the appropriate level. When all six categories, 32 items, and 5 levels have been completed, a comprehensive view of the child and her or his accomplishments and needs is available. Training is recommended for first-time users.

Developmental Screening

Another type of child assessment known as **screening** is often done at the beginning of the program year to identify children who may experience developmental lags, learning problems, or disabilities that call for further investigation. Screening helps children who need services to gain access at an early age in order to prevent more severe problems later. Should such problems be identified, further assessment and evaluation will be necessary. Head Start and many state prekindergarten programs are required to perform such screening. A selection of **standardized screening instruments** is listed in Table 1.3.

THE PROBLEM WITH TESTS AS ASSESSMENT INSTRUMENTS

As noted earlier, the reasons to assess young children are many and varied. Some early childhood programs do assessments of children as a program evaluation tool. Are the children progressing as they should? Should changes be made in the curriculum? Other programs do assessments because they are mandated by the state or federal government to prove their effectiveness to receive ongoing support and funding.

The 21st century is an accountability era. The No Child Left Behind Act of 2001 required states across the nation to develop standards-based assessment (i.e., tests) for kindergarten through 12th-grade students in order to receive benefits. States

Table 1.3 Selected Preschool Screening Instruments

Ages & Stages Questionnaires, 3rd Ed. (ASQ)	Parent-completed; self-regulation, communication, social interaction
AGS Early Screening Profiles (ESP)	Cognitive, language, motor, self-help, social
Denver II	Observation or parent interview format; gross & fine motor, communication
Developmental Indicators for the Assessment of Learning, 3rd Ed. (DIAL-3)	Identifies children with potential learning problems or giftedness
Early Screening Inventory-Revised (ESI-R)	Visual/motor, language, cognition

Source: Based on Meisels & Atkins-Burnett, 2005; Wortham, 2012

failing to comply fully would lose benefits. By 2003 testing of students had reached down into preschool with the Head Start Bureau's test *National Reporting System* being administered to 4- and 5-year-olds—with mixed results.

Testing, the traditional means for evaluating children, should work if the testing instruments have been carefully developed and validated by researchers in the field, shouldn't they? However, when applied to young children, the results are often mixed. What works with older children does not seem to work as well with preschoolers and kindergartners. Test developers sometimes blame the validation procedures used in developing the tests. Early childhood educators nod wisely and think to themselves: "It's the kids."

Young children have little interest in tests. Why should they? They don't need to prove to anyone what they can or cannot do. It's true that they can be talked into cooperating with a test-giver. The teacher can administer a test to a child and occasionally get valid results on a particular day. Next week the results may be different with the same child. Honest researchers have had to admit that the major conclusion of their study is that it is inadvisable to routinely test young children prior to or immediately after their entry into kindergarten (Wenner, 1988). Wenner found that even highly respected and widely used tests predicted little more than a quarter of the actual academic performance of kindergarten children.

Romero (1999) pondered the problem of distinguishing the young child's inability from his or her refusal to cooperate. Sometimes a child's response of "I don't know" may really mean just that, but often it can mean "I don't want to." Nevertheless, assessment procedures routinely include tests of many kinds. Although many are reliable and valid instruments, for their results to be used with confidence, teachers and testers alike need to be aware of this "young child factor."

Young children do not test well. Thus assessors need to include other more informal but reliable types of assessment—such as observations of children in the regular classroom—to round out the picture when they are evaluating young children.

Dodge, Heroman, Charles, and Maioca (2004) also pointed out that **government mandates** to test preschoolers are the wrong reason for administering tests. Ongoing assessment should support children's learning and lead to appropriate curriculum, not gather statistics about children and programs for a political agenda. The tests used for such purposes are often inappropriate as well. These writers say that researchers recommend assessing children based on observations of the processes children use rather than on simple, concrete, disconnected **indicators** or **milestones**.

Teachers as Testers

If formal tests are used, it is especially important that the classroom teachers learn to administer the instrument themselves whenever possible. If an outside tester is the administrator, be sure to help such a person establish rapport with individual children. Invite the tester to the classroom ahead of time. Help her or him to become acquainted with individuals by playing with them, reading to them, and talking with them before the testing begins. Otherwise, results for young children are sure to be suspect.

Much testing of young children constitutes misassessment because the testing is not developmentally appropriate. Tests often present young children with a series of demands to answer here and now, although young children may not be inclined to respond immediately. Classroom teachers who need child assessment data to plan activities that will support individual needs must first understand the meaning of **developmentally appropriate assessment** before choosing such a test or other data-gathering procedure. This means the assessment must be age appropriate, individually appropriate, and culturally appropriate for the children.

It should be stressed again that the classroom teacher, rather than a tester from outside the program, should be the **primary assessor**. The assessment should be based on activities in which children typically engage within the classroom, and not **contrived activities** in **artificial situations**. Assessment should not threaten children, nor should it focus on wrong answers or what children cannot do.

It is important that the teacher be the tester.

Figure 1.4 Observing, Documenting, and Assessing to Support Young Children and Families

3a. Understanding the goals, benefits, and uses of assessment

3b. Knowing about and using observation, documentation, and other appropriate assessment tools and approaches

3c. Understanding and practicing responsible assessment to promote positive outcomes for each child

3d. Knowing about assessment partnerships with families and with professional colleagues

NAEYC STANDARDS FOR EARLY CHILDHOOD PROFESSIONAL PREPARATION

Learning standards for preparing teachers of preschool children have been developed in most states following the trend of standards for kindergarten through 12th grade. If they are used carefully, standards can become a helpful tool to identify expectations in the many diverse early childhood programs (Gronlund & James, 2008). Our national organization, the National Association for the Development of Young Children (NAEYC), has developed its own Standards for Professional Preparation to ensure high-quality early childhood education. Its position statement is available online at http://www.naeyc.org.

There are six core standards, each of which describes what well-prepared students should know and be able to do:

Standard 1. Promoting child development and learning
Standard 2. Building family and community relationships
Standard 3. Observing, documenting, and assessing to support young children and families
Standard 4. Using developmentally effective approaches to connect with children and families
Standard 5. Using content knowledge to build meaningful curriculum
Standard 6. Becoming a professional

This text focuses on Standard 3 as shown in Figure 1.4.

ALTERNATIVE APPROACHES TO ASSESSMENT OF YOUNG CHILDREN

In addition to testing instruments, the assessment of preschool children can be done using alternative techniques. Many of them include child observation, but also the collecting of representative work in **play-based assessment**, **child interviews**, and **visual documentation**.

Play-Based Assessment

Because play is young children's natural means of interacting with the world around them, it makes sense to assess children's development while they are engaged in play activities. Toys and specific artificial play situations have long been used by psychologists to observe and record children's behavior using standardized instruments. Play-based assessments, on the other hand, vary from these traditional assessments in that the child is observed doing whatever the child typically does in the environment. Although standardized assessment instruments may be used for the observations and analysis of children's behavior, in this assessment the observer records the child interacting naturally with play materials, peers, or even parents or teachers in the classroom environment. Three types of play-based assessment are typically used:

- *Nonstructured:* identifies all behaviors occurring during a play session; assessors often watch a parent playing with the child
- *Structured:* uses a previously designed set of play behaviors using specific play items
- *Transdisciplinary:* uses a team of assessors observing the child simultaneously, each team member looking for specific information

Play-based assessment (Figure 1.5) has also become the method of choice for assessing children with special needs (Ahola & Kovacik, 2007).

Child Interviews

Assessment interviews done by a teacher and a child can provide important information about a child not easily obtained by any other means. Wortham (2012) tells us about interviews being especially appropriate for young children who are just beginning to develop literacy skills and cannot yet express themselves with paper-and-pencil tests. The strategies followed can be similar to those used by Swiss psychologist Jean Piaget to understand children's thinking. He used questioning, then asked more questions based on children's initial responses.

Such interviews are best conducted on an informal basis during a free-play situation. As the teacher interacts or plays with the child, she or he can talk about what

Figure 1.5 Advantages of Play-Based Assessment

- Provides an opportunity to assess behavior of a child who cannot or will not perform in formal testing situation.
- More can be seen in observing children at play than in asking them to perform.
- All the development domains of a child can be witnessed at the same time.

is happening. For example, while making an animal puzzle with Nicole, the teacher can make remarks about Nicole's skill in finding and matching the puzzle pieces. This may lead Nicole to tell how she does it. What does she guess the animal will look like when the puzzle is finished? If teachers listen closely to what children have to say, they can use children's responses to lead them to new questions that will elicit further information about their development. Teachers can then record their interviews either on a recording device or by writing them down afterward.

Interviews should be short. Ten minutes is an appropriate length of time. Children should also be given plenty of time to think about and respond to the teacher's questions. Reading a picture book to an individual child can serve as an informal interview if the book is carefully chosen and the questions carefully framed to elicit desired information.

Most teachers find such simple informal interviews to be so valuable that they tailor book readings to particular children and develop forms for recording elicited information. These forms are kept in a child's documentation folder or portfolio along with other observational data. You can develop your own interview questions on a recording form or use questions like those in Figure 1.6.

Visual Documentation

Visual documentation is also something we can look at to gain insight into a child's development. With young children, it can take many forms: photographs of children involved in activities, photographs of children's work, video recordings, audio recordings, or samples of children's work.

You can add another dimension to your observation of children by using digital cameras, smartphones, video cameras, or digital audio recorders in addition to conducting play-based assessments, interviews, or traditional classroom observations.

Figure 1.6   Book Interview Protocol

Describing:
What's happening on this page?
Predicting:
What do you think will happen next?
Problem solving:
How else could the character solve the problem?
Empathizing:
How does the characters feel about what's happening?
Creating:
What would you do if you were the character?
Recalling:
Do you remember what the character did first?

Figure 1.7 Uses for Photos
in Child Assessment

- Captures image of child at moment of action
- Serves as memory aid for teachers
- Promotes child's self-image
- Can be used in assessment interviews
- Can be used in parent conferences
- Can be used in book child creates
- Can be used in portfolios, document panels
- Helps staff interpret child's development
- Helps staff plan for child

Such visual documentation can capture important moments to be used to document observational data already gathered about the children. They also can serve as foci for team discussion regarding each child's development or to help make decisions on follow-up activities for the children in question. These observations can then be placed in each child's portfolio or documentation folder.

Photographs

Photos of children are easy to take with digital cameras or smartphones these days, so be sure to take a series of the same child or same incident for later recording. These photos are for your use, not the children's. They should be captioned with content descriptions, dated, and placed in the same file as your recorded notes—perhaps in a child's portfolio.

Photos have other uses as well (Figure 1.7). You can use the photo of a child interacting with others or engaged in a classroom activity as the focus of an **assessment interview**, just as you would use a picture book. Jot down simple questions you will want to ask the child about the photo to elicit assessment information. Be sure the questions are open ended enough for the child to respond in creative ways you may not expect. You may want to audio record your conversation or make a written record of the results on file cards with the picture attached.

Photographs of individual children taken with a digital camera open other avenues for child assessment. Using appropriate software, these photos can be printed on regular computer paper, making several copies of each for use in child or parent interviews, or for inclusion in child portfolios. They also can be used as pages in a book children can create with their own stories written under the photos. Digital photos can also be shown on computer or television screens for use in staff planning sessions on individual children or for parent conferences.

Digital photos are especially well suited to on-the-spot recording. In areas where a child needs strengthening, such photos can be especially useful. For example, if Jessica experiences difficulty at arrival time in making the transition from home to school, be sure to take photos of her every morning for several days, whether or not she continues to encounter the difficulties. Keep a running record of her actions at

Many programs use videos for child observations.

the same time and then mount the daily photos together with your written observations on file cards or portfolio pages. Interpreting children's behavior and making plans to help them improve it are more effective when you can see firsthand the visual evidence of their actions long after it occurs (Good, 2009).

Videos

Videos serve the same purpose as photos. Use a video camera or smartphone to capture a child's actions for later observation and discussion with other staff members or parents. After you have previewed the video and know what areas of development it documents, ask staff members to check off that particular section of the Child Development Checklist when they view the video. Checklists can be used like this with videos, treating them like live observations. A group discussion of the video can be recorded and added to the observational data for making individual plans or for documenting the assessment.

Audio Recordings

A digital audio recording or smartphone recording can also add depth to your written observations by recording a child's spoken language or verbal interactions with other children. Speak the child's name, your name, the date, and the classroom location into the recorder before placing it on a table or countertop near the child. After listening to the recording, make notes or check off appropriate items on a checklist to be placed in the child's portfolio. Audio recordings can also be made of child interviews, as noted previously. Some observers also prefer to speak softly into a smartphone recorder instead of taking notes during their observations of children. Later, the recording can be downloaded into a computer and printed.

Document Panels

Another alternative assessment method for observing children's development is the document panel. Photographs of children along with their products (e.g., painting, writing, and science collections) are displayed on a board or a panel on the wall of the classroom. The Reggio Emilia schools in Italy promoted this approach, believing that documentation should be a part of the learning process. Teachers and parents alike need to see visually what children have accomplished.

For instance, the children in Noah's Ark Preschool in Taos, New Mexico, built their own playhouse outside on their playground over several weeks from adobe bricks they made. Fathers of the Hispanic children helped them plan the dimensions, mix mud and straw, fill square frames, set the bricks out to dry, and then build up the walls and roof. Each step of the process was photographed. Children audio-recorded what was happening. Then they wrote stories and made drawings. This material was then assembled on poster board panels as a visual day-by-day diary of the project.

Although the children and parents often view these panels simply as pictures of an exciting project, teachers understand that this is a permanent record of how the children are developing. It is a form of **summative evaluation**. The playhouse panels displayed children's large- and small-motor accomplishments over time. Their cognitive skills of measuring and counting emerged. Turn-taking and helping one another were captured on video. Their creative skills of making up stories about the playhouse and then reenacting them in real life materialized. These document panels could then be shared with other professionals and afterward kept for future planning.

Other, shorter projects can be documented on panels when they are finished. The "Buddies not Bullies" project illustrated in the accompanying photo was completed in three weeks after a bullying problem was discovered. Teachers did the photography, but children listened to stories, wrote stories, illustrated their stories, interviewed other children, did puppet role-plays, and started a Kindness Classroom.

Portfolios

Many early childhood educators have adopted the portfolio as one of the best methods for assessing the ongoing development of each child. A portfolio is an individual

This document panel shows what children learned about bullying.

systematic collection of documents that reflects what a child does in a classroom. It is usually assembled by both teachers and children, and emphasizes both process and product in the documents collected.

The teacher must provide the framework for collecting items; otherwise, the results may become a meaningless hodgepodge. Helm, Beneke, and Steinheimer (2007) tell us about the many different approaches to systematizing a portfolio collection process. They discuss a variety of portfolios that have been effectively used in early childhood programs. Some programs use a three-folio system with separate portfolios for ongoing work, current work, and permanently kept work.

The purpose for creating the portfolio may be the deciding factor in how to assemble it. Teachers who need to document a child's development will be assembling a **developmental portfolio**. If the primary purpose is to chart development, then the portfolios should emphasize work in progress.

Such portfolios can be used for assessment of a child's development by the teachers, the program, outside evaluators, and the parents. This author suggests using the Child Development Checklist as an outline for collecting documentation materials. Observing and documenting can then go hand-in-glove in helping teachers, children, and parents to illustrate where the child stands in each of the development areas. See Figure 1.8.

Before beginning to create a portfolio for each child, it should be clearly understood what the portfolios will be used for, thus what work samples will best illustrate this use. Mindes (2011) believes that observational notes form the foundation of the portfolio. Also included should be a collection of children's paintings, drawings, and stories; lists of books read; transcripts of discussions with children about their work; and other products collected throughout the year.

At first this may look like an overwhelming task, but once the observers realize the portfolio can be assembled over the entire school year, they may be more willing to take on the task of adding a piece of evidence to one of the nine areas of development only when appropriate. For example, the teacher may add a sample of a child's writing at the beginning, middle, and end of the year. Or she or he may decide to include only a copy of a child's journal. Photos of children at work and play can be excellent illustrations of their development products for the nine checklist areas.

BECOMING AN OBSERVER

To become an observer of children, you must first step out of the role you normally hold. If you are a teacher or teaching assistant, you must temporarily give that role to another staff member. This can be planned ahead of time at a staff meeting. Each staff member should take on an observer's role for brief periods every week. Student interns can participate, adding another dimension to this important information-gathering task.

Figure 1.8 Portfolio
Items Based on Child
Development Checklist

Self-esteem
- Photos of child showing classroom accomplishments
- Anecdotal records about child from classroom meetings
- Parents' communications about child at home

Emotional competence
- Teacher's records of how child handles stress, anger, joy
- Photo of books child likes to hear when under stress
- Finger painting child made to relieve stress

Social competence
- Photos of child playing with others
- List of dramatic play themes child participates in
- Parent communication about child playing in neighborhood

Physical development
- Photo of child on outside climber
- Photo of large hollow block building child helped build
- Parent communication on child climbing stairs up and down
- Sample of cut-and-paste artwork
- Photo of child pounding nails into wood

Cognitive development
- Pictures with colors child identified
- Photo of block building showing patterns
- Caption dictated by child on drawing he makes

Spoken language
- Audio recording of story child tells
- List of songs child sings
- Funny words child likes to say

Emergent writing and reading skills
- Page of scribbles child makes
- List of books parent has read to child
- Sign-up sheet with name child prints

Art, music, and dance skills
- Sample of easel painting
- Audio recording of child singing, dancing
- Photo of play dough creation

Dramatic play skills
- Hand puppet child made for pretending
- Video of child in dramatic play role
- Running record of child pretending with small figures

Where to Observe

As an observer, you should step back unobtrusively and position yourself close to, but not interfering with, the child you are to observe. You may be seated, standing, or walking around—whatever it takes to get close enough to the child without calling attention to yourself. Try to avoid making eye contact with the child you are observing. If he or she looks your way, you can look around at the other children.

Young children are often much more observant than we give them credit for. Despite your best efforts, the child you are observing will often pick up the fact that you are watching him or her if you keep at it long enough. Most children soon forget about the scrutiny they are undergoing and continue their participation in their activity. If you find, however, that a child seems uncomfortable with your presence and even tries to get away, you should break off your observation. Try again another day, or let another staff member or student observe that particular child.

Children actually like teachers to observe them in this focused way. They relish such one-on-one attention. Children who are not being observed sometimes complain about it. The problem is that you, the observer, want to see what your child is doing with materials and with other children without her looking over her shoulder at you. If she realizes she is being watched, her normal behavior may change. Psychologists call this the Hawthorne effect (Ahola & Kovacik, 2007). Thus, you must try your best to observe a child without being noticed.

What Tools to Use

Many observers prefer to use a clipboard with paper or the Child Development Checklist on it for recording their observations. Several such boards can be left on countertops or the tops of room dividers in each learning center, to be picked up and used by observers whenever the occasion calls for it. If children see you writing on a clipboard for any length of time, some will come over to see what you are doing and want to write with your pencil. Tell them you are busy with your work this morning and that they need to do their own work now. If they persist in wanting to write with your tool, direct them to the classroom writing center, where you can keep a similar clipboard with pencil and paper.

Because children love to imitate you, you could ask those children to observe something like the guinea pig. If they continue to demand your attention, tell them you are busy at the moment but you will attend to them when you are finished. Some observers redirect other children to another staff person or give them a chore to accomplish in one of the learning centers.

Do not announce to the class that you are now doing observations and should be left alone. For youngsters of this age, such an announcement only calls attention to yourself, making everyone stop to look at you. Instead, you should be doing just the opposite: making yourself invisible. Then the child you are observing will continue his or her actions undisturbed. Once you have started observing regularly, most children will soon understand and respect your need for privacy.

Figure 1.9   Getting
Started

- Start at the beginning of the day.
- Walk around watching several children before settling down.
- Keep in mind how interesting the child is.
- Think about painting this child's picture in words.
- Just take the plunge and do it!

How Do You Get Started?

Once you begin observing regularly, you will soon find yourself getting hooked and never want to stop. The problem is getting started. If observing is something you have never done before, you may keep putting it off. What will the children think? Won't you look foolish just standing around? Even though you understand that making observations of individuals is just as important as teaching, it may still be hard for you to drop your regular tasks and begin. Getting started demands conscious effort. Some ideas for getting started are listed in Figure 1.9.

When and How Long Should You Observe?

When is the best time to observe? Any time! You understand how important it is for you to acquire baseline data about each of the children in your program to plan for them. You must therefore *make* time in your busy schedule to gather the necessary information about each child through observation. The time of day to do your observing depends on what you want to learn about a child.

Do you want to see how she makes the transition from home to school in the morning? Which learning centers attract her attention? How long she stays with an activity? How she interacts with others in the dramatic play center? How she handles tools such as scissors, paintbrushes, or pencils? Whether she knows how a particular book "works"? Plan to observe her, then, in each of the centers where these activities take place any time of day.

It does not take long. Only *5 to 10 minutes a day* of focused observing on the part of each staff member will produce a surprising amount of information on children. Make plans to spend your 5 to 10 minutes observing a child you would like to know better. Every day for a week observe the same child for a different 5- to 10-minute period, and soon you will accumulate enough data for a nearly complete profile of her development.

How Should You Plan for Observing?

Because observing and recording are such important aspects of a teacher's commitment to child development, you should explore ways to make it easier for yourself and other staff members to carry out this responsibility. Some teachers plan to do their most in-depth recording during free-choice time, when children are busily engaged in all the classroom learning centers. Others preplan by placing an "observation chair" in an unobtrusive spot near children's activities. Having notebooks or clipboards and pencils ready at strategic locations also helps.

Some programs include a smartphone as a tool so teachers can record their observations for computer downloading later instead of writing them down at the time. This material can then be transcribed on a checklist. You should consider anything that makes your task easier. Share ideas with other staff members and find out what works best for them. Then everyone can get into the act of observing, recording, and planning for children. This entire process is known as **systematic observation**.

FOLLOW THE STEPS IN SYSTEMATIC OBSERVATION

Systematic observation—using a particular system to look at and record children's behavior—has thus become an important part of a classroom staff's daily responsibilities. Systematic observation of young children requires that you have a plan you will be following to do the observing and recording of a child. Steps in such a plan may include those in Figure 1.10.

SHOW THAT YOU KNOW HOW TO SEE

Before you become too deeply involved in child observation, you need to ask yourself: "What do I really see when I look at a child?" Most of us tend to take a cursory look, make some sort of judgment, and then dismiss it. Bentzen (2005) explains about our brains enabling us to see in ways that far exceed the camera's ability to see. Then observation becomes complicated because we do more with sensory information than the camera is able to see. All of us look at and organize the objects according to our past experiences, what we know, and what we believe. In other words, we judge what we see.

This means that two people looking at the same child engaged in play will come away with two different views. On the other hand, the more each of us knows about child development, the more similar our observations of the same child will be. As

Figure 1.10 Systematic Observation

1. Identify the information you want to gather.
2. Identify the child you plan to observe.
3. Identify the method you plan to use.
4. Set up a schedule for observation.
5. Follow the observation schedule.

you practice observation according to this text's suggestions, try doing it with a partner so you can compare your notes. You will find the more you observe, the better you become. The more you learn about young children, the more you will see when you observe. The old adage "We see what we look for" holds true with child observations. When we are not looking for specific details, we tend not to see them. Thus it behooves us to become aware of as many details as possible.

Children "see" with all their senses, not just their eyes. They use sight, sound, touch, smell, taste, and movement to "see" the environment that surrounds them. As an observer of young children, you will need to use as many of these senses as possible for every observation you make. You will also need to record as many details as possible for each of these five senses plus movement.

Practicing Observation Skills

It is important to practice your observing skills before you begin observing children. Look at a person near you or a photo of a person and jot down all the descriptive details you can see. Do this exercise with a team member and compare your results. Do it again and try doubling the details. Next zero in on one aspect of a person, for instance, his or her facial expression, and describe it in detail: eyes, eyebrows, lashes, nose, mouth, lips, cheeks, chin, forehead, ears, and movements. Now take the eyes alone and describe them in detail: eye color, winking, blinking, twinkling, flashing, sparkling, staring, gazing, glancing, opening, closing, squinting, peeking, peering, laughing, scowling. Be careful about being judgmental. Use objective terms only.

Read to a child from a picture book that focuses on careful observation. See if the child can discover hidden objects. See if you can. In **Looking for a Moose** (Root, 2006), four children hike into the woods, a swamp, the bushes, and up a hillside in search of a moose. Only parts of the moose are visible in each location, but no one sees anything at all until the moose finally bugles its call. Zany sound words that accompany the search add to the excitement.

Observation of young children is critical for a number of reasons. Bentzen (2005) goes on to mention how we learn about reality by observing it, by having contact with it through one or more of our five physical senses. Therefore, if we are to understand children, we must watch them, listen to them, and even touch them. Then we need to make some sense of this data in order to act toward children in appropriate and meaningful ways.

LEARNING ACTIVITIES

1. Write a brief report explaining what makes child observation the best way to assess children's development and why.

2. Choose one of the standardized tests discussed and explain how it can be used in a child assessment.

3. Choose one of the standardized tests that present problems and describe how teachers can overcome some of the problems.

4. Use one of the alternative methods for assessment such as child interviews, document panels,

videotapes, or portfolios and show what kinds of data you can gather on child development.

5. Use the steps in systematic observation of a child and describe in detail the plan you would use to determine the child's development.

6. Work with a partner in observing a child in all the developmental domains mentioned. Write up the results separately and then compare them. What did you learn?

SUGGESTED READINGS

Curtis, D. (2011). Changes in how we see children. *Exchange,* July/August, 20–25.

Garrigues, S. M. (2012). Competency-based behavioral interviewing. *Exchange,* February, 37–41.

Gibson, C. Jones, S., & Patrick, T. (2010). Conducting informal developmental assessments, *Exchange,* May/June, 36–40.

Harris, M. E. (2009). Implementing portfolio assessment. *Young Children, 64*(3), 82–85.

Ogunnaike-Lafe, Y., & Krohn, J. (2010). Using document panels to record, reflect, and relate learning experiences. *Exchange,* May/June, 92–96.

Reifel, S. (2011). Observation and early childhood teaching: Evolving fundamentals. *Young Children, 66*(2), 62–65.

CHILDREN'S BOOK

Root, P. (2006). *Looking for a Moose.* Cambridge, MA: Candlewick Press.

WEB SITES

UCLA Center for the Study of Evaluation
http://www.cse.ucla.edu

The National Center for Fair and Open Testing
http://www.fairtest.org

HighScope Educational Research Foundations
http://www.highscope.org

KidSource Online (issues related to assessment and observation)
http://www.kidsource.com

Early Childhood Direction Center Behavioral Observation Checklist
http://www.thechp.syr.edu

The National Association for the Education of Young Children (NAEYC)
http://www.naeyc.org

CHAPTER 2

Recording and Collecting Observational Data

In this chapter you will learn to:

____ Make an anecdotal record and running record of a child's actions

____ Record information using your own shorthand

____ Make samplings, rating scales, and rubrics of children's actions

____ Choose a new method of observing and recording

____ Use the Child Development Checklist in two of the domains to observe and record a child's actions

____ Interpret the data and fill out a Learning Prescription for a child

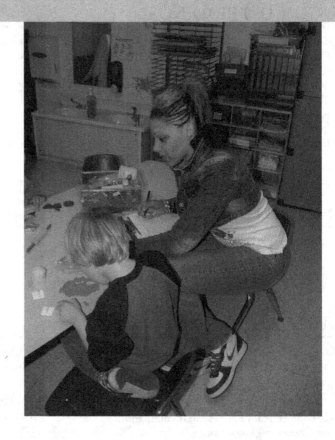

METHODS FOR RECORDING AND COLLECTING OBSERVATIONAL DATA

As you begin the actual observation of young children, you need to keep in mind that important criteria apply to the details you are discovering and recording. They include those in Figure 2.1.

Figure 2.1   Criteria for
Observing Children

- **_Objectivity:_** You must observe each child without judging.
- **_Confidentiality:_** You must keep the information you obtain to yourself.
- **_Recording details:_** You should look for and record even the smallest details.
- **_Using direct quotes:_** You should listen closely and record what each child says.
- **_Using mood cues:_** You should describe the emotional mood of the child.

Systematic observation of young children always implies recording. Not only must observers have a particular reason to observe a child and know what to look for, but they also need a method for recording the information they gather. Mindes (2011) reminds us to to make multiple measures, collecting several samples of observations on all the children. A sampling of these methods is included for discussion in this chapter (Figure 2.2).

ANECDOTAL AND RUNNING RECORDS

The most popular methods for recording child observations fall under the heading of "narrative recording," that is, written descriptions of children's actions. Three of the several types of informal narratives most widely used are anecdotal records, running records, and logs.

Figure 2.2   Recording
Methods

- <u>**Narratives**</u>
   Anecdotal records
   Running records
   Learning Center logs
- <u>**Sampling**</u>
   Time sampling
   Event sampling
- <u>**Rating scales**</u>
   Graphic scales
   Rubrics
- <u>**Checklists**</u>
   Developmental

Anecdotal Records

Anecdotal records are brief narrative accounts describing an incident of child behavior that is important to the observer. Anecdotes (a) describe what happened in a factual, objective manner, (b) telling how it happened, (c) when and where it happened, and (d) what was said and done. Sometimes they include reasons for the child's behavior, but the "why" is better kept in the commentary part of the record. These accounts are most often written *after* the incident has occurred, by someone who witnessed it informally, rather than *during* its occurrence, by someone who was formally observing and recording. Anecdotal records have long been made by teachers, psychologists, social workers, and even parents who record when their babies first walk and talk.

Although anecdotal records are brief, describing only one incident at a time, they are cumulative. A series of them over a period of time can be extremely useful in providing rich details about the child being observed. Teachers can also use anecdotal records with the Child Development Checklist to describe more fully the evidence they offer when checking an item. When combined with photos, anecdotes written as captions for photos provide very rich visual information about each child's development. Other advantages of using anecdotal records include the following.

Advantages

1. The observer needs no special training to record.
2. The observation is open ended. The recorder writes anything and everything he or she witnesses and is not restricted to one kind of behavior or recording.
3. The observer can catch an unexpected incident no matter when it occurs, for it is usually recorded at a later time.
4. The observer can look for and record the significant behavior and ignore the rest.

As in all observational methods, there are also disadvantages. Observers need to decide (1) why they are observing, (2) what they want to find out, and (3) which method will be most useful. Some of the disadvantages of the anecdotal method include the following.

Disadvantages

1. It does not give a complete picture because it records only incidents of interest to the observer.
2. It depends too much on the memory of the observer because it is recorded after the event. Witnesses to events are notoriously poor on details.
3. Incidents may be taken out of context and thus be interpreted incorrectly or used in a biased manner.
4. It is difficult to code or analyze narrative records; thus, the method may not prove useful in a scientific study.

Such records can be more useful if recorded on a vertically divided page with the anecdote on the left side and a space for comments or interpretation on the right,

ANECDOTAL RECORD

Child's Name _____*Stevie*_____   Age ____*4*____   Date ___*2/23*___

Observer _____*Anne*_____   Place _____*HS*_____   Time ___*9.00-10.00*___

INCIDENT

Stevie went over to the block corner and asked two boys, Ron and Tanner, if he could help them build. They told him it was okay. As they were building he accidentally knocked some blocks down. "I can put it back up," he said, and handed the blocks to Ron. For awhile he watched Ron build and then said, "I found a smokestack, Ron," and handed him a cylinder block. Ron told him where to put it, and Stevie began getting cylinders off the shelf and handing them to Ron and Tanner to place. Finally he started placing his own cylinders around the perimeter of the building. The teacher asked him if he wanted to finger paint but he replied, "I'm not gonna finger paint unless Ron finger paints."

COMMENT

Stevie is often involved in a lot of dramatic play with several other boys. He especially likes to be near or play with Ron. He seems to look up to him. Whatever rules Ron sets in the play, Stevie follows. Once engaged in play, he likes to continue, and will usually not let another child, or even the teacher, distract him.

Figure 2.3   Anecdotal Record of Observation

or the page can be divided horizontally with the anecdote at the top and the commentary at the bottom. Figure 2.3 is an example of the latter format.

This anecdote tells what happened in an objective manner. Especially good are the direct quotes. The anecdote could have included more details about the child's facial expression, tone of voice, and gestures. The reader does not get the feeling of whether the boy was enjoying himself as a helper, trying to ingratiate himself with another child who was not paying much attention, or desperately trying to gain the attention of the other boy. Such details are sometimes missing from anecdotes because they have not been written down until the end of the day or even later. By then, much is forgotten.

The comments contain several inferences and conclusions based on insufficient evidence. Obviously this observer has spent some time watching Stevie, based on her comments, "Stevie is often involved" and "Once engaged in play, he likes to continue, and will usually not . . ." She would need an accumulation of such anecdotes to make valid statements like this based on evidence. If this were one page in an accumulation of anecdotes about Stevie, the comments would perhaps be more accurate.

The observer infers that Stevie "likes to be near or playing with Ron," although there is not sufficient evidence here to make that definite an inference. Perhaps she should have said: "Whatever rules Ron sets in the play, Stevie follows," if Stevie actually placed a cylinder block where directed. However, this was only hinted at and not stated. Particular words are very important in objective recording. Her conclusion

The observer needs to make careful inferences about the boys.

about Stevie not letting another child or even the teacher distract him is only partially accurate because the observer recorded no evidence about another child.

If you were writing the comments about this particular anecdotal record, what might you infer from the incident? Can you make any conclusions based on this information alone, or is it too limited? Are there things you might want to look for in the future when observing this boy that you would include in the commentary?

It is also helpful to indicate what the purpose is for the particular observation. Most observation forms do not provide a space for this, but the usefulness of the observation is enhanced if it is included. In this case, the observer was looking for evidence of involvement in social play for this child.

Running Records

Another popular informal observing and recording method is the **running record**. It is a detailed narrative account of behavior recorded in a sequential manner as it happens. The observer sits or stands apart from the children and writes down everything that occurs to a particular child over a specified period, which may be as short as several minutes or may be recorded from time to time during a full day. The running record is different from the anecdotal record because it includes all behavior and not just selected incidents, and it is written as the behavior occurs instead of later. Sentences are often short, and words are abbreviated to keep up with the pace of the action. Ahola and Kovacik (2007) point out how the running record is beneficial because it allows us to record minute details, but it is not considered practical when trying to collect a great deal of information about a child. Information you should record in a running record includes the items shown in Figure 2.4.

Figure 2.4   Information
to Record

- Facial expressions
- Interactions with materials
- Interactions with people
- Body movements
- Body langauge
- Spoken language
- Attention span

As with all factual recording, the observer must be careful not to use descriptive words and phrases that are judgmental. The running record has a number of advantages for persons interested in child development.

Advantages

1. It is a rich, complete, and comprehensive record not limited to particular incidents.
2. It is open ended, allowing the observer to record everything he or she sees, and not restricting the observations to a particular kind of behavior.
3. Because it is written at the time of the incident, it tends to be more accurate than accounts written later.
4. It does not require that the observer have special observational skills and therefore is particularly useful to the classroom teacher.

There are also several disadvantages to using this method, once again depending on the purpose for gathering the information.

Disadvantages

1. It is time consuming, making it difficult for observers to find periods of uninterrupted time.
2. It is difficult to record everything for any length of time without missing important details.
3. It works best when observing an individual, but it is inefficient when observing a group.
4. Observers must keep themselves apart from the children for long periods.

Observer Errors

Insufficient Evidence

Look at the running record for Katy (Figure 2.5). Has the observer, Rob, omitted any information that would be important for any conclusion he might make about Katy?

RUNNING RECORD

Name _____ Katy _____ Age ___ 4 ___ Date ___ 2/9 ___

Observer _____ Rob _____ Place ___ SPreschool ___ Time ___ 930-10 ___

Observation

Katy is playing by herself with plastic blocks, making a gun; she walks into playroom; "Lisa, would you play with me? I'm tired of playing by myself; They walk into other room to slide & climber area.
K: "I am Wonder Woman."
L: "So am I."

K: "No. There is only 1 Wonder Woman. You are Robin."
L: "Robin needs a Batman because Batman and Robin are friends." All this takes place under slide & climber; Lisa shoots block gun Katy has given her; Katy falls to floor.
L: (to teacher) "We're playing super friends and Wonder Woman keeps falling down.

K: Opens eyes; gets up; says: "Let's get get out our Batmobile & go help the world." She runs to other room & back making noises like a car.
L: "Wonder Woman is died. She fell out of the car." She falls down.

K: "It's only a game; wake up, Lisa. You be Wonder Woman. I'll be…….
L: Let's play house now."

Katy begins sliding down the slide. Says: "Robin is coming after you!" she shouts to Lisa, running from slide to other room.
L. "Katy, here is your doll's dress." John joins girls.
L. "I'm Wonder Woman."
K. "I'm Robin."
J: "I'm Batman. Where is the Batmobile?"

K. "John, we are not playing Superfriends any more."

Comments

Clips blocks together to make gun; copies it to make gun for Lisa; clever; shows creativity; does teacher allow guns?

Seems to be the leader here as in other activities I have observed. Lisa is the friend she most often plays with.

Katy switches roles here. She shows good concentration & spends much time on one play episode.

She can distinguish reality from fantasy.

Shows good large motor coordination. Spends much time every day like this, running around room. Seems to know she is good at this & spends a lot of time doing it.

Seems to be more comfortable playing with only 1 child at a time.

Figure 2.5 Running Record for Katy

Look at the "information to record" in Figure 2.4. Check off each item as you reread the running record for Katy. Was anything overlooked or omitted? What about "facial expressions" and "body language"? Can you comment on the "emotional mood" of the child from this running record? What conclusions can you make about Katy from this record?

In another situation, if we see a child come into the room in the morning, refuse to greet the teacher, walk outside and sit on a trike without riding it, shoo away another child who tries to talk to her, and shake her head in refusal when the teacher suggests an activity, how can we record it? A running record of the situation might read like this:

> Jennifer walks into the room this morning as if she is mad at the world. She will not look up at the teacher or respond to her greeting. She sort of slumps as she walks out to the playground with the others. She plunks herself down on a trike but doesn't ride it. When Monica comes over to talk to her she shoos her away. The teacher goes over and asks her if she wants to ride in the trike parade but she shakes her head no.

This record is rich enough in detail for us to visualize it, but is it factually objective? No. The words *as if she is mad at the world* are a conclusion based on insufficient evidence. The recorder might better have described Jennifer's entrance objectively like this:

> Jennifer walks into the room this morning with a frowning kind of look on her face. She lowers her head when the teacher greets her and does not respond.

This behavior is unusual for Jennifer, the staff knows. Later the teacher found out that she was not "mad at the world," but sad because her pet cat had been killed by a car the night before. We realize that frowning looks, lowered head, and refusal to speak

Does this girl look angry or sad?

or participate may be the result of emotions other than anger. If the observer first thought about recording the child as "acting grumpy this morning," he needs to avoid this judgment and instead record the actual details that explain what happened, such as: *"Jennifer wouldn't respond to the teacher's greeting at first, and when she did, she muttered 'good morning' in a low voice with head bent down."* It is up to us to sift out our inferences and judgments and make sure we record only the facts.

Omitting or Adding Facts

Other observer errors include (a) omitting some of the facts, (b) recording things that did not happen, and (c) recording things out of order. Here is the "Jennifer incident" again with some of these errors included. Can you find them?

> Jennifer walks into the classroom this morning. She doesn't look at the teacher but goes out on the playground with the others and sits on a trike. The teacher wants her to join the trike parade but she refuses. Monica comes over to talk with her, but she shakes her head no.

Facts *omitted* from the observation:

1. Has a frowning look on her face.
2. Does not respond to teacher's greeting.
3. Walks out to the playground with shoulders slumped.
4. Drops herself down onto a trike but doesn't ride it.

A fact *added* to the observation:

1. She shakes her head no to Monica.

Such errors can creep into an observation almost without the recorder being aware. You need to practice with at least two observers recording the same incident, and then compare results. If you find discrepancies between the records, check carefully that you have followed the guidelines in Figure 2.6.

Learning Center Logs

Some programs have found that the best way to observe and record on-the-spot actions is to keep a small spiral notebook on the top of the room divider for each learning center. Staff members are asked to briefly record what they see happening in a center whenever they are in the vicinity and to date their observations. The

Figure 2.6 Guidelines for Objective Recording

- Record only the facts.
- Record every detail without omitting anything.
- Do not interpret as you observe and record.
- Use words that describe but do not judge or interpret.
- Record the facts in the order that they occur.

teacher later gathers these **logs** and transfers the information onto the Child Development Checklists being used for each of the children.

This is a way to collect data for several children at once, as well as data for child interactions in several learning centers at once. Some programs divide the pages of their logs into the headings of *Child, Actions,* and *Language* to help remind observers of what information to record. If the teacher notes that nothing has been recorded in one of the centers by the end of the day, she or he can discuss this with the staff. Did no children play in that particular center, or did none of the staff happen to observe what was going on there?

Using learning center logs like this helps to alert staff members not only to what is occurring throughout the classroom during the day, but also as a reminder to record what they see happening. As a result, the teacher can piece together a record for more than one child's entire day of activities as seen by several different observers. In addition, no one feels burdened by stepping out of the role as a teacher to observe. Child observation occurs naturally as a part of the staff's normal checking of learning centers to see how children are doing.

All the staff, including the teacher, benefit from this sort of ongoing assessment of children. They learn where each child is developmentally, which centers and which activities seem to attract the most children, and which centers need changing. Learning center log recording like this gives the entire staff a better feel for what is really happening in the program. Martin (1994) also pointed out, "The log system requires a teacher to be diligent in record keeping. It can provide a detailed analysis of what the child is doing. For the child who has a diagnosed special need, this type of record keeping can provide data which can be interpreted and form part of the planning process" (p. 227).

RECORDING INFORMATION

Using Your Own Shorthand

Children often move from one area to another very rapidly. Even within the same learning center they may not settle down. To catch all the action in your notes, you will want to develop your own shorthand by using abbreviations. Use children's initials for their names and abbreviate words: *child* = ch, *teacher* = tch, *with* = w/, *different* = dif, and so on. Use descriptive verbs whenever you can. Instead of "walks over to sink," can you be more specific? Try to paint a picture with words. Figure 2.7 suggests descriptive verbs to be used for the word *walks*.

Figure 2.7 Descriptive Words for *Walks*

marches	prances	strolls
stomps	tiptoes	skips
shuffles	toddles	strides
plods	trudges	tramps

Figure 2.8 Descriptive Words
for *Said*

whispered	stammered	muttered
shouted	grumbled	mumbled
argued	declared	insisted
announced	uttered	stated

Practice makes perfect, and you will soon be developing your own observational shorthand and vocabulary. Complete sentences are not necessary on a running record. Instead, catch the moment on paper as quickly and completely as you can. Afterward, you can draw a line under the recording and write any comments or interpretive remarks that may help explain what you saw happening. Your first 5-minute running record may be rather short, perhaps not more than a half-page of notes. But as you hone your skills, you will soon be filling up more than one page because the more experienced you become, the more you will see.

Be sure to record as much of the spoken language as possible. Also include how the child sounds as she or he speaks. Figure 2.8 lists some of the many verbs describing speaking that you can use instead of the word *said*.

You may want to keep a card with you listing descriptive verbs to substitute for *walks* and *said* and other frequently used but nondescriptive verbs.

What about judgmental words? Be careful that the words you use do not carry judgments that will give a unintended meaning to the observation. Figure 2.9 lists judgmental phrases and sentences sometimes found in observation records. Should they ever be used? If not, why not? What could you substitute for them?

✓ SAMPLINGS, SCALES, AND RUBRICS

A different way of observing children is to look at samples of certain behaviors to discover how often, how long, or when a particular behavior occurs. When using samples, it is important to combine them with other forms of recording—such as developmental checklists—so that a whole picture of the child emerges.

Time Sampling

Because many of young children's behaviors are brief, the observer can gain comprehensive information by using time sampling (Wortham, 2012). In time sampling,

Figure 2.9 Judgmental
Phrases

He was a good boy today.	*Lost his temper*
Marcie was mad at Elena.	*Got upset*
Shouted angrily	*Made a big mess*
Acted happy	*Couldn't wait to go home*

the observer records the frequency of a behavior's occurrence over time. The behavior must be overt and frequent (at least once every 15 minutes) to be a candidate for sampling. For example, hitting or crying are behaviors that a teacher might want to sample for certain children because they can be seen and counted. Laughing and helping to pick up are other overt behaviors. Problem solving is not a good candidate for time sampling because this behavior is not always clear to the observers, nor can it be counted easily.

Time sampling thus involves observing a specified behavior of an individual or group and recording the presence or absence of this behavior during short time intervals of uniform length. The observer must prepare ahead of time, determining what specific behavior(s) to look for, what the time interval will be, and how to record the presence or absence of the behavior. Such time sampling is often used in **behavior modification** interventions. If the behavior is an inappropriate one, it is also important to use other assessment tools (such as a developmental checklist) to give a complete picture of the child.

For example, to help Jamie change his bullying behavior, the teacher needed to know how frequently the behavior occurred. The teacher noted that it included the following behaviors, determined by previous observations:

Hitting = h

Pushing = p

Kicking = k

Holding another against his will = hd

Taking another's toy = t

Next the teacher needed to decide about the time intervals to observe and record. She decided she wanted to sample Jamie's behavior for 5-minute intervals during the first half hour of the morning for a week. This seemed to be the most difficult time for him. Then the teacher had to decide what and how to record on the sheet she had blocked off in time intervals. Often an observer simply records "1" if the behavior occurs and "0" if it does not. This is called **duration recording**.

Check marks and tally marks can also be used if the teacher wants to know how many times the behavior occurred, rather than just its presence or absence. If the teacher is more concerned with specific categories of bullying, each of the categories can be given a code. The teacher can then set up her recording chart like the one in Figure 2.10 or in any way she wants, since this is an informal type of observation. This chart also involved **frequency counts**.

How would you interpret the results gathered on the first day as shown in Figure 2.10? The teacher could see that Jamie's bullying during the first 15 minutes of the day involved mostly hitting and pushing certain children. That also seemed to be the case on the following mornings. She decided to set up a home-to-school transition activity for Jamie to get involved in interacting nonaggressively with other children. Future observations would help the teacher determine if the intervention strategy had been successful. Time sampling is thus a useful method for observing children for some of the following reasons:

Figure 2.10 Time
Sampling

	Time Intervals (5 minutes each)					
Duration Recording (presence or absence)	1	2	3	4	5	6
	1	1	1	0	0	0
Event Recording (frequency)	IIII	II	I	0	0	0
Event Recording (presence or absence)	h, p	h, p, t	h	0	0	0

Advantages

1. It takes less time and effort than narrative recording.
2. It is more objective and controlled because the behavior is specified and limited.
3. It allows an observer to collect data on a number of children or a number of behaviors at once.
4. It provides useful information on intervals and frequencies of behavior.
5. It provides quantitative results useful for statistical analysis.

Disadvantages

1. It is not an open method and therefore may miss much important behavior.
2. It does not describe the behavior, its causes, or results because it is more concerned with time (when or how frequently the behavior occurs).
3. It does not keep units of behavior intact because its principal concern is the time interval, not the behavior.
4. It takes the behavior out of its context and therefore may be biased.
5. It is limited to observable behaviors that occur frequently.
6. It usually focuses on one type of behavior (in this case an inappropriate behavior) and thus may give a biased view of the child.

Event Sampling

Event sampling is used instead of time sampling when a behavior tends to occur in a particular setting, rather than a particular time period (Wortham, 2012). The observer waits for and then records a specific preselected behavior. Event sampling is used to study the conditions under which particular behaviors occur. It may be important to

---

Event Sampling

Name _____Darrell_____   **Age** ___3½_____

Center ____Head Start_____   **Date** ___10/5_____

Observer ___Sue S._____   **Time** ___9:00-12:00___

Behavior: Kicking: striking out at other children or teacher with right foot, hard enough to make children cry.

Time	Antecedent Event	Behavior	Consequent Event
9:13	Darrell playing alone in block corner; Rob comes in & puts block on Darrell's building	Darrell looks at Rob with frown; stands; pushes at Rob; Rob pushes back; Darrell kicks Rob on leg	Rob cries & runs to teacher
10:05	On playground; Darrell waiting turn in line with others to go on slide; Sally tries to cut in	Darrell kicks Sally hard on leg Darrell kicks teacher	Sally cries; teacher comes & takes Darrell away by arm to talk to him

---

Figure 2.11   ABC Event Sampling Observation

learn *what triggers* a particular kind of behavior—biting, for instance—to find ways to control it. Or the observer may want to find out *how many times* a certain behavior occurs. Time sampling could be used if time intervals or time of day were the important factor. If the behavior occurs at odd times or infrequently, event sampling is more appropriate.

The observer must first define the event or "unit of behavior." Then, the setting in which it is likely to occur must be determined. The observer takes the most advantageous position to observe the behavior, waits for it to occur, and records it.

Recording can be done in several ways, depending on the purpose for the observation. If the observer is studying causes or results for certain behaviors, then the so-called ABC analysis is especially useful (see Figure 2.11). It is a narrative description of the entire event, breaking it down into three parts: A = antecedent event, B = behavior, and C = consequent event. Each time the event occurs, it is recorded.

If subsequent observations of Darrell show the same sort of sequence as in the event sampling, the teacher could interpret this to mean that Darrell does not initiate the kicking, but rather responds to interference with his activities in this inappropriate manner. The teacher may need to help him learn an acceptable way to vent his frustration other than kicking. Until this issue is resolved, he may need to keep his shoes off in the classroom. This may also help him learn that kicking hurts. The advantages and disadvantages for using event sampling include the following:

Advantages

1. It keeps the event or behavior intact, making analysis easier.
2. It is more objective than some methods because the behavior has been defined ahead of time.
3. It is especially helpful in examining infrequent or rarely occurring behaviors.

Disadvantages

1. It takes the event out of context and thus may minimize other phenomena that are important to the interpretation.
2. It is a closed method that looks only for specified behavior and ignores other important behavior.
3. It misses the richness of detail that anecdotes, specimen records, or running records provide.

Rating Scales

Rating scales are observation tools that indicate the degree to which a person possesses a certain trait or behavior. Each behavior is rated on a continuum from the lowest to the highest level (or vice versa) and is marked off at certain points along the scale. The observer must make a judgment about where on the scale the child's behavior lies. As an observation tool, rating scales work best where particular degrees of behavior are well defined or well understood by the observer and where there is a distinct difference in the behavior at the various points on the scale.

These tools are useful in diagnosing a child on several behaviors at the same time. The observer watches the child and checks off or circles the point on the scale that indicates the child's current position in regard to the behavior or ability. Such scales are simple to make: Simply state the behavior, draw a line, then mark off a number of points or intervals along the line. Five intervals are often used so that there is a middle (neutral) position, with positive and negative intervals on either side of it (see Figure 2.12).

Graphic Scale

The rating scale in Figure 2.12 shows only one item of behavior. Many similar behaviors could be listed on this same scale. Such scales are called **graphic scales** and can be drawn either horizontally or vertically. Many traits can be listed on one sheet. Graphic scales are often easier to construct than to use. The observer must know the children well, be able to interpret their behavior, and be able to make an objective judgment within a limited time. For example, how would you rate the girl in the accompanying photo?

Shares toys					
	Always	Often	Sometimes	Seldom	Never

Figure 2.12   Graphic Scale for Single Behavior

Rating Scale Observer Errors

A different kind of observer error can affect the use of rating scales. Contrary to other types of observation, this tool calls for the observer to make an on-the-spot judgment, rather than an objective description. It is extremely difficult for observers to be totally unbiased and objective. They may be influenced by other things they already know about the child or the child's family, or by outside influences completely unrelated to the situation they are observing. For example, one observer persistently gave lower ratings to an overweight child. When asked about it later, the observer admitted a prejudice against overweight children because he had been one himself.

To guard against these tendencies, the observer should rate all of the different children being observed on the same trait before going on to another trait. To check objectivity, a second rater can observe the same children and compare results.

Rating scales may be used on their own, implemented with other observation methods as a part of the procedure, or filled in after the observation is completed

This girl has trouble sharing toys.

from data gathered from running records. As with the other observation methods, rating scales have certain advantages and disadvantages.

Advantages

1. They are easy to design and less time consuming to use.
2. They provide a convenient method to observe a large number of traits at one time or more than one child at a time.
3. They make it possible to measure difficult-to-quantify traits—shyness, for example.
4. They can be used by nonspecialist observers.
5. They are easier to score and quantify than most other methods.

Disadvantages

1. Rating scales use a closed method. They examine specified traits and may overlook other important behavior.
2. They feature the negative as well as the positive side of each trait.
3. Clearly differentiating between each point on the scale is sometimes difficult, both for the designer and the observer.
4. It is difficult to eliminate observer bias when judgments must be made quickly on many different traits.

Rubrics

Rubrics are a set of guidelines that evaluate performance. They have a range of criteria, like rating scales, but have indicators that determine the quality of performance from one level to the next (Wortham, 2012). There are three types of rubrics: holistic, analytic, and developmental.

Holistic Rubric

This type of rubric has a number of indicators that describe the quality of work or performance arranged in a progression from worst to best. It is scored with points for the level a child obtains. See Figure 2.13

Attention Span

1—Rarely finishes task, moves rapidly from one task to another
2—Usually needs encouragement to stay with task until complete
3—Can usually remain with task appropriate to age level until it is finished
4—Can stay with a chosen activity for very long periods, even returning next day

---

Figure 2.13 Holistic Rubric for Attention Span

Analytic Rubric

Describes and scores each task attribute separately with limited descriptors. For example, for "Rarely finishes task" the descriptors could be: 1—Gets up and leaves before starting task; 2—Starts a task but leaves before finished; 3—Stays with task for a while before leaving; 4—Stays with task almost to the end before leaving. This kind of rubric is used for diagnostic purposes.

Developmental Rubric

This type of rubric is used to serve a multiage group of children over a long period of time, often several grade levels. A child is assessed on a continuum of skills that shows developmental progress (Wortham, 2012).

Advantages
1. They provide guidelines for a child's performance.
2. They can be designed for many uses and ability levels.
3. They can easily meet changing needs.
4. They can be used to discuss children's performance with parents.

Disadvantages
1. Teachers may have difficulty determining the assessment criteria.
2. Rubrics may be limited or too specific.
3. Holistic rubrics may lack validity and reliability.
4. Teachers may focus on the wrong characteristics of student work.

Checklists

Checklists are lists of specific traits or behaviors arranged in a logical order. The observer must indicate the presence or absence of the behaviors either when observing them or when reflecting on the observation. Checklists are especially useful for types of behaviors or traits that can be specified easily and clearly. We tend to see what we look for. Thus a checklist can prove to be a valuable tool for focusing attention when many different items need to be observed. A survey or inventory of a situation can be done more efficiently with a checklist than with almost any other observation tool. If the observer needs to know whether a child displays the specified behavior, a checklist is the instrument of choice to use.

Both checklists and rating scales often include large numbers of traits or behaviors. The difference between the two is not necessarily in their appearance but in their use. An observer using a checklist merely checks off the presence of the trait (a blank denotes its absence). The observer using a rating scale must make a snap judgment about the degree to which the trait is present.

A separate checklist can be used for each child in the class.

Checklists can be used in a number of ways, depending on the purpose for the observation. For instance, a separate checklist can be used for each child in the class, if the results are to be used for individual planning. Or all of the children's names can be included on the same checklist along with the checklist items, if it is the observer's purpose to screen children for certain traits.

The items on a checklist can simply be checked off, or the date or time when they first appear can be entered to make a more complete record. A different checklist can be used for each observation, or a single checklist can serve in a cumulative manner for the same child all year if dates are recorded for each item. A single checklist can be used by one observer or by several observers who will add to the cumulative data over a period of time.

Finally, information gained from anecdotal and running records can be transferred to checklists to make interpretation easier. It is much simpler to scan a list of checked behaviors than to read through long paragraphs of wordy description when attempting to interpret observational evidence. However, it is obvious that checklists need to be prepared carefully.

Whether you plan to make your own checklist or use a prepared list, make sure the items listed are specified very clearly in objective, nonjudgmental terms. The user should be able to understand the items easily; thus, it makes sense to put items through a pretest before actual use in an observation tool. All checklist items should be positive, unlike rating scale items, which include a range of behavior from positive to negative.

Checklist items not observed are left blank, indicating absence of the particular behavior. If the observer does not have the opportunity to witness certain behaviors, these items should not be left blank, but denoted by some symbol (e.g., N, meaning no opportunity to observe). Some suggestions for developing checklist items are listed in Figure 2.14.

Overall, the checklist format should allow the observer to scan the items at a glance. The Child Development Checklist is an example of an observation tool that

Figure 2.14 Checklist
Items

- Short, descriptive, understandable
- Parallel in construction (word order, verb tense)
- Objective and nonjudgmental
- Positive in nature
- Not repeated elsewhere in checklist
- Representative of behavior, not all-inclusive

looks at nine important areas of child development, breaking down each area into six observable items: Each item is brief, represents an important aspect of development, is parallel in construction (beginning with a verb), and is positive. The six items are listed in either a sequence or a progression of known child development. Together, they form the profile of a whole child as he or she works and plays in the environment of an early childhood classroom. Advantages for using checklists of this nature include the following:

Advantages

1. They are easy, quick, and efficient to use.
2. The nonspecialist observer can use them with ease.
3. They can be used in the presence of the child or later from remembered behaviors or recorded narrative observation.
4. Several observers can gather the same information to check for reliability.
5. These checklists help to focus observation on many behaviors at one time.
6. They are especially useful for curriculum planning for individuals.

Checklists have a number of disadvantages as well. Observers must weigh one against the other, always keeping in mind their purpose for observing.

Disadvantages

1. They are closed in nature, looking at particular behaviors and not everything that occurs; thus they may miss behaviors of importance.
2. They are limited to recording the presence or absence of behavior.
3. They lack information about the quality and duration of behavior and a description.

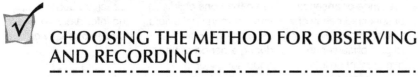

CHOOSING THE METHOD FOR OBSERVING AND RECORDING

Table 2.1 compares six of the methods for observing and recording young children discussed in this chapter. Each has advantages and disadvantages that an observer needs to consider before choosing a particular method. The final choice often depends on the purpose for the observation.

Table 2.1 Comparison of Methods of Observing and Recording

Method	Purpose	Advantages	Disadvantages
Anecdotal Record:			
A narrative of descriptive paragraphs, recorded *after behavior occurs*	To detail specific behavior for child's record; for case conferences; to plan for individuals	Open-ended; rich in details; no special observer training	Depends on observer's memory; behavior taken out of context; difficult to code or analyze for research
Running Record:			
A narrative written in sequence over a specified time, recorded *while behavior is occurring*	To discover causes and effects of behavior; for case conferences; to plan for individuals	Open-ended; comprehensive; no special observer training	Time-consuming; difficult to use for more than one child at a time; time-consuming to code and analyze for research
Time Sampling:			
Tallies or symbols showing the presence or absence of specified behavior during short time periods, recorded *while behavior is occurring*	For behavior modification baseline data; for child development research	Objective and controlled; not time-consuming; efficient for observing more than one child at a time; provides quantitative data for research	Closed; limited to observable behaviors that occur frequently; no description of behavior; takes behavior out of context
Event Sampling:			
A brief narrative of conditions preceding and following specified behavior, recorded *while behavior is occurring*	For behavior modification input; for child development research	Objective; helpful for in-depth diagnosis of infrequent behavior	Closed; takes event out of context; limited to specified behaviors
Rating Scale:			
A scale of traits or behaviors with checkmarks, recorded *before, during, and after behavior occurs*	To judge degree to which child behaves or possesses certain traits; to diagnose behavior or traits; to plan for individuals	Not time-consuming; easy to design; efficient for observing more than one child at a time for many traits; useful for several observers watching same child	Closed; subjective; limited to specified traits or behaviors
Checklist:			
A list of behaviors with checkmarks, recorded *before, during, and after behavior occurs*	To determine presence or absence of specified behaviors; to plan for individuals; to give observer an overview of child's development or progress	Efficient for observing more than one child at a time for many behaviors; useful for an individual during a period of time; a good survey or inventory tool; useful for several observers at once; no special training needed	Closed; limited to specified behaviors; no information on quality of behavior

A checklist was chosen as the basis for this book because of checklists' unique ability to give the observer an overview of child development. It is a teaching tool as well as an observational tool. The Child Development Checklist will thus assist the observer not only in gathering information to help plan for specific children, but also in learning the sequences of child growth in the areas of emotional, social, physical, cognitive, language, and creative development. Ahola and Kovacik (2007) concur, saying: "Checklists that are well-designed and appropriately used can be useful in understanding children's development and in developing curriculum" (p. 27).

USING THE CHILD DEVELOPMENT CHECKLIST

The Child Development Checklist in Table 2.2, around which this text is written, is as much a learning device for the observer as it is a planning tool for helping the child. With sequences of child development as its focus, it presents the areas of emotional, social, physical, cognitive, language, and creative development by dividing most of these domains into two major areas, then subdividing each area into six representative items of development.

Emotional development, for example, is divided into "self-esteem" and "emotional competence" (shown here) with a chapter devoted to each of these topics. These chapters illustrate representative behaviors in the sequence of emotional development that can be seen in the early childhood classroom.

Using One Checklist Section at a Time

As a learning device for the observer, the checklist is best used one section at a time. To understand the sequence of emotional development as it appears in the early childhood classroom, for instance, the observer should first plan to use the Self-Esteem section of the checklist in observing a child *for enough time to see if all six items are present*. This means coming into the classroom early enough to see how the child enters the room, what she does when her parent/caregiver leaves, and how she interacts with the teacher(s). It also means coming early to the classroom *more than once* to observe how the child behaves on different days and to record this information. The observer should not only check off the items as they appear, but also record evidence for each item in the space provided.

Using the Entire Checklist

Once you are familiar with each of the checklist areas and items, you can use the entire checklist (Table 1.1) for one child to gain a complete overview. How should you begin? You may want to learn something about a particular child in a certain area of development. Perhaps she has difficulty getting involved with the others in the pretend play during free-choice period. Plan to begin your observation during this period. You will want to look at the items in the social competence section. Other

Table 2.2   Child Development Checklist (Self-Esteem; Emotional Competence)

CHILD DEVELOPMENT CHECKLIST

Name _____   Observer _____

Program _____   Dates _____

<u>**Directions:**</u>

Put an **X** for items you see the child perform regularly. Put an **N** for items where there is no opportunity to observe. Leave all other items blank.

Item	Evidence	Dates
1. Self-Esteem		
_____ Separates from primary caregiver without difficulty		
_____ Develops a secure attachment with teacher		
_____ Completes a task successfully		
_____ Makes activity choices without teacher's help		
_____ Stands up for own rights		
_____ Displays enthusiasm about doing things for self		
2. Emotional Competence		
_____ Releases stressful feelings in appropriate manner		
_____ Expresses anger in words rather than negative actions		
_____ Can be calmed in frightening situations		
_____ Shows fondness, affection, love toward others		
_____ Shows interest, excitement in classroom activities		
_____ Smiles, seems happy much of the time		

checklist areas that can often be seen at the same time as Social Competence include the items under Self-Esteem, Emotional Competence, Spoken Language, and Dramatic Play Skills. Either check off the items as you see them, writing in the evidence, or do a running record of everything the child does and says and convert it to the checklist afterward.

Be sure to make notes after each item, jotting down the evidence that prompted you to check the item (or leave it blank). If you leave the item blank, it is still important to write down your reason—the evidence for leaving the item blank. If you use the same checklist on more than one day in a cumulative manner, be sure to put the date after each item as well.

The time of your next observation may be determined by the areas you have not had the opportunity to observe. For Self-Esteem, for instance, you will want to observe the child when she arrives in the morning, especially at the beginning of the year. Emotional Competence items also need to be observed during lunch or snack time, toileting, and naptime.

✓ INTERPRETING AND USING THE DATA

Once you have observed a child and recorded data about her in a running record, then transferred the data to the Child Development Checklist, the next step is to interpret the information. Learning to know and understand a child is a fascinating process. Objective observing and recording like this make possible a deeper understanding than a lifetime of merely being around children can do. We need to step back from children and look at them impartially and objectively. Only then do we truly see who they are and what they are. Only then do we begin to understand how we can help them reach their greatest potential.

Interpreting the information your observations have provided takes knowledge and skill. You need to know a great deal about child development both from reading and studying about children and from actual experience with them. Then you can begin to make valid inferences and conclusions about children based on your observations.

However, the data you have gained about a child from the Child Development Checklist observation can help you plan activities for the child to help in his or her development. Go over the checklist carefully making notes of the particular strengths of a child whom you have observed. Also note the areas needing strengthening (not weaknesses). Make what we call a Learning Prescription for the child by listing three areas of strengths and three areas needing strengthening. Using the child's strengths, decide on three activities that can help the child in the areas needing strengthening (see Figure 2.15). Set up these activities and observe to see how the child responds over time. New activities can be added if necessary.

Use of the Checklist by Preservice Teachers and Student Teachers

Preservice teachers and student teachers can use the Child Development Checklist just as a classroom teacher does, making a series of observations of a single child

Figure 2.15 Learning
Prescription

Learning Prescription

Name_____Age_____Date_____

Areas of Strength and Confidence

1._____

2._____

3._____

Areas Needing Strengthening

1._____

2._____

3._____

Activities to Help

1._____

2._____

3._____

until all the items have been noted. In case the observer has no access to live children in a classroom, it is possible to observe and record using prerecorded videos or CD-ROMs of children in a classroom.

For student observers who observe and record live children, you need to rewrite your notes as soon as possible after you have finished your observations. As an experienced observer notes:

Memory is a poor recorder. Therefore you will want to make it a practice to transcribe your notes soon after you visit a classroom.

OBSERVATION OF EACH CHILD

It is important to observe each of the children in this kind of detail throughout the year. Teachers report that they can learn more about each child by stepping back and making a relatively brief, focused observation like this, than by having the child in their program for an entire year. It is an eye-opening experience to look at one child in depth from an observer's point of view, rather than from the perspective of a busy teacher involved with the activities of many other lively youngsters.

Child development students report that an in-depth examination of a real child makes textbooks and courses come alive, as well. Parents, too, benefit from the information that objective observations provide. Not only do the parents learn new activities to use with their children at home, but they also often become involved in the fascinating drama of how their own children develop, why their children act the way they do, and how they, as parents, can best help their children realize their full potential.

LEARNING ACTIVITIES

1. Have a team of observers record a 10-minute observation of a child at play in a preschool classroom. One team member should record a running record of the child at the time of the observation. The other member should make a running record of the same observation at the end of the day. Compare the results. Write up which one showed the most details and which worked best for the observers.

2. Write up the results of the time sampling, event sampling, and rubric you used to observe a child. Tell which of these methods was more satisfactory and why.

3. Write up a comparison of the six methods of observing and recording shown in Table 2.1 as they apply to a specific child of your interest. What would you want to find out about the child? Which method worked best and why?

4. Write up your use of the Child Development Checklist in two of the domains to observe a different child's actions. Summarize your findings about this child.

5. Fill out a detailed Learning Prescription about the child based on your observations.

SUGGESTED READINGS

Burke, K. (2011). *From standards to rubrics in six steps* (3rd ed.). Thousand Oaks, CA: Corwin.

Gibson, C., Jones, S., & Patrick, T. (2010). Conducting informal developmental assessments. *Exchange* (May/June), 36–40.

McAfee, O., & Leong, D. J. (2011). *Assessing and guiding young children's development and learning* (5th ed.). Boston, MA: Pearson.

McFarland, L. (2008). Anecdotal records: Valuable tools for assessing young children's development. *Dimensions of Early Learning, 36*(1), 31–36.

Nilsen, B. A. (2010). *Week by week: Plans for documenting children's development* (5th ed.). Belmont, CA: Wadsworth/Cengage.

Puckett, M. B., & Black, J. K. (2008). *Meaningful assessments of the young child* (3rd ed.). Upper Saddle River, NJ: Pearson.

WEB SITES

American Educational Research Association
http://www.aera.net

Kidsource Online (assessment and observation)
http://www.kidsource.com

Lesson Planz (suggestions for assessment)
http://www.lessonplanz.com

A quick program for creating rubrics
http://www.ribistar.41teachers.org

Focuses on building rubrics
http://www.teachnology.com/web_tools/rubrics/

An early childhood behavioral checklist
http://www.thechp.syr.edu/Behavioral_Observation_Checklist.pdf

CHAPTER 3

Self-Esteem

In this chapter you will learn to observe if children can:

____ Separate from primary caregivers without difficulty

____ Develop a secure attachment with teacher

____ Complete a task successfully

____ Make activity choices without teacher's help

____ Stand up for own rights

____ Display enthusiasm about doing things for self

____ Be observed by using running record and checklist

 DEVELOPING SELF-ESTEEM

From the moment of birth, the young human being is engaged in the dynamic process of becoming himself or herself. The child continually develops into a whole person with a temperament, personality, and value system—with a physical, cognitive, language, social, emotional, and creative makeup that is uniquely his or her own. It is an engrossing process that may take most of a lifetime to complete, but its early stages are perhaps its most crucial, for they set the pattern for all that is to follow. Using observational methods such as the Child Development Checklist, running records, child interviews, rubrics, and others, you will be able to determine where a child stands in his or her development of self-esteem.

Among the most important aspects of the child's growing persona is his development of **self-concept**: his sense of self that includes both his **self-image** (his inner picture of himself) and his **self-esteem** (his sense of self-worth). Although these three terms are often used interchangeably, they actually refer to different aspects of the self. A person's self-image is his internal image or picture of himself that includes his looks, his gender, his ethnicity, his standing in the family, and his abilities. A child acquires this image as he grows and sees himself as a separate individual. Self-image is not judgmental, it is descriptive.

On the other hand, self-esteem is an emotional evaluation of these aspects: the child's feeling about her looks, her gender, her standing in the family, and her abilities. She needs to feel that she is capable, significant, successful, and worthy. She acquires this sense of self-worth through her interaction with the other people around her as well as her own judgmental view of herself and what she is able to do. Frost, Wortham, and Reifel (2012) believe that when preschoolers begin to make judgments about their own worth and competence, they feel that they are liked or disliked depending on how well they can do new things. Self-image and self-esteem come together to form a child's self-concept.

Self-esteem formation is a continuous process, but once it has taken some form, it is difficult to change as the child gets older. As the child receives incoming information about the way she is treated by others or by her experiences of success or failure, she uses such data to confirm what she already feels about herself. For example, if the child feels good about herself because of the way she is treated in her family, then she will see a teacher's good treatment of her as confirmation of what she already knows. She then acts out these feelings in the classroom by being happy and cooperative. This, in turn, keeps those around her treating her positively.

If, on the other hand, a child has negative feelings about himself because of the way he is treated in his family, even a teacher's good treatment may not change his self-esteem readily. Instead, he may rationalize it by thinking that the teacher is being nice to him because she feels sorry for him because he is so bad. He may act out his negative feelings about himself by being aggressive toward other children, disruptive of activities, or by withdrawing into himself and not participating. Any scolding or other negative response to such behavior only promotes a feeling that he is no good.

How then can a teacher of preschool children help youngsters become convinced that they are truly worthy people? Teachers must be persistent and consistent in their positive messages to *every* child *every* day. Sometimes we think we have done our duty by greeting a child whenever we have time as long as some staff member is at the door to do the greeting in the morning. This is not enough. You must personally deliver your positive messages *every* day to *every* child.

This chapter will discuss some of the developmental progressions that are observable in children 3 to 5 years of age as they strive to develop a healthy sense of self in the early childhood classroom. Although children carry with them their own unique package of genetic traits and home influences, the teachers they meet and the daily care they receive in the classroom have a strong bearing on their future development.

Each item of the Child Development Checklist will be discussed separately. Each checklist item is positive in nature and should be checked if the observer sees the child performing in the manner described. An item left unchecked may indicate help is needed for that particular item. Suggestions for helping and supporting the child's development in the unchecked items will follow the discussion of the item.

The six items in the Self-Esteem Checklist section show a progression of steps many children take as they separate from their parents or primary caregivers and make the sometimes difficult transition into preschool. It is important for a teacher to determine at the outset where each child stands in this progression to assist the children in developing a strong, positive sense of self.

☑ SEPARATES FROM PRIMARY CAREGIVER WITHOUT DIFFICULTY

Initial Attachment

Most studies of young children agree that a key ingredient in their successful development is a strong **initial attachment** to a primary caregiver, usually the mother. Many psychologists, in fact, regard attachment as the **seminal event** in a person's emotional development. It seems a great paradox, then, to suggest that for successful development to continue, the young human must learn at the same time to separate from the parent. But such is the case. This **separation** should occur first in the home—not only with the child, but also with the parents, who must let go of the child and encourage the child to become independent of them.

Many current attachment/separation studies are based on the initial work of John Bowlby (1969) and Mary Ainsworth (1974), who talk about children's attachment to their parents as a condition of trust in their parents' reliability. Attachment occurs during the first year or two of life as a result of many interactions between infants and parents. The first separation of the child from the mother is, of course, the physical one that occurs at birth. Some psychologists believe that much of life thereafter is the developing person striving to achieve that perfect state of oneness once again with another human.

This is the beginning of the strong initial attachment that both the infant and caregiver need for later separation to occur successfully. Such an attachment leads to a sense of security and trust on the part of the infant. The lack of such an attachment often interferes with the child's ability to build trust in future relationships.

Psychologist Erik Erikson describes young children's psychosocial development in terms of ages and stages. In each stage he noted that a particular task

Initial school separation from a parent is sometimes difficult for a child.

must be accomplished for the personality to develop smoothly. Erikson called the important task during an infant's first year "trust versus mistrust." How infants are treated by those around them helps them to develop feelings either of trust or mistrust of people. These feelings can affect a person's actions or interactions for the rest of his life, Erikson believed (Mooney, 2000).

Initial Separation

The initial separation of the infant from its mother or primary caregiver begins when he first recognizes he is separate from that person. This develops within the first 6 months of life as the baby recognizes there is a difference between himself and the caregiver—and later, between himself and others. At this time, his first memories—visual in nature—are occurring. Some psychologists call this the "psychological birth" of the baby. It is the first glimmering of self-identity.

Toward the end of the first year, as the infant learns to move about by creeping and by taking her first unsteady steps, an interesting pattern of interaction with the caregiver often emerges. The youngster uses the caregiver as a base from which to explore her environment. She moves out a bit and comes back, moves farther and returns, moves out again, and this time may only look back, making the eye contact that will give her the reassurance to continue exploring.

During the last half of the child's first year (or sometimes before), **separation anxiety** also emerges: The infant sets up a strong protest of crying or clinging if the caregiver attempts to leave. This pattern of distress is also exhibited when a stranger appears, making it obvious that the baby recognizes the difference between the caregiver and others. Thus self-esteem develops as the toddler ventures out and scurries back, clings and pushes away, holds on and lets go. But the stronger the initial attachment, the more secure the developing child should feel each time he or she lets go.

The young human learns who he is by the way other people respond to him (how others seem to be affected by his behavior). Hopefully, this response is mainly positive, so that by the time he enters child care, preschool, or Head Start, he already will be feeling good about himself.

School Separation

No matter how good the young child feels about herself, the initial **school separation** from a parent is often difficult. At 3 years old, the sense of self is still a bit shaky. Although the child has an identity at home, at school the child is in a strange environment. Balaban (2006) talks about separation from the parents or primary caregiver making young children unhappy. They often feel abandoned, sometimes frightened or angry. To complicate matters, the parent/caregiver may be experiencing the same "separation anxiety" and may not want to let go of the child, which the child often senses.

Each child handles the situation in his or her own way. One child may be accustomed to being taken to the home of a loving babysitter and will take this new "playroom" in stride. Another may cling to her mother and scream whenever the mother attempts to leave. The child who is used to playing with others may quickly join the group in the block building center. A shyer child may need the teacher's urging to join in. One fussing, crying child may stop crying as soon as his mother leaves. Another may withdraw into herself and sit in a corner sucking her thumb.

You—as a teacher, student intern, or assistant—hope that children will become adjusted to this separation within a few days or a week or so. Most of them will. One or two may not. How can you help them develop a strong enough sense of self that they feel free to let go of their primary caregiver?

If You Have Not Checked This Item: Some Helpful Ideas

One or more of the children in your classroom may have self-esteem checklist items that are not checked. Because you are aware that each item represents a step in the developmental progression of young children, you may be able to lend children support at the outset by arranging your schedule or setting up your classroom ahead of time to address their problems. Here are some ideas that may help preschoolers separate from their parents or caregivers with less difficulty.

■ Make Early Initial Contact with Parent/Caregiver and Child

If the child and the parent have met you ahead of time, they may feel less reluctant to separate on the day that school begins. For the child, it is better if this meeting takes place close to the time of school opening rather than the spring before. Memories of a brief visit several months before school begins have little meaning for the young child. An immediate follow-up is more effective. If you visit the child's home, take a camera to make a photo for later use in the classroom to help the child make an easier transition from home to school.

■ Try Staggered Enrollment

Rather than having all the children in your class begin school on the same day at the same time, you might consider having half of them begin on the first day and half the second—or half in the morning and the rest in the afternoon. This will allow staff members to devote more time to the individual children and their parents. In addition, the first day may not be so overwhelming for the children if only half of the class is present at once.

■ Create a Simple Initial Environment

The more complex the classroom environment, the more overwhelming it is for certain children. You might plan to have the classroom arranged with fewer activity areas for the first weeks, and less material on the shelves. As the children settle in and become more secure, you can add activities and materials as needed.

■ Use Transition Materials

Children can make the transition from home to school and separate more easily from their parents if familiar materials help bridge the gap. Water is one such material. A water table or basin with an egg beater, funnel, and squeeze bottles may take a child's mind off his parent long enough to get him happily involved in the center. Toy trucks and dolls often have the same effect. Have a special set of little toys you can allow children to take home with them at the end of the day and return again in the morning to make the transition less difficult.

■ Utilize Parent/Caregiver Visits

Allow the parents to stay as long as necessary on the first days or come in for visits from time to time. The shy child may use her parent as a base for exploration in the classroom, venturing away from the parent and returning just as she did as a toddler at home. If the separation is a difficult one, have the caregiver return early to pick up the youngster. Little by little the children should be able to stay longer without their parents.

■ Show and Foster Acceptance of the Child

Up until now the child's self-esteem has evolved from the reactions of his family to him. Now that he is in your classroom, you and your coworkers and the other children will be adding details to the child's interior picture of himself. These details need to be positive, happy ones. You need to support this process first by accepting the child and his family unconditionally. Information is relayed to children through words, facial expressions, and actions.

Nilsen (2010) talks about setting the mood for the day by greeting every child upon arrival. This lets the child know he or she is important. You need to smile at the child frequently. Greet him personally *every day*, telling him how glad you are to see him. Say goodbye to him at the end of *every day*, telling him "See you tomorrow, don't forget!" Demonstrate that you enjoy being near him and having him near you. You are the behavior model for the other children as well. If they see that you accept a child no matter what, they will be more likely to do the same.

■ Read a Book

Children like to hear stories about other children that have feelings the same as theirs. Try reading a book about separation to children having difficulty in this area. If the characters of the story are children from a different culture, all the better. Children learn to accept one another when they see picture books featuring various cultural and ethnic characters. In *See You Later, Mom!* (Northway, 2006), the story of the first week in preschool for William, an Anglo boy, shows his teacher to be Asian and his best friend, African. William wants to play with the other children, but he is too uncomfortable to let go of his mother for long. Little by little he lets go of her until on Friday, he quickly joins the others and waves goodbye to Mom.

✓ DEVELOPS A SECURE ATTACHMENT WITH TEACHER

Children who have already formed a secure attachment with their parents or primary caregivers usually have little trouble developing a secure relationship with their teachers as well. Balaban (2006) says that when a child trusts her parents, she transfers her loving feelings from parents to teachers. Such securely attached children tend to view teachers as trustworthy and themselves as worthy of care. They are willing to enter into a cooperative relationship with their teachers in which the teacher guides and supports them, and the children comply with the teacher's requests. They trust that the teacher will help them when they need help and protect them from danger when necessary.

Riley, San Juan, Klinker, and Ramminger (2008) discuss studies showing how "four-year-olds who were securely attached to their current teacher seemed to engage in more complex play, were friendlier, and were less aggressive with peers."

This girl has developed a secure attachment with her teacher.

Figure 3.1 Behaviors Showing Secure Attachment with Teacher

- Asking the teacher to help them solve a problem
- Accepting help or support from the teacher
- Allowing themselves to be comforted by the teacher in times of stress
- Showing affection toward the teacher
- Wanting to be close to the teacher
- Paying attention and listening to the teacher
- Complying with the teacher's requests
- Taking part in conversations and activities with the teacher

Teachers, on the other hand, need to expect and welcome such an attachment on the part of the children. They need to be there for the children in good times and bad, to provide support and opportunity for children to establish friendships, to know individual likes and dislikes, to provide a stimulating environment where children can become involved in exciting activities, and to give children choices as well as time to complete their projects. They need to show a caring attitude toward each child and display an interest in things the child does or says.

Lucos (2007–2008) talks about how emotional togetherness along with a passion for working with children helps a teacher not just to be present, but to be wholly available to children on emotional, cognitive, and physical levels. For appropriate engagement with a child to take place, a teacher needs to know where each child stands developmentally.

As an observer of the children, how will you know if children have developed this secure relationship with their teacher? Their behavior toward their teacher is the best indication. Some of their behaviors are shown in Figure 3.1.

Children with Insecure Attachments

Children with insecure attachments to parents or primary caregivers often view themselves as unworthy or incompetent. This feeling frequently follows them into the classroom and affects their relationships with teachers and staff members. They may feel that they cannot rely on any adults to meet their needs, thus their classroom relationships are built on mistrust rather than trust. They may show little interest in becoming involved in classroom activities or with other children. Some may be disruptive, interfering with what other children are doing or calling attention to themselves in other inappropriate ways. They expect to be scolded or punished, and if this does not happen, they may act out in an even more disruptive manner.

If you notice that a disruptive child continues to look over at you once he has interfered with another child, it may be a sign that his behavior is really directed at you rather than the other child. It is almost as if his behavior is calling out to you: "What are you going to do about me?" or "I want attention, too!" If your attention takes the form of making the child sit in the "time-out chair," this is a punishment response and is not conducive to building a trusting relationship with the child.

What should you do, then, to help this child build a secure attachment relationship with you? Balaban (2006) tells us that teachers must remain calm and supportive and give a child the opportunity to recover from the upset of the separation. Play helps and may be children's most satisfactory means of coming to terms with and mastering their reactions to separation.

If You Have Not Checked This Item: Some Helpful Ideas

■ Stay in Physical Proximity to the Child

When she first enters the classroom, if the insecure child sees you standing or working nearby, she may begin to relax and feel better about being in a new environment. You can look up and smile at her from time to time, or walk over and say a few words of encouragement. Be sure to show the child on a daily basis that you are aware of her. She may eventually come over and stand by you for a few minutes and then return to her activity.

■ Provide Positive Individualized Attention

You need to show genuine interest in the child. If this is a child who has made you feel annoyed, find a way to change your feelings. Make a daily list of positive things about the child and tell the child how you appreciate what he is doing or saying. Find out what he likes to eat, do, wear, or play with. Look through a back issue of a magazine or catalogue together. Have him cut out the items that interest him and start a scrapbook of "Things I Like." By giving him positive individualized attention like this, you are helping to break down the child's mistrust and his old patterns of interaction with an adult who has perhaps mistreated or neglected him.

■ Engage in Joint Activities with the Child

Eventually you should be able to play with the child, ask her to help you, share ideas with the child, and ask for her input. You can be her partner for a while, but eventually she will need to partner with another child as she becomes acclimated to the classroom and able to trust that you care about her and will take care of her no matter what. Having more than one adult in the classroom makes it possible to spend such time with children in need—and every child.

COMPLETES A TASK SUCCESSFULLY

You are also helping the child to construct a new and secure relationship by showing him he is a competent human being who can succeed in things. Perhaps he has been overly criticized at home and therefore has little confidence in his ability to

Observe to see which children can successfully complete an activity you have set up.

succeed at anything. Once you know what things interest him, bring in some books he will enjoy about these topics. Set up a simple art project that he can complete. Have him collect some natural objects and display them in the science center. Help him write his name as large as he can and outline each letter with glitter sprinkled on transparent glue. Then he can see who he is: big and strong and beautiful!

Observe to see which children are successful in the activities you have set up in art or science or matching games. Watch to see which ones can perform self-help skills such as getting dressed. Success is such an important ingredient of self-esteem. Even a child's partial success in a task should be recognized. Giving descriptive praise to even the smallest of children's efforts helps them toward mastering a complex skill—and feeling good about themselves. Look at that! You laced both your shoes by yourself! (no mention of the skipped eyelet). Being recognized for accomplishments is the major and most essential component of a child's self-esteem.

Because "we see what we look for," have you actually looked for such successes? Keep track of successful accomplishments, no matter how small, for each of the children. Be sure to acknowledge them with descriptive praise, describing exactly what they have done, and not empty praise (phrases such as "good job").

Some children are afraid to start anything, let alone finish it. Also watch for children who enter an activity area, start an activity, but leave before it is finished. Sometimes a first step is all a child needs. Sit next to the child who tells you he can't make the puzzle and put in a piece yourself. Then ask him to look for the next one. Stay with him until he completes the puzzle. Then ask him to try it again on his own. Give him positive verbal support all the way, but refrain from helping this time. When he has finished, recognize his accomplishment with descriptive praise and/or a photo of him and his puzzle.

If You Have Not Checked This Item: Some Helpful Ideas

■ Create a Sorting Task with Child's Favorite Items

If you know the child has a cat for a pet, bring in a set of dog and cat counters and a sorting tray or plastic containers. Ask the child to sort out items that are alike.

■ Read a Book

Read a picture book about a character who has a problem to solve and stays with it until it is solved. In **Drum, Chavi, Drum** (Dole, 2003), the Hispanic girl Chavi wants to play the conga drums in Miami's Calle Ocho Festival, but she is not allowed to because she is a girl. Nothing stops Chavi, the best drummer on the street, who finally wins by dressing like a boy and fooling everyone. In **Jingle Dancer** (Smith, 2000), Jenna, a Muscogee Creek Indian girl, dreams of doing a jingle dance at the next powwow just like her grandma did. But her dress has no jingles. Jenna uses her wits to acquire one row of jingles at a time until she has enough for her dress.

Feeney and Moravcik (2005) believe that picture books for young children play a major role in shaping their emerging images of themselves and others.

■ Use the Computer

Take special time in helping the child who seldom completes activities successfully to use the computer. Choose a simple program (e.g., *Dr. Seuss's ABC*). Stay with him until he learns how to use it. Then have him use it on his own. Using the computer successfully is an especially strong booster of a child's self-esteem.

MAKES ACTIVITY CHOICES WITHOUT TEACHER'S HELP

One of the next observable indicators of a child's feelings about herself in your classroom is her willingness to choose on her own the activity she wants to engage in. Once she feels confident enough to leave your side, she needs to explore the new environment and try out the various materials and activities on her own. Many children have strong enough self-esteem to go immediately to the activity areas upon first entering the room. Others use the adult who accompanies them as a base for their explorations, going into an area and coming back to the person.

The more secure the child–teacher attachment relationship, the less likely the young child is to be irritable and isolated. Thus, it is important to help a child build this relationship initially. It is also important to observe which children are able to become involved with activities independently—and which are not quite ready, possibly because their teacher attachment or self-esteem is not yet strong enough.

Do the children know what activities are available in the classroom? Be sure to spend time early in the day talking about what activities are available. Figure 3.2 shows the floor plan of a typical preschool. Be sure your classroom is arranged

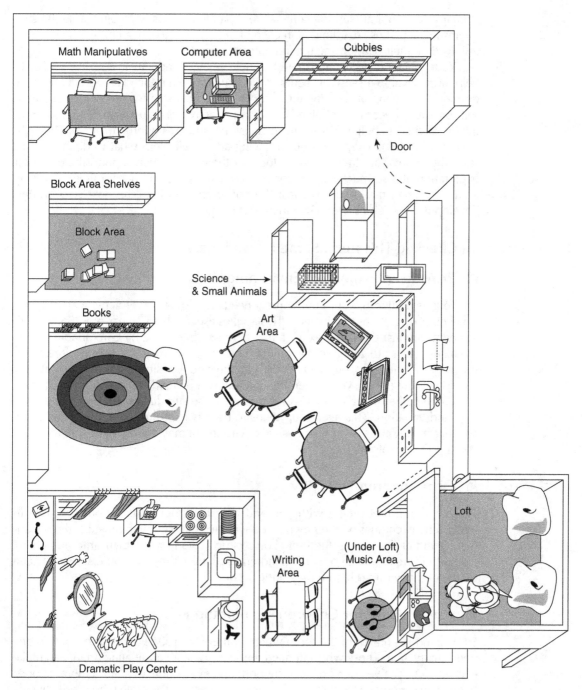

Figure 3.2   Floor Plan of Preschool

similar to this so that learning centers are separate and easily recognizable. Be sure interesting activities are going on in each of the centers to entice children to become involved on their own during the free-choice period.

Your goal for children who do not participate independently in activities will be to help them develop a sense of security with you and within the classroom. Once they develop this feeling of security, they may take the next step toward developing their self-esteem by becoming involved in classroom activities on their own. It is so tempting for teachers to help children make decisions, and the children to agree. They will even ask for help. They are used to having adults tell them what to do. You must resist the temptation. Invite them to look for themselves, then support them in their exploration. It is so much simpler for you to make up their minds for them, you may argue. But then they will have lost the opportunity to take the next step in their development of self-esteem. Give them this chance.

If You Have Not Checked This Item: Some Helpful Ideas

■ Provide an Explorable Environment

For younger children, your environment needs to display fewer activity areas and a small number of items within each. This applies especially to 3-year-olds. Some environments are just too complex for many of these children to be comfortable. When too many things are going on, the children may respond by refusing to explore or get involved. For this age group you need to simplify your physical environment—at least at the beginning of the year. Later, the children will be ready for additional activities.

On the other hand, 4- and 5-year-olds need the stimulation of complexity, novelty, and variation. This age group tends to be less fearful of new things and more adventurous. A more complex physical environment may encourage rather than discourage their exploration.

■ Give Children Time

Once children feel secure with you and your classroom, they should be able to make activity choices on their own if you will give them enough time. Let them wander around at first during the free-choice period. Don't force them into an activity before they are ready to go. Some children need more time than others. Others need to try out many things before they settle on one.

■ Act as a Base for Children's Explorations

Sit or stand in an area of the room where children can see you, near but not in any one activity area. Those who still need the security of an adult attachment can make eye contact, receive your smiles of support, and even come over for a moment or so before you encourage them to go off on their own again. The child who is still clinging can explore with her eyes. When she feels secure enough, she will join the others, knowing you are nearby.

■ Read a Book

Hearing a book read about a preschool classroom and all the interesting activities it contains may motivate the insecure child to look around her own classroom and be more willing to make activity choices on her own. Invite an insecure child to hear you read a book such as **See You Later, Mom!** (Northway, 2006), mentioned earlier, where children are playing with trucks and play dough, doing painting, singing, and dancing. What would be going on in your classroom?

✓ STANDS UP FOR OWN RIGHTS

For preschool children to stand up for their rights within the classroom, they need to have developed strong enough self-esteem to believe in themselves as individuals with a point of view worth other people's consideration. Thus far in their development of self-esteem, they have been able to make the separation from their parents, develop a secure attachment relationship with the teacher, complete various tasks successfully, and choose activities on their own. Now the children are progressing further by developing their own points of view they feel are worthy of other children's consideration.

What are some of the classroom rights such a self-confident child might insist on? One is *the right of possession* (see Figure 3.3). If a child is playing with a piece of equipment, he should be able to continue using it unless some previous turn-taking rule is in effect. Many childhood squabbles take place over toys or materials, often because of children's egocentric perspectives. A child believes he should have a toy because he wants it. The fact that another child is playing with it does not count in his mind. The development of mutual respect is difficult among 3- and 4-year-olds because many of them lack the ability to understand the other's perspective. The child who feels his right is worth defending will often refuse to give in.

A child's *choice of participation* is another personal right often established in early childhood classrooms. If a child opts to join or not join a particular activity, you and the other children need to honor her choice. Use enticements rather than force if you feel the child should be involved when she chooses not to be.

Completing independent projects in her own way is a right that self-confident children will defend. If a child is doing a painting, modeling clay, constructing a building, or dressing a doll on her own, she should be able to do it as she sees fit as

Figure 3.3   Children's Rights

- The right of possession
- The choice of participation
- Completing independent projects
- Protecting personal property
- Playing without fear of bullying

long as she is not interfering with others. Similarly, others should not be allowed to interfere with her. The child with strong self-esteem will continue in her own manner, disregarding or rejecting the attempts of others to impose their will.

Protecting property is another right that self-confident children will insist on. Toys or games they have brought from home are often the focus of conflict. You need to provide a private space like a cubby for each child to store his possessions. Block buildings are also important to the children who have built them. The child who insists on saving his building may want help in making a sign informing others: "Please Leave Dion's Building Standing."

Playing without fear of bullying is another right all children may need to learn to do, especially on the playground with no teacher around. Too often these days a child's right to play unmolested by another child who would tease, taunt, push, hit, or chase him is being violated. Such bullying needs to be stopped. It needs to be reported to the teacher by the victim and other witnesses. Teachers need to talk to the children about bullying and that reporting it is not tattling. The class as a whole may need to start a "kindness to others" project.

Children may stand up for their own rights in a number of ways. They may physically prevent another child from doing something or make the child do something. They may verbalize their position with the other child. They may tell the teacher. Some of their actions may not be acceptable in a classroom full of children. Use of power or aggression is not appropriate. You need to help such children find more acceptable means of standing up for their rights.

As you observe your children on this particular item, look to see which ones do not allow another child to urge or force unwanted changes on them and which ones do not back down or give up a toy or a turn. At the same time, take note of children who always give up or give in to the demands of another. They may also need your support in strengthening their self-esteem.

Cultural Differences in Standing Up for Own Rights

Whereas Western cultures consider a child's standing up for his rights as an indication of his self-esteem, Eastern cultures place a greater emphasis on maintaining harmonious relationships. Parents from Chinese families teach their children self-restraint and control of their emotions. Their children might very well give in to the demands of another because they have been taught self-restraint. They consider their children competent if they are shy, reticent, and quiet, whereas North American teachers may see such children as lacking self-confidence. Puerto Rican mothers focus on respectfulness of others, and traditional Navajo mothers teach their children to stand back and observe rather than go forward in their play. Many African, Latin American, and southern European cultures also bring up their children to have respect for others rather than asserting themselves.

If you find that nonassertive children in your classroom are from another culture, you need to look for other indications of their self-esteem, including respect for others and being sensitive to others' points of view.

If You Have Not Checked This Item: Some Helpful Ideas

■ Model Your Own Behavior

You need to model the behavior you want your children to follow. Stand firm on your decisions. Let your children know why. If you are "wishy-washy" or inconsistent in your treatment of them, they may have trouble standing firm themselves.

■ Allow Children Choices

One way to help a child learn that her rights can count is to give her a chance to make choices that are important to her. Let her choose a favorite activity to participate in or a toy to take home, rather than forcing your choice on her.

■ Stand Up for the Child

When it is clear to you that a child's rights have been infringed upon by another child, you should take a stand supporting the child, and at the same time let the others know "why Shandra can finish her painting now and Tyrell can't," for example.

■ Read a Book

Reading stories to children about bullying and how to respond to it is important these days. Three books you might consider are shown in Figure 3.4. Ask your children how the bullied character in the book responded to the bullying. What would your children have done?

In *Bullies Never Win* Jessica tells her mother about Brenda, the bully, and finally gets enough courage to stand up to her. Brenda never bothers her again. In *Freckleface Strawberry and the Dodgeball Bully* Freckleface finally confronts Windy Pants Patrick and scares him with her monster song. They become friends. In *Lucy and the Bully*, an animal story, Lucy compliments Tommy on his drawing (a first) and they become friends.

DISPLAYS ENTHUSIASM ABOUT DOING THINGS FOR SELF

The lifelong pursuit of a self-concept is, in the final analysis, a struggle for autonomy. If young children are successful in this quest, they will be able and willing to behave independently in many ways. Your observations in the area of self-esteem will help

Figure 3.4   Books About Bullying

Bullies Never Win (Cuyler, 2009)

Freckleface Strawberry and the Dodgeball Bully (Moore, 2009)

Lucy and the Bully (Alexander, 2008)

The most successful learners are often those who want to do things for themselves.

you determine which children in your class are well on the road to developing strong self-concepts and which ones are not. The most successful learners will be those who can and want to do things for themselves. They will have achieved enough self-assurance about their own abilities to be able to try and eventually succeed in doing things on their own. Achieving this competence will then allow them a measure of independence from the adults around them.

What are some of the activities you may observe such children performing independently in your classroom? Figure 3.5 is a partial list.

The adeptness of 3-, 4-, and 5-year-old children in these various activities depends on their self-esteem, the practice they have had at home or elsewhere, and

Figure 3.5 Independent Classroom Activities

dressing and undressing	*painting with brush*
tying or fastening shoes	*mixing paints*
using own cubby	*getting out toys*
toileting	*putting toys away*
washing hands and face	*returning blocks to shelves*
brushing teeth	*dressing dolls*
setting table for eating	*handling hammer*
pouring drink	*cutting with scissors*
dishing out food	*cutting with knife*
handling eating implements	*mixing dough*
eating	*using climbing equipment*
cleaning up after eating	*making puzzles*
using computer	*using audio recorder*

the encouragement or discouragement the adults around them have offered. Children who have always had things done for them by the adults around them often give up the struggle for autonomy. You and your coworkers need to beware of the temptation to "help the little children" more than necessary. Children can do many more things for themselves than we realize. You need to allow time for children to learn to zip up their jackets and pour their own drinks. Otherwise, you are denying them an unparalleled opportunity to develop their independence.

The way adults behave toward children during these formative years can indeed make a difference in children's feelings about themselves and thus in the way they behave. Research regarding gender stereotyping has found that mothers and fathers often treat their young daughters differently when it comes to independent behavior.

Parents often allow and encourage boys to behave independently earlier than girls in such areas as using scissors without adult supervision, crossing the street alone, playing away from home, and riding the bus. When girls ask for help they often get it, but boys more often receive a response telling them to do it themselves. Boys are encouraged to manipulate objects and explore their environments, whereas girls are more often discouraged. Thus it seems that many parents value independence in boys more than in girls. This behavior is changing, you may say. True, but many parents still start this way.

This type of discriminating behavior may of course result in girls feeling less capable than boys and therefore attempting fewer things on their own. Or this behavior may cause girls—and therefore women—to become dependent on men and less willing to risk using their own capabilities. Is this still the case among your children even with all the focus in the world around them on gender equality?

You and your coworkers need to take special care that stereotyped attitudes about the roles of men and women do not color your behavior toward the boys and girls in your classroom, or that such stereotyped ideas brought in by the children are handled appropriately. As in all areas of development, your goal should be to help each child become all he or she is capable of being. When each shows enthusiasm about doing things independently, you know they are well on their way to developing strong self-esteem.

If You Have Not Checked This Item: Some Helpful Ideas

■ Assess Your Classroom for Independent Possibilities

What can children do in your classroom? It gives them great satisfaction to accomplish difficult tasks on their own. Walk around your physical area and make a list of things that children can do. Figure 3.6 lists items on your daily job chart for individuals or teams to choose.

■ Encourage Performance of Self-Help Skills

Teach children how to tie their shoes when their small-motor coordination allows them this capability. Or have another child help them get started with buttons, zippers,

Figure 3.6 Job Chart Chores

feeding the rabbit	*taking own attendance*
cleaning the aquarium	*getting out playground toys*
watering the plants	*sweeping the floor*
scraping carrots for snack	*sponging off the tables*
delivering mail to the office	*getting out cots for naptime*
audio-recording a story	*turning on and using the computer*

or Velcro tabs. Allow enough time for even the slowest child to perform this task on his or her own.

■ Be Enthusiastic Yourself

Enthusiasm always scores very high on lists of the competencies of successful teachers. You, as a behavior model in your classroom, need always to be enthusiastic and positive about everything you do. If children see you acting vigorously on your own, they will want to do likewise.

OBSERVING BY USING A RUNNING RECORD AND CHECKLIST

Self-esteem was chosen as the first topic on the Child Development Checklist because this is the first area of child development a teacher should be concerned with when she meets new children in her classroom for the first time. Here is an example of how one teacher used the checklist.

To use the checklist most effectively, many observers prefer to make a running record of the child they are observing. Afterward they transfer the data they have gathered by checking items on the checklist that they observed the child performing and by recording running-record evidence for their check mark in the space provided. This combines the best of both methods of observation: the open-ended and rich descriptive advantages of the running record with the focus on a particular sequence of behaviors from a developmental checklist. Here is a running record for 3-year-old Sheila on October 22:

Sheila's mother brings her into classroom.

Sheila holds tightly to her hand. She begins to cry.

Mother says: "Now, Sheila, you like it here. Be a good girl. See you later."

Mother leaves. S. stands at entrance to room crying.

When teacher comes over S. looks at her & takes her hand.

Tch. takes S. over to girls in doll corner & says something.

S. shakes her head "no."

When tch. lvs. S. begins following tch. around.

Tch. sits S. down at small table with box of crayons in middle & blank sheets of paper in front of 2 chairs.

S. finally takes 2 crayons & starts coloring on paper.

Beth comes over & sits down at table.

Beth takes crayon out of box & starts coloring on her paper.

No talking at first.

Then Beth asks S. "May I borrow your orange?" It is on table.

S. says "No" & covers crayon with hand.

Beth grabs her hand, takes crayon with other hand & pops it into her mouth!

S. says "That's not fair!" and calls tch.

When tch. comes S. says, "She ate my orange crayon so I can't finish my pumpkin!"

Tch. says to Beth, "People shouldn't eat crayons."

Tch. is distracted by other ch. & leaves area.

S. gets up & goes to book corner & takes book.

S. carries book around room, looking carefully at what is going on, but not joining in.

S. whispers to Brian, "Becky painted yesterday & she's going to paint again today. See!" & points to easel.

Brian doesn't respond. S. whines to tch., "I wanna paint!"

Tch. tells her she can paint when Becky is finished.

The observer then takes this running record and fills out the Self-Esteem section of the checklist, as shown in Figure 3.7. As the observer reads the chapter on self-esteem, she should pay special attention to the items that she did not check. She will learn from her reading that a 3-year-old like Sheila may still not be secure enough to let go of her mother easily when she first comes to the preschool. The observer then notes that Sheila does transfer her clinging to the teacher, just as 3-year-olds often do at the beginning of school. But she does not play with the other children. The Helpful Ideas section after each item in Chapter 3 gives suggestions that may assist this child to make the transition from home to school more easily. Because Sheila has been in school for a month and still has difficulty making this transition, she may need this special help.

Evidence

It is important to record evidence as brief, nonjudgmental statements of what you actually saw. If you are observing and recording directly onto the checklist, these statements can be brief descriptions of the child's actions and language that you see and hear. If you are transferring data from a running record, enter that evidence. If you did not have the opportunity to observe the child for a particular item, place *N* instead of a check mark beside it. If the child has the opportunity to perform a checklist item, but does not do it, leave the item blank, but write an explanation.

CHILD DEVELOPMENT CHECKLIST

Name	Sheila age 3	**Observer**	Connie R.
Program	Head Start	**Dates**	10/22

Directions:

Put an X for items you see the child perform regularly. Put an *N* for items where there is no opportunity to observe. Leave all other items blank.

Item	Evidence	Dates
1 .Self-Esteem		
_____ Separates from primary caregiver without difficulty	*clings to mother & cries*	10/22
__X__ Develops a secure attachment with teacher	*clings to teacher when mother leaves*	10/22
_____ Completes a task successfully	*starts coloring;stops when beth comes*	10/22
_____ Makes activity choices without teacher's help	*teacher places her at art table*	10/22
__X__ Stands up for own rights	*tries to stop Beth from taking crayon*	10/22
_____ Displays enthusiasm about doing things for self	*watches others; does not play with them*	10/22

Figure 3.7   Self-Esteem Sections of Child Development Checklist (for Sheila)

For example, in Figure 3.7, the observer leaves the first item blank but includes under Evidence what she saw the child doing. Instead of checking "Separates from primary caregiver without difficulty," the observer notes that "Sheila clings to mother & cries." It is important for the teaching staff to have such information in interpreting the checklist results and making plans for this child.

From the running record previously made about Sheila, the observer can continue to complete the Child Development Checklist under the other areas, checking off items and filling in the Evidence column. Obviously a number of other observations need to be made of Sheila at various times during the day and on different days during arrival, free choice, snack, outdoor play, lunch, nap, and departure to provide a comprehensive picture of the child.

As you can see, the Child Development Checklist *is not a test,* but a listing of developmental items that children may or may not perform. If observers leave certain items blank because the child does not perform them, this may mean one of several things:

1. She cannot because she has not yet reached that level of development.
2. She does not because she is not interested in doing what the item describes.
3. The classroom itself is not set up to encourage the child's performance.

You should not ask children questions about whether they recognize certain colors, for instance. The youngsters' performance on the items should become evident as you observe the children in their natural play activities. Set up activities that will engage the children in the areas you wish to observe. Be sure these activities are spontaneous and not forced. If a child does not get involved in Art Skills, even though art activities are available every day, you should leave the items blank. Do not use *N*, no opportunity to observe, when in fact the child has the opportunity to participate in art activities, but chooses not to. You may want to make a note, though, after the items that "Easel painting and art activities are available, but B. does not get involved in art."

From the running record previously made, the observer can check off items and fill in evidence for Sheila under Emotional Competence or "Shows interest, excitement in classroom activities"; under Social Competence for "Plays by self with own toys/materials"; under Spoken Language for "Speaks in expanded sentences"; and under Art, Music, and Dance Skills for "Makes pictorial drawings." Other observations on Sheila can be made, recorded, and dated on the same checklist until a comprehensive picture of her emerges.

Learning Prescription

Creating a **Learning Prescription** for Sheila is the next step in the process of planning for an individual child based on interpreted observational data. To create such a prescription, you should look over the Child Development Checklist to find at least three *areas of strength*. Although her checklist is far from complete, it is still possible to come up with real strengths for Sheila. For example, she:

1. Stands up for her own rights
2. Speaks in expanded sentences
3. Enjoys art and displays art skills

These three areas of strength can be entered on Sheila's initial learning prescription. *Making a reliable overall assessment of a single child should not be done based on only one observation.* You should have as much information as you can gather from as many different days, activities, and points of view as possible. The best overall records are a compilation from the entire classroom staff. Have each person put a date by the items observed. Individuals may want to indicate their check marks and evidence with a symbol, initials, or color coding if everyone is using the same checklist for all the observations.

In Sheila's case, for the purpose of illustrating the checklist planning process, we will make an initial learning prescription based on this one observation. After you have decided on Sheila's strengths, you need to look for her areas that need strengthening. We do not call these *weaknesses*, a negative term, because they are not weaknesses. Words are important, as previously noted, and we should use them carefully. If we talk in terms of negatives, we will think in terms of negatives regarding Sheila and our other children. If we think in terms of areas that need strengthening, we should be able to plan a positive program for Sheila that will help her to continue in her development and improve in areas that need improvement.

Three areas that need strengthening can also be taken from Sheila's checklist from items not checked. For example, Sheila:

1. Needs to separate from her mother more easily
2. Needs to make activity choices on her own
3. Needs to play with other children

Finally, the Learning Prescription needs to include specific ideas for helping the child to improve by *drawing on her strengths*. Specific ideas for activities can come from your own experience or from the ideas listed in the various chapters after every checklist item under the heading "If You Have Not Checked This Item: Some Helpful Ideas." Because Sheila speaks well and seems to want to do particular things, it might be well to get her involved as a leader with one other child. Presenting such an activity as a transition from home to school when she first arrives might help her separate from her mother more easily. Being the leader in another activity with the same child might help her to make activity choices on her own. Her interest in painting could also keep her involved with the other child and the classroom activities.

With these thoughts in mind, the staff proposed the three Activities to Help as shown on an initial Learning Prescription for Sheila (Figure 3.8). Future observations

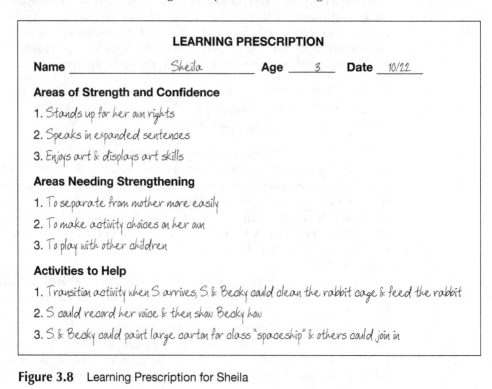

LEARNING PRESCRIPTION

Name _____ Sheila _____ **Age** ___ 3 ___ **Date** _ 10/22 _

Areas of Strength and Confidence

1. Stands up for her own rights
2. Speaks in expanded sentences
3. Enjoys art & displays art skills

Areas Needing Strengthening

1. To separate from mother more easily
2. To make activity choices on her own
3. To play with other children

Activities to Help

1. Transition activity when S. arrives; S. & Becky could clean the rabbit cage & feed the rabbit
2. S. could record her voice & then show Becky how
3. S. & Becky could paint large carton for class "spaceship" & others could join in

Figure 3.8   Learning Prescription for Sheila

would help the staff determine if these activities did help Sheila or if different activities would be more appropriate. The teachers in Sheila's class will want to continue their observing and recording to evaluate how these activities help Sheila and the other children, as well as to determine what other individual plans are needed.

Be sure that observation of such children is an ongoing process in your center. Do a follow-up of children who seem to need special help. Has your Learning Prescription been helpful? Did the activities you planned really help this child? Share your observations with your classroom team and with the child's parents. Ask them to make similar observations. Include their ideas, as well as your team's, in your individual plans for each child.

LEARNING ACTIVITIES

1. Observe all the children in a classroom each morning for 3 days of school, using the items in the Self-Esteem checklist as a screening device. Note which children can *separate without difficulty from their parents* and which children cannot. What could you do for those who need help? Write up the results of your efforts.

2. Observe all the children in a classroom for several days on the Self-Esteem item from the checklist, *Develops a secure attachment with teacher,* using it as a screening tool. Check off children who demonstrate this, writing down evidence. What other characteristics do they demonstrate?

3. Put out several puzzles and invite children to make them. Note which ones complete the task and which do not. How would you help the children who do not complete their puzzle?

4. Choose a child who seems to have difficulty getting involved with activities without the teacher's help. Make a running record of everything the child does or says during three different arrival periods. Transfer this information to the Child Development Checklist under Self-Esteem. How do you interpret the evidence you have collected? Can you make any conclusions yet about this child?

5. Observe children on the playground for several days looking for indications of bullying actions by any child. Do any of the children stand up to this child? Make a running record of what happens.

6. Choose a child for whom you have checked *Displays enthusiasm about doing things for self.* Observe this child during the first half-hour of class for 3 days. Which of the other items can you check for this child based on your observations? What physical evidence can you place in the child's portfolio about her self-esteem?

SUGGESTED READINGS

Balaban, N. (2006). Easing the separation process for infants, toddlers, and families. *Young Children, 63*(6), 14–20.

Curtis, D., & Carter, M. (2011). *Reflecting children's lives: A handbook for planning your child-centered curriculum* (2nd ed.). St. Paul, MN: Redleaf Press.

Evans, B. (May/June, 2012). What adults can do to stop hurtful preschool behavior before it becomes a pattern of bullying. *Exchange,* 58–61.

Gallagher, K. C., & Meyer, K. (2006). Teacher-child relationships at the forefront of effective practices. *Young Children, 61*(6), 44–49.

Gropper, N., Hinitz, B. F., Sprung, B., & Froschl, M. (2011). Helping young boys be successful learners in today's early childhood classrooms. *Young Children, 66*(1), 34–41.

Mindes, G. (2011). *Assessing young children* (4th ed.). Upper Saddle River, NJ: Pearson.

CHILDREN'S BOOKS

Alexander, C. (2008). *Lucy and the bully.* Morton Grove, IL: Albert Whitman.

Cuyler, M. (2009). *Bullies never win.* New York: Simon & Schuster.

Dole, M. L. (2003). *Drum, Chavi, drum!* San Francisco, CA: Children's Book Press.*

Moore, J. (2009). *Freckleface Strawberry and the dodgeball bully.* New York: Bloomsbury.

Northway, J. (2006). *See you later, Mom!* London, England: Frances Lincoln's Children's Books.

Pullen, Z. (2008). *Friday my Radio Flyer flew.* New York: Simon & Schuster.*

Smith, C. L. (2000). *Jingle dancer.* New York: Morrow Junior Books.*

Soman, D., & Davis, J. (2011). *The amazing adventures of Bumblebee Boy.* New York: Dial Books.

WEB SITES

http://thechp.syr.edu/Behavioral_Observation_Checklist.pdf

National Association for the Education of Young Children
http://www.naeyc.org

National Head Start Association
http://www.nhsa.org

Center on the Social and Emotional Foundation for Early Learning
http://www.vanderbilt.edu/csefel

Responsive Classroom
http://www.responsiveclassroom.org

Schrock's Guide for Educators
http://www.school.discoveryeducation.com/schrockguide/Kathy

*Multicultural

CHAPTER 4

Emotional Competence

In this chapter you will learn to observe if children can:

_____ Release stressful feelings in appropriate manner

_____ Express anger in words rather than negative actions

_____ Be calmed in frightening situations

_____ Show fondness, affection, love toward others

_____ Show interest, excitement in classroom activities

_____ Smile, seem happy much of the time

_____ Be observed by using sampling and checklist

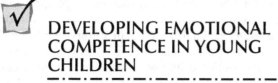

DEVELOPING EMOTIONAL COMPETENCE IN YOUNG CHILDREN

The emotional development of the preschool child is somewhat different from other developmental aspects. Although emotional growth happens simultaneously with physical, social, cognitive, language, and creative development and is interdependent with them, it may seem as if youngsters do not stay developed. They seem to repeat the same sequences of emotional reactions over and over—throughout life. However, it is not the emotion itself that is repeated, but the response to it.

It is the *response* to this feeling that needs to be controlled. Developing control over one's emotions is known as *emotional competence*. Emotional competence is the aspect that needs to be developed by young children. Nissen and Hawkins (2010) tell us that emotional competence has three specific aspects: *emotional expressiveness, emotional knowledge,* and *emotional regulation*. They describe each as playing a key role in determining young children's ability to interact and form relationships with others.

Emotional expression is what we call the emotion itself. Positive emotional expressions include happiness, love, and excitement, while negative expressions are often distress, anger, and fear. Children who can identify the emotional display in others are exhibiting emotional knowledge. But most important to teachers in preschool programs is children's emotional regulation, the ability to manage arousal and behavior during social interactions.

Young children are often overwhelmed by emotions, both positive and negative. They have limited resources for emotional regulation, which may in turn lead to upsetting behaviors. Nissen and Hawkins also note that a child's state of emotional development impacts development in all domains, especially social, emotional, and cognitive learning, which are interconnected in younger children. Building emotional competence can help children form positive social relationships and positive self-esteem, leading to ongoing academic success.

In order to help young children build their own emotional competence, you as a teacher, teacher assistant, student intern, or volunteer need to learn as much as you can about emotions and their expressions. Emotions originate in the brain and nervous system. But can emotions be inherited and then develop through maturation and surroundings just like the ability to think? Yes. Brain research makes it clear that brain maturation influences much of what children are capable of emotionally at different ages. Developmental researchers also recognize that certain emotional expressions seem to be universal. Separation anxiety, for instance, occurs at about the same time and for the same reasons in infants and toddlers around the world. Similarly, other types of emotions seem to trigger the fight-or-flight response in humans everywhere.

Developmental psychologists studying universal responses talk in terms of the functions of emotions (i.e., how they help the human species adapt and survive). These scientists note that certain emotions that trigger necessary survival responses in infants have outlived their usefulness when they occur in older children. The acute distress the infant feels and expresses in tears and screams when his mother leaves the house, for example, has outlived its usefulness if it is a daily occurrence for a 4-year-old whose mother leaves him at preschool. Although such basic emotions seem to serve in helping to preserve the self or the species, the higher emotions serve social purposes, and their appropriate expressions must be learned in a social context.

Brain research has given us more clues about emotional control. For instance, the right hemisphere of the brain is more responsible for processing negative emotions, intense emotions, and creativity. The left hemisphere is more responsible for positive emotions, language development, and interest in new objects and experiences, Gallagher reports (2005). Because the right hemisphere experiences greater growth during the first 3 years of life, it is important that early childhood teachers work closely with young children helping them learn to regulate their emotions. Such self-regulation is difficult for many children without adult help.

This chapter, then, looks at observable emotional expressions of young children in six different emotional areas: distress, anger, fear, interest, affection, and joy. Each discussion is followed by suggestions for helping the child improve his or her behavior if the particular response is not demonstrated. Each of the checklist items refers to a particular emotion. It should be noted, however, that the order in which the items are listed is not a developmental sequence, because sequence as such does not seem to be an important factor in emotional development.

Many psychologists recognize 10 or 12 basic sets of emotions. These are sometimes listed as interest-excitement, enjoyment-joy, affection-love, surprise-startle, distress-anguish, anger-rage, disgust-revulsion, contempt-scorn, fear-terror, shame/shyness-humiliation, sadness-grief, and guilt-remorse. The emotional responses of preschool children seem to be involved principally with the six emotions shown in Figure 4.1.

To help children develop emotional competence, the preschool teacher should be concerned with promoting positive responses and teaching management of inappropriate responses. Although techniques to accomplish this control may vary depending on the emotion and the situation, the five strategies in Figure 4.2 can be used in helping most children manage their inappropriate reactions.

Figure 4.1 Emotions

1. Distress	4. Affection
2. Anger	5. Interest
3. Fear	6. Joy

Figure 4.2 Teacher's actions to help children manage emotional expression

- Remove or reduce the cause of the emotion.
- Diffuse child's negative response by allowing him to cry or talk.
- Offer support, comfort, and ideas for self-control.
- Model controlled behavior yourself.
- Give children the opportunity to talk about negative feelings appropriately.

What might Ron say if Gina knocks down his building?

Helping Children Manage Inappropriate Emotional Expressions

Once a child can verbalize, she can begin to take charge of her emotions. She may be able to tell you what happened or how she feels. This is the first step toward self-mastery of emotions, in other words, emotional competence. But many children do not possess what Deerwester (2007) calls "emotional literacy," that is, the proper words that express how we feel.

She says we can teach children to identify emotions by looking at the face and body language of the person expressing the emotion. She tells about the need for children to build an emotional vocabulary of words like *happy, sad, angry, surprised, disappointed, excited, grumpy, jealous,* and others. These are new words for many 3-, 4-, and 5-year-olds. They may have heard them, but have little idea what they mean.

For you as a teacher, you can start with emotion word games, word songs, word books, word puppets, and word stuffed animals. At a time when everyone is calm, you or they can act out such feelings one at a time.

Your goal for the children should be the same as in the other aspects of their development—for them to gain self-control. To help children acquire this control, you first need to find out where they stand in their present responses. Do they cry, whine, or complain much of the time? Do they ever smile? Do they show anger or aggression toward others? The Child Development Checklist lists six representative items of emotional behavior that can be observed in preschool children; each item represents one of the six emotions previously listed. Observe the children in your class to determine which youngsters have accomplished the emotional self-control described in the checklist. Children who have not exhibited these checklist behaviors may benefit from the ideas and suggestions discussed in the remainder of the chapter.

✓ RELEASES STRESSFUL FEELINGS IN APPROPRIATE MANNER

Distress

Children who cannot handle their feelings during stressful times are exhibiting the emotional expression known as distress. At its lower extreme, distress may result from physical discomfort due to pain, extremes of temperature, or noise; at its upper level, distress may take the form of anguish or depression due to loss. A basic cause of distress throughout life is physical or psychological separation, especially from a loved one. Children who perceive themselves as having been abandoned by an adult, even when this is not the case, experience the same emotion as children who actually have been abandoned. Children also feel distress when negative things happen to them at home, especially abuse and neglect.

Brain research tells us that the body produces chemicals called hormones that help regulate body functions and reactions to the environment. One such hormone is cortisol, which is released in response to stress and helps the body respond to challenging situations. Even daily stressors such as being hungry or hearing a loud noise can cause increases in cortisol levels. Gallagher (2005) talks about too much cortisol production over a long period of time leading to problems with memory and self-regulation. Thus, it is important for teachers in preschool programs to create a calm environment where children feel cared for and secure, and where children can learn to regulate stress-producing emotions.

Children express distress by crying, whining, or showing a sad face. Sometimes they cling to an adult caregiver. Distressed children may feel uncomfortable, disappointed, or rejected. Because distress is not the most severe negative emotion found in children, adults do not always take it seriously. They should. Distress is an indication that all is not well with a child. Failure to reduce the distress or its causes over time tends to break down children's trust in adults. Furthermore, they may learn to become unsympathetic to others who are distressed because that is the way they have been treated.

What are the principal causes of distress in the preschool classroom? For many youngsters, separation from their mother or primary caregiver is the greatest stressor. Physical discomfort or pain, rejection by peers, bullying by peers, dissatisfaction with a performance, and lack of a skill are other causes of distress. A stressful situation in the family, such as the birth of a new baby, a death, a hospitalization, a move, or a divorce, may also be carried over into classroom behavior by the child who is disturbed by it. Even such a simple thing as a change in schedule may be a source of stress for some children. Some causes of distress are listed in Figure 4.3.

Figure 4.3   Causes of
Distress

> - Separation from mother
> - Physical pain
> - Rejection by peers
> - Bullying by peers
> - Not performing well
> - Change in schedule

The Teacher's Role

How can you help? Your principal role in the children's development of emotional competence should be to help them master or regulate their feelings. You should not be the controlling device yourself, but instead you should help them find a way to control their feelings from within.

Adults are often tempted to take control of an emotional situation. Young children, in fact, look to you to solve the emotional problems that so often overwhelm them. You do children a disservice if you comply. Your role should be that of a facilitator, not a controller. Otherwise, without you, the children will be no better off the next time the emotional situation occurs. As with other aspects of development, your overall goal for children should be to help them develop emotional competence themselves, in other words, emotional self-control.

Although the particular situation may determine your response, distress most often requires that you first give comfort to the child. She is upset and uncomfortable; she may be whining or crying. You can show your concern through comforting words and actions such as holding or hugging.

Requiring a child to stop crying right away is not usually the way to help him master his emotions. Venting through tears is, after all, a catharsis. He may think you are not sympathetic to his plight if you insist he stop crying. He may in fact stop on his own when he hears your comforting words or feels your touch. Recent studies have found that crying is of therapeutic value not only psychologically, but also physically. Chemical toxins that build up during stress are released in tears. Even blood pressure, pulse rate, and body temperature seem to be lowered by crying. Psychologist Solter (1992) tells us crying is not the hurt but the unhurt.

Where do such feelings go when they get stopped? Bowling and Rogers (2001) tell us what every teacher knows. Either the feelings erupt as kicking, hitting, and screaming or they are pushed inside, and the child withdraws and clings to a blanket or thumb. They suggest that the best way to help children release feelings and heal emotionally is to give them complete focused attention, one-on-one. During this special time, the teacher can interact with the child using one or more of the strategies in Figure 4.4.

As for mastering distress so that it will not happen again, this is probably not possible and certainly not appropriate. Distress may be relieved and perhaps controlled

Figure 4.4 Relieving
Stress

- Give comfort
- Allow child to cry
- Redirect attention
- Help child to verbalize

to some extent, but not completely mastered. Nor should we want it to be. Distress is a necessary symptom signaling that all is not well with the individual. In your classroom, you should hope to relieve, not prevent, distress in a child. If you are successful, a distraught child will allow herself to be comforted or redirected. But if her sense of self is not strong enough or if the distress is too overwhelming, she may not even allow this. What can you do to help such a child?

If You Have Not Checked This Item: Some Helpful Ideas

■ Hold and Rock

It's a good idea to have an adult-size rocking chair in your center. Sometimes the best help for a distraught child is to hold and rock him.

■ Have Child Hold a Huggable Toy

A child is often comforted by holding something soft. That is why toddlers carry "security blankets." Your classroom should have cuddly stuffed animals or similar toys available, not only for play but also for stressful situations.

■ Use Materials with Soothing Properties

Water play and finger painting are activities with soothing qualities. Distressed children can take out their frustrations by moving paint around a surface with their hands or by swishing water and squeezing sponges, thus transferring their negative energy in a harmless fashion.

■ Have Child Talk to a Puppet

Verbalizing distraught feelings is one of the best ways to defuse and control them. You could designate one of the puppets in your room as a "feelings" puppet and keep it in a special place for the times when children are feeling upset. They can talk to the puppet about how they feel and ask the puppet how it feels. Model the use of this puppet yourself when upsetting occasions arise so that the children can follow your lead when they feel bad.

Have the child talk to a puppet.

Figure 4.5   Books for
Stressful Situations

- ***The Story of My Feelings*** (Berkner, 2007)
- ***The Way I Feel*** (Cain, 2000)
- ***Grumpy Gloria*** (Dewdney, 2005)
- ***Yesterday I Had the Blues*** (Frame, 2003)
- ***My no, no, no day*** (Patterson, 2012)

■ Read a Book

Sometimes distraught children will allow you to read a favorite book to them. You might also keep particular books for them to look at on their own during troubling times. The books in Figure 4.5 are especially suitable for stressful situations.

✓ EXPRESSES ANGER IN WORDS RATHER THAN ACTIONS

Anger

Anger is the emotion of most concern not only in the classroom, but also in society at large, perhaps because anger has the potential for such harm. We are very much concerned that people learn to control their anger. Therefore we begin teaching what to do—or rather what not to do—very early. We are usually not very successful. There is, however, a positive approach to controlling anger that can diffuse the anger so that children do not turn it against others or themselves.

First, we need to look at the emotion itself to understand what it is, what causes it, and what purpose it serves. Anger is the emotion or feeling that results when we are physically or psychologically restrained from doing something, frustrated in our attempts, interrupted, personally insulted, or forced to do something against our will. We feel hurt, disappointed, and irritated. We frown, our face gets hot, our blood "boils," our muscles tense, our teeth clench, our eyes stare. At anger's highest level, we feel rage that threatens to erupt in an explosive manner. At the other extreme we feel hostility, a cold type of anger.

With anger comes a sense of physical power and greater self-assurance than with any other negative emotion. The body, in fact, rallies its resources in readiness to strike out against the cause of the anger. In primitive humans, anger mobilized the body's energy quickly and was important for survival. In modern humans, the anger still appears, but its primary purpose has all but vanished. This energy needs to be released or somehow diffused, otherwise we will turn it against ourselves. Repressed anger has been implicated as one of the causes of skin diseases, ulcers, migraines, hypertension, and certain psychological disorders (Izard, 1977).

Most parents teach their children from the start not to display anger. When they allow angry feelings to begin to show on their faces, children sense their parents' displeasure. Many children soon learn to conceal or disguise anger. Others let anger out in acts of aggression. Neither response is satisfactory, yet many of us carry these responses throughout life.

Instead, we need a positive approach that teaches children from the start what they should do (expression) rather than what they must not do (repression). Anger definitely calls for some sort of release, but children and adults need to "let off steam" harmlessly.

One of the most satisfactory methods used by many preschool teachers coaches children to verbalize their feelings as they did during stressful situations. Verbalizing involves neither yelling nor name-calling, but expressing in words how the child feels about whatever is causing the anger. This approach has at least two advantages: It gives children an acceptable release for their strong feelings, and it puts the children in control. They—not adults—deal with the situation. And solving the problems on their own strengthens the children's self-esteem.

Strong feelings such as anger overwhelm and thus frighten young children. A method for learning control from the inside and not being controlled from the outside will help children in the future when adults are not around. The anger emotion calls for action. But if children learn to speak out rather than strike out, they will not have to suffer the guilt or remorse afterward for an unacceptable act. What will they say?

Adams (2011) believes that children can be taught to name their feelings. She calls the understanding of emotions *emotional literacy*. She suggests that adults can support children's expanding emotional vocabulary by making a Feelings Word List—words that the children can use instead of striking out when they are angry. Figure 4.6 lists some of the words for anger: These are words the teacher can use at first when something upsetting happens. Then children can learn to use them.

Figure 4.6 Words for
Anger

Angry	Cross	Furious
Mad	Grumpy	Disgusted
Upset	Crabby	Frustrated
Irritated	Annoyed	Enraged

Expressing anger in words is not easy in the beginning. It does not come naturally for young children, whose communication skills are still limited. It is even more difficult for the child caught in the throes of an overwhelming emotion who finds it simpler to strike out physically, shout, or cry. Yet 3-, 4-, and 5-year-olds can learn the response of telling how they feel in words.

How do you teach them? First, you need to model this behavior yourself. When you become angry, use your serious tone of voice to tell the children how you feel and why you feel this way: "I feel very upset to see you dropping the CD player on the floor like that! If you break it no one can enjoy the music anymore," or "Luis and Victor, I am so angry to see you ganging up on Juan again! Two against one is not fair!"

You must also convey to your children that their actions—not them as individuals—make you angry. You must show you still respect and like the children no matter how angry they get or how upset you feel over their actions. Show the children both verbally and nonverbally that you still accept them as good people.

You also must intervene *every time* the children display temper, and you must help them repeatedly to express their own feelings in words: "Sarah, tell Jessica how you feel when she takes your book." "Roberto, don't hit Luther. Tell him how you feel." Make eye contact with the children. Help them to make eye contact with one another to diffuse their anger: "Roberto, look Luther in the eye and tell him."

Obviously, some of the words in Figure 4.6 are adult words, but if you use them yourself, as well as going over your list every time someone expresses anger, you may be surprised to hear children using them, too.

Teaching children to express anger in words is a time-consuming process, but so is all learning. If you believe children must gain inner control over their anger, and if you understand they must have some acceptable way to vent their feelings, then you will find it worthwhile to put in the time and effort necessary to divert anger's destructive energy into words. You will know you have been successful when the children begin telling one another, "Don't hit him, Jamar, tell him!"

If You Have Not Checked This Item: Some Helpful Ideas

■ Talk About Feelings

Establish a "feelings" corner in your room with pictures of people looking sad, angry, and glad. Ask the children to tell you what they feel when they look like that. If you have no pictures, make photocopies of feelings pictures from books. Provide a feelings hand puppet that the children can hold and talk to about the feelings they have.

Figure 4.7   Books
About Anger

> - ***Llama Llama Mad at Mama*** (Dewdney, 2007)
> - ***When Sophie Gets Angry—Really, Really Angry*** (Bang, 1999)
> - ***Sometimes I'm Bombaloo*** (Vail, 2002)

■ Read a Book

Read books about feelings (see Figure 4.7) to a child or small group at any time of day, not only when tempers are short.

When the little llama gets angry in the story and starts throwing things, his mama takes him out of the shopping cart and invites him to help her shop. When Sophie gets so angry she kicks and screams and wants to smash the world to smithereens, she takes herself outside and climbs a tree. When Katie Honor loses her temper she finds something funny to laugh at. How would your listeners handle losing their tempers? Can they express their feelings in words? Have them try it.

CAN BE CALMED IN FRIGHTENING SITUATIONS

Fear

Fear first appears as an emotion in the second half of the first year of infancy, according to many psychologists. Somewhere between 5 and 9 months of age, babies begin to notice an unfamiliar face and are afraid of it. Before that point, their physical and cognitive development have not progressed to allow them to distinguish between friend and stranger. After that recognition occurs, infants see unfamiliar faces as a possible threat—until they learn differently.

Fear may result when the possibility of harm appears, when a strange person, object, or situation is confronted, and when specific fright-producing elements—heights, the dark, thunderstorms, emergencies, violent scenes on TV, and certain animals such as dogs and snakes—are present. When humans are afraid, they feel anxious and alarmed. They may tremble, cower, hide, run away, cling to someone, or cry, depending on their degree of fright. They often seek protection.

Fear is in some ways age-related. Young children are generally not afraid of heights, the dark, or animals before their second year. It is as though they really don't know enough to be frightened before then. As they grow older, children add new fears and drop some of the old ones. Fear seems to serve as a warning signal for the human species. Reduce the threat or seek protection. When this warning feeling persists but is no longer useful to the young human, you as a teacher need to intervene.

We know, of course, that extreme fear can be paralyzing, but we need to realize that even lesser fears like anxiety produce tension of some sort: a tightening up of the body and the mind. The anxious person has trouble relaxing and feeling at ease in tense situations.

Tense situations that may cause children to be fearful in a preschool classroom these days can be caused by any number of things: an adult raising her voice at a child, an out-of-control child hurting someone, an emergency such as a building evacuation because of fire or a bomb threat, a storm or natural disaster, or an accident causing personal injury. Even loud noises such as an emergency vehicle siren going by outside or the sudden loud banging of doors inside may cause children to tighten up, huddle together, or cry. When children see, hear, or sense the presence of something threatening, they become afraid.

It is up to you and your staff to help the children remain calm and in control no matter what happens. How can you do it? First of all, you must remain calm and in control yourself. Try to anticipate what emergencies you might face. Practice evacuation drills ahead of time. Show the children by your facial expression, voice, and actions that you are calm and not panicked. They will look to you to see how you are handling any tense or threatening situation. Be ready to show them your unruffled composure, your quiet voice, your confident actions.

For you to show fear in the face of danger can cause panic among the children. How will you respond to such an emergency event as a shooting, bombing, or explosion? If you fall apart, many of the children may too.

You will need to anticipate such emergencies and discuss with the staff how each of you will handle them. Taking roles and acting out emergency situations with the staff ahead of time helps everyone understand their role and gain control of themselves. Walk staff through a practice fire drill without children before you involve the children. Afterward, observe to see which children follow your lead during emergencies or tense situations, and which cry or lose control. Should only one or two children be unable to contain their fear, you or one of the staff members can give support and comfort to them while you involve the others in a calming activity to take their minds off the situation.

If You Have Not Checked This Item: Some Helpful Ideas

■ Remove or Reduce the Cause of Fear

If you know what is causing the fear in a child, it may be possible to remove the cause. If you don't know, ask the child. Let her know that you will be right there with her no matter what happens. If a child is afraid of a dog on the playground, you can take the child inside while another staff member shoos the dog away. If children express fear of lightning or thunder, you can reduce the cause by pulling the curtains shut, gathering everyone together in a Happiness Circle on the floor, and singing some funny songs (Beaty, 2012). When children see violent scenes on television, it is important to talk about them in a class discussion where children can express their fears, and you can help them feel safe at school.

■ Give Support and Comfort to the Child

Fearful children can be comforted by being touched, hugged, held on your lap, rocked in a rocking chair, or seated close to while you talk quietly or read a story to them. Neuroscientists have found that a soothing touch causes the brain to release growth hormones. On the other hand, emotional stress needs to be released or it can cause the release of the steroid cortisol, high levels of which may interfere with connections between brain cells in children.

■ Allow Child to Cry

As mentioned previously, chemical toxins that have built up during stress can be released in tears. Do not stop a frightened child from crying. Talk soothingly to her and tell her it's okay to cry. Many young children release their fearful feelings through tears. Venting through crying is a catharsis. Later, when it is appropriate, you can try to calm her down by holding her or talking softly to her.

■ Redirect Children's Attention with Calming Art Activities

Children in the grip of fear may be calmed down by certain art activities. Have them work with play dough. Squishing dough through their fingers or rolling it out on a countertop helps them release pent-up feelings. Finger painting is another activity that allows children to paint out their fears by swishing paint around with their fingers. Or they can get down on the floor and move the paint around on butcher paper with their arms and hands, or stamp their handprints on the paper with slaps that dissipate their fear. Play at the water table is also calming. Children can squirt water into containers with squeeze bottles, whip up bubbles with eggbeaters, blow bubbles in the water through straws, or pour water from one container to another.

■ Involve Children in Helping Others

Helping another child in a fear-producing situation can take the helpers out of themselves and their own fears. Not all children are able to do this, but those who can often find that their own fears are lessened. They can look at a book together, play with puppets, put a puzzle together, or listen to a music CD with a child who seems upset by the situation. Children are more likely to give help to another when they are with someone. You can ask two children to help a third by playing with materials together. All three children will then be distracted from the fear situation.

■ Read a Book

Books that can help children dissipate fear are listed in Figure 4.8. These books are lead-ins to activity about being fearful. Sometimes the activity is just talking calmly with the children about the situation. Other times they may paint, do water play, or build blocks enclosures.

The Scaredy Cat overcomes his fears by going out in the storm to rescue his master, Ben. Baby owl overcomes his fear of the dark when his father reads to him and tells him it's okay to be a little scared of the dark. Jessica, who worries that she

Figure 4.8 Books
About Fears

- ***Francis the Scaredy Cat*** (Boxall, 2002)
- ***"I'm Not Scared!"*** (Allen, 2007)
- ***Stop, Drop, and Roll*** (Cuyler, 2001)
- ***Aunt Minnie and the Twister*** (Prigger, 2002)
- ***Don't Forget to Come Back!*** (Harris, 2004)
- ***Scare a Bear*** (Wargin, 2010)
- ***Snip Snap! What's That?*** (Berman, 2005)

won't remember what to say, finally gets the words right and says them. Aunt Minnie teaches her orphaned youngsters what to do in case of a tornado and they do it by holding onto each other. Babysitter Sarah helps the little girl overcome her fears by playing silly games. The children at the camp don't have any luck scaring away the bear in rhyming words until they say BOO. The children in ***Snip Snap!*** who are threatened by an alligator finally stand up to the beast and make it scared.

☑ SHOWS FONDNESS, AFFECTION, LOVE TOWARD OTHERS

Affection

Young children learn affection when those around them are affectionate. They learn to love when those around them show them love. They develop fondness when their caregivers give them consistent caring and love. From infancy on, fondness, affection, and love are as necessary for children's growth and development as food and water.

If such affection has not been expressed between children and their primary caregivers at birth or soon after, young children may have difficulty showing fondness, affection, or love to others around them. It is not too late for you and your team of teachers or caregivers to help correct this situation. As "significant others" in a child's life, you may be the ones to offer such unconditional affection and love to each child in your class—no matter who they are, what they look or act like, or where they come from. All young children need this warmth from the adults around them if they are to reciprocate and learn to show warmth to others. You need to forge a real connection with them, if they are to fashion one with you and the others in the class.

Do you have trouble with such a notion? Are you, perhaps, not an affectionate person yourself, and thus find it difficult to show affection to others? It is important that you review your role as a teacher or caregiver of young children. Young children need warm and affectionate adults around them. You may want to reconsider your position if you cannot respond in this manner.

Even though the child may not have received such unconditional love from an adult in his or her family as described earlier, classroom adults can show such affection and love through actions listed in Figure 4.9.

Figure 4.9 Showing Affection

- Nearness (standing, sitting, holding on lap)
- Touch (hugs, pats, arm around shoulders)
- Nonverbal cues (smiles, eye contact, nods, waves, handholds)
- Verbal affirmations ("I'm so glad to see your happy face today!")

Children need to feel affection from other children in the classroom, as well. If you serve as the model for showing affection to them, they should be able to pass it along to others. Most children will respond to your warm attention with smiles, touches, and hugs. But some may hold back and be slower to show affection or make genuine connections with the adults and children in the classroom. These may be the children who have not formed a strong attachment with the primary caregivers in their family. Do not give up on them. If you observe that any of your children do not seem to exhibit some of the four displays of fondness, affection, or love listed, you may want to try the following.

If You Have Not Checked This Item: Some Helpful Ideas

■ Read a Book

Certain books on love and affection have become classics, such as Joosse's *Mama Do You Love Me?* Its success prompted her to write two more. (See Figure 4.10.)

The child character in all three of Joosse's books challenges the adult to tell how much they love the child in all sorts of conditions. But of course their love is unconditional, and the child feels secure. *Homemade Love* is a simple but

It's nice to find someone who likes you on the playground.

Figure 4.10 Books
About Love

- ***Mama, Do You Love Me?*** (Joosse, 1991)
- ***Papa, Do You Love Me?*** (Joosse, 2005)
- ***Grandma Calls Me Beautiful*** (Joose, 2008)
- ***Homemade Love*** (Hooks, 2002)
- ***Because Your Daddy Loves You*** (Clements, 2005)

powerful African American story written in large-font type with huge colorful characters that show Girlpie being loved, no matter what. The girl in Clements's story mentions all the usual things a daddy could do on a trip to the beach, but he doesn't. Her daddy finds her lost shoe, rescues her drifting beach ball, plays as long as she wants, reads her favorite story over again, and tucks her in at night saying "I love you."

■ Bring Two Together

Start with two children whom you will bring together to hear one of the preceding stories or to tell one to you. One of the children can be openly receptive of affection and love; the other, more reticent. Be sure to show them both your affection and love. Afterward, ask them if they can include one other child in this reading group and show him or her the book just read while you remove yourself. Later do the same with two other children and little people figures to act out the story.

✓ SHOWS INTEREST, ATTENTION IN CLASSROOM ACTIVITIES

Interest (Excitement)

Interest is the most frequent and pervasive positive emotion that human beings possess. Children show interest by directing their eyes toward an object or person who catches their attention, and then exploring it with their eyes and, if possible, their other senses. Interested people are alert, active, self-confident, and curious. Interest is the motivator for much of children's learning, as well as for their development of creativity and intelligence. Thus it is crucial for growing children to have their interest stimulated by the interesting people, materials, and ideas in their environment.

Psychologists believe that change or novelty is the basis for the interest emotion. The novelty of an object first attracts the person's attention. Once he is aroused and curious, he is motivated to find out more about the object, thus increasing his knowledge, skill, and understanding. Interest, in other words, is the impulse to know, which then sustains our attention in the things we are curious about. Excitement is the most intense form of interest.

The interest emotion appears very early in an infant's life. Interest is evident in the attention she shows to the human face: eyes riveted to her mother's face and turning to follow it. Objects such as rattles, bottles, mobiles, her own fingers and toes are fascinating fields for exploration with her eyes and then her mouth. Later she shifts from external exploration to manipulation. What will objects do when you kick them, throw them, drop them?

Poverty frequently interferes with the development of strong interests and attention because the variety of objects or activities available in the child's environment is often limited. In cases where the parents must also spend much of their energy struggling to survive, they may have little or no time to interact with their youngsters. The parents may, in fact, actively discourage them from exploratory endeavors. If, in addition, negative emotions dominate the atmosphere, interest quickly fades away.

Thus it is important for you to know which children in your classroom have retained their native curiosity and which have not. The interest and attention individual children pay to classroom activities may give you a clue. But you need to remember that interest is stimulated by novelty and change, so a truer test might be to set up a new activity area and observe which children notice it, who plays in it, and for how long. Because interests by now are very much individualized and personalized, what interests one child will not necessarily cause a flicker of attention in another. For this reason you must provide a wide range of activities and materials for your group. Remember also to add something new once in a while.

The basic interest emotion also affects attention span. Children must first be attracted to an activity through interest that is activated by change or novelty. If they find the activity interesting, they are likely to spend more time doing it and pay more attention to it. Although we know that age and maturity have a great deal to do with how long a child's interest can be held (i.e., the older, the longer), we can also increase the attention span by providing highly attractive materials and activities. Because children must attend (i.e., pay attention) to learn, the length of attention span is crucial in every learning situation. Teachers thus need to know what kinds of things 3-, 4-and 5-year-olds find attractive.

If You Have Not Checked This Item: Some Helpful Ideas

■ Focus on the Self

Although children's interests are widely varied, all humans—especially egocentric youngsters—have a basic interest in themselves. Think of something new and different about the child who shows little interest in center activities. Make it some kind of question, problem, or challenge that is intriguing and fun. Then turn the child loose with it. For instance, have a Cool Shoe Contest that the child who shows little interest can start. Have her make some kind of paper design that she can tape to the top of her shoes. This makes her Ms. Cool Shoe for the day. Then have her slap out a rhythm with her shoes, which you record. Play the recording. Let other children try to copy it and record their own shoe slaps. Let her choose who will be the next Mr. or Ms. Cool Shoe.

This boy is zooming his "jet plane" across the playground.

■ Arouse Curiosity

Children love mysteries. Invite a mystery guest (an adult dressed in a costume and mask) to visit the classroom. Let children guess who it is. Or bring a big stuffed animal in a bag and let the children guess what it is. Give them hints about what it eats or the noise it makes. Maybe the slow-to-respond child would like to think of a name for it once it is out of the bag. Simple things often interest children, for example, a cardboard carton, or a box full of plastic items.

■ Read a Book

Books these days are full of outrageous kids, zany animals, and outer space oddities just waiting to grab children's attention. Figure 4.11 lists a few. These books are for more than just reading. They invite children to participate in their wild adventures. Who can resist?

Girls can be pilots like Violet and build their own boat-planes from cardboard cartons. Boys can fly their own red Radio Flyer wagons. The whole class can convert their "school bus" to a "sailbus" and race through the ocean to victory with Hispanic Captain Cheech.

Or if dinosaurs pique their interest they can take cardboard cutouts of these prehistoric monsters to school for Pet Day. Afterward, children can make dinosaur heads from paper bags, or have dinosaur races with dinosaur toys in trucks from the block center.

Yolen's *How Do Dinosaurs Go to School?* (2007) always arouses the instant curiosity of children who can't get enough of these prehistoric creatures. A giant yellow- and blue-striped ceratosaurus on the cover not only shows off for the teacher but grabs a reader's attention right away. Your children can enjoy making

Figure 4.11 Attention-Getting Books

- *Friday My Radio Flyer Flew* (Pullen, 2008)
- *Violet the Pilot* (Breen, 2008)
- *Captain Cheech* (Marin, 2008)
- *Dino Pets Go to School* (Plourde, 2011)
- *How Do Dinosaurs Go to School?* (Yolen, 2007)
- *Boogie Monster* (Bissett, 2011)

their own outrageously colored dinosaur masks from paper bags and playing these roles themselves.

Finally, the **Boogie Monster** (Bissett, 2011) from outer space can drop into your classroom for a jam session with your children. The orange monster cheers children on to make their moves just like hopping kangaroos, stiff-legged robots, or waddling penguins. Observe all the children carefully and ask those who fail to participate in any of these activities what they would like to try.

✓ SMILES, SEEMS HAPPY MUCH OF THE TIME

Joy

Joy, the most positive of the emotions, is also the most elusive. Seek it and you may not find it. Try to experience it directly, and it may elude you. But live a normal life, and it will appear spontaneously. Joy does not occur so much on its own as it does as a by-product of something else: a pleasant experience, a happy thought, a good friendship. In other words, this emotion is indicative of feeling good about oneself, others, and life in general.

Ward and Dahlmeier (2011) talk about two kinds of joy: *affective joy*, which is experienced in relationship to others, and *cognitive joy*, the sense of accomplishment. They worry about the absence of joy in some classrooms these days. They say: "The current emphasis in early childhood and elementary programs on assessment, accountability, and increased academic expectations can deprive some children and their teachers of the experience of joy" (pp. 94–95).

We believe that using the assessment tools provided in this text will promote, not negate joy. Observing children using the Child Development Checklist, a positive tool, should, in fact, be a happy experience for all involved, as you watch children playing in a natural environment.

For children the absence of joy tells us that the child is not feeling good about things. We need to observe children carefully to see where they stand in regard to this important indicator of inner feelings, and we need to take positive actions if this emotion is missing.

Joy is the feeling of happiness that may precede or follow a pleasant experience: sensory pleasure such as a hug, a kiss, or a back rub; psychological pleasure such as the remembrance of good times; and the anticipation of seeing a loved one or of having fun with friends. For young children the most reliable source of joy is play.

People express joy with smiles, laughter, the lighting up of eyes, increased heartbeat, an inner feeling of confidence, a sense of well-being, or a glow. The emotion itself is fleeting, but the good feeling it creates may color a person's actions and responses for many hours.

As with the other emotions, the capacity for joy is inherited and is different for each individual. Its development, however, depends greatly on how the mother or primary caregiver responds to joy in the infant. A person cannot teach another person

Seeing smiles tells you children feel happy.

to be happy, but she can influence the occurrence of happiness by creating a pleasant, fun-filled environment in the first place, then responding positively when joy occurs.

Babies may smile during the first days of life. At first they smile in reverie or dreams, then during waking hours when a pleasant, high-pitched voice talks to them, and finally, by the fifth week at the sight of a friendly face coming close. The elicited smile that comes as a result of a voice occurs within the first week. By the second or third month, infants are smiling spontaneously without seeing or hearing anyone—that is, if they have been responded to pleasantly by their caregivers. But the human face remains the single most effective stimulus to smiling.

Laughter has its own developmental sequence. It first occurs between 5 and 9 weeks, usually in response to patty-cake-type games or tickling. Scientists believe a child's motor development has some relationship to development of laughter. But both laughter and smiling can be stimulated by the same expressions of joy on the part of another person. Situations that discourage or prevent the emotion of joy from occurring are listed in Figure 4.12.

Recognition of a familiar person, object, or situation helps stimulate or encourage the expression of joy. Whereas change and novelty seem to stimulate the emotion of

Figure 4.12 Situations to Discourage Joy

- Poor physical health
- Fatigue
- Boredom
- Harsh treatment
- Neglect
- Poverty
- Caregiver's lack of joy

Figure 4.13   Situations
to Encourage Joy

- Having a positive self-image
- Being around happy people
- Being successful in activities
- Finding a friend to play with
- Hearing laughter around you
- Choosing your favorite activity
- Hearing your favorite story
- Playing with your favorite toy

interest, familiarity and being comfortable with things set the stage for joy. Keep this in mind in your classroom. A little change is challenging, no change at all is boring, and too much change is overwhelming for young children. They need a stable schedule of daily events they can depend on and a physical arrangement of equipment that does not change too drastically overnight. Then they can look forward with joy to coming to the center every day (see Figure 4.13).

Humor

McGhee (2005) believes that the relationship between joy and humor is a two-way street. In other words, children are more likely to experience humor when in a happy, joyful state. They sometimes seem to think everything is funny and burst into giggles, silliness, and laughter. But they can also create joy and happiness that wasn't previously there by engaging in humor. Thus, some of the children's books described in Figure 4.14 are about creating joy by doing or having funny things happen.

If You Have Not Checked This Item: Some Helpful Ideas

■ Talk with Parents

Children who express no joy probably are not very happy. You will need to converse with the joyless child's parents in a sensitive manner, trying to elicit how the child reacts at home, whether any particular problems or pressures are affecting him, and what his basic personality is like. Is the child fundamentally happy? What are his

Figure 4.14   Books to
Promote Joy

- *Shoe-la-la!* (Beaumont, 2011)
- *Aliens Love Underpants* (Freedman & Cort, 2008)
- *Smile* (Hodgkinson, 2009)
- *Ha, Ha, Baby!* (Petty, 2008)
- *Grandma's Smile* (Siegel, 2010)

favorite foods, colors, toys, activities? What makes him laugh? Perhaps you can use some of these favorites as a focus for an activity to make him feel joyful.

■ Be a Joyful Person

Children and others feel joy when they meet a person who thinks they are delightful and wants to be around them. Make yourself that kind of person.

■ Read a Book

Books that can elicit joy and happiness in young children may include those in Figure 4.14.

In *Shoe-la-la!* four wonderful multicultural girls go on a shopping spree for shoes to match their party dresses. What a glorious romp in the shoe store as they try on every pair, but can't decide which. They end up making their own gorgeous creations at home. In *Aliens Love Underpants* just the word "underpants" will start your listeners giggling. These aliens who land in the backyard grab underpants off the clothesline and tumble on playground equipment donned in fancy pants. What a great art project for your children who can draw after they finish laughing.

The last three books are about smiles that have been lost by a little girl, a baby, and a grandma. How do they finally find them? Read the books to find out. Ask your listeners what they would do if their smiles were lost.

CHILDHOOD EMOTIONS IN THE CLASSROOM

Table 4.1 helps you see at a glance the causes and results of these common feelings. Such awareness can assist you in helping children develop more positive responses in emotional situations.

Table 4.1   Childhood emotions in the classroom

Emotion	Common Cause	Possible Results
Distress	Separation from loved one, abandonment	Crying, whining, clinging
Anger	Physical or psychological restraint, insult	Red face, loud words, screaming, aggression
Fear	Presence of threat	Tightening of muscles, trembling, clinging, crying
Interest	Change, novelty	Looking at something, exploration with senses, wide eyes
Affection	Displays of affection toward child	Standing, sitting near teacher, others; touches, hugs others; smiles, holds hands
Joy	A pleasant experience, happy thoughts, friendship	Smiling, laughing, lighting up of eyes, talking happily

OBSERVING EMOTIONAL COMPETENCE WITH CHECKLIST AND SAMPLING

Checklist

To understand and interpret the emotional growth of individual children, it is helpful to fill out the Emotional Competence section of the Child Development Checklist for specific children. Using data gathered during observations, the teacher filled out this section of the checklist for Sheila, as shown in Figure 4.15.

Sheila has connected with the teacher. However, she does not seem to be all that comfortable with the other children: She does not play with them yet, and she runs to the teacher whenever anything upsetting happens. The other important indicator is the fact that she does not smile or seem happy. Perhaps Sheila does not display happiness because she is ill at ease with the other children.

CHILD DEVELOPMENT CHECKLIST

Name _Sheila_   **Observer** _Connie_

Program _Head Start_   **Dates** _10/22_

Directions:

Put an **X** for items you see the child perform regularly. Put an **N** for items where there is no opportunity to observe. Leave all other items blank.

Item	Evidence	Dates
2. Emotional Competence		
__x__ Releases stressful feelings in appropriate manner	Lets teacher calm her down when Beth takes her crayon	10/22
__x__ Expresses anger in words rather than negative actions	When Beth takes her crayon she says to her: "That's not fair!"	10/22
__N__ Can be calmed in frightening situations	No opportunity to observe	10/22
__x__ Shows fondness, affection, love toward others	Touches, stays close to teacher	10/22
__x__ Shows interest, excitement in classroom activities	Goes around room trying out everything	10/22
_____ Smiles, seems happy much of the time	Rarely smiles, no evidence of being happy	10/22

Figure 4.15   Emotional Competence for Sheila

This observation was made at the beginning of the school year before all of the children were used to each other and to the center. Some of the activities listed in the section "If You Have Not Checked This Item: Some Helpful Ideas" may help Sheila feel more comfortable with the others. The fact that Sheila goes around the room trying out everything is a sign that she will eventually want to get involved in everything. Perhaps Sheila can do an art activity with another child. Her teacher may want to pair Sheila with a child who is already at ease and will thus help Sheila feel more at home in the classroom.

Screening Method

The six emotional competence checklist items can also be used as a screening tool for the entire class if this information is important for the teacher. She should then list each item down one side of a page. After each item she can list the name of every child she sees accomplishing it. When the list is completed the teacher can see at a glance the emotional state of the children. Items with few names often indicate areas where children need more help. Appropriate activities for the whole class will also help these children.

Sampling

Emotional competence in children can be observed in other ways. The expression of anger is often difficult to deal with. One teacher noticed that Neil was always getting angry and fighting with the other boys. They came to her saying "Neil started it." But Neil disagreed. The teacher decided to observe and record situations where Neil was involved in fighting from beginning to end.

She started observing and recording Neil's actions on a running record. Whenever fighting occurred, she put the information on an ABC Event Sampling chart she had made. The A action was the "antecedent event," what happened before the fighting. The fighting itself was the B action, the "behavior." The C action was what happened afterwards. (See Figure 4.16). After three fighting episodes she was able to determine what caused the fighting.

Time	Antecedent Event	Behavior	Consequent Event
10:15	Richie starts teasing Neil by running his truck into Neil's block building over & over.	Neil gets mad; starts hitting Richie	Teacher stops fighting; Richie keeps saying "He started it!"

Figure 4.16   ABC Event Sampling for Neil

She found that two brothers took turns secretly teasing Neil until he got so mad he struck out at them. She talked to each of the brothers about what they were doing, and what they could do to get along with Neil. She talked to Neil about what he could say to them in words instead of hitting if they teased him again. She talked to all three together about the problem, and they agreed to change their behavior. This was a good use of event sampling, she decided, and she would use it again.

Emotional events like this are common in early childhood classrooms. Aware teachers can help all the children develop emotional competence if they use their observation skills to understand what is happening in the classroom and who may need special help.

LEARNING ACTIVITIES

1. Observe the children in your classroom for a week to determine which children seem to release stressful feelings inappropriately through emotion. How would you help them regain emotional control? Write out and discuss a plan with your supervisor.

2. Choose a child who has trouble allowing his or her angry behavior to be redirected. After the angry episode talk to the child about what words he might use instead of aggressive acts. Write out what happened and what follow-up actions you might take.

3. Work with a child who seems to exhibit fear, and read one of the books described in the chapter. Describe the results.

4. Do a screening of the children in the class to determine who does not show fondness or affection toward any of the other children. Work with these children individually, helping them feel liked and wanted in the classroom. Pair them with another child in certain learning activities. Observe them later to see if their positive emotions have improved.

5. Put out a new and different exhibit and observe who notices it and shows interest or excitement. For those who do not, try to find out what their favorite things are (e.g., pets, food, TV shows, games, etc.). Have them help you set up an activity about one of these.

6. Choose a child for whom you have checked "Smiles, seems happy much of the time." Observe this child on three different days. Which of the other items can you check on the checklist based on your observations? What is your evidence for each checkmark? What conclusions can you make about this child based on these observations? Do you need any additional evidence to make conclusions?

SUGGESTED READINGS

Bruno, H. E. (2011). Using our brain to stay cool under pressure. *Young Children, 66*(1), 22–27.

Carlson, F. M., & Nelson, B. G. (2006). Redirecting aggression with touch. *Dimensions of Early Childhood, 34*(3), 9–15.

Fallin, K., Wallinga, C., & Coleman, M. (2001). Helping children cope with stress in the classroom setting. *Childhood Education, 78*(1), 17–24.

Fox, L., & Lentini, R. H. (2006). "You got it!" Teaching social and emotional skills. *Young Children, 61*(6), 36–42.

Riley, D., San Juan, R. R., Klinkner, J., & Ramminger, A. (2008). *Social and emotional development.* St. Paul, MN: Redleaf Press.

Riley, J. G. (2007). Buddying or bullying? A school-wide decision. *Dimensions of Early Childhood, 35*(1), 3–9.

CHILDREN'S BOOKS

Allen, J. (2007). *"I'm not scared!"* New York: Hyperion Books for Children.

Bang, M. (1999). *When Sophie gets angry—really, really angry*. New York: Blue Sky Press.

Beaumont, K. (2011). *Shoe-la-la!* New York: Scholastic Press.*

Berkner, L. (2007). *The story of my feelings*. New York: Orchard Books.

Bergman, M. (2005). *Snip snap! What's that?* New York: Greenwillow Books.

Bissett, J. (2011). *Boogie monster*. Seattle, WA: Compendium/Kids.

Boxall, E. (2002). *Francis the scaredy cat*. Cambridge, MA: Candlewick Press.

Breen, S. (2008). *Violet the pilot*. New York: Dial Books for Young Readers.

Cain, J. (2000). *The way I feel*. Seattle, WA: Parenting Press.

Clements, A. (2005). *Because your daddy loves you*. New York: Clarion Books.

Cuyler, M. (2001). *Stop, drop, and roll*. New York: Simon & Schuster.

Dewdney, A. (2005). *Grumpy Gloria*. New York: Viking.

Dewdney, A. (2007). *Llama llama mad at mama*. New York: Viking.

Frame, J. A. (2003). *Yesterday I had the blues*. Berkeley, CA: Tricycle Press.*

Freedman, C., & Cort, B. (2007). *Aliens love underpants*. Hauppauge, NY: Barron's.

Harris, R. H. (2004). *Don't forget to come back!* Cambridge, MA: Candlewick Press.

Hodgkinson, L. (2009). *Smile*. New York: Balzer+Bray.

Hooks, B. (2002). *Homemade love*. New York: Hyperion Books.*

Joosse, B. M. (1991). *Mama, do you love me?* San Francisco: Chronicle Books.*

Joosse, B. M. (2008). *Grandma calls me beautiful*. San Francisco: Chronicle Books.*

Joosse, B. M. (2005). *Papa, do you love me?* San Francisco: Chronicle Books *

Marin, C. (2008). *Captain Cheech*. New York: Harper/Collins.*

Patterson, R. (2012). *My no, no, no day!* New York: Viking.

Petty, K. (2008). *Ha, ha, baby!* London: Boxer Books (New York: Sterling Publishing).

Plourde, L. (2011). *Dino pets go to school*. New York: Dutton's Children's Books.*

Prigger, M. S. (2002). *Aunt Minnie and the twister*. New York: Clarion.

Pullen, Z. (2008). *Friday my Radio Flyer flew*. New York: Simon & Schuster.

Vail, R. (2002). *Sometimes I'm Bombaloo*. New York: Scholastic.

Siegel, R. (2010). *Grandma's smile*. New York: Roaring Brook Press.

Wargin, K-J. (2010). *Scare a bear*. Ann Arbor, MI: Sleeping Bear Press.

Yolen, J. (2007). *How do dinosaurs go to school?* New York: The Blue Sky Press.*

WEB SITES

Center for Early Childhood Mental Health Consultation
www.ecmhc.org

Center on the Social and Emotional Foundations for Early Learning
http://csefel.vanderbilt.edu/index.html

Early Childhood Behavior Project
http:/slhslinux.cla.unm.edu

Pyramid Plus: The Colorado Center for Social and Emotional Competence and Inclusion
www.pyramidplus.org

*Multicultural

CHAPTER 5

Social Competence

_____ Play by self with own toys/materials

_____ Play parallel to others with similar toys/materials

_____ Play with others in group play

_____ Gain access to ongoing play in positive manner

_____ Make friends with other children

_____ Resolve play conflicts in positive manner

_____ Be observed by using running records and checklist

 **DEVELOPING SOCIAL COMPETENCE**

The social competence of the preschool child is revealed in how he or she gets along with peers. Research suggests that children who fail to achieve social competence in the early years are at risk of developing maladaptive behavior later in life (Nissen & Hawkins, 2010).

Young children frequently struggle to develop social skills. Children start out completely self-centered, which seems to stem from a survival mechanism in infancy. By the time they arrive in your classroom, children have begun to know themselves as individuals but mainly in relation to their adult caregivers. Now they must deal with their peers.

Children who have developed strong self-esteem should do well away from home. They will be able to let go of their primary caregiver more easily and will be more willing to try new things and to experience new people. Reviews of research support this point of view: Kemple (1991) examined studies that showed how the quality of the child's attachment relationship with his mother in infancy predicted the child's social acceptance in preschool.

Peers in the early childhood classroom, however, pose a different problem for the young child. Many, if not most, 3- and 4-year-olds simply have not developed the social skills for making friends or getting along with others. The focus of these children is on themselves. For many, everything has been done for them. Even if a new baby has replaced them as the youngest in the family, they still struggle to be first in the eyes of their parents.

This egocentric point of view does not serve them well in the world at large because sooner or later they must learn to deal with others and be treated as part of a group. They may have been enrolled in your program to learn precisely this. The purpose of many preschools is to help young children develop basic social skills. What exactly do these preschoolers need to learn? Some important aspects include those listed in Figure 5.1.

Preschoolers' success in developing these skills, either on their own or with your help, may make the difference in how they get along with others for much of the rest of their lives.

This chapter is particularly concerned with the young child's ability to make contact, interact, and get along with peers. To determine where each of your children stands in the development of these skills, you need to be aware of behaviors that indicate their development level. Frost (Frost, Wortham, & Reifel, 2012), a recognized play specialist, believes much of children's social development occurs through play. He talks about how their social development helps them understand

Figure 5.1 Social Skills for Preschool Children

Important Social Learning for the Preschool Child
- Making contact and playing with other children
- Interacting with peers, to give and take
- Getting along with peers, interacting in harmony
- Making friends with other children
- Seeing things from another child's point of view
- Gaining access to ongoing play
- Resolving interpersonal conflicts

themselves and others, and how they establish friendships through play. Social competence is a factor in their successful play relationships.

THE IMPORTANCE OF PLAY

Vygotsky (1976) was one of the first early childhood researchers to be concerned primarily with the social interactions of children. He coined the term *zone of proximal development* (ZPD) to refer to the conditions through which children's comprehension is furthered as a result of social interactions. He looked at children's social play as the essential ingredient. Although Piaget, too, considered play and social experience to be important, his work focused mainly on individual children rather than their social interactions (Van Hoorn, Nourot, Scales, & Alward, 2003).

OTHER EARLY PLAY RESEARCH

Many early childhood specialists have been interested in determining how children develop the skills to get along with one another. Social play has been the focus of such research since Parten first looked at "Social Participation Among Pre-School Children" in the late 1920s and published her findings in 1932. She found that social participation among preschoolers could be categorized and that the categories correlated closely with age and maturity.

Parten (1932) identified six behavior categories that have since served as a basis for determining children's social skills level in several fields of study. Her well-known categories include

1. *Unoccupied behavior:* The child does not participate in the play around him. He stays in one spot, follows the teacher, or wanders around.

2. *Onlooker behavior:* The child spends much time watching what other children are doing and may even talk to them, but he does not join or interact with them physically.

3. *Solitary independent play:* The child engages in play activities, but he plays on his own and not with others or with their toys.

4. *Parallel activity:* The child plays independently, but he plays next to other children and often uses their toys or materials.

5. *Associative play:* The child plays with other children using the same materials, but he acts on his own and does not subordinate his interests to those of the group.

6. *Cooperative play:* The child plays in a group that has organized itself to do a particular thing and whose members have taken on different roles (pp. 248–251).

Since 1932, many other researchers have used Parten's categories and find them still observable. Frost, Wortham, and Reifel (2012) noted that the validity of Parten's stages has been confirmed by numerous researchers over the years, and that these stages are also useful in describing many other social events, not just play. Although they see that many of today's children may be progressing through these stages at an earlier pace, they tell us that for any child, we see a developmental progression in the type of social involvement that a child exhibits, and the onset of each type is roughly linked with age.

Researchers like to use Parten's "play categories" when observing children at play because these behaviors can readily be seen in the play interactions of young children. Yet since Parten's day, a great deal of new information about the social development of young children has surfaced. Today we acknowledge that these early play categories are indeed a valuable beginning point for gathering observational data about a young child's social development, but we also need to incorporate other up-to-date information.

NEUROSCIENCE RESEARCH

Frost et al. (2012) discuss this new research, called "brain science," about the functioning of the human brain and how it affects young children's development. They tell us (with great excitement) about the findings being so compelling and far-reaching that people of all ages and persuasions will be affected. That means adults who work with children will need to become brain literate. Using brain scans such as computerized axial tomography (CT scan), magnetic resonance imaging (MRI), and positron emission tomography (PET), these scientists have found important linkages between brain development and children's play (see Figure 5.2).

What is really important happens during the first years of life, say Frost and colleagues. Playful activity makes a positive difference in brain development and subsequent human functioning. They also note that this brain development is well disguised in the "seemingly innocuous cloak of play." Only brain scientists get to see the physical evidence, the brain scans, that reveal the consequences of environmental stimulation or neglect on young children.

There is, however, another piece of physical evidence—a most important one in the preschool teacher's arsenal of educational tools: **child observation**. You can indeed learn to understand the results of brain development through systematic

Figure 5.2 Linkages Between Brain Development and Children's Play

- All healthy young children play.
- The range and complexity of play quickly increase as neurons start hardwiring brain connections at a remarkable rate.
- Their early play equips young children for the skills they will need later in life.
- Early childhood experiences exert a dramatic, precise impact on the wiring of the brain and children's formation of various developmental abilities.

Observation is your "brain scan evidence" of children's development.

observation of the children. You might even say *careful observation is your brain scan evidence!*

SOCIAL PLAY DEVELOPMENT

Because development of social play is very much age-related, the preschool teacher can observe it in a particular sequence as children progress from solitary play through parallel play to cooperative play. "Age-related development" (brain development) thus signifies that the child's social skill level depends on cognitive, language, and emotional maturity. It also infers that the older the child, the more experience he probably has had with social contacts. Observers have noted that infants first begin to imitate one another in play toward the end of their first year.

Early in their second year, they are already engaging in peer play whenever they have the opportunity. Two-year-olds often begin peer play by playing alongside another toddler in a parallel manner. If they interact with an age mate, it is with only one. Two-year-olds have difficulty handling more than one playmate at a time. A threesome does not last long for children of this age.

Three-year-olds, as they become more mature and experienced, are able to play with more than one other child at the same time. As they become less egocentric and more able to understand another child's point of view, 3-year-olds have more success with social play. Using more mature language, listening to their play partners, and adjusting their behavior to the situation all support such play. (See Figure 5.3.)

Figure 5.3   Social
Play Development

1-year-olds
Begin to imitate one another in play

2-year-olds
Play alongside another child; sometimes interact
Have difficulty handling more than one playmate

3-year-olds
Can play with more than one child at same time
Less egocentric; more able to see other's point of view
More successful in social play

THE TEACHER'S ROLE

Many teachers today are concerned about the apparent increase in the number of children who exhibit poor emotional regulation, undeveloped social skills, and a fascination with violent play themes.

How can teachers help children overcome these problems? Many children learn how to interrelate and play with peers in an early childhood program without the teacher's assistance. Others, however, need your help. Newcomers, shy children, immature children, and children from dysfunctional families often have difficulty on their own. Rodrigues, Smith-Carter, and Voytechi (2007) also tell about preschoolers with developmental delays. They have lower rates of social interaction and fewer friendships.

If yours is a multiage classroom, it is often the youngest children who have the most difficulty gaining access to group play, sustaining their role in the play, or resolving conflict when it appears. These children definitely need your help. Yours is a special role in helping children develop the social skills for peer acceptance. It involves several steps:

Helping Children Develop Social Skills for Peer Acceptance

Figure 5.4 lists strategies for helping children develop social skills for peer acceptance.

How the teacher carries out this important role in children's social skills development is discussed under each of the checklist items to follow. All of the checklist items—solitary, parallel, group play, gaining access, making friends, and resolving conflict—are, of course, descriptive rather than judgmental. We are interested in observing individual children on each item to try to discover the child's level of social skills. We must be careful not to judge a child negatively if we do not check a certain item. The items themselves are neither negative nor positive; they merely describe behavior. What we infer from the checkmarks or lack of them will be more

Figure 5.4 Social
Skills for Peer
Acceptance

- Set up the physical arrangement of the classroom to accommodate small-group activities.
- Observe and record the social skills of the children to determine: (a) who plays alone, (b) who plays parallel to others, (c) who plays with a group, (d) who gains access to play, (e) who makes friends, and (f) who can resolve conflict.
- Help children initiate friendly contacts with other children.
- Help children gain access to ongoing play.
- Help children learn to resolve conflicts with others

meaningful if we also look at the recorded evidence on which the checkmarks or blanks are based. It is just as important to record descriptive evidence on *items not checked* as on those items you have checked.

PLAYS BY SELF WITH OWN TOYS/MATERIALS

Many young children, when they first enter a preschool program, start out playing by themselves. This may occur because of the strangeness of the situation or their lack of self-confidence with unfamiliar children. Solitary play also occurs because children are attracted by the toys and materials and want to try them out by themselves. Some solitary play may occur because certain programs encourage it or because children have an independent project they want to accomplish. You will need to observe and record the child's actual activity during solitary play, as well as the youngster's overall involvement or lack of it with other children. Even after children have advanced to cooperative play, many continue playing by themselves on projects of their own and should not be discouraged from doing so.

Parten (1932) described "solitary independent play" as follows:

> The child plays alone and independently with toys that are different from those used by the children within speaking distance and makes no effort to get close to other children. He pursues his own activity without reference to what others are doing. (p. 250)

For some children, solitary play is truly a beginning level of social play that precedes their becoming involved in playing with others. If your children do not play at all with others or only play parallel to them, you might consider solitary play as a beginning level of play for such youngsters.

Research by Smilansky in the 1960s and Rubin in the 1970s and 1980s has looked at children's play in terms of their cognitive development in addition to their social skills. They maintain that levels of play are determined not only by whether children play by themselves or with others, but also by what children do during play.

To determine whether your solitary players are, indeed, at a beginning level of social play, you should note in your observational data what they are doing. If children

*Some children gain satisfaction
doing solitary constructive play.*

are manipulating toys and materials or trying them out to see how they work, they are at a beginning level of play. In block play, for instance, beginners often pick up a block, put it down, pound with it, or put it in a container and then dump it out. More mature players stack blocks into towers, line them up into roads, or build buildings with them.

If you observe a child constructing or creating something by herself, this may indicate something altogether different from the beginner who is manipulating materials alone. If the builder is purposefully using materials toward some end—for instance, making a building, a painting, or a play dough creation—she may be exhibiting higher-level creativity skills. This higher level of skill development may have enabled such children to get satisfaction from making something on their own. Instead of discouraging these children from solitary constructive play, you should provide them with many opportunities for expressing this creativity. Such children will join in group play again when the time is right for them.

Our high-tech society is creating another type of solitary player these days: the young child who spends large amounts of time playing by himself with play stations or interactive video games. Such children may need your program to introduce them to traditional play materials as well as to other players. Does your program include a television or any high-tech play materials? Such materials, with the exception of the computer, belong in the home rather than the preschool if you plan to help children develop social skills. Even children's use of the classroom computer should not be a solitary activity, but needs to involve two children together at the keyboard. However, if a child is neither engaged in solitary play nor any other kind of play during the free-choice period, you can help her in several ways.

If You Have Not Checked This Item: Some Helpful Ideas

■ Give Child a Familiar Material

Many children are familiar with dough at home but have not had an opportunity to play with it. Have the nonplaying child help you mix a bowl of play dough. Then give him some implements such as a small rolling pin and cookie cutters—and let him play.

■ Read a Book

Read a moving, grooving book such as **Pete the Cat: Rocking in My School Shoes** (Litwin, 2011). Pete discovers the library, the lunchroom, and the playground. What can your solitary listener discover in your classroom as he or she rocks around it?

In **Kindergarten Rocks** (Davis, 2005) your listeners can follow scared little preschooler Dexter around as he starts his first day of kindergarten. Can they find the same things to do as Dexter did? (Art, cooking, Play-Doh, letters, blocks, dress-up, and books?)

PLAYS PARALLEL TO OTHERS WITH SIMILAR MATERIALS

Parallel play is a fascinating phenomenon. If you are unfamiliar with this type of play, you have to see it to believe it. Parallel play often involves two children who seem to be playing together. As you get close enough to witness what is going on, you find that each child is actually playing a different game from a different point of view but often with similar toys. If language is involved, the two children seem to be talking to themselves rather than each other.

Parten (1932) described parallel play this way:

> The child plays independently, but the activity he chooses naturally brings him among other children. He plays with toys that are like those which the children around him are using, but he plays with the toy as he sees fit, and does not try to influence or modify the activity of the children near him. He plays beside rather than with the other children. There is no attempt to control the coming or going of children in the group. (p. 250)

All kinds of parallel play go on in the preschool setting. More seems to occur with younger children than with older ones. Parallel play, as previously mentioned, seems to enable younger children to learn to play cooperatively with others in an early childhood classroom. This idea makes a great deal of sense when you consider that your room consists of a large group of highly egocentric youngsters who are strangers for the most part. They come together in a physical setting full of toys and activities just for them. How are they to deal with such a setting?

They begin by trying out things on their own. Then they play side by side using the same materials but playing a different game. Finally the children begin to cooperate, to interchange ideas, and to come together to play as a group with self-assigned

roles and tasks. It was once thought that children who have learned to play cooperatively may abandon parallel play altogether. Researchers Anderson and Robinson
(2006) are more inclined to believe that parallel play can also serve as a bridge for
children moving from one play state to another. How is it in your classroom?

If You Have Not Checked This Item: Some Helpful Ideas

■ Try Finger Painting for Two

Set up a small table where two can sit side by side; put out finger paints to be
shared. Invite one of your reluctant participants and one other child to paint. Do
not force the reluctant child. Perhaps you could first involve him in a solitary manner and then ask him if another child could work next to him. This time he will be
working not only parallel to the other child, but also with the child, because the
paints have to be shared.

■ Set Up Audio Recording for Two

It is important to have two recorders in your program. They are invaluable because
they provide an opportunity for two people to play individually with the same materials in a parallel manner. Recording is personal and fun. Even the shy child can talk
as softly as she wants as long as she holds the mike up close. Then comes the fun of
listening to what she has spoken. Two children can record at the same table if they
each talk into their own microphones. They may eventually want to talk into each
other's mikes.

Observe closely to decide if these two are really doing parallel play.

■ Set Up a Computer Program for Two

Place two chairs in front of the computer and bring up a simple program that two children can take turns using. If no one is using the computer, ask a child who knows how to use it to try the program you have set up. Suggest to a child who usually plays by himself that there is an empty computer chair waiting for him—that the other child will help him get started if he wants.

✓ PLAYS WITH OTHERS IN GROUP PLAY

When children play together in a group using the same materials for the same purpose or doing pretend play around a common theme, we say they are engaging in group or "cooperative" play. A great deal of group play occurs in most early childhood programs, although not every child joins in. The observer can often spot children engaged in group play in the block center where they are building structures together or in the dramatic play center where they are playing house or doctor.

Group play like this is the principal activity for many children during free-play time, whereas others have not yet learned the social skills necessary to enter the play or sustain their roles. They are the children often engaged in parallel play alongside the group players. Some children are perfectly content to play alongside others without joining in, whereas other youngsters may need your help to join the fun.

Whatever you do, don't force the issue. Some children are not yet enough at ease in the classroom to join in with others in their group play schemes. Give them a chance to get used to the program. Children fare very well on their own, and most will join in their own good time. Because this is the most sophisticated type of play in preschool, many children need time to play on their own or in a parallel situation. They need to become acquainted with the other players and perhaps make friends among them. They also need to have an interest in what the group is doing.

Your role should be to encourage group play by giving children the opportunity for it to occur during the free-choice period, by supporting children in their own play schemes or giving them ideas for new play projects from time to time, by giving them plenty of time to carry on this play, and by inviting anyone interested to join the play.

For children who want to play but do not know how to join in, see the suggestions in the following section. If you do not see much group play of any kind occurring in the classroom, you may need to take stock of your room arrangement or materials. Is your classroom divided into learning centers or curriculum areas with enough space for several children in each area? The block area should have room for at least four to six children to create structures on the floor, but not be so large or open that all the children try to occupy it at once. Block shelves can be pulled away from the walls to partially enclose the area. The shelves themselves should be filled with wooden unit blocks, enough for groups of children to build really large structures. Building accessories can include people, animals, small vehicles, and dollhouse furniture.

*Here is a small play group in the
dramatic play area.*

Many children first come together in group play in the block center. They may
start by playing with blocks by themselves, then build parallel to other builders, and
finally join in with a group. Do your space and materials allow for this to happen?

A second area highly conducive to group play is the dramatic play center. Most
classrooms have a housekeeping area with child-size kitchen furnishings, a full-
length mirror, dolls, and dress-up clothing. In addition, you can add shelves, a desk
and toy cash register, and empty containers and bags for creating a pretend store. If
there is space for several children and materials for several play themes, you may see
more than one play group in operation at once.

If You Have Not Checked This Item: Some Helpful Ideas

■ Follow-Up Field Trips

Whenever you go on a field trip, whether near or far, be sure to set up some trip-
related props in one of the learning centers for children to play with cooperatively.
Children can then spontaneously re-create the trip or play out some aspect of it that
interests them. For example, put out firefighters' gear (hats, raincoats, boots) in the
dramatic play center; or put out little fire trucks, plastic tubes for hoses, and figures
of people in the block center.

■ Follow-Up Book Readings

Another way to initiate spontaneous group play is to read a favorite story and then
put out props for children to reenact or follow up some aspect of the story. ***This Is***

the Firefighter (Godwin, 2009) is an especially good book to have available after a trip to the fire station. The exciting story in rhyme takes the firefighter and all his equipment to an apartment fire where he rescues people. Can your youngsters reenact their own drama in the block center?

In *The Moon Over Star* (Aston, 2008) five African American children in a family group build their own spaceship and pretend to be Neil Armstrong and the astronauts who go to the moon. It is a story for older children but still simple enough to be understood by all.

Children of every race enjoy pretending to be book characters. Whether or not you have African American children in the class, your youngsters can identify with the book characters in *The Moon Over Star* and thus feel good about such children. That is why it is so important to have picture books showing people of many races and cultures available for your children to look at. Ramsey (1991) feels that by engaging children in these stories they empathize with the characters and can be in another person's shoes.

Ellis, Gallingane, and Kemple (2006) agree. They tell us about researchers finding how children's stories, fables, and fairy tales have a profound effect on children's social skills. This means you must be sure to talk with the children afterward about whether their own experiences are like those in the books. (See Figure 5.5.)

Start a Play Group Yourself

Children love to have the teacher play with them. If you take on a role and pretend, all the better. Choose an unoccupied learning center and set out a few props to entice children to participate. Perhaps the sand table is free. You can be a paleontologist going on a dig for dinosaur bones for a museum. Put on safety goggles and your explorer's hat, and take a little shovel along. Bury some of the block center toy dinosaurs in the sand. If no children have noticed what you are doing, make an open invitation: "I need four children to go on an expedition with me to the Gobi Desert to search for dinosaur bones." If more than four want to participate, have them sign up for the next turn. Be sure to have a dinosaur picture book on hand for identification purposes, as well as the class camera to take photos of the finds. Once the children are involved, you can withdraw quietly and let the players carry on.

Afterward read to a small group at a time the simple book *Bones, Bones, Dinosaur Bones* (Barton, 1990) about six diggers who look for dinosaur bones, find them, dig them up, wrap them up, transport them to the science museum, and assemble

Figure 5.5 Books
to Stimulate Play

Kindergarten Rocks (Davis, 2011)
The Moon Over Star (Aston, 2008)
Pete the Cat: Rocking in My School Shoes (Litwin, 2011)
This Is the Firefighter (Goodwin, 2009)
Bones, Bones, Dinosaur Bones (Barton, 1990)

them into the bones of *Tyrannosaurus rex*. Will your children want to create their own museum?

✓ GAINS ACCESS TO ONGOING PLAY IN A POSITIVE MANNER

Access Rituals

The trick for many children in your classroom, you will note, is to gain access to play already in progress. Sociologists call these maneuvers "access rituals." Children new to the group may try different strategies to get involved:

(a) The youngest children may use nonverbal appeals such as smiles or gestures of interest as they stand nearby and watch, hoping a player will take note and invite or allow them in.

(b) Other children may walk around and watch, or stand and watch, waiting for an opportunity to insert themselves.

(c) They may engage in similar play parallel to the original players, hoping to join the original players if their own parallel play is accepted.

(d) They may intrude in a disruptive manner claiming that the space or the toys are their own.

(e) The oldest preschoolers often use words, asking "Can I play?" or "What are you doing?" to gain access.

Some children may stand around and watch, waiting for an opportunity to insert themselves.

During free-play periods in most preschool classrooms, you see groups of children busily engaged in building in the block center, dressing up for pretend roles in the dramatic play area, playing with table blocks, painting, molding play dough, or playing with puppets in the reading area. Not every child is engaged. Onlookers, shy children, new children and others may want to get involved, but don't know how. Some have tried but been rejected. Others may need your help to get started.

But why should child players keep other children out once their play has started? Corsaro's (2003) research has shown that kids realize how difficult it is to be accepted into ongoing activities so they concentrate on protecting their own play. While some children use aggression

Figure 5.6   Positive
Strategies to Gain
Access to Ongoing Play

- Observing the group to see what is going on
- Adopting the group's frame of reference as in parallel play
- Contributing something relevant to the play
- Acting interested, walking round and round the play
- Asking more than once if one can play

to force their way into ongoing play, children who successfully enter ongoing play have learned to adopt positive strategies such as those in Figure 5.6.

Communication skills also seem to play an important role in children's gaining access to group play. Outsiders need to talk with the players, understand what their replies are, then respond again, replying to their concerns. If the group is pretending to take their babies to the doctor, for instance, a successful strategy Charlene might use for gaining entrance is to get a doll from the dramatic play area and bring it along with the others, saying, "My baby needs to be examined, too." In this case, she had adopted the group's frame of reference (doctor play) as well as contributing something relevant to the play. But just as important, she uses words and does not crash unannounced into the play. Instead, she gets a doll, brings it along with the others, and then communicates clearly.

Had she merely asked, "Can I play?" it would be easy for the group to reject her. Had she taken one of the other children's dolls or tried to take over the role of the doctor, she would certainly have been rejected. Children who have difficulty seeing things from another person's point of view may not understand what is required of them to join in ongoing play. Then it may be up to you to help.

Rosa, a shy little girl in Head Start, had trouble gaining access to much of the group play because she tended to be so unassertive. She would watch the others play, but whenever she shyly asked if she could play, she was refused. Then she would go off by herself. She should not have given up so easily. Over half of the requests made to join preschool play groups are denied, Corsaro discovered. But because group play in preschool is so fluid with children coming and going, outside children have many opportunities to join in. Just because a child is denied access once does not mean she will be denied if she tries again—or again.

Many children like Rosa do not try again. Then it is up to the teacher to coach them on their next step, or to model a successful strategy herself that they might try. If nothing seems to work for Rosa and the group will just not accept her, then the teacher may want to spend some time coaching the group later on how to admit an outsider.

The most successful strategy for a child to gain access to ongoing play seems to be engaging in parallel play. The least successful strategy is to be disruptive. Researchers have noted that parallel play among preschoolers decreases as group play increases. Still, parallel play seems to be one of the principal modes of social play for 3- and 4-year-olds in most classrooms.

Whatever she does, the teacher should not force the child on the group. Being the adult in charge, the teacher has the power to make the group accept Rosa, but she will not be solving Rosa's problem by doing so. Instead, the group may become resentful toward Rosa, because she was forced on them by the teacher. The social dilemmas that preschool children face are actually important learning situations for them. If the teacher solves the problem, then the child has missed the opportunity to try to work it out for herself. Whenever a teacher intervenes, it should be as a last resort after a child has had more than one chance to attempt the resolution herself.

If You Have Not Checked This Item: Some Helpful Ideas

■ Use Puppets with the Child and/or the Group

When it seems appropriate, bring out two hand puppets and introduce them to Rosa with names such as Ollie Outsider and Purely Personal. Tell her that little Ollie wants to play but Purely won't let her. Ask Rosa what she thinks Ollie can do to get Purely to let her play. Whatever Rosa suggests, you can try out with the puppets. Let Ollie succeed if Rosa's suggestions seem appropriate. Give your own suggestions if nothing of Rosa's seems to work. Use this same sort of puppet play to coach a group that will not let an outsider join. Have children put the puppets on their hands and be the characters.

■ Provide a Time for Everyone to Join a Group

It is much easier for children to join a play group at the outset. Once the group has started, the outsider usually encounters resistance. Thus it is important for the teacher to provide a time and opportunity for everyone to become involved in playing with someone else. At morning circle or at the beginning of the free-choice period the children can learn what activities are available and make their choices.

✓ MAKES FRIENDS WITH OTHER CHILDREN

Is making friends with peers really important to young children, you may wonder? For instance, are they worried about finding a friend when they first come to school? Whether they express this idea openly, it is often uppermost in the minds of many youngsters when they first come into the unknown environment of the preschool classroom. Will the other children like them? Will there be a friend waiting for them? Just like human beings everywhere, young children also need to feel welcomed and accepted wherever they go.

This is part of being human. All human beings need to be accepted as part of a group outside our families. And within that group, we need at least one other person we can relate to and who relates to us as a friend. The needs of preschool children are no different. But they are different in their ability to make friends. How does one go about making a friend when one is 3 or 4 or 5 years old?

Some children have no difficulty. Others seem to bumble about without much success. A few others don't even try. Not so many years ago, friendship was the main reason that parents enrolled their children in preschools. They called it "socialization." They wanted their children to learn socialization skills before they went to elementary school. In other words, they wanted their children to learn to get along with other children.

Somehow, in the intervening years, many people have changed their goals for preschool children. When parents, teachers, and society at large talk about preparing children for elementary school, they seem to mean children's learning of academic skills such as reading, writing, and numbers. What happened to the social skills of making friends and learning to get along with peers? Don't children still have to learn that?

This text takes the point of view that all development occurs simultaneously. Social skills are just as important as cognitive skills, and support for their development should not be neglected. For preschoolers who do not develop competence in interpersonal social skills, the results can be disastrous in later years, as noted earlier.

As children move away from their families by coming to preschool, they necessarily form new relationships with the people around them, especially their peers. Although such relationships are usually thought of as friendships, they are quite different from the friendships of older children or adults. Being preoccupied with their own interests and needs makes it difficult for preschool children to form friendships based on personality. They are more likely to look on a friend as a momentary playmate who is doing something interesting or is fun to play with. Ramsey (1991) describes friendship among preschool children as "playmateship" in which children think of their most frequent companions as their friends. Some friendship choices may reflect convenience more than personal preference.

Until children can truly see things from another person's perspective, their relationship with that person will always be somewhat one-sided. For the egocentric child of 3 to about 6 years, friendship is more of a one-way street than a two-way relationship with each partner contributing. Young children are preoccupied with their own needs. They believe that others want what they want. That is the reason that play among preschoolers may suddenly break down into conflict, because the players cannot see things from the other person's point of view.

How does friendship come about, then, among young children? When toddlers and the youngest preschoolers talk about a friend, they usually apply the word to any special person who has been called a friend for them. They do have favorite peers and can form strong attachments, but the concept of friendship itself does not have much meaning for them at first.

With older preschoolers, friendship often starts with two children coming together. Each needs to be recognized as a person by the other, and then accepted. These children may indeed be true friends, but often the reason for their friendship in preschool is based on playing together rather than liking one another's personality. The most important aspect of this type of friendship in an early childhood program is whether the child is *included* in the play with a partner or a group.

It is important for teachers to help children make friends for a number of reasons. Riley, San Juan, Klinker, and Rammminger (2008) talk about preschool-aged friends being happier during their interactions and better at dealing with conflict than nonfriends. They also are more skilled and competent when interacting with a friend than a nonfriend.

Teachers can best help young children make friends with others first by observing and then recording the children to determine who has been included or excluded from group activities. Keep your eye on disruptive children who often engage in verbal and physical aggression; they may be children who have not found friends. They may wander around the room, hovering close to others but not really included. Other onlookers may be shy or withdrawn children who have not been rebuffed but ignored by their peers. And still others may be children who are new to the class and have not yet found a way to be included by others. Children who are perceived by others to be different because of looks, language, age, or a physical disability are also sometimes excluded.

Once you have determined which children do not seem to have a friendly attachment to anyone in the group, you can decide whether such youngsters need to resolve their own friendship problems or if you should intervene to help them. If children come to you or cling to you, it may be a sign for you to bring them together with one other child. On the other hand, if an onlooker seems content to play parallel to the others, she may need more time to become comfortable with the activities and children before finding a friend on her own. Children with disabilities may also need your help to find a friend. About 50% of inclusive preschool children with disabilities are at risk for social rejection by peers. They require intervention to promote their social competence, according to Rodrigues et al. (2007).

If You Have Not Checked This Item: Some Helpful Ideas

■ Help Children Find Partners (Playmates)

Play singing games or circle games where children have a partner to participate with. Do not ask children to go around choosing a partner, because some children, such as shy children, will be left out. Instead, the teaching staff can help children pair up quickly and quietly without a fuss. Playing partner games like this every day may help outsiders feel included enough to begin playing with their partner in an unstructured activity afterward.

■ Do Not Make a Fuss About Friends

Teachers who talk a great deal about which children are friends with which other children may unknowingly be putting pressure on children who do not have identifiable "friends." Finding a personal friend is not the point in preschool. Most children have not yet developed to this level. Having a playmate is more important, but talking about it is not.

■ Create Size-Restricted Play Spaces

Have a number of spaces or tables set up for two children. For example, two to tape record their names; two to listen to a book CD; two to build with Lego blocks; two to paint with finger paint; two to count with tiny dinosaur counters. Children, especially those with visual or hearing impairments, can be directed to these activities to play with one other child. Be sure to call their partners by name so they will get to know the other child better.

■ Model the Contact Behavior

If the child seems unable to make any contact with someone to play with, you can model the behavior yourself. "C'mon, Terrell, you take that car, and I'll take this car. We're going to build a garage for our cars. Let's see if we can get someone to help us. Let's ask Lavon. Hi, Lavon. We're going to build a garage for our cars with the blocks. Want to help us?"

You should be successful because children enjoy playing with the teacher and like to be chosen by the teacher to do things. However, if Lavon refuses, then approach another child with the same request. This helps Terrell learn what to do should he be refused. You can extract yourself unobtrusively from this play once the children are engaged.

■ Read a Book

Some preschool children may have an imaginary friend at home, but seldom does this "friend" come to preschool. In *I Am Too Absolutely Small for School* (Child, 2004), a humorous Charlie and Lola book, Lola tells Charlie all the reasons she can't go to school, one being that Loren Sorenson, her invisible friend, is feeling slightly not very well. Charlie replies to all her reasons, so off she goes with Loren. When she returns she is with a real visible friend and they sit down together at home to have a glass of pink milk. But there is a space between the two girls. You know who is there.

In another Charlie and Lola book, *My Best, Best Friend* (Child, 2010), Lola and her best friend Lotta do everything together both in and out of school. Then one day a new girl, Evie, comes to school, and Lotta is asked to show her around. Soon Lola feels left out, until Charlie and his friend give Lola a big lift and that brings Lotta back. Talk with your listeners about their own experiences with friends.

RESOLVES PLAY CONFLICTS IN A POSITIVE MANNER

Not only does group play teach children the social skills of gaining access and finding a friend, but more important, it also gives young children the opportunity to learn to get along together. This is not always easy to learn. Conflicts of all kinds occur with high frequency in an early childhood classroom. Children need to learn how to resolve such disagreements in a positive manner. Unfortunately, many children have learned from television that it is acceptable to resolve conflicts with violence. Your job is to help them learn a different type of resolution. During group play, major conflicts often focus on:

- Roles
- Direction of play
- Turns
- Toys

Pretend roles are important to the children who take them. In spontaneous dramatic play, certain children often insist on being mother, or father, or doctor. If several children want the same role, a conflict often results. This does not necessarily mean a physical fight, but usually an argument and sometimes tears. If the children involved cannot resolve the conflict quickly, play is disrupted and sometimes disbanded.

Conflict also occurs over play themes in dramatic play (e.g., "Let's play doctor." "No, let's play superheroes"), as well as the direction of the action, which is generally made up on the spot. Egocentric young players often want their own way and frequently disagree over who will do what, what they are going to do, and what's going to happen next.

"It's my turn!" or "It's my toy!" are other comments frequently heard during group play in early childhood classrooms or playgrounds. Youngsters 3, 4, and 5 years old are still for the most part focused on themselves and their desires. It is most annoying for them to find that someone else got there first, or has what they want, or won't listen to them.

Often children turn to the teacher to resolve these conflicts. You need to be aware, however, that the youngsters themselves have the capability to resolve social play conflicts on their own. That, in fact, should be your goal for the children: to help them resolve play conflicts by themselves in a positive manner. How do you do it? To begin with, your observation of individual children will tell you which youngsters are able to resolve conflicts on their own and which ones are not.

Rather than focusing on the negative behaviors during such conflicts, spend some time observing how certain children are able to settle their disputes positively. We can learn a great deal from children if we are willing to try. Consider the following running record that looks at 4-year-old Alex:

Alex, Calvin, and Dominic are on top of the indoor climber/slide pretending to be astronauts in outer space. Alex is the captain of the space shuttle. All three boys make zooming noises and motions. Alex pretends to steer. Two other boys climb up the ladder to try to join the group but are ignored and finally leave.

Alex:	*"Duck! There's a meteor!"*
Calvin:	*"It's my turn to be captain, Alex."*

Alex ignores Calvin and continues steering.

Dominic: *"No, it's my turn. I never get a turn."*

Alex: *"We're being bombarded by meteors! You need to duck!" (He ducks his head.)*

Calvin: *"I'm captain now."*

Alex ignores Calvin and continues steering.

Dominic (to Calvin): *"You can't be captain. Alex is still captain."*

Alex: *"You can be copilot. They always have copilots."*

Calvin begins pretending to steer.

Alex: *"Bang! We've been hit by a meteor! Abandon ship!" (He slides down to floor and runs across room; other boys follow.)*

This exciting adventure in outer space is typical of the vigorous dramatic play preferred by 4-year-olds. It should also be exciting for an observer to see a 4-year-old like Alex handle a role conflict with such composure and success. Alex is often the leader in such play, and from the way he uses ideas and words, it seems obvious that he is an experienced player. Children who play together a great deal learn by trial and error what works in resolving conflicts and what doesn't. They also find out what works with particular children and what doesn't work.

The first strategy Alex uses is *ignoring*. Alex ignores the boys who try to join his shuttle play. They finally go away, so he certainly notes that this kind of ignoring is a successful way to keep out unwanted players. Then another potential conflict emerges: Calvin wants a turn to be captain.

Alex prepares for his role of captain of a space shuttle.

At first Alex ignores this request as well. Then Dominic joins in and also wants to be captain. Now Alex tries another strategy: *distracting*. He tells them that they are being bombarded by meteors and wants them all to duck. A strategy like this may sometimes work. In fact, here it seems to work with Dominic, who gives up his own demand to be captain and cooperates with Alex. But it does not work with Calvin because he has not given up his demand to be captain. So Alex tries another strategy: *negotiating*. He offers Calvin another role: copilot. Calvin accepts and the play continues. This does not mean that either boy knows exactly what a copilot is. But it must sound satisfactory to Calvin because he *compromises* his demand to be captain, accepts the new role as copilot, and plays the role the same as Alex plays the captain's role.

Alex may very well have known that he had to do something to satisfy Calvin, or perhaps Calvin would have: (a) gotten up and left or (b) continued his complaints and disrupted the play. Obviously Alex wanted the play to continue and wanted to keep his own role as captain and leader. He was successful in *negotiating a compromise*.

Did all of this actually happen in so short a dramatic play incident, you may wonder? Yes, it did. Observe a child involved in group play for yourself and record everything that happens. Then step back and interpret what you have seen. Obviously the children do not talk or think in terms of strategies. These are adult interpretations. Young children do not conceptualize in this manner. They just do it. Trial and error has taught certain alert youngsters what works for them and what doesn't when conflict arises. Children who are successful in resolving play conflicts in a positive manner often use strategies such as those in Figure 5.7.

If your observations turn up children who do not seem to know how to resolve play conflicts like this, then you may want to consider some of the following solutions.

If You Have Not Checked This Item: Some Helpful Ideas

■ Have Child Observe and Discuss Play with You

For a child who often tries to resolve play conflicts by hitting or shouting, you can have him observe a group play situation with you and then discuss it. If the child had

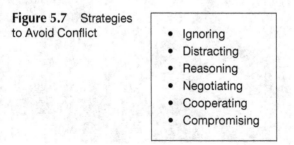

Figure 5.7 Strategies to Avoid Conflict

- Ignoring
- Distracting
- Reasoning
- Negotiating
- Cooperating
- Compromising

sat next to you as you observed and recorded the Alex-Calvin-Dominic play incident, you might say to him:

> Alex is captain of the space shuttle, isn't he? But Calvin wants to be captain, and so does Dominic. What does Calvin do? Yes, he tells Alex that he wants to be captain. Does Alex let him? No, he doesn't pay attention to him. So then what does Calvin do? Does he yell at Alex? No. Does he hit Alex? No. He tells him again that he wants to be captain. Does Alex let him? He lets him be a copilot. Is that like being captain? What would you do if you were on the space shuttle with Alex, Calvin, and Dominic? Do you think your ideas would work?

If the play scenario you observe with the child contains some aggressive behavior, ask the child what the result of the behavior was. Most children will not continue to play with peers when they act aggressively. Often they won't allow such peers in their play groups in the first place.

■ Use Puppets

For a child who gets into arguments frequently with his playmates, try using two puppets to enact a similar situation. Name your puppets something like Tong-Talk-Back and Fronz-Friendly. Put one on each hand and enact a play situation where Tong argues with Fronz over something, with the result that the playing is discontinued. Ask the child what Tong could have said to keep the play going. Ask what the child would have done.

■ Coach the Child on How to Act

Sometimes you need to go to a child and coach him or her on how to act or what to say in a conflict situation. You must make it clear to children that you will not let them hit anyone or hurt anyone or call them names. When they are upset about something, children must learn to express their feelings in words. You may need to coach those who do not know how:

> Tell Jenny how you feel, Teresa, because she took your eggbeater. Don't call her names. Tell her why you are upset. Say it in words. Say: "Jenny, you took my eggbeater. That makes me feel bad. I wasn't finished using it. Please give it back."

■ Do a Group Role-Play

Sometimes the play group itself doesn't know how to resolve conflicts peacefully. In that case, you can consider having a group role-play sometime after the children have settled down. The players should be other children, so that the children having conflicts can watch. Take a role yourself if it seems appropriate. Then you can help direct the play. Give a few other children names and roles to play. Describe a brief conflict situation. Then have the children act it out. Stop the play

Figure 5.8 Books for
Friends and the Moon

Hedgie Blasts Off (Brett, 2006)

I Am Too Absolutely Small for School (Child, 2004)

If You Decide to Go to the Moon (McNulty, 2005)

My Best, Best Friend (Child, 2010)

On the Moon (Milbourne, 2006)

---

at any time to discuss what has happened and whether there is a better way to
resolve the conflict. Try each of these techniques to see which ones work best with
your particular children.

■ Read a Book

For children who want to pretend about astronauts there are several good books.
Hedgie Blasts Off (Brett, 2006) is an exciting adventure of a hedgehog astronaut
who flies to the planet Mikkop to save Big Sparkler, the volcano that shoots out
sparkles. *If You Decide to Go to the Moon* (McNulty, 2005) is a more scientific
but imaginary journey of a boy blasting off and traveling to the Moon and back,
with a foldout of the beauty of Earth and all its creatures. *On the Moon*
(Milbourne, 2006) is a child's imagining of what it would be like to go to the
Moon, riding on the Moon in a Moon buggy, and returning in a spaceship (see
Figure 5.8).

Group Dramatic Play

No matter what children choose to dramatize in their dramatic play, you should
keep your observer's eye peeled for these unique spontaneous performances. Be
as unobtrusive and inconspicuous as possible as you record their actions in a
running record. Then ask yourself if the players have shown evidence of learning
any of the social skills listed in Figure 5.9. You may be amazed at what you
discover.

Figure 5.9 Social
Skills Learned Through
Group Dramatic Play

- Adjusting your actions to the requirements of your role
- Being tolerant of others and their needs
- Not always expecting to have your own way
- Making appropriate responses to others
- Helping others and receiving help from them

OBSERVING, RECORDING, AND INTERPRETING SOCIAL COMPETENCE

How should you use the Social Competence Checklist section with your children? The following description shows how one classroom team put the checklist to use:

When 3-year-old Lionel entered the classroom as a new child in January, he seemed to have a great deal of trouble interacting peacefully with the other children. By the end of the third week he still had not joined any of the group activities. The staff members decided to make a running record of Lionel during the free-play period for several days and then transfer the results to the Child Development Checklist. Figure 5.10 is a typical example of a running record made of Lionel.

When the staff members reviewed the running records and checklist information recorded for Lionel (see Figure 5.10), they concluded that he knew where to find materials and toys in the classroom and how to use them. They also interpreted his Social Competence Checklist results to mean that Lionel played by himself and in parallel play as closely as possible to other children because he wanted to join them. His methods for gaining access to a group (e.g., driving his car up the block building wall and crashing his car into the wall) were neither successful nor acceptable.

Staff members also determined from a Language Skills checklist that his language development was not as advanced as that of many of the children in the classroom. That may have been the reason he did not express his wants verbally. Perhaps because he was a new outsider, he had not made friends with the other children, and his aggressive actions had prompted some of the boys to keep him out of their play. (See Figure 5.11.)

The staff decided to try pairing up Lionel with Adrian, a more mature player, who might help Lionel get acquainted with the others and gain access to their play. They asked Lionel and Adrian (who also liked cars) to build a block garage for the little cars and said they could then take a photo of it with the school smartphone. Eventually two other boys joined them in this activity.

Figure 5.10   Running Record of Lionel

Lionel gets two little cars from box in block corner & sits on floor moving cars around, one in each hand. Makes car noises with voice. Plays by himself with cars for five minutes. Moves closer to block building that two other boys are constructing. Plays by himself with his cars. Then L. tries to drive his cars up wall of building. Boys push him away. L. waits for a minute, then tries to drive car up wall of building again. Boys push him away. L. crashes one car into building & knocks down wall. One of boys grabs L's car & throws it. Other boy pushes L. away. L. cries. Teacher comes over & talks with all three. L. lowers head & does not respond. Boys say: "He was trying to knock down our building with his cars" and "We don't want him to play with us."

CHILD DEVELOPMENT CHECKLIST

Name _Lionel_   **Observer** _Barb_

Program _Preschool–K2_   **Dates** _1/20_

Directions:

Put an **X** for items you see the child perform regularly. Put an **N** for items where there is no opportunity to observe. Leave all other items blank.

Item	Evidence	Dates
3. Social Competence		
_x_ Plays by self with own toys/ materials	Plays with little cars	1/20
_x_ Plays parallel to others with similar toys/materials	Moves close to block building with his cars	1/20
___ Plays with others in group play		1/20
___ Gains access to ongoing play in positive manner	Tries to gain access by driving cars up building—then crashes car	1/20
___ Makes friends with other children		1/20
___ Resolves play conflicts in positive manner	Crashes car into bldg when boys won't let him play	1/20

Figure 5.11   Social Play Development Observation for Lionel

This type of observing and recording can assist individual children in their development of social competence and help them grow and learn in your program.

LEARNING ACTIVITIES

1. Use the Child Development Checklist, Social Competence, as a screening tool to observe all of the children in your classroom. Which ones engage mainly in solitary play? In parallel play? In group play? Are any unoccupied or onlookers?

2. Choose a child whom you have observed engaging in solitary play. Do a running record of the child on three different days to determine what kind of solitary play was performed. How could you involve the child in the next level of play? Should you do it? Why or why not?

3. Choose a child whom you have observed engaging mainly in parallel play. What kind of play does the child do? How can you help the child get involved in the next level of play? Use one of the suggested activities and record the results.

4. Choose a child who is not able to gain access to ongoing group play and use one of the activities described to help the child enter and play with a group.

5. Observe the children during a free-choice period for three days. Pay special attention to any children who play consistently with a particular child. Follow one of these pairs throughout the day to see if they do other activities together. Take note over several days on how long this pairing lasts. Record your feelings about this "friendship."

6. Make a running record of a child observed in group pretend play. Afterward, determine which of the discussed strategies the child used to resolve conflicts. If the child is not successful, describe why and how you would propose to assist him or her.

SUGGESTED READINGS

Kostelnik, M. J., Whiren, A. P., Soderman, A. K., & Gregory, K. (2009). *Guiding children's social and emotional development: Theory to practice* (6th ed.). Clifton Park, NY: Thomson-Delmar-Cengage.

Lynch, S. A. & Simpson, C. G. (2010). Social skills: Laying the foundation for success. *Dimentions of Early Childhood, 38*(2), 3–11.

Meece, D., & Soderman, A. K. (2010). Positive verbal environments: Setting the stage for young children's social development. *Young Children, 65*(5), 81–86.

Moody, A. K. (2012). Family connections: Visual supports for promoting social skills in young children, a family perspective. *Childhood Education, 88*(3), 191–194.

Willis, C. A., & Schiller, P. (2011). Preschoolers' social skills steer life success. *Young Children, 66*(1), 42–49.

CHILDREN'S BOOKS

Aston, D. H. (2008). *The moon over star.* New York: Dial.*

Barton, B. (1990). *Bones, bones, dinosaur bones.* New York: HarperCollins.*

Brett, J. (2006). *Hedgie blasts off.* New York: G. P. Putnam's Sons.

Child, L. (2004). *I am too absolutely small for school.* Cambridge, MA: Candlewick.*

Child, L. (2010). *My best, best friend.* New York: Dial.*

Davis, K. (2005). *Kindergarten rocks.* Orlando, FL: Harcourt.

Godwin, L. (2009). *This is the firefighter.* New York: Hyperion.

Litwin, E. (2011). *Pete the Cat: Rocking in my school shoes.* New York: HarperCollins.

McNulty, F. (2005). *If you decide to go to the moon.* New York: Scholastic.

Milbourne, A. (2006). *On the moon.* London, England: Usborne Publishing.

WEB SITES

Center on the Social and Emotional Foundations for Early Learning
http://csefel.vanderbilt.edu

Pyramid Plus: The Colorado Center for Social Emotional Competence
www.pyramidplus.org

Technical Assistance Center on Social Emotional Intervention for Young Children
www.challengingbehavior.org

*Multicultural

CHAPTER 6

Physical Development

In this chapter you will learn to observe if children can:

____ Run with control over speed and direction

____ Climb up, down, and across climbing equipment

____ Throw, catch, and kick balls

____ Turn knobs, lids, and eggbeaters

____ Pick up and insert objects with dexterity

____ Use tools (scissors, hammers) with control

____ Be observed by using rating scales, checklists

 LARGE-MOTOR SKILLS

Physical development for young children involves two important areas of motor coordination: movements controlled by the large or gross muscles and those controlled by the small or fine muscles. The first half of this chapter will focus on observing large-motor development involving movements of the whole body, legs, and arms. The second half will focus on observing small-motor development involving fingers and hands.

We understand that a child's physical development depends largely upon his biology, but we need also to consider Vygotsky's contention that environmental conditions are just as important. In the classroom it is the teacher who provides assistance (scaffolding) according to the child's zone of proximal development—the level of difficulty at which he can accomplish a task with the help of an adult. Thus, teacher-designed activities for individuals and small groups play an important role in this chapter.

Because motor development is so obvious and visible an aspect of children's growth, we sometimes take it for granted. Of course children will grow bigger, stronger, and able to perform more complicated motor tasks as they increase in age. Of course they will learn to run and jump on their own. Why should we be concerned with motor development in preschool? Sanders (2006) explains that most children naturally develop at least a minimal level of physical skills simply by moving through their home and school environment. However, some children do not get the opportunity to refine these physical skills to a level where they feel competent to participate in physical activities. Children who do not participate and are not physically active are the ones who are more likely to become overweight or obese.

Need for More Exercise

The fact that many youngsters today are leading much more sedentary lives than children did formerly causes great concern among health professionals. The increase in television watching along with the decrease in safe outdoor play areas has cut down tremendously on the motivation and opportunity for young children to run, jump, and move their bodies. Up to half of U.S. children may not be getting enough exercise. We know that exercise and physical activity are necessary to build healthy bones and muscles, to control weight, to decrease blood pressure, and even to reduce the risk of later heart disease and diabetes. Current brain research adds impetus to the need for physical exercising in preschool children.

Frost, Wortham, and Reifel (2012) describe what happens in the brain when young children are involved in physical activities. These experiences exert a dramatic impact on the wiring of the neural circuits and the selecting out, that is, "pruning," of synapses. Physical activity makes a positive difference in brain development and subsequent human functioning.

Even more important, these motor pathways in the brain of the developing child are refined through use. The more a particular pathway is activated through consistent use, the likelier it is to be stabilized. Hunter (2000) makes it more imperative when he tells us that sitting still makes us dumber; that the brain doesn't grow. Without movement, the body doesn't grow either.

Lack of exercise in the early years has other serious consequences. When children sit watching television, they often snack on junk food. Soon they are putting on excess body weight that may lead to obesity. Obesity, in turn, may lead to childhood diabetes and other serious ailments.

Preschool teachers often feel that their programs already serve the physical needs of their children by providing first-rate playgrounds for daily use with swings and slides, climbing and balancing equipment, and trike paths with trikes, scooters, and wagons. Isn't this enough, they ask? Not according to many specialists. They say that many 4- and 5-year-old children on playgrounds for one half-hour of free play were not participating in vigorous activity. More than half were sitting, standing, or talking (Staley & Portman, 2000).

That was a number of years ago, you may argue. Surely it is different today with better equipment and more motivated children and teachers. Is it? How is it on your playground? Are your children getting enough exercise? Use the checklist in Figure 6-1 to observe each child on your outside playground to see who is running, jumping, climbing up ladders, sliding down slides, pumping swings, negotiating monkey bars, making hoops with basketballs, or pushing medicine balls across the playground. Record the names of children engaged in vigorous play and those who are not. Do you agree or disagree with the specialists about the percentage of children involved? They also say that a total of 30 to 60 minutes of daily vigorous exercise is necessary for the optimal health of children under 18 years of age. How long are your children involved?

For most programs this means that teachers must do more than merely provide children with equipment and time to use it. It means *you will need to lead all the children in exercising every day*. Young children can complete such a 30-minute regimen in several short time bursts of 10 minutes either inside or outside the classroom. Make it fun and they will love to do it. Take a tambourine outside and beat it when you shout LET'S MOVE! Have everyone make some kind of movement as long as you beat the tambourine.

Figure 6-1 Vigorous Playground Exercise

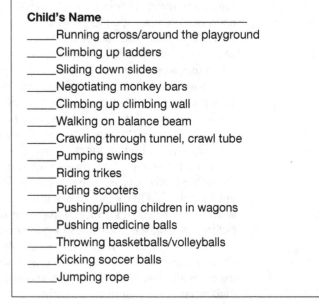

Child's Name_____
_____Running across/around the playground
_____Climbing up ladders
_____Sliding down slides
_____Negotiating monkey bars
_____Climbing up climbing wall
_____Walking on balance beam
_____Crawling through tunnel, crawl tube
_____Pumping swings
_____Riding trikes
_____Riding scooters
_____Pushing/pulling children in wagons
_____Pushing medicine balls
_____Throwing basketballs/volleyballs
_____Kicking soccer balls
_____Jumping rope

Children love to move on the playground.

This chapter includes a number of creative activities for everyone—including you. In addition, some preschool children may need special help with large-motor skills. To determine who they are, you should observe and record how each child accomplishes the skills on the Figure 6-1 checklist and Figure 6-2 rating scale. Although all children develop physically in a predictable sequence of skills that can be observed, there are definitely individual differences. These can be determined through observation.

Child's Name_____

	Always	Sometimes	Never
Walks down steps alternating feet			
Walks across balance beam easily			
Crawls through tunnels, crawl spaces			
Runs with control over speed and direction			
Jumps with feet together			
Hops on one foot			
Climbs up, down, across climbing apparatus			
Throws, catches, kicks balls			
Rides trikes, bikes, scooters			
Pushes, pulls wagons, medicine balls			

Figure 6-2   Large-Motor Skills Rating Scale

You also need to become familiar with the sequence of normal large-motor development. You can then apply this knowledge to particular children to determine whether they are developing predictably within the normal range, or whether they may need some special help. Finally, you can assemble a repertoire of activities to motivate all the children in your program, including those who may be lagging behind in this development.

Motor Skills in the Classroom

It is important to screen all the children in your classroom at the outset using the Figure 6-2 rating scale or a similar list of skills to identify children needing special help. You and your coworkers can play physical games with the children doing hopping and jumping while another staff member observes and records on a single sheet. At another time, walk up and down stairs or a step stool with children and give them opportunities to move their legs and feet and arms and hands in rhythm as someone observes. Still another time, toss various types of balls to the children for catching, throwing, and kicking practice.

You can rate either with check marks or numbers (e.g., 1, 2, 3). Such a scale is easy to make to represent the children's accomplishments in your own program. You can then count the number of check marks for each child or add up the number of points. Remember, this should not be a test, but an observation of natural accomplishments from activities set up in the classroom or on the playground. Take as many days as necessary to complete these observations. You will then have an idea of the nature of the large-motor skills each child possesses. But be sure to keep these observations ongoing throughout the year to record each child's improvements.

Setting up developmentally appropriate activities is possible once you have this important baseline information about the children. Observe and record individual accomplishments whenever children become involved in these activities. Newman and Kranowitz (2012) explain that motor development is sequential, with each skill emerging from a previous one. That makes it important for your program to provide a sequence of materials and activities that help children develop and improve their large-motor skills.

RUNS WITH CONTROL OVER SPEED AND DIRECTION

Running may be the large-motor skill you think of when you consider young children. They seem to be perpetual motion machines. This is the principal method of movement for some children. Others run awkwardly and spend much less time doing it than the rest of your children. What should you expect of the 3-, 4-, and 5-year-old children in your program? You will need to know about the range of development for this skill before you can decide where each of your children stands and how you best can help.

Running is smoother for 3-year-olds than it was when they were younger. Their body proportions have grown and changed from a top-heavy appearance. Their legs are now longer and more coordinated in their movements. They have more control over starting and stopping than 2-year-olds, but they still have not mastered this skill completely. Because their large motor skills are so much more automatic, they can abandon themselves to the pure enjoyment of running.

Then at about 3½, many children go through an awkward stage where some of the smoothness of their large-motor movements seems to disappear. Teachers need to be aware of these "disequilibrium" times so they can support the child during his "difficult days," knowing he will reacquire his smoothness of motion sometime soon. This support is particularly important for so-called "awkward" children. Pica (2011) tells us that such children may feel clumsy and inferior and therefore may shun physical activity to avoid humiliation. This belief can affect them their whole lives and prevent them from engaging in any physical activity.

The sensitive teacher needs to work with each child, encouraging and supporting him to accomplish all he is capable of. Pressure and ridicule simply have no place in the early childhood classroom. The teacher needs to find interesting motor activities in which children showing awkwardness can succeed and to avoid activities that pit one child against another. A wide range of individual differences exists in physical development as in every other aspect of development. Some children simply will never be highly coordinated. Others may grow up to be professional athletes.

Providing a wide range of interesting motor activities that are fun to participate in seems the best answer. Three-year-olds are at an ideal age to begin such a program. And because some so-called awkward children are simply beginners in skill development, they should not be labeled as such or treated differently. Children are children; they are all different in looks, likes, and abilities. Each of them needs your special affection and support as he or she progresses through the sometimes rocky road of physical development. Using a rating scale like Figure 6-3 can help you observe to determine the skills of your children and who may need help. Make your own simple scale like this example.

Child's Name	Always	Sometimes	Never
Runs fast			
Runs smoothly			
Stops and starts easily			
Zooms around corners			
Stays upright when running			
Gallops			
Skips			

Figure 6-3   Running Skills Rating Scale

You need to be aware of the ages and stages as they apply to your children. Take time to visit this year's class next year and you may see some surprises. This year's awkward boy may be the best runner in another year. The sedentary girl who would never join in may be the leader of the physical activities. A year makes such a difference in the development of young children.

Expansive 4-year-olds are usually good runners. Their movements are strong, efficient, and speedy. They can start and stop without difficulty, and they like to zoom around corners. They seem to know what their bodies can do and enjoy putting them through their paces. Give them space and time to run. Play running games in and out of the classroom to get them started. Avoid games where there are winners and losers.

Five-year-olds seem to spurt up in height, mostly in their legs. They are more mature runners than 4-year-olds, and many love to join in games that test their abilities. Their speed and control have increased, and they seldom fall when running across uneven surfaces as 4-year-olds sometimes do. Their running games, like the rest of their actions, are usually not as noisy and out-of-bounds as those of 4-year-olds.

Other children's leg movements include galloping and skipping. Galloping is a combination of a walk and a leap. The child takes a step with one foot, then brings the other foot behind it and leads off with the first foot again. In other words, one foot always leads. Children often pretend to be horses galloping around the room to music or tambourine beats.

Skipping is a much more complex skill. It is a combination of a step and a hop. Most children do not master this skill much before age 5 or 6 or even later. But some 4-year-olds will want to try it, especially if you've read them the book *Ready, Set, Skip!* (O'Connor, 2007). The little girl character demonstrates how she can leap, creep, twirl, and skate. But she can't skip. Her mother shows her how to hop on one foot and then the other. That is skipping, says her mother. Other movement books children enjoy hearing and then trying out are in Figure 6-4.

If You Have Not Checked This Item: Some Helpful Ideas

■ Offer Simple Running Games

Preschool running games should not be competitive. The "awkward" child may give up trying if he or she is always last. Instead, simple circle games may serve the same

Figure 6-4   Movement Books Children Enjoy

Bounce (Cronin, 2007)
Faster! Faster! (Patricelli, 2012)
How Do You Wokka-Wokka? (Bluemle, 2009)
Move! (Jenkins, 2006)
Ready, Set, Skip! (O'Connor, 2007)

purpose. Old classics like "Duck, Duck, Goose" are still favorites of 3- and 4-year-olds. No one wins or loses. Games with rules are often too complicated for pre-schoolers, but they can learn to make the right responses in simple games like this and enjoy the running portion. You can join in too and let some of the less-skilled runners catch you.

■ Employ Directed Running

You can make up all kinds of inside and outside running activities. For instance, one child at a time can run to the tree and back until all have had a turn. Make the activity more complicated by having them follow a second direction: run to the tree, run around it once, and then run back.

■ Have the Children Run to Music

Have children run to music in the large motor area. Have them run fast or slow, loudly or quietly, according to the music. Then have them run like animals to music. How would a deer run through the woods?

■ Try Imaginative Running

Let children pretend to be cowboys or cowgirls riding stick horses or be jet planes zooming down the runway. Have them pretend to be animals that run, such as deer or dogs. Put up pictures of animals that run and have the children imitate them. Have an imaginative "Running Romp" in the classroom for 10 minutes at a time. If you have no room, they can run in place. Clements and Schneider (2006) remind us that preschool children should not be sedentary more than 60 minutes at a time except when sleeping. How is it in your classroom?

CLIMBS UP AND DOWN CLIMBING EQUIPMENT

Climbing involves use of the arms as well as the legs. It is, in fact, an outgrowth of creeping. Most children begin climbing as soon as they can creep over to an item of furniture and pull themselves up. If they are allowed, they will creep up the stairs. They will try to creep down, too, and soon find out that a backward descent is the only kind that works.

Many 3- and 4-year-olds enjoy climbing on all sorts of things: jungle gyms, ladders, ladder climbers, dome climbers, slides, rope climbers, trees, rocks, and poles. By the time they are in your program, children this age should be able to climb up and down with ease.

Although it takes bravery as well as muscle strength and coordination to be a successful climber, many of your children will be able to accomplish this skill if they have the opportunity. You should consider providing climbing equipment and

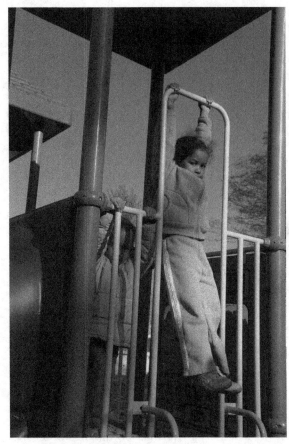

To swing from the top bar makes this child feel great.

climbing possibilities both inside and outside your classroom. First of all, safety factors need to be considered. Because falling is the main concern with climbing, be sure that floor or ground surfaces are cushioned. Padding can be used inside. Sand or wood chips are preferable to grass or hard surfaces outside.

Not all children will attempt to climb. Do not force the reluctant ones. You can encourage them and help children if they try to climb, but if they refuse, they should not be forced to try. Not all children will want to accomplish climbing skills, which is perfectly acceptable. Children have as much right to personal choices as adults. Were you a climber when you were 4?

On the other hand, the excitement of accomplishing a physical feat such as climbing to the top of a climber is wonderful to behold. For children who indicate they would like to attempt this sort of climbing, you can help them best by standing close enough to catch them if they should falter, to encourage them if they turn to you for help, and to congratulate them when they succeed. They may climb only halfway to start. Then, little by little, they gain courage and expertise enough to complete their climb. You should accept any attempt they make, but not prod them to go all the way if they are not ready.

Some children may need to strengthen their leg muscles before they can succeed in climbing very high. One fun method is to have them practice using leg muscles with the traditional song "The Grand Old Duke of York." Have the children sing it as they sit in a line or a circle and stand all the way up on the word "up," sit down on the word "down," and "stand half-way up" on those words. You try it with them. You may be the only singer at first as they try to do the movements.

(Tune: "The Farmer in the Dell")

The Grand Old Duke of York	*And when you're **up**, you're **up**,*
He had ten thousand men,	*And when you're **down**, you're **down**,*
*He led them **up** the hill*	*And when you're only **half-way up**,*
*And then he led them **down** again.*	*You're neither **up** nor **down**.*

Go very slowly at first until the children get used to what they are supposed to do. Some may just not be able to follow it. But those who can will enjoy it even more as you speed up the song. Soon they will be all mixed up trying to go up or down. It all ends in laughter—and stronger leg muscles! Do it again, teacher.

If You Have Not Checked This Item: Some Helpful Ideas

■ Provide a New Piece of Climbing Equipment

A packing crate (with splintery edges sanded down) is often a tempting piece of homemade climbing equipment that can be used either inside or outside. Ladder steps can be fastened to the outside of the crate or children can use a step stool to climb to the top. Cargo netting is also a fine piece of climbing equipment.

■ Build a Loft

Lofts not only give preschool children extra space for various new activities, they also provide a new perspective on the activities below. Some lofts use ladders to reach their tops, others use steps or stairs. Some have several means of entrance and exit. Even nonclimbers often learn to manage all the methods of access because being up in the loft is such fun.

■ Have a Multiple-Access Slide

A multiple-access slide is one of the most valuable pieces of large-motor equipment you can purchase if your center can afford only one piece of equipment. Children are motivated to learn to climb to get to the platform at the top of the slide. If you have space inside, an indoor multiple-access slide can serve as a loft as well as a large motor device.

■ Make an Obstacle Course

Use planks, sawhorses, barrels, ladders, and boxes to create an obstacle course for climbing. Rearrange them frequently. Children can climb up, over, and under. Children use all of their large-movement skills to negotiate an obstacle course. (See Table 6-1.)

THROWS, CATCHES, AND KICKS BALLS

Many preschool children do not get the opportunity to play with balls until they are older, perhaps when they enter primary school. Although their arm, hand, and leg muscles are not so well developed and coordinated during the preschool years, your program can encourage this coordination. Children enjoy playing with balls when it involves balls they can handle at their level of accomplishment. Using the smaller, softer balls available for indoor play makes this possible.

Throwing

Throwing and catching are two important upper body large-motor skills. Throwing appears first. There are several ways to throw, such as overhand, underhand, and

Table 6-1   Large-motor skills

Age	Walking	Running	Jumping	Climbing
8 months–1 year	Walks in a wide stance like a waddle			Climbs onto furniture and up stairs as an outgrowth of creeping
1–2 years	Walks in a toddle and uses arms for balance (arms are not swung)	Moves rapidly in a hurried walk, in contact with surface	Uses bouncing step off bottom step of stairs with one foot	Tries climbing up anything climbable
2–3 years	Walks upstairs two feet on a step	Runs stiffly, has difficulty turning corners and stopping quickly	Jumps off bottom step with both feet	Tries climbing to top of equipment, although cannot climb down
3–4 years	Walks with arms swinging; walks upstairs alternating feet; walks downstairs two feet on step	Runs more smoothly, has more control over starting and stopping	Springs up off floor with both feet in some cases; jumps over object leading with one foot	Climbs up and down ladders, jungle gyms, slides, and trees
4–5 years	Walks up and down stairs alternating feet; walks circular line; skips with one foot	Displays strong, speedy running; turns corners, starts and stops easily	Jumps up, down, and forward	Climbs up and down ladders, jungle gyms, slides, and trees
5–6 years	Walks as an adult; skips alternating feet	Shows mature running, falls seldom, displays increased speed and control	Jumps long, high, and far; jumps rope	Displays mature climbing in adult manner

sidearm, and with two hands or one. Young children seem to go through a general progression, starting with infants who throw small objects overhand but downward, to the two-hand underhand throw, the one-hand underhand throw, and finally the one-hand overhand throw. The size and heaviness of the thrown object also make a difference as to the type of throw (Pica, 2011).

Two-year-olds frequently try to throw things such as food or clothing, sometimes in frustration. Their throwing action is more of a jerky, sidearm movement. If they should try to throw a ball, they often stand facing the target, using both forearms together to push a ball forward. The ball often dribbles away, almost accidentally.

Some youngsters who have the smaller, softer indoor balls at home may develop one-hand overhand throws even before preschool. How accurate they eventually become depends on maturity and practice.

The children in your classroom should be able to develop throwing skills. Throwing takes practice—not so much instruction as opportunity. Children have to work out how to throw by themselves as their muscles and coordination mature. Give the youngsters many throwing opportunities, and they will do the rest.

What can they throw? Let them try inflated beach balls, yarn balls, sponge balls, Nerf balls, foam balls, squeezable balls, squish balls, beanbag balls, grip balls, tactile balls, and punching balloons. Balls come not only in dozens of materials these days, but also in a huge variety of sizes and shapes, from golf-ball size to giant balls as big as the children. Some are made from soft materials to resemble soccer balls, footballs, basketballs, and baseballs.

Where can children throw? Because accuracy is not the point at first, they will need to become familiar with the throwing action itself. Have them throw foam or yarn balls against a wall. When they are ready, have them throw at a large target like a hula hoop hung on the wall or a box standing upright against a wall. A freestanding basketball backboard at preschoolers' height can be used even in the classroom if a foam ball is thrown. Girls and boys alike enjoy throwing balls. But neither will develop this skill to a mature degree without practice.

Evidence shows that practice counts with this large-motor skill. Earlier, our society considered boys to be better throwers than girls. "To throw like a girl" was a derogatory comment often made about boys who threw poorly. It describes the throwing stance of stepping forward on the same foot as the throwing arm and throwing from the elbow: the stance of an immature thrower.

In order to develop their arm muscles children need to be involved in many of the activities your classroom provides. Block building is one that offers special strengthening of arm muscles. It also activates the brain. Gellens (2005) tells us that children's entire brain is activated. Brain connections are made in many parts of the brain simultaneously. Repetition of both large- and small-motor movements brings permanence in brain connections. Not the small unit blocks but large plastic bricks, big cardboard blocks, or hollow blocks require the use of large muscles.

Giant balls like medicine balls can also promote large-motor development. Children can learn to somersault over them. They can also take turns pushing the huge balls across the playground. Looks like work, but it turns out to be fun for the pushers.

Catching

Because catching a ball is more difficult than throwing, it develops later. In addition to having upper body maturity, children also need eye–hand coordination to track the thrown ball and catch it with their hands. Many of your children may not develop this skill as easily as they did throwing. Some young children fear the object as it approaches them. Pica (2011) explains that using soft colorful objects such as scarves, beanbags, balloons, or yarn balls and large, soft beach balls or foam balls can alleviate fear and make visual tracking easier.

Children can learn to somersault over a medicine ball.

In addition to the necessary practice, this particular skill also requires nervous system maturity. The child is being asked to respond to moving objects of varying speeds. His response time is much slower than that of an older child or adult. Even when he seems to be ready for the ball to arrive in his hands, he may not be able to bring them together in time.

It's fun to see how far you can push this giant ball.

Preschool girls seem to be more successful than boys in ball catching, perhaps because they have more mature eye–hand coordination. All children need as much practice in catching as in throwing. You, however, need to be aware that they may not succeed as well in catching because they are not developmentally ready.

Have children begin by catching their own bounced ball. Once they are used to this activity, you can stand close to them and toss a large, soft ball to them. Catching success does not happen in one day or even one week. Let children take their time, but be sure to provide frequent opportunities. Once children have achieved some success, challenge them to catch an object they themselves have tossed up in the air—the hardest challenge of all.

Kicking

Kicking a ball with the leg and foot is not as easy as it looks for preschoolers. Besides having leg muscle development, children need balancing skills and eye–foot coordination to kick a ball, a skill that is not fully developed until age 9 or 10 (Pica, 2011). Kicking for distance and not accuracy is more important for preschoolers.

Have children start by placing their nonkicking foot next to the ball. Tell them to look at the ball, then kick with their other leg. They can begin by kicking a beach ball any way they want. Once they get the hang of it, have them kick smaller foam balls at a wall. If you have little space for kicking balls, have children kick punchball balloons. If children want to kick harder rubber balls, find a space outside where they will not kick the ball into another child.

If You Have Not Checked This Item: Some Helpful Ideas

■ Try Some Kicking Games

Have children take several steps backward from a ball on the ground, then run up and kick the ball. How far can they kick? Another day, put two traffic cones about 6 feet apart. Have children stay behind a line at about 6 feet and try kicking a ball between the cones.

■ Use Targets for Throwing

Make targets out of cardboard boxes. Paint a simple animal face or clown face on the box. Cut a large hole for the mouth, much larger than the ball or beanbag. Have children stand behind a line not too far away and try to throw into the hole.

■ Throw Newspapers

A fun throwing activity is throwing rolled-up newspapers into a box placed in front of a drawing of a house. Children can pretend to be newspaper boys and girls delivering the morning paper. Can they throw it in the box while moving in front of the house? How close do they need to be for accuracy?

Figure 6-5 Ball Books
Children Enjoy

> ***Hit the Ball Duck*** (Alborough, 2006)
> ***Luke Goes to Bat*** (Isadora, 2005)
> ***Just Like Josh Gibson*** (Johnson, 2004)
> ***Hoops with Swoopes*** (Kuklin, 2001)

■ Use Pillows

For children who are having difficulty catching a ball, try throwing a small soft pillow to each one. Stand close enough at first for them to succeed without difficulty. Then step back a little at a time until you are farther away when you throw and they must track the pillow with their eyes.

■ Read a Ball Book

You are not going to be teaching or playing baseball in preschool programs, but such a game promotes the skills of throwing and catching that young children need to practice. Basketball is different. Your children can practice throwing child-size basketballs into baskets both outdoors and indoors. Several baseball books and one basketball book in Figure 6-5 are appropriate for young children. The first one has humorous animal characters. The next one has a boy character, and the following two have girl characters.

✓ OBSERVING AND RECORDING LARGE MOTOR SKILLS

Some teachers prefer to use rating scales or simple checklists for recording observational data on their children's large motor skills. Others develop their own checklists showing particular skills and with space for recording observed evidence. (See Figure 6-6.)

✓ DEVELOPING SMALL-MOTOR SKILLS

Small-motor development involves the fine muscles that control the extremities. In the case of young children, you should be especially concerned with control, coordination, and dexterity in using the hands and fingers. Although this development occurs simultaneously in children along with large-motor development, the muscles near the trunk mature before the muscles of the extremities, which control the wrists and hands.

Thus it is important for young children to practice use of the large muscles as they become involved in small-motor activities. Delays in developing large-motor coordination may very well have a negative effect on the development of small-motor

---

LARGE MOTOR CHECKLIST

Name_____

Item	Evidence	Dates
_____Walks down steps alternating feet		
_____Runs with control over speed and direction		
_____Jumps with feet together		
_____Hops on one foot		
_____Climbs up, down, across climbing equipment		
____Throws, catches, and kicks balls		

Figure 6-6   Large-Motor Checklist

skills. But once children can accomplish small-motor movements, preschool teachers should encourage them to engage in all types of manipulative activities so they can learn and then practice the skills needed to use their hands and fingers with control and dexterity.

Reflexes

You may note that infants and toddlers use their hands and fingers without much previous experience. Why, then, do 3-, 4-, and 5-year-olds have a different situation? The difference is important. It involves voluntary versus involuntary movements through reflexes. Reflexes are unlearned, automatic responses to stimuli resulting from earliest neuromuscular development (Puckett, Black, Wittmer, & Petersen, 2009).

Infants move their arms, hands, and fingers through these reflexes, not voluntary movements. The nervous system assimilates these involuntary movements as it matures, allowing children to control their movements voluntarily. As these initial reflexes disappear, children must purposefully learn to replace them by using and controlling their hands and fingers.

A very large number of reflexes are present in the infant. They include the Moro, or startle reflex, in which the infant throws out its arms with a jerk and lets out a cry; the rooting reflex, in which the infant turns its head and opens its mouth when touched on the side of the cheek; the sucking reflex, in which the infant sucks if its lips or mouth are touched; the walking reflex, in which the infant makes stepping movements when held in an upright position on a surface; the swimming reflex, in which the infant makes swimming movements when held in the water with its head supported.

The reflex most connected with small-motor hand skills is the grasping reflex or palmar grasp in which the baby clamps its fingers around anything put in its palm. This grasp is so strong in the beginning that it will support the infant's weight and can be used to lift the baby entirely off the surface on which it is lying. It is difficult, in fact, for the infant to let go. You may have to pry its fingers apart.

Involuntary responses such as this have their origin in the lower brain stem and spinal cord and eventually come under the control of the higher brain centers of the nervous system as the child matures. This higher part of the brain inhibits these initial reflexes after they have finished their task of aiding the survival of the helpless newborn; the higher brain center then allows voluntary movements to replace them.

The grasping reflex lasts until about 9 months. Infants cannot start to control hand and finger actions voluntarily before this. Infants may reach for things—but not very accurately—before the age of 6 months; letting go is the infants' main problem. Even year-old children may struggle to release an object voluntarily, and some do not gain control of "letting go" before 1½ years of age. This is called "prehension," the ability to grasp an object and let go. Children in your program will be using prehension to handle painting and writing tools as well as small manipulative objects.

Timing

We understand that, like the large-motor skills, voluntary small-motor skills do not just happen; they must be learned naturally and then practiced by young children. Is there a certain time period when particular skills can be learned best? When is the child's neuromuscular system mature enough for him to control his movements and perform certain actions? Should we wait until he is ready? Not really. As with large motor skills, we should encourage children to use their small muscles as soon as they can. Because each child's development is different, this time period may differ with various children.

All of us carry within us an inherited biological clock. For some of us, small-motor development occurs in textbook fashion, just as the charts for average physical growth indicate. For others, this development happens just a bit behind or ahead of the charts. This staggered individual development will exist in all the children in your program. Each child has his or her own built-in biological clock. Neither you nor the child knows what time it is for the child, except in general terms. Because everyone's development occurs in a particular sequence, the best we can do is to assess the child's development through observation and provide him or her with appropriate activities, materials, and encouragement.

Is there a "critical moment" when small-motor skills must be learned or it will be too late? Again, not really, except in broad general terms. The best time to learn a

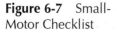

Figure 6-7 Small-Motor Checklist

Child's Name_____

_____Uses paper punch

_____Pours liquid without spilling

_____Squeezes water from baster

_____Turns knobs, lids, eggbeaters

_____Screws/unscrews nuts and bolts

_____Clips clothespins to cup

_____Inserts puzzle pieces correctly

_____Fastens/unfastens zippers, buttons

_____Strings beads

_____Paints with a brush

_____Traces objects with felt-tip pen

_____Writes with an implement

_____Cuts with scissors

_____Cuts with a knife

_____Pounds nails with a hammer

small-motor skill seems to be when the skill is changing most rapidly. But because this is not easy to determine, it is best to offer many types of activities for all your children and to help them get involved with activities that offer both success and challenge.

In other words, all your children are "ready" to begin developing their small-motor skills when they enter your program. You do not need to wait. The question is not whether they are "ready," because they are, but whether *you* are ready to assist them in this important area of development. To do this successfully, you will first need to know where each child stands in small-motor development, so that you can help them continue in their growth and learning.

You may want to screen them using a Small-Motor Checklist like Figure 6-7, or one of your own making. These items are observable behaviors that demonstrate acknowledged small-motor skills of young children in the areas of rotation, manipulation, and dexterity.

Dexterity and Handedness

Dexterity calls for quick, precise movements of the hands and fingers. Four- and 5-year-old children must be dexterous to manage small buttons and zippers and write legible letters and numerals. Young 3-year-olds may not have matured to this level. It all depends on a neurological process, with certain abilities becoming localized in the left and right hemispheres of the brain. Handedness is an outgrowth of this process but may not be fully dominant until 6, 7, or 8 years of age (Puckett et al., 2009).

Encouraging the use of one hand over the other is not necessary. The process is governed by neurological connections in the brain. On the other hand, children need to succeed. A strong hand preference may help them perform small-motor tasks with dexterity. If you know what that preference is for any of your children, you can help them develop it further with practice and positive feedback.

Stages of Small-Motor Development

Huffman and Fortenberry (2011) explain that there is a sequence in developing muscles. Four stages of fine-motor development set the stage for early writing success—*whole arm, whole hand, pincer,* and *pincer coordination*. We understand that body development occurs from the trunk outward. Arm muscles must develop first before hand and finger muscles.

Children will be refining *whole arm* muscles during their playground equipment play and classroom play with balls. Then they need to strengthen their *whole hand* muscles by pouring liquids, using a paper punch, and squeezing water from a baster at the water table. Holding an object while making a turning movement with their hand is another important hand muscle strengthener.

✓ TURNS KNOBS, LIDS, EGGBEATERS

Twisting or turning movements—done with the wrist, hand, and fingers by rotating the wrist and/or forearm—take several forms. The child may enclose a doorknob with her hand and try to twist and then pull it to open the door. Depending on the size and stiffness of the knob and door, she may or may not succeed at first. Or she may not be tall enough to make her small-motor skills work effectively. Turning a key in a lock involves this same type of motion.

Another form of small-motor rotating involves vertical turning at the wrist or rotating the forearm while the fingers are gripping an implement: a cranking type of movement. Manual eggbeaters, food mills, and can openers use this motion. Still another type of small-motor rotating involves using the fingers to twist a nut onto a bolt, turn a screw into a hole, or twist a lid onto or off a jar or bottle.

Children at an early age can accomplish this motor skill. Two-and-a-half and 3-year-olds, for instance, can turn a doorknob if they can reach it. They love to screw and unscrew lids or tops on jars and bottles. Have parents collect empty plastic bottles and containers of all sizes along with their screw-top lids, and keep the items in a box in the manipulative area of the classroom for the children to practice on.

Small-motor control is far from perfect, especially with the younger children; things have a way of slipping out of their fingers from time to time. Thus it is important to use only unbreakable containers such as plastic—never glass—in the classroom.

Puzzles

This same hand-rotating skill is used by 3-year-olds and older children as they try to put together a puzzle. Whereas 2-year-olds will often try to jam a puzzle piece into place and will give up if it doesn't fit, older children will rotate the piece to try to match the shape of the hole. Watch and see how your children make puzzles. Obviously perceptual awareness (i.e., what the piece looks like) is also at work in this instance, but children first need the small-motor rotating skill to use their shape recognition ability.

Wooden puzzles of differing complexities should be an item on your shelves of manipulative materials. These puzzles offer excellent practice for finger dexterity and eye–hand coordination, as well as the cognitive concepts of matching shapes and part-to-whole relationships. Puzzles can teach teachers, too.

Two preschool teachers at a faculty meeting happen to make the comment that one child had brought to school a 100-piece puzzle and another had brought a 150-piece puzzle and was making it with his classmates. Could 3- and 4-year-old children actually make puzzles of such size and difficulty? No one had ever given them the opportunity. But when they had the chance, yes, they were able to work on such complex multipiece puzzles successfully and, over time, complete them.

Cooking

Three-year-olds can also use this hand-turning skill to operate an eggbeater, and they love to do it. Be sure to have more than one eggbeater at your water table because the eggbeater is usually a favorite implement and the focus of many squabbles if only one is available. Children like to try turning food mills and can openers as well, but do not always have the strength to succeed if the items to be ground or opened are too difficult.

Objects of differing shapes and those that can be modified are more interesting to children than rigid and unchangeable objects. Novelty is also an important quality in encouraging children to handle and manipulate objects. When the novelty wears off, children are less interested in playing with the items. Teachers should respond to such findings by including a variety of items in the manipulative area and by changing them from time to time.

In addition, teachers should include cooking experiences in the classroom on a daily or weekly basis. Children can help with "cool cooking," that is, food preparation without heat, such as daily snacks. They can scrape carrots and cut celery for dipping; mix cream cheese with flavorings for dips; whip cream into butter and grind peanuts into peanut butter (check first for peanut allergies). They can also help with "hot cooking" by whipping eggs with eggbeaters for scrambled eggs or grinding cooked apples or pumpkin through a food mill.

Gellens (2005) explains that children not only enjoy preparing food, but that every sense is engaged, so multiple areas of the brain are stimulated simultaneously. Measuring, cutting, stirring, and pouring are good for eye–hand coordination but also for large muscular development. The more the senses are associated with a given activity, the stronger the synapses and the stronger the memory.

More and more teachers are making food preparation a part of their curriculum with the advent of appliances such as electric fry pans, hot pots, microwaves, and toaster ovens. It is an activity with special significance for children's development of small-motor skills. But before you begin hot cooking, be sure to check on safety codes followed in your building or community.

If You Have Not Checked This Item: Some Helpful Ideas

■ Provide a Collection of Food Utensils for Cooking and Play

Visit a hardware store having a large assortment of food preparation utensils and stock up on all kinds of grinding, squeezing, and cranking types of implements. Better still, visit a flea market and buy the same sorts of things secondhand. Some of the old-fashioned hand tools of great-grandma's kitchen will make a big hit in your classroom. Keep some of the items in your housekeeping area for pretending, and some near the water table or on your manipulative shelves for small-motor practice. But be sure to let children use these utensils when you do real cooking.

■ Use a Food Mill

Using a food mill to strain cooked apples to make applesauce requires arm strength and stamina. Children see sequencing firsthand when they follow recipes and see foods change from one state to another.

■ Make a Nuts-and-Bolts Board

Fasten bolts of differing sizes to a sanded-down board, and give children a box of nuts to screw onto the bolts. The children will need to use their size-sorting as well as small-motor skills. Such boards are also available nowadays from educational supply houses, but creating your own makes the activity more natural and personal.

■ Collect Old Locks and Keys

Have a box of old locks and keys for children to experiment with. The youngsters will need persistence as well as motor skills to match up and make the locks and keys work. But it is an exciting challenge for them.

■ Get a Toy Hopper with a Hand Crank for the Sand Table

Children love to play with sand. Toy stores, toy catalogs, and stores selling beach toys offer sand implements for sifting and grinding that certain children will use for hours. With a hopper, they can grind sand enough to fill every container available. Don't forget to have children wear safety goggles at the sand table.

■ Try a Citrus Reamer

Bring in a citrus reamer that works by hand and let your children take turns twisting half an orange on it to make their own juice for a snack. You may need to help them get started.

Figure 6-8   Fun Food
Picture Books

The Runaway Wok (Compestine, 2011)
Chopsticks (Rosenthal, 2012)
Oliver's Milk Shake (French, 2000)
Whopper Cake (Wilson & Hillenbrand, 2007)
Duck Soup (Urbanovic, 2008)

■ Read a Book

Duck Soup (Urbanovic, 2008) is a wacky animal tale about Maxwell Duck deciding to make a soup that will be his masterpiece. Ooo-la-la! So he does. Can your children guess what happens next? Other fun food picture books are listed in Figure 6-8.

✓ PICKS UP AND INSERTS OBJECTS WITH DEXTERITY

Manipulative Materials

Picking up and inserting objects is the small-motor skill most frequently promoted in the early childhood classroom. This skill involves manipulation of items by gripping them between thumb and fingers and inserting or placing them somewhere else. It strengthens the *pincer* muscles of the fingers. Using pegboards and stacking toys; lacing, sewing, weaving, stringing beads; counting, sorting, and matching small items call for this skill. Playing with Lego bricks, geoboards, formboards, bristleboards, and many plastic table games also call for the picking up and inserting skills.

All classrooms should have a permanent space for manipulative activity of this sort, with shelves at the children's level equipped with many such materials for easy selection and return. There should be a table in the area next to the shelves, as well as floor space for playing with the larger toys. Some classrooms call this area the "manipulative/math center" because preschool math concepts are learned through the manipulation of small objects. The selection of materials should cover a wide range of children's abilities. Table block sets should include large blocks as well as Lego bricks.

It is not necessary to put out all the manipulative materials that the program owns at once. Add a few new ones to the area every month and remove some of the old ones. Remember that novelty motivates children to use the materials. Save some of the more complicated table toys for challenging the experienced children later in the year. If you have a limited supply of materials, consider trading with other programs.

Children's Skills

You will want to know which children visit the manipulative area during your free-play period. Use the Small-Motor Checklist, Figure 6-7, as a screening device to help you find out. Are children avoiding the area because they are not comfortable using small-motor skills? Are boys the ones who avoid the manipulative materials?

Once you identify which individuals avoid manipulative activities, you will be able to sit down at a table with a single child and challenge him or her to make a puzzle with you, stack blocks, or sort shapes into a formboard. If you are keeping file card records of each child, you can add this information to these cards. You or your coworkers may need to spend time every day with children who need extra practice with small-motor skills. You may need to encourage these children to complete some of the small-motor activities on their own. It is important for children to succeed in something on their own.

Gender Differences

Our society still seems to encourage girls to engage in small-motor activities more than boys. Boys are encouraged to run outside and play ball. Girls are given manipulative-type toys for their play. As a result, many girls are more dexterous with their fingers, whereas many boys are more skillful in large-motor activities such as running and throwing.

In the end, all children need to be skillful and at ease with both large- and small-motor activities. Once involved with formal education, both genders will need to handle writing tools and reading activities. Girls who are more skillful with finger dexterity and eye–hand coordination have an edge over boys in writing and reading at present. Is this small-motor skill imbalance perhaps the reason more boys than girls have problems in learning to read?

If You Have Not Checked This Item: Some Helpful Ideas

■ Use Bead-Stringing

Put out all kinds of materials for both boys and girls to use in making necklaces. Have macaroni and all sorts of pasta shapes available. The children can color them first by painting. Bring in little seashells with holes drilled in them (hobby shops do this), as well as acorns and horse chestnuts in the fall, plastic or wooden beads, and any other small items you can find. If bead-stringing catches on, your children may want to go on a field trip to a bead store or hobby shop.

■ Make a Geoboard

Make a 1-foot-square wooden board about ½-inch thick and pound in headless nails over the surface of the board in rows 1 inch apart. Allow the nails to protrude above the surface about an inch. Let the children string colored rubber bands over the tops of the nails, making all kinds of designs. Older children can try to copy design cards you have made, as well.

■ Make Pegboards

Ask a building supply company for scraps of pegboard it normally would throw away. You can cut the scraps to child-size shapes and sand down the edges. The pegboards do not have to be squares. Triangular pegboards are just as useful and appealing. Get boxes of colored golf tees for pegs, and let the children use the tees the same way colored rubber bands are used on the geoboards.

■ Ask Parents to Help

Have a parent "Board-Making Bee" to help stock your classroom as well as make enough extra boards to take home for their children to play with. You can almost always attract parents or other family members to help your program if they know they will be making educational games they can also take home.

Besides helping their children both at home and at school, the parents themselves can be learning the importance of small-motor activities for their children. Parents need to be aware that play is essential to their children's physical, mental, creative, and social development as human beings. Such parent group activities may change parents' outlook.

■ Hide Objects in Sand Table

No need to purchase manipulatives if you use your imagination. For instance, use your sand table as a beach that the children pretend to visit to look for shells. Collect little shells from a real beach (or a bead store) and bury them in the sand table. Have several children at a time dig for them with their fingers.

The sand table can also be a forest floor, where children hunt for acorns you have buried. Or perhaps it can be a dinosaur dig, where the children need to dig up the little plastic dinosaurs you have buried. All these are wonderful for finger exercising. If your program has no funds for purchasing such items, call a company for one of their toy catalogues, cut out and duplicate pictures of the items, laminate them, and bury them in the sand table.

USES SCISSORS WITH CONTROL

Learning to cut with scissors takes a great deal of practice. This is the final stage in the sequence of small-motor development: *pincer coordination*. Children who have had practice cutting at home may be ahead of those who have not, regardless of age. Sometimes the scissors themselves make it difficult for youngsters to learn how to use them. The blunt scissors found in many preschools are often dull and difficult to manipulate, even by adults. Really good scissors are expensive, but a worthwhile investment when you consider what fine practice they give children in developing strength and coordination in hands and fingers.

A variety of scissors is now available from educational supply companies. Most preschoolers can learn on conventional scissors, but spring-action scissors are also available for beginners and children with limited muscular control. Because you want your children to develop small-muscle control, try conventional scissors first. Be sure they are child-size with stainless steel blades and with large enough plastic hand grips for both righties and lefties.

You can help children who have not learned to cut in several ways. Show them how to hold the scissors with their favored hand. As with crayons, children sometimes pick up scissors with either hand, but they will not have much success if they are trying to use the nondominant hand. You may also have to model the use of scissors.

To help children hold the paper they are cutting with the opposite hand, you might put a dot on that side of the paper to remind children to hold it with the dot under their thumb. You can then tell them to cut with their thumbs up. Some teachers start by holding a narrow strip of paper stretched taut between two hands for the child to cut in two. Once a child can do this cutting without difficulty, get another child to hold the paper and let each take a turn holding and cutting. Give them a task of cutting all the yellow strips into small pieces.

On another day, show the child how to hold the strip of paper in her own hand and cut with the other hand. She needs to keep her scissors in her dominant hand. Let her practice on different kinds of paper, including construction paper, typing paper, and pages from magazines. Finally, draw a line on a sheet of paper and let the child practice cutting along a line. Be sure to have at least one pair of left-handed scissors.

Most 4-year-olds can learn to cut along a straight line, but many have trouble turning corners and following a curved line. Children need practice of all kinds in cutting. Whenever you are preparing art materials for the children to use, especially cutouts that need to be pasted, try to involve the children in helping to do the cutting.

You can show the child how to hold the paper and cut.

If You Have Not Checked This Item: Some Helpful Ideas

■ Use Wrapping Paper Ribbons

Let children practice cutting wrapping paper ribbons into confetti. Ribbons have more body than ordinary paper and cut easier. Someone may need to hold the ribbon while the other cuts. Save the confetti for a celebration.

■ Use Squeeze Bottles and Sponges

If children have difficulty making scissors work, it may be they need help strengthening finger muscles. Put several squeeze bottles in the water table and let them squirt water into containers, or take them outside and squirt designs on the sidewalk. Make rules ahead of time about not squirting each other or they will lose their bottle. Also cut up sponges into sizes small enough for children to hold and squeeze. They can use them to sponge off art tables or lunch tables—another small-muscle strengthening activity.

■ Set Up a Cutting Table

Put out several pairs of scissors and different kinds of paper scraps to be cut into small pieces: letter paper, wallpaper, old greeting cards, drinking straws, coupons, wrapping paper, and so on. Save the cuttings for later use in making collages.

■ Read a Book

In *I Had a Favorite Dress* (Ashburn, 2011) a little girl outgrows her favorite dress, so her mother cuts and sews it into something new, which she also outgrows—so more cutting and more outgrowing. In *Kite Day* (Hillenbrand, 2012) bear and mole cut and glue the paper and string into a kite, which a storm carries into a tree. *Crafty Chloe* (DiPuccio, 2012) cuts out a special birthday present.

These books can be lead-ins to cutting activities you have set up. Read them one at a time and then involved small groups in an activity (see Figure 6-9). For dresses, scan pictures of clothes in catalogues or magazines and have children cut them out. Cutting should not be sexist. Read books on cars and trucks, scan them, and have children cut out these figures, too. Everyone can fold squares and cut off corners to makes snowflakes.

Figure 6-9 Good Cutting Picture Books

I Had a Favorite Dress (Ashburn, 2011)
Crafty Chloe (DiPuccio, 2012)
Kite Day (Hillenbrand, 2012)
Hot Rod Hamster (Lord, 2010)
Trucks Roll! (Lyon, 2007)

✓ USES A HAMMER WITH CONTROL

Holding a nail and pounding it with a hammer held in the opposite hand is the most complicated small-motor skill thus far discussed. Many children will not be able to do it well until they are older and more coordinated. Even adults often have difficulty. Try it yourself and find out.

Arm and wrist strength make a difference. The small toy hammers in play sets should not be used. They are not heavy or strong enough to have much effect other than frustrating the pounder. A small adult hammer is better for pounding in real nails.

Both boys and girls should be encouraged to pound. It is an excellent activity to develop small-motor strength and coordination. If you do not have a carpenter's bench in your room, you can set up a woodworking area by hanging tools on the wall from a pegboard and using a tree stump as a pounding surface. Slices can also be cut from a stump and placed on a table for pounding. Nails go into tree stumps easier than into boards. Place a towel or rug sample under each stump to absorb the sound. When the top of the stump is completely covered with nails, it can be sliced off, making a clean surface for new pounding.

Children's first hammering of nails into stumps is random. You can control for safety by limiting the number of hammers or tree stumps available for pounding. Also be sure the pounders wear safety goggles and that an adult is present when tools are being used.

Safety seems to be the primary concern for teachers. But with basic safety limits established before the children use the center or its tools, the possibility for injuries is reduced. If a teacher is uncomfortable using the tools, she or he should ask a carpenter or a parent to demonstrate their use.

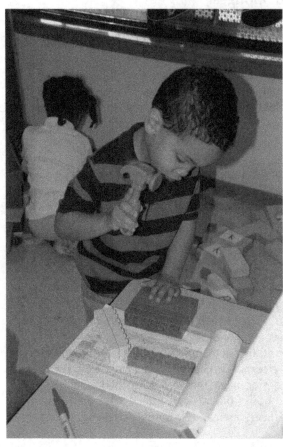

Pounding is an excellent activity to develop small-motor strength.

If You Have Not Checked This Item: Some Helpful Ideas

■ Use Soft Pounding Materials

Do not start your pounding activities with wood. Most children need to acquire the skill before they can drive a nail through wood easily. Start with a softer material such as fiberboard, ceiling tiles, or Styrofoam.

■ Use Large-Headed Nails

Children should use large-headed nails at first. Most tacks are too short for the pounder to hold, but roofing nails or upholstering tacks are large enough and long enough to work well.

OBSERVING, RECORDING, AND INTERPRETING MOTOR DEVELOPMENT

Using the Physical Development section of the Child Development Checklist at the head of the chapter to observe and record each child's development will give you an overall view of their motor progress. For a more in-depth look at small-motor skills you will need to observe children using Figure 6-10, the Small-Motor Checklist. Figure 6-10 shows observations of Lionel's small-motor skills as an example.

SMALL-MOTOR CHECKLIST

Name _Lionel_ **Observer** _Barb_

Program _Preschool—K—2_ **Dates** _1/20_

Directions:

Put an **X** for items you see the child perform regularly. Put an **N** for items where there is no opportunity to observe. Leave all other items blank.

Item	Evidence	Dates
Small Motor Development		
__X__ Turns knobs, lids, eggbeaters	Plays with eggbeater at water table	1/20
__X__ Pours liquids without spilling	Pours own milk at lunch	1/20
__X__ Fasters/unfastens zippers, buttons, Velcro	Dresses & undresses self	1/20
__X__ Picks up & inserts objects with dexterity	Makes puzzles easily	1/20
__X__ Molds play dough/clay with dexterity	Likes to roll out play dough	1/20
_____ Uses drawing/writing tools with control	Does not use markers or writing tools	1/20
_____ Uses scissors with control	Does not use scissors	1/20
__N__ Uses hammer with control	Woodworking not available	1/20

Figure 6-10 Small-Motor Checklist Observation for Lionel

LEARNING PRESCRIPTION

Name _____ Lionel _____ Age _____ 3 _____ Date __1/20__

Areas of Strength and Confidence

1. Does manipulative activities by self

2. Performs or participates in music/rhythm activities

3. Has good small-motor coordination

Areas Needing Strengthening

1. Needs to develop large-motor skills

2. Needs to learn to play with others

3. Needs to develop small-motor skills of writing, drawing, cutting

Activities to Help

1. Bring in pair of left-handed scissors & have Lionel cut out car pictures to make a scrapbook with one of the other boys

2. Bring in hammer, nails, & tree stump; ask Lionel to help another child make rhythm instrument shaker

3. Have Lionel & other children paint rhythm instruments they make

---

Figure 6-11   Learning Prescription for Lionel

Finally, you should make an individualized Learning Prescription for each child needing special help. The activities you choose to help the child in "Areas Needing Strengthening" should be based on his or her "Areas of Strength and Confidence." Using the information gained on other checklists, the staff put together the Learning Prescription for Lionel (Figure 6-11).

Because Lionel shows the ability to make puzzles and to fasten and unfasten zippers and buttons, the staff thought he could use his small-motor skills to work with another child in a class project. He likes art activities such as using play dough and finger painting, but he does not use paintbrushes, writing tools, or scissors. He is left-handed and seems to have trouble with scissors. The staff says that they will provide him with left-handed scissors and give him support in the activity of cutting out pictures of cars for the class scrapbook. They do not have a woodworking bench, but Lionel says he has helped his grandfather pound nails. Perhaps he and other children could pound together simple rhythm instruments from wood, paint them, and use them in a rhythm activity (Lionel excels in rhythm). Using things Lionel likes to do and is good at doing may help him get involved with the other children.

LEARNING ACTIVITIES

1. Use the Large-Motor Skills Rating Scale in Figure 6-2 to observe all the children. Which ones are the most physically accomplished? Which need the most help? What are their ages? How do you plan to help them? Record the results.

2. Choose a child who seems to need a great deal of help running with control. Use the rating scale in Figure 6-3 to further determine his or her running skills. Do an activity with the child to promote this skill. Record the results.

3. Observe a child who does not climb on climbing equipment. How would you help him to strengthen his leg muscles? Does this help him climb? Record the results.

4. Observe the children to determine which ones need help throwing balls. Play games with small groups, including these children, that involve throwing balls of different kinds and sizes to see which ones work best. What else could you do? Record the results.

5. Observe a cooking activity involving opening jars and using an eggbeater to determine which children need help with turning skills. Put out plastic containers of water with a squirt of detergent and several eggbeaters to see how long these children can churn up bubbles to strengthen their hand muscles. What else could you do? Record the results.

6. Put out several cutting materials and several kinds of scissors on a cutting table and observe which children are successful, which need help, and which do not participate. Work with children who need help, giving them different interesting cutting challenges. Which one works best? Record the results.

SUGGESTED READINGS

Izumi-Taylor, S., Morris, G., Meredith, C., & Hicks, C. (2012). Music and movement for children's healthy development. *Dimensions of Early Childhood, 40*(2), 33–39.

Marigiliano, M. L., & Russo, M. J. (2011). Moving bodies, building minds: Foster preschooler's critical thinking and problem solving through movement. *Young Children, 66*(5), 44–49.

Newman, J., & Kranowitz, C. (2012). Developing gross motor skills: Moving experiences that will last a lifetime. *Exchange, 34*(1), 97–99.

Nilsen, B. A. (2010). *Week by week: Plans for documenting children's development.* Belmont, CA: Wadsworth/Cengage.

Orlowski, M. A., & Hart, A. (2010). Go! Including movement during routines and transitions. *Young Children, 65*(5), 88–92.

CHILDREN'S BOOKS

Alborough, J. (2006). *Hit the ball duck.* La Jolla, CA: Kane/Miller.

Ashburn, B. (2011). *I had a favorite dress.* New York: Abrams.*

Bluemle, E. (2009). *How do you wokka-wokka?* Sommerville, MA: Candlewick.*

Compestine, Y. C. (2011). *The runaway wok.* New York: Dutton's Children's Books.*

Cronin, D. (2007). *Bounce.* New York: Atheneum.

DiPuccio, K. (2012). *Crafty Chloe.* New York: Atheneum.

French, V. (2000). *Oliver's milk shake.* New York: Orchard Books.

Hillenbrand, W. (2012). *Kite day.* New York: Holiday House.

Isadora, R. (2005). *Luke goes to bat.* New York: G. P. Putnam's Sons.*

Jenkins, S. (2006). *Move!* Boston: Houghton Mifflin.

Johnson, A. (2004). *Just like Josh Gibson.* New York: Simon & Schuster.*

Kuklin, S. (2001). *Hoops with Swoopes.* New York: Hyperion.*

Lord, C. (2010). *Hot rod hamster*. New York: Scholastic.

Lyon, G. E. (2007). *Trucks roll!* New York: Atheneum.

O'Connor, J. (2007). *Ready, set, skip!* New York: Viking.

Patricelli, L. (2012). *Faster! Faster!* Sommerville, MA: Candlewick.

Rosenthal, A. K. (2012). *Chopsticks*. New York: Disney Hyperion.

Wilson, K., & Hillenbrand, W. (2007). *Whopper cake*. New York: McElderry.

Urbanovic. J. (2008). *Duck soup*. New York: Harper/Collins.

WEB SITES

Body, Mind, and Child Ratio
www.bodymindchild.com

Centers for Disease Control and Prevention
www.cdc.gov/HealthyYouth/KeyStratgies

National Association for the Education of Young Children
www.naeyc.org

National Association for Sport and Physical Education
www.aahperd.org

PE Central
www.pecentral.com

President's Council on Fitness
www.fitness.gov

*Multicultural

Cognitive Development

In this chapter you will learn to observe if children can:

_____ Classify objects by shape, color, size

_____ Place objects in a sequence or series

_____ Recognize, create patterns

_____ Count by rote to 20

_____ Display 1-to-1 correspondence with numbers

_____ Problem-solve with concrete objects

_____ Make thinking visible

_____ Be observed by using documentation and checklist

☑ DEVELOPING COGNITIVE CONCEPTS

Cognitive development of preschool children is concerned with how their thinking abilities evolve. We are only beginning to understand how this takes place. The work of pioneer researchers like Swiss psychologist Jean Piaget in his investigation of how knowledge is created has given us new insights into how children think as well as how their thinking evolves. The research of Russian psychologist Lev Vygotsky has added his own theories on cognitive development and helped to apply this information to the classroom. Studies by more recent psychologists have refined those earlier premises and developed theories of their own. The research of neuroscientists continues to provide more insights into how the brain develops and how this affects young children's thinking processes and behavior.

One of the surprising findings resulting from all this research is the fact that young children's thinking is not the same as that of adults. Piaget's Stages of Cognitive Development in Table 7.1 show how children below the age of 7 think mostly in concrete terms and have not yet developed the abstract thinking of older children and adults. Not all modern researchers agree with Piaget's stage theory, although McDevitt and Ormrod (2004) believe that Piaget's stages provide a rough idea of when new abilities are likely to emerge. But perhaps the most startling finding to those unfamiliar with this research is that children actively construct their own knowledge.

Using the physical and mental tools they are born with, children interact with their environment to make sense of it, and in so doing, they construct their own mental concepts of their world. The brain seems to be conditioned to take in information about objects and their relationship to one another. What do things look, feel, taste, sound, and smell like? What can they do? How are they like one another? How are they different? What happens if you touch, push, or throw them?

As children manipulate the objects in their environment, they learn to make different responses to different objects. The new knowledge that they gain is assimilated into their previous knowledge, thus helping their thinking patterns evolve. To Piaget, children's cognitive development comes from biological maturation, their interactions with their environment, and their spontaneous discoveries about it. Piaget puts the knowledge that children are constructing into three categories:

- *Physical knowledge.* Children learn about objects in their environment by physically manipulating them. They begin constructing the mental concepts of shape, size, and color about these objects.
- *Logico-mathematical knowledge.* Children construct relationships about the objects such as alike and different, more and less, which ones go together, how many, how much.
- *Social knowledge.* Children learn rules for behavior and knowledge about people's actions through their involvement with people.

As they interact with the objects and people in their environment, young children acquire physical knowledge and logico-mathematical knowledge simultaneously. As the physical characteristics of objects are learned, logico-mathematical categories are constructed to organize information. Thus cognitive concepts are formed. Such concepts are the building blocks of knowledge that allow children to organize and categorize information.

This chapter will look at children's development of particular logico-mathematical concepts as observable examples of where they stand in cognitive maturity. Although

Table 7.1   Piaget's Stages of Cognitive Development

Sensorimotor Stage (Birth to Age 2)

Child thinks in visual patterns (schemata).

Child uses senses to explore objects (i.e., looks, listens, smells, tastes, and manipulates).

Child learns to recall physical features of an object.

Child associates objects with actions and events but does not use objects to symbolize actions and events (e.g., rolls a ball but does not use ball as a pretend car).

Child develops object permanence (comes to realize an object is still there even when out of sight).

Preoperational Stage (Ages 2–7)

Child acquires symbolic thought (uses mental images and words to represent actions and events not present).

Child uses objects to symbolize actions and events (e.g., pretends a block is a car).

Child learns to anticipate effect of one action on another (e.g., realizes pouring milk from pitcher to glass will make level of milk decrease in pitcher as it rises in glass).

Child is deceived by appearances (e.g., believes a tall, thin container holding a cup of water contains more than a short, wide container holding a cup of water).

Child is concerned with final products (focuses on the way things look at a particular moment, "figurative knowledge," and not on changes of things or how things got that way, "operational knowledge"), and he cannot seem to reverse his thinking.

Concrete-Operational Stage (Ages 7–11)

Child's thoughts can deal with changes of things and how they got that way.

Child is able to reverse her thinking (has ability to see in her mind how things looked before and after a change took place).

Child has gone beyond how things look at a particular moment and begins to understand how things relate to one another (e.g., knows that the number 2 can be larger than 1, yet, at the same time, smaller than 3).

Formal-Operational Stage (Ages 11+)

Child begins to think about thinking.

Child thinks in abstract terms without needing concrete objects.

Child can hypothesize about things.

Vygotsky's theories support many of Piaget's findings, Vygotsky believed that after age 2, culture and cultural signs are necessary to expand children's thinking. In other words, cognitive development does not come from the child alone but also from the adults and mature peers around him, as well as from mental tools (Vygotsky called them "signs") that the child develops such as speech and, later, writing and numbering.

Good teaching means presenting material a little ahead of a child's development.

Whereas Piaget emphasized children as explorers and discoverers, constructing their knowledge independently, Vygotsky developed the concept of the *zone of proximal development,* or ZPD, defined as the area between where the child is now in mental development and where she might go with assistance from an adult or a more mature child.

To gain cultural knowledge, the child needs assistance or scaffolding, which is provided by more mature learners. To Vygotsky, good teaching involves presenting material that is a little ahead of the child's development. Teachers know they have identified a child's ZPD when the child responds with enthusiasm to the activities the teacher provides.

Both Piaget's and Vygotsky's points of view are incorporated into quality early childhood programs today by giving children opportunities to explore and discover on their own, as well as to interact with adults who support their efforts and challenge them in making new discoveries. However, neither Piaget nor Vygotsky had access to the brain research technology currently being used to discover how the brain develops and functions. Although many of these findings support the theories of those pioneer researchers, we are still at the beginning of our knowledge about this amazing organ we all possess: the human brain.

BRAIN RESEARCH

New findings about infants' and young children's brain development are opening our eyes to the importance of early adult–child interactions and a stimulating environment. As recently as 30 years ago, many psychologists believed that the genes children were born with determined the structure of their brains, which could not be changed. Brain research, however, has disproved such a theory. Heredity determines only the basic number of neurons (brain cells) children are born with, but this is just the framework. New brain-imaging technologies such as positron emission tomography (PET) that allow neuroscientists to study how the brain develops over the first 6 years of life have come up with surprising findings (Sprenger, 2008).

The weight of the brain increases from about 1 pound at birth to 2 pounds by age 1. It is the electrical activity of the neurons that is most important. Even before birth, these cells fire electrical charges that carve mental circuits into patterns in the brain, actually changing the structure of the brain. *You could say that the brain is wiring itself for use.*

Are you brain-imaging-literate? You need to know the vocabulary of what is happening inside your brain. Children want to know, too. You can draw a simple round picture of a *neuron*, a brain cell. Show little branches coming out of it. These are *dendrites,* little appendages through which information flows into the neuron. A longer appendage also attached to the neuron is called an *axon,* where information flows out of the neuron and into the dendrites of adjacent neurons. This space between neurons where dendrites and axons meet is called a *synapse,* a connection (Sprenger, 2008).

Immediately after birth, an explosion of learning occurs caused by these same electrical processes. What happens next is up to the people and the environment surrounding the infant. The brain changes dramatically as trillions more synapses (connections) than it can possibly use are produced, laying out circuits for vision, movement, language, thinking, and the functions necessary for life itself. By age 2 the number of synapses reaches the adult level, and incredibly, by age 3 the brain's synapse density is twice that of the adult brain. This time the neural activity is no longer spontaneous as it was before birth, but is driven by the sensory experiences the child encounters in his environment. In other words, for neurons to make connections in the brain, they must be activated through experiences. The synapses that are used tend to become permanent fixtures. Those that are not used are eliminated.

The brain's neurons continue to develop and disappear throughout most of our lives, according to Rushton and Juola Rushton (2011). Those neurons that are not stimulated to make connections to other neurons are eventually pruned away and dissolve. However, we experience the greatest growth of dendrites as well as a high volume of pruning in early childhood. The more experiences a child is engaged in, the more potential there is for dendrite growth. Strong connections between dendrites that develop through repetition help create and strengthen neural pathways of learning.

This new understanding of how the brain develops makes it clear that positive emotional experiences are crucial in a young child's growth of intellectual capacities. Thus, as we look at the cognitive development of preschool children in this chapter, we must keep in mind that for intellectual competence to occur, the activities and experiences we provide must be accompanied by positive interactions with caring adults.

USING PLAY

Both Piaget and Vygotsky agreed that children create their own knowledge through exploratory play. They do it by playing with things, people, and ideas. Most people think of play as something recreational, something we do for enjoyment, and something rather inconsequential. For adults, this definition of play may be true, but for infants and young children, play is their way of learning: of trying out and finding out about the world around them. Youngsters use their senses of taste, touch, sound, sight, and smell in a playful manner with anything and everything they can get their hands on, to find out what an object is, what it feels like, what it sounds like, and what you can do with it. The fact is that child's play is sensory practice in learning to think.

From the time he is born, the human infant pursues such information with a single-minded determination. At first, everything goes into the mouth. Then the infant bangs objects against the side of the crib to see what they sound like, to see what they will do, or to find out what will happen. The toddler has an extra advantage. He has expanded his field of exploration by learning to walk. Suddenly the world's objects are his to touch, pick up, shake, throw, taste, and take apart. He uses his senses to "play" with his world and to find out what it is about. And as soon as he can talk, he plays with words and word sounds as well.

All the information extracted through this playful exploration of the environment is filed away in predetermined patterns in the brain, to be used to direct or adjust the child's behavior as he continues to respond to the stimuli around him. We now know that this knowledge is organized by the brain in predictable patterns from a very early age.

STAGES OF EXPLORATORY PLAY

Exploratory play itself occurs in predictable, observable patterns as young children grow and develop. All children seem to go through three definite stages of play every time they explore the possibilities of a new object or activity on their own. To make such stages easy to recognize and remember, we call them "the 3 Ms": manipulation, mastery, and meaning. Children progress through these developmental stages by being allowed to explore new objects and activities on their own. If we make children do things our way, we are short-circuiting their learning process. Our guidance should come after children have a chance to try out things on their own (Beaty, 2012).

When children of any age first begin to explore a new object, they play around with it, turning it upside down or inside out, or using it in ways it was never meant to be used. For example, when children first use unit blocks, they often fill containers or trucks with them and then dump them out. Building with the blocks comes later, after children have become acquainted with the possibilities of blocks through *manipulation*. With paints, children start by messing around with the brushes and paints, perhaps filling a page with color and then covering it with another color. They are manipulating the medium. With a computer, children often start by "piano-playing" the keys; that is, pressing all the keys instead of pressing one at a time and watching what happens. Children need this manipulation experience to discover how things work.

Once they are familiar with the medium, they quickly go on to the next stage of exploratory play: *mastery*. To master the use of a material or activity, young children need to try it out over and over, much to the distraction of many adults. Repetition is the hallmark of the mastery stage, almost as if children were setting up a natural practice session for themselves. With blocks, they build endless roads or walls or towers. With paints, they often repeat a scribble or line on page after page. With the computer, they call up their favorite screen again and again. You are probably witness to the story-reading mastery phase when children want the same story repeated endlessly. They are wiring their brains to remember; in other words, they are developing memory.

After they have satisfied this urge to master the material, many children go on to a new exploratory stage in which they put their own *meaning* into the activity. With blocks, they construct buildings. With paints, they create pictures. With computer programs, they may add their own twist such as playing an invented "I stopped you!" game with a partner. With familiar stories they often rename characters, change the plot, or make up their own story. Not all preschoolers reach this meaning stage, but many do if they have been encouraged to develop naturally through exploratory play.

CLASSIFICATION

Classification, one of the basic processes children use to develop reasoning abilities, is the method of placing objects that are alike in the same class or category. For the brain to classify, children first need to be able to tell what things look like: their shape, color, size, and other attributes. Then they must be able to tell which objects are alike according to particular attributes and which ones are different. Complex mental and physical abilities come into play as children develop classification skills: language and vocabulary; identification of shapes, colors, and sizes; and visual perception in identifying likeness and difference.

How do children learn these complex skills? They learn them through the exploratory play stages previously discussed. Once they have begun to notice the similar properties of objects, children can begin to separate or classify them, a necessary ability in cognitive development for the brain to sort out and process the wealth of incoming data obtained through sensory activities. Sorting objects and materials gives children practice in this skill and involves identifying the similarities of objects as well as understanding their relationships. The more we learn about young children's development of thinking abilities, the more we realize that thinking is concerned primarily with information processing and retrieval.

Piaget and other researchers have noted that children progress through a sequence of sorting skills, and that each skill is more complex than the previous one.

The earliest sorting skill to appear is simple classification, which many 2- and most 3-year-olds can do. Children doing simple classification can sort or group objects that actually belong together in the real world. For example, they can group together all the toy animals that live on the farm in one set and all the fish and creatures that live in the ocean in another set, if the youngsters have had the appropriate experiences concerning such animals. This activity is not quite true classification, because it is based on associations between the animals and their homes, rather than the animals' likenesses or differences.

Another type of simple classification in which young children place things that "belong together" into a group involves putting all of the toy trucks, cars, and motorcycles together in a group because "you can drive them," or putting the proper hats on all the dolls, or putting all the blocks together because they make a house.

A more mature type of classification that many 3-year-olds and most 4- and 5-year-olds can do involves classifying objects into separate sets based on a common characteristic like color, for instance. You can ask the children to sort out a group of red blocks and blue blocks by color. If they understand classification they will put red blocks in one pile and blue blocks in another.

Children need to practice with all kinds of sorting games, activities, and collections—and the youngsters love this practice. Give a child a box of mixed buttons and let him sort it any way he chooses. Talk with the child afterward, and ask how he decided on which buttons to put in each pile. Look around your classroom for other objects to sort, such as dress-up clothing, blocks, and eating utensils. By age 5, children with experience can sort objects into intersecting sets based on more than one characteristic: color as well as size, for instance. The problem most young children have in doing this kind of sorting involves consistency.

They have difficulty keeping in mind the rule on which the sorting is based. Often, they will start sorting objects on the basis of color but will switch in the middle of the task to some other property, like shape, and may even switch back again before they are finished. Willis (2007) tells us that the more ways something is learned, the more memory pathways are built in the brain. She calls teachers "memory enhancers"—not just "information dispensers" (pp. 311–312).

What other ways can children classify in your classroom? What about organizing collage materials in art, gathering role props in dramatic play, choosing picture books on a certain subject, sorting objects collected on a field trip through the park, choosing musical percussion instruments? Children need to use more than their sight in classifying. They should also use touch, taste, smell, and sound when appropriate

 ## ASSESSING DEVELOPMENT

How have your children fared in constructing their own knowledge? They need to have built up:

1. Mental representations of objects
2. Ways to differentiate things by their appearance or by their sound or feeling

3. Ways of telling how things are alike or different

4. Ways to decide how things fit together as a part of a sequence or a series

These are the patterns or concepts the brain forms in organizing the data it takes in. You will need to assess each of your children by observing their ability to accomplish the skills of classification, understanding sequences, creating patterns, counting, using numbers, and problem solving. Your careful observation of each child in these areas will help you to identify the state of their cognitive development.

☑ CLASSIFIES OBJECTS BY SHAPE, COLOR, SIZE

Shape

Children identify and classify objects by their shapes. Development of thinking begins with the infant's seeing, hearing, and feeling things in her environment: her mother's face, or her bottle or mother's breast. Her brain takes in these important visual perceptions and stores them in particular schemes or patterns that are mental representations for the objects and events she experiences. Her brain seems to be conditioned to pay attention to certain things in her environment and ignore the rest.

Research has shown, for instance, that an infant looks longer at the human face than at anything else around her. She seems to have an innate preference for faces or facelike objects. The infant seems, in fact, to prefer visual stimuli that have a contour configuration. She is beginning her construction of knowledge.

The first checklist item on shape is concerned with refinement of the child's perceptual recognition. To think, reason, and problem-solve, the child needs to know and discriminate among basic shapes of things. We start with geometric shapes because the concept of shape is one of the first concepts to emerge in the child's cognitive development. He needs to distinguish among a circle, a square, a rectangle, and a triangle—not to do math problems, but to be able to categorize and distinguish mentally among the objects in his environment.

Young children need to begin sorting and classification activities as soon as they enter your program. Put out a set of plastic shape blocks. They may be red, blue, green, and yellow squares, circles, rectangles, and triangles. Observe to see how the children play with them. Does anyone group all of the circles together? That child is demonstrating discrimination abilities: that one shape is different from the other shapes. Can anyone tell the names of the different shapes? Those children are demonstrating labeling abilities. What about matching? Can anyone find other blocks to match a shape you put out? Can they do sorting; that is, separating the mixed group of shapes into sets of similar shapes? Remind the children they need to be looking at the shapes of the blocks, not the colors.

After children have played with all kinds of concrete materials like this, they may be ready to find shapes in the classroom environment. Play shape-finding treasure hunts with them. At an even higher and more abstract level, they can try to find the shapes they know in pictures. Finally, some should be ready to reproduce certain

This girl is looking for matching cubes.

shapes in their art, on geoboards, or in block buildings. As you can see, this learning takes place not just by a teacher telling the child, "This is a square," "This is a circle," but more effectively by children's hands-on playing or exploring with all their senses about what makes a particular object a circle or what makes another shape a square.

Your program should provide the children with many such experiences. Because the children learn these classification skills through the senses, you should give the youngsters all kinds of sensory play opportunities. Playing with dough, for instance, allows children to make dough balls, which the youngsters flatten into circles with their hands or roll flat with a rolling pin and cut into circular cookies. Sensory learning involves taste, touch, smell, and sight in this instance.

Children in this preoperational stage of development learn best from three-dimensional objects first, before recognizing more abstract symbols such as pictures. Seeing pictures of the various shapes is helpful, but it is too abstract as the only method from which young children can learn. Youngsters first need hands-on activities with concrete materials.

Block building is an excellent medium for creating circles, squares, rectangles, and triangles. In the beginning, you may need to name the shapes the children are making. They probably already know "circle" and perhaps "square," but "rectangle" and "triangle" are interesting new grown-up words. Can the children build a triangle, one of the most difficult shapes for youngsters? Their triangles may be rather rounded in the beginning, because corners are hard for the children to deal with. The diagonal line is the last to appear in children's cognitive learning. This is why triangles and diamonds are very difficult for children to make. Put masking tape on the floor in the shapes of circles, squares, rectangles, and triangles and let children try to build these shapes with their blocks.

Color

Another way the brain classifies things is by color. Research shows that infants as young as 4 to 6 months old begin discriminating colors. Most young children recognize red, green, yellow, and blue along with black and white first before they recognize secondary colors such as violet, pink, and brown. Children develop color perception shortly after shape recognition, although they seem to talk about colors first. Adults make more reference to color than shape, and children quickly pick up this fact.

Your children may, in fact, be able to name many colors just as they name numbers, without truly knowing what the name means. Naming colors is a function of language development in which children must link a visual image with a recalled name. Just because a child says "red" does not mean that she can identify the color. Ask the child the color of her shirt. Ask the youngster to find something red in the classroom.

Color, like shape, is an aspect of visual perception that the child's brain uses to help her classify objects and discriminate their differences. Although the child sees colors from the beginning, she now needs to put names to the different ones.

Again, concentrating on a single color at first and then adding other colors is best. Although basic colors are usually easier for children to recognize, you must take advantage of seasonal and holiday colors as well. Orange should certainly be a part of your classroom during the fall pumpkin, Halloween, and Thanksgiving seasons, and pink as well as red for Valentine's Day.

Allow children to play with colors as they do with blocks. Give them things like poker chips or golf tees and let the children see if they can find all the reds. Some children will be able to sort all of the items by color, but don't expect everyone to be so accurate at first. Let the children experiment with the look and texture of "redness" in all of its shades as they mix it with white paint. Give the children plenty of time to experience one color before you focus on another.

As your group begins its investigation of other colors, you can add paint colors one by one to the easel. Have colored lotto cards, colored plastic blocks, and many other table games featuring colors. Be sure to bring in many different items of the color you are exploring. If you have bilingual children, be sure everyone learns color names in both languages.

Differently abled children can learn color concepts along with all of the other youngsters. Set up your activities to allow children with physical and mental challenges to participate. If you keep concept games in the manipulative area, be sure the shelves are low enough for everyone to reach.

Size

As the young child constructs his own knowledge by interacting with the objects and people in his environment, his brain seems to pay special attention to the relationships between things. Size is one of those relationships. Is it big? Is it small? Is it bigger or smaller than something else? The property of size, like the properties of shape and color, is an essential understanding the child needs to make sense of his world.

Early in life the infant develops size constancy, the ability to see the size of an object as constant no matter if it is close or far away. By the time they are in preschool, children need to be able to compare objects that look the same but are of different sizes. These various orders of size are often thought of in terms of opposites: big-little, large-small, tall-short, long-short, wide-narrow, thick-thin, and deep-shallow. Once again, language plays a part because the child has to link a visual image with a recalled descriptive word. Direct comparison of objects based on one of the opposites just listed seems to be the best way for young children to learn size.

Comparing

Comparing one object with another is one of the best ways to investigate the properties of something new or different. This is, in fact, how the brain works. It focuses on, takes in, and evaluates data about the new object on the basis of what the brain has previously processed about a similar object. Charlesworth and Lind (2007) tell us that as children develop skills in observation, they naturally begin to compare and contrast and identify similarities and differences. The comparing process, which sharpens their observation skills, is the first step toward classifying.

When you are first using comparisons with your children that focus on the concept of size, be sure to use objects that are alike in all their properties except size. This is not the time to use different color or shape items. Instead, try using two similar items, one large and one small. Then talk to the children about how the objects are alike and how they are different.

Opposites

Making a direct comparison of two objects that are similar in every aspect except size is one of the best methods for helping children learn the concept of size. (See Figure 7.1.) Use things such as two apples (a big and little one), two cups, two blocks, two books, or two dolls. Be sure to talk in positive terms ("This one is big. This one is little."), rather than in negative terms ("This one is not big."), which may only confuse the child.

Use the size opposites big and little in all sorts of comparisons in your classroom before you move on to another aspect of size, such as tall and short. Be sure that you use the words for size opposites whenever you can in the classroom: "Look, Kenya has built a tall building and Rhonda has made a short one." "Can someone bring me a large block from the shelf? Can you find a little one, too?" "Who can find a thick

Figure 7.1　Basic Comparisons

large	small	thick	thin
big	little	wide	narrow
long	short	near	far
tall	short	later	sooner
fat	skinny	old	young
heavy	light	high	low
fast	slow	loud	soft

pencil? Who can find a thin one?" A pretend shoe store in the dramatic play area is a fine opportunity to feature size concepts.

Collections

Once children are familiar with various size, shape, and color categories through their own explorations and the games you have played with them in identifying and naming objects, let them try to apply their skill to collections with more than one attribute besides size. Children enjoy playing with collections of natural objects just to discover what they feel like, see what they look like, and explore how they can play with them. A collection of shells, acorns, or rocks can be kept in plastic containers on the shelves of the manipulative/math area for children to bring to a table in the area and play with. They need to find out how the items are alike. Once the items are sorted, can they find the biggest one? The littlest? Keys and buttons also make fine collections or for sorting.

If You Have Not Checked This Item: Some Helpful Ideas

■ Start with One Shape at a Time

Children need to focus their attention on one concept before expanding it to include other aspects. The circle is good to begin with because children are used to the roundness or ovalness of the human face. They need to experience examples of all kinds of circles. Let the youngsters find out how many circles they can discover in the classroom. Did they find the wheels on toy vehicles, the casters on the doll bed or office chair, the clock, or the mark on the table made by a wet glass?

■ Let Children Mix Colors

Let children have the fun of mixing colors. Put out squeeze bottles of food coloring, spoons for stirring, and plastic cups or muffin tins full of water. You may want to use only one or two colors at first, or you may want to let children discover how mixing blue and yellow together makes green because this is such a dramatic change. At another time, use cups of predissolved colors, medicine droppers, and muffin tin cups full of clear water.

Children can play with mixing colors in many ways. The youngsters can finger paint with the color you are focusing on. When the children add a new color to their repertoire, add the same one to the finger painting table. Have them mix the old and new colors together to see what happens.

■ Play Size Transition Games

When you are waiting with the children for lunch to be served, for the bus to come, or for something special to happen, it is a good idea to have a repertoire of brief transition games, finger plays, or stories to tell. This time provides an excellent opportunity for concept games, such as: "The girl wearing the shirt with wide stripes may stand up." "The boy wearing the T-shirt with narrow stripes may stand up." Or play a guessing game with your fingers. Hold your hands behind your back and ask the children to guess which hand has a big finger held up and which has a little finger held up. Then show them. Can one of your children then be the leader of this game?

■ Sort Blocks During Cleanup

Have children help sort out the largest unit blocks during cleanup before putting them back on the shelves. This activity will give you an indication of who can and cannot sort objects based on size. Make the activity a game, though, and not a task.

☑ PLACES OBJECTS IN A SEQUENCE OR SERIES

In observing children to determine their cognitive development, we have been concentrating thus far on the classification aspects of what is known as "logico-mathematical knowledge." Children display three aspects of this knowledge:

- *Classification abilities*: The ability to understand particular characteristics or attributes of objects and the ability to group things into classes with common properties
- *Seriation abilities*: The ability to understand "more than" or "less than," and the ability to arrange things systematically in a sequence or a series based on a particular rule or order
- *Number abilities*: The ability to understand the meaning and use of numbers, and the ability to apply them in counting and ordering

This next checklist item involves seriation abilities in children. To arrange objects in a sequence, the child first has to recognize their properties and relationships. How are they alike? How different? What is the common thread that connects them? Then the child must understand order: that one comes first (perhaps the biggest), one comes next, and next, and finally last. His practice in sorting items by likenesses should help him note both properties and relationships among objects as well.

Just as the young child often changes the rule he is using as he sorts a number of things, he also displays inconsistency in arranging objects in a sequence. It is as if his immature mind cannot hold for long the rule on which the sequencing is based. Simple seriation asks us to observe children to see if they can arrange objects in a series from the largest to the smallest or vice versa. Children's previous activities with opposites should prepare them for identifying extreme differences among objects. Because young children can think of only two things at one time, they can usually identify the first and last objects in seriation, but may mix up those in between. However, young children can usually arrange items in a series if they are provided with cues.

Montessori size-cylinders, for instance, can be arranged in a board containing a series of graduated holes. Children try to fit the cylinders from large to small in the increasingly smaller holes. They match the size of each cylinder with the size of each hole by trial and error to see which cylinders do fit or do not fit. Once they have learned the concept, many children can line up the cylinders in the proper order without cues from the board.

Stacking blocks, boxes, and rings work on the same principle of arranging items in a series, usually from the largest to the smallest. Even toddlers soon learn that the smallest ring will not go down all the way on the stacking column. Instead, they have to put the largest ring on first. Then, if one ring is left over, they will need to start over again to find their mistake. Russian matreshka dolls, a classic folk art, are a series of hollow wooden dolls, each smaller than the next, that fit inside one another. The point is that children play these learning games on their own, and thus come to discover the concept of sequencing through their own play.

Most preschoolers understand the concept of bigger and smaller, but when this concept is applied to a series, the complexity of the many comparisons seems to confuse some youngsters. How can an object that is bigger than one item also be smaller than the item that precedes it?

You may find that you have not checked this particular checklist item for any but the most mature children. This finding is to be expected with 3- and 4-year-olds. Five-year-olds, on the other hand, usually are more successful. You may decide to add a number of new series games and activities to your manipulative or science/math areas to promote this skill. Be sure the new materials provide enough cues for your children to succeed. Most of all, be sure these activities are fun to do.

If You Have Not Checked This Item: Some Helpful Ideas

■ Arrange Children

Have groups of three children at a time arrange themselves from shortest to tallest on three boxes of graduated sizes. Let them tell who is tallest. Then let them shift around on the boxes. Now who is tallest? Give everyone a chance to be tallest. To arrange children without the graduated boxes may make the truly shortest child feel bad because children have gotten the idea from us that tallest is best.

■ Read a Book

The traditional classic stories of *Goldilocks and the Three Bears, The Three Little Pigs,* and *The Three Billy Goats Gruff* all feature a graduated series of characters from the littlest to the biggest along with their graduated series of furniture, cereal bowls, houses, and even noises. ***The Three Little Tamales*** (Kimmel, 2009) is a modern Hispanic version of *The Three Little Pigs.*

Hit the Ball, Duck (Alborough, 2006) is a book full of comical sequences all shown on pages divided in two lengthwise. Listeners need to sit close to see the ball being thrown by Goat, being hit by Duck, landing in a tree; the bat being thrown, landing in the tree; the glove being thrown, and so on. Then they all come down in sequence. Lots of sequence practice for your children.

You can cut out the characters from scanned pictures from each of these books. Then mount the cutouts with sandpaper or Velcro and use them with flannel board activities. Can your children arrange the characters in proper order from littlest to biggest? Children need this hands-on activity to develop the abstract concept of seriation.

✓ RECOGNIZES, CREATES PATTERNS

The cognitive concept of patterning involves recognizing or creating a series of objects, words, sounds, or colors that occur in a certain order and are repeated. Why involve preschool children in learning about patterns? Research focusing on the concept of patterns facilitates children's ability to make generalizations about number combinations, counting strategies, and problem solving, according to Copley (2000). Learning about patterns also helps preschoolers to predict what will happen next, especially in a story. Many children's lives are governed by patterns (rituals) that must be followed to the letter or loud protests will ensue, even though the term "pattern" is seldom used.

Patterns surround children. The daily schedule occurs in a pattern. The chorus of a song or the words of a jump rope rhyme are patterns. Children enjoy being involved in hand-clapping patterns. Some patterns follow repeated sequences of a preset rule such as designs in wallpaper or tiles. Most children intuitively recognize patterns once the concept is pointed out. Have them look around to find patterns inside and outside the classroom. Rainbows are patterns of color. Dances are patterns of steps. Gardens may be planted in patterns of flowers. Floor tiles may be arranged in patterns. Children's pants and shirts often contain fascinating patterns.

Once children understand what makes something a pattern, they will be happy to search for patterns in their everyday life if you make it a game. They can be "pattern detectives" seeking patterns everywhere. Put a sticker on the shirt of each one who discovers a pattern. Use different stickers so that a row of them on a shirt also forms a pattern. Perhaps they will note that letters can be arranged in patterns; so can numbers.

You can soon tell who understands this concept by the number of stickers they wear. If some children have not received a sticker, play a game with them until they do, perhaps in the book center, so they can find a book with a pattern in it; or in the dramatic play center where the plastic dishes and tablecloth may contain patterns.

Now it is time for them to create some patterns of their own. Bring out sets of manipulative objects such as tubs of little jungle animals or sea creatures, and sets of giant beads, colored blocks, or tiles. First have them sort them into piles according to one attribute (e.g., color, size, or species). Then have children line up or arrange several of them in patterns. One child can start. Try not to use more than three different attributes at first (e.g., red, blue, and yellow; or tigers, elephants, and monkeys). Ask those who are watching: "What is the rule for this pattern?" "Yes, it is first red, then blue, and then yellow." Or "Yes, it is first tigers, then elephants, and then

This girl is trying to line up a repeated pattern of animals.

monkeys." What comes next? Do children understand that each pattern starts all over like the first one?

Find out through your observation which children can keep the pattern going. Inconsistency is also a problem here with many young children. They start out with the pattern in mind, but soon forget which color comes next and don't understand they can look back at the first pattern to find out. The more they practice, the more accurate they will become. Activities like this give them practice in keeping track of what comes next.

If You Have Not Checked This Item: Some Helpful Ideas

■ Have Children Become a Pattern

If you recall that young children learn best when they are involved as persons, invite those who are interested to make a pattern of themselves. Have six children tie different single-color scarves around their necks. Use only three colors (e.g., red, blue, and yellow). Can they stand in a line so the six are in a pattern?

■ Find Hair Patterns

Hairstyles are patterns, too. Have the children look for different patterns among children's hair in their class. Do they have names? Then read them **Hats off to Hair!** (Kroll, 1995) with impressive pictures of children's faces and hair illustrating 36 different hair patterns! Does anyone understand that the rhyming words of the story are also in patterns?

Figure 7.2   Books with
Colorful Patterns

> ***My Painted House, My Friendly Chicken, and Me*** (Angelou, 1994)
>   African houses
> ***Kente Colors*** (Chocolate, 1996) African patterns
> ***Luka's Quilt*** (Guback, 1994) Hawaiian quilt patterns
> ***Grandma Calls Me Beautiful*** (Joosse, 2008) Hawaiian dress patterns
> ***Papa, Do You Love Me?*** (Joosse, 2005) African shields and robes
> ***Mama, Do You Love Me?*** (Joosse, 1991) Alaskan dress patterns
> ***Stitchin' and Pullin'*** (McKissack, 2008) Southern quilt patterns

■ Read a Book

Although books are more abstract than blocks or paints or people's hair, certain
books contain fantastic patterns that even the youngest children can recognize. Here
are some in Figure 7.2.

Find older books at www.Amazon.com.

Have your children make a house out of a cardboard box and decorate it with
a pattern.

COUNTS BY ROTE TO 20

No need to emphasize how important the learning of the number concept is for the
children. They will be dealing most of their lives with numbers involving size, distance, amount, time, temperature, cost, money, and measurement. In their mind's
quest to create its own knowledge, the children will be going through a predetermined sequence of development, internalizing the information gained from their
sensory interactions with the world around them.

Rote counting involves reciting the names of the numerals in order from memory. It seems such a simple thing to do, but it involves memory skills (remembering
the names of the numbers), seriation skills (remembering the order of the numbers),
and even patterning skills (understanding that numbers from 1 to 10 are repeated in
a pattern as the counting proceeds to higher numbers).

Even 2-year-olds display a rudimentary knowledge of numbers when they hold
up two fingers to show you their age and count aloud "one-two." For most, this
counting is more of a parroting response than a true understanding of "two years."
However, some 2-year-olds can count by rote to 10, and many 3- and 4-year-olds
are able to count by rote to 20.

Again, this rote counting does not mean the children understand the concept of
numbers at first. Often, in fact, children do not get the sequence correct in their
counting or may even leave out a number or two. These mix-ups and omissions are
understandable because the children are performing a memory task, not a concept
task. Their counting is really chanting, as in a nursery rhyme. You will find that many

Children need to be able to count out numbers to make moves on board games.

children do not know the meaning of each number word. In fact, their chanting of numbers seems more like one long word instead of 10 separate ones:

"onetwothreefourfivesixseveneightnineten."

Nevertheless, chanting numbers like this is important in the cognitive development of the child. Cognitive development, like physical development, proceeds from the general to the specific. Children first chant a line of numbers and then begin to understand specific number names from the line. Listen to the children as they chant. Are they getting the number names right and in the right order? Chant along with them to help them hear the correct pronunciation.

This type of counting is due in part to the children's limited language experience. To understand the meaning of each number word, the child must form a mental image of it. You cannot expect this mental image formation in many 2-year-olds. By age 3, some children will have formed mental images of certain numbers because of their sensory experience with these numbers in their environment. It is therefore important for parents and other adults to use numbers frequently in the children's everyday living, and to involve children in the use of numbers with activities such as chanting, measuring, weighing, counting out items, counting out money, and playing games involving the counting of moves.

Children need to be able to place objects in a series and understand that the objects are more than or less than one another. The youngsters need to know the answers to questions such as, "Which group has the most?" And, of course, they need to know the names of the numbers. Some of these skills are just developing in the preschool classroom, but many children will not fully grasp the concepts of seriation and number much before the age of 7.

For children who can count to 10 or 20, but have no real understanding of numbers or of what counting really means, try having them count to 7 or to 13. The children will have to slow down and think about what they are doing. They may not be able to stop at a number other than 10 or 20 at first. Play games with individuals or small groups, asking each to count to a number other than 10 that you will call out. Make such games exciting. Children who have not learned to count will soon be picking up this skill to play the game. Children love to count. Charlesworth and Lind (2007) tell us that children need repeated and frequent practice to develop counting skills, but this practice should be of short duration.

Rote counting needs to evolve into *rational counting* in which children match each numeral name in order to an object in a group. This is a complex task involving a child's coordination of eyes, hands, speech, and memory. A teacher should not push children to do rational counting with more things than they can count easily and with success.

Be sure bilingual children learn to count along with you. They can also count in their home language for the others to hear and learn. Make counting by rote fun for all, but be sure to do it often for short durations. Familiarity with numbers can only happen for preschoolers if the numbers and number games are repeated frequently.

If You Have Not Checked This Item: Some Useful Ideas

■ Chant or Play a Jump Rope Rhyme

Have children learn a jump rope rhyme that includes numbers. There may be as many "how many?" rhymes as there are children in the school. Some involve Cinderella:

Cinderella dressed in white,
Went upstairs to say goodnight.
How many seconds did it take?
One, two, three, four, five. . . .

Cinderella dressed in yellow,
Went inside to eat marshmallows.
How many marshmallows did she eat?
One, two, three, four, five. . . .

Use chants from **Mother Goose: Numbers on the Loose** (Dillon & Dillon, 2007), which includes familiar and not so familiar Mother Goose rhymes containing numbers. Beginning with rhymes containing 1, the verses take readers through all the numbers up to 30.

Make up some of your own chants using children's names. Have two adults turn a long jump rope outside on the playground while children clap and chant the numbers each time the rope hits the ground. One child at a time can run through the turning rope or stop and jump.

■ Sing Songs Involving Numbers

Sing "Hickory, Dickory, Dock." Have the clock strike a different number and the mouse do something different for each verse: The clock struck two, the mouse said "boo." The clock struck three, the mouse had tea, and so forth. Sing the "One little, two little . . ." song using different objects (fire trucks, baseballs, rubber bands, etc., but not Indians).

Figure 7.3 Countdown Books

> *The Moon Over Star* (Aston, 2008)
>
> *Click, Clack, Splish, Splash* (Cronin, 2006)
>
> *On the Moon* (Milbourne, 2006)
>
> *Construction Countdown* (Olson, 2004)
>
> *Pete the Cat and His Four Groovy Buttons* (Litwin, 2012)

■ Read a Countdown Book

Can your children count down? They probably can if they have followed spaceship takeoffs. In ***The Moon Over Star*** (Aston, 2008) for older children, a group of African American youngsters on vacation at Gran's build their own spaceship and count down for a liftoff to the moon. In ***On the Moon*** (Milbourne, 2006) for younger children, a little girl visualizes what it would be like going to the moon with its big countdown at the Kennedy Space Center. ***Construction Countdown*** (Olson, 2004) shows a countdown from 10 to 1 showing earthmovers, payloaders, and other construction vehicles. All are great lead-ins to pretending activities (see Figure 7.3).

In ***Click, Clack, Splish, Splash*** (Cronin, 2006), the animals on Farmer Brown's farm, led by Duck, sneak into his house and take all the goldfish out of his aquarium one by one. Another simple "countdown" book—or you could say subtraction—is ***Pete the Cat and His Four Groovy Buttons*** (Litwin, 2012). As each button pops off his shirt, how many are left?

DISPLAYS 1-TO-1 CORRESPONDENCE WITH NUMBERS

Next, children must master simple one-to-one correspondence for them to develop number sense. This is what we are asking them to do when they count objects. Learning that a number stands for an object is their next step in the sequence of learning number concepts. At first, many youngsters try to rush through their counting without actually including all the objects. The children seem more concerned with saying all the numbers than with making sure each number represents an object. They eventually learn the key principles governing counting (Figure 7.4).

Figure 7.4 Key Principles Governing Counting

- The number names must be matched one-to-one with the objects being counted.
- The order of the number names matters.
- The order in which the objects being counted are touched does not matter.

This is part of rational counting. It will assist children in their awareness of quantity. They come to understand that the last number they name tells how many there are. Preschool children learn these principles not by being taught, but by being involved playfully in hands-on counting. As with learning shapes and colors, concrete objects should be used first, pictures later, and finally numerals.

Children become familiar with the names and the task by repeating them many times in many forms. Through repetition and trial and error, they finally get it right. Most adults are not aware of the importance of learning to count. If children are unable to count rationally, they are not ready to start more formal math activities.

Thus, it is important that children count or hear you counting every day in the classroom and that you provide youngsters with many opportunities for doing so on their own. Start with fewer items than 20 in the beginning, just as you did with number chanting. Then the children will need to stop before they get to 20. Also have the children touch each item as they count. If they skip one, have them try again. Or have them hand you an item as they count it. But be sure it is fun or interesting for them, and not a task involving right or wrong.

Learning to sort also is good preparation for counting things. Putting a cup with a saucer or a hat on a doll helps them understand one-to-one correspondence. Now they must apply their learning to numbers. They learn by their sensory actions that the number "one" represents the first object, that "two" represents the second, and so on. This learning is a first step. But counting in a progression still is not the same as understanding one-to-one correspondence.

Children may be able to count a row of 10 or even 20 children, and still may not be able to choose four of them. Give them practice. Once they are able to count up to 10 objects in a progression, the youngsters can practice picking out a particular number of items, such as three dolls, five blocks, or seven dominoes. Phrase your questions or directions to give the children practice with both activities. "How many red markers are there?" asks them to count in a progression. "Bring me four napkins" takes them one step further in their development of number concepts.

Put out small collections of items in margarine tubs on the tables of your manipulative area and have children count them. They can do it on their own and record their number on the audio recorder if you have it set up for them. Have "Count Me" signs hanging around the room on objects like your fish aquarium, your painting easel paints, and the hats in your dramatic play area. What other things would the children like to count on their own? Ask them. If they want you to check on their accuracy, you will have to count these things, too—a good modeling behavior.

Using Marks, Picture Symbols, and Number Symbols to Record

To support children's number activities, you or your children can record their counting. You should not use number symbols at first, but simple marks to represent the numbers. For example, keep an attendance chart with all the children's names and mark a symbol for each child present. Then the children can count the marks. Have children keep track with marks on a pad or punches on a card with a paper puncher of how many times they feed the guinea pig or water the plants, or of how many cars pass by the building. Then have them count the number of marks or punch holes to get the total.

Use shape symbols, stick figures, or picture symbols for numbers, too. Put signs in each activity area with a particular number of stick figures or peel-off picture symbols to represent the number of children allowed in the area at once. Have a certain number of hooks on the wall with tags on them for use in each area. Have children take the tags while in the areas. Check from time to time with the children in the area, having them count how many participants are in there and whether this is the proper number.

Use charts and bar graphs at appropriate times to record numbers. Hang a calendar chart near the guinea pig's cage and record the number of carrots the guinea pig eats every day by drawing carrot symbols. Record how tall each child's seeds grow every week by posting a chart with the child's name and having him or her measure the height with a ruler. Help children record the height after their names. Or use a bar graph that can be colored to the height the plant has grown.

Later in the year when the children have shown that they understand one-to-one correspondence, you may want to use the actual numerals along with the picture symbols. Numerals alone are often too abstract for many of the children at the beginning of the year.

If You Have Not Checked This Item: Some Helpful Ideas

■ Have Children Count One Another

Any activity is more meaningful to a young child if it involves her and her peers directly. Have children help you take attendance in the morning by going around and counting how many children are present. Have the counting child touch each child. Give the counters help if they need it with numbers above 10.

■ Have Many Counting Materials

Fill your manipulative or math area with counting materials or games. Use egg cartons for children to fill the sections with items and count how many there are. Use buttons, shells, dominoes, spools, paper clips, and macaroni as items to fill the sections.

■ Do a Follow-the-Leader Counting Walk

Walk around the room with three or four children doing a follow-the-leader, touch-and-count walk. Do it aloud the first time and then silently once children know how. For example, after touching three items silently yourself, stop and ask, "How many did we touch?" Congratulate the ones who get it right, and continue your walk. When all the children have caught on, let one of them be the leader.

Figure 7.5   Counting Books

> *Max Counts His Chickens* (Wells, 2007)
>
> *Ten Little Caterpillars* (Martin, 2011)
>
> *Ten Terrible Dinosaurs* (Stickland, 2009)
>
> *We All Went on Safari: A Counting Journey Through Tanzania* (Krebs, 2003)
>
> *Zero, Zilch, Nada: Counting to None* (Ulmer, 2010)

■ Have Children Set the Table

Let the children set the table for meals and snacks. They may need eight spoons and eight forks for each table, along with eight plates, cups, and napkins. Can they do it? This real task is an especially powerful activity for teaching one-to-one correspondence.

■ Read a Book

Counting books are as popular as ABC books these days. Some are shown in Figure 7.5.

We All Went on Safari: A Counting Journey Through Tanzania (Krebs, 2003) shows an extended family of African people walking through various animal habitats. Each day a different child tells the number of the particular species they see from 1 to 10. This book is a lead-in to taking your children on a counting safari around your classroom to look for toy animals.

In *Max Counts His Chickens* (Wells, 2007), the Easter Bunny has hidden 10 hot-pink marshmallow chicks all over Grandma's house. Big sister Ruby finds most of them. Grandma quickly calls the Easter Bunny, and soon yellow marshmallow chicks come popping through the mail slot in the door. Your children will have to count them. Little Max says: "One, three, ten, two, six, four, seven, eight, nine, five!" Can your children correct his one-to-one correspondence?

■ Use a Computer Program

Computers in preschool programs are sometimes seen as controversial. But for teachers who know how to use them, how to select appropriate software, how to help children learn to use them on their own, and how to integrate the software into the curriculum, computers can be powerful learning tools for young children. The strength of the computer is its ability to bridge concrete and abstract thinking and learning. Children seem to learn in the same way computers teach: by trial-and-error.

The key to successful computer use with preschool children is in the software you select. In this instance, you will be looking for CD-ROM programs that feature activities to help children strengthen cognitive skills such as sorting, classifying,

Figure 7.6   Criteria for Children's Computer Programs

- Tried out by teacher ahead of time
- Attractive to young children
- Based on children's book being used
- Easily used and understood by children
- Teaching appropriate skills
- Tied in to learning center activities

sequencing, and patterning, as well as programs that feature counting, numbers, and one-to-one correspondence.

Because computer programs are more abstract than the concrete materials in the classroom, it is important for you to try them out ahead of time to determine how they can lead to concrete activities in the learning centers. Choosing programs based on one of your picture books is one way of tying them into your classroom activities (Beaty, 2012). As you look for appropriate programs, keep the criteria in Figure 7.6 in mind.

You can introduce a new program to two children at a time who are seated at the computer. Others can watch and take their turns later. Cooperative learning like this is the best way for them to make use of the computer. They learn to take turns, to talk together, and to teach each other how the program works.

You will already have installed the program they are to use on the hard drive. Children will then be able to access the program themselves. Use only one program at a time until all the children are thoroughly familiar with it. Most software contains multiple games and activities at increasing levels of difficulty, so you will need to know which game is the one your children should start with. What your children need to know about operating a computer is shown in Figure 7.7.

Repetition is the key element here. Turn off the program and let them start it up over and over. With two children at the computer, one can remind the other of the next step. After the children have demonstrated their ability to access the program, you can put out extension activities involving blocks, books, and manipulative materials. Here are some computer CD-ROMs appropriate for cognitive learning:

Adventure Workshop: Preschool—1st Grade: Dr. Seuss (The Learning Company)

Figure 7.7   What Children Need to Know About Operating a Computer

- How to turn on the computer
- How to wait until the main menu appears
- How to double-click the mouse on the proper icon
- How to wait until the program menu appears
- How to click on the activity they want to pursue

By choosing the math section, the Cat-in-the-Hat invites the children to proceed. Horton the elephant then leads them into a problem-solving situation to find Sweet Alma Sue's mother. To start the adventure, an outdoor scene appears as a nonverbal picture menu with four activities embedded in it: *Fox in Socks Sorting, Yertle's Counting Turtles, Fish Follies,* and *Sneezlebee's 1,2,3s.* Children need to run their mouse around on the scene to find these games. When the right area lights up, they should click on it and wait for the activity to appear.

In *Fox in Socks Sorting,* children are directed by voice to help Fox sort out his two different-color socks hanging on a clothes line into two different-color boxes. They must click on each sock of the right color and drag it down to the box of that color. Two higher levels of this game are included. In *Yertle's Counting Turtles,* the scene is a pond with turtles in it. Yertle asks children to choose turtles with a particular number on them and to stack them on top of one another for Yertle to climb on. *Fish Follies* has an octopus asking children to choose one of six colors and color in the white fish displaying a circle, a triangle, or a square.

Some of these may seem rather sophisticated games for 3s and 4s, but as soon as they catch on, they will be completing the activities with glee. You may want to go through each game at first with the children, always asking them what to do when each direction is given orally. Don't show them. Let them try it. Or simply let them figure out how the games work by trial-and-error.

Be sure to acquire the Seuss books *Fox in Socks, Yertle the Turtle,* and *One Fish Two Fish Red Fish Blue Fish* for reading to the children before they play the computer games. Then make up your own sorting and coloring games. Bring in colored socks and shoe boxes. Have children draw fish with two simple curved lines, color them in, and cut them out. They can be used in a sorting, numbering game you invent. Children can make turtles out of colored play dough to predict and count how many turtles they can stack up before they all fall over.

Dr. Seuss character dolls can be found in children's book sections of book stores. The computer programs can be purchased in computer stores and office supply stores, or ordered online. See Figure 7.8 for other computer programs appropriate for preschool children.

Figure 7.8   Computer Math Programs

Blue's 123 Time Activities (The Learning Co.)
Counting game; weighing game;
shape and number game; cash register
Disney's Mickey Mouse Preschool
Opposites; cause and effect
Disney's Winnie the Pooh Preschool
Classification; discrimination
Millie & Bailey Preschool (Edmark)
Matching shoes; cash register; numbers game;
build a mouse house; Cookie Factory

✓ PROBLEM-SOLVES WITH CONCRETE OBJECTS

Problem solving involves young children in using higher levels of thinking. They must use creative thinking in which they create new ideas or use materials in new ways. They also use critical thinking to mentally break down a problem into its parts, in other words, to do reasoning.

Types of Reasoning

Several types of reasoning are often employed by young children in their problem-solving efforts. *Intuitive reasoning* is based on appearances of things. They may think one object is bigger than another because it looks that way: for example, the tall thin glass holds more water than the short wide glass. With more information available through measuring, they may find that both glasses hold the same amount. When youngsters do intuitive reasoning like this, you need to ask them "why" they think something is so and "how" they can tell.

Inductive reasoning is based on perceptions of regularity. Children use it when they are looking for a pattern or for something several things may have in common. Their conclusions may be accurate when applied to specific examples, but may not fit all situations. *Deductive reasoning,* on the other hand, is based on conclusions drawn from information gathered over a period of time.

As children do reasoning, they will be using many of the concepts they have developed previously, especially classification and numbers. The best way for pre-school children to apply their newly acquired cognitive concepts is through problem solving with concrete materials. They will be manipulating materials in a trial-and-error exploration of what works and what doesn't work.

Teachers can start with a small group of children at a time in a particular class-room learning center, posing a simple problem. For example, in the block center the teacher might ask: How can you build a road wide enough for two little toy cars to travel side by side? Some children may solve the problem by building a road with two parallel lanes. Others may make one wide lane. If it works for both little cars, then it is a good solution.

Another time, the teacher may put down a wide piece of blue construction paper to represent a river and ask the builders what they can build so their cars can get across the river without getting wet. This more complex problem calls for bridg-ing the river by placing a block on either side for a support and then finding blocks or a board long enough to span the river between the two supports. You may want to talk with them about how they will go about finding a solution. Listen to what they have to say and jot it down. They will need to break down the problem into parts: finding a block or blocks long enough to span the river and finding a way to raise the blocks above the river.

No fair laying the blocks lengthwise in the river, as some builders will say. Ask them what would happen in a real river if they did this. Do they know how the water in a real river flows? Finding a block or board long enough to reach the supports is one solution. Often children have trouble finding the right length block and continue trying out blocks that are too short to reach the supports. The concept of length is still a bit fuzzy for many. Can they find another way besides guessing? Trial and error is one way. Someone else may suggest measuring it. Yes. Then they will need to apply this measurement to the blocks on the shelf until they find the right length. Take photos of their various trials.

Measuring Devices

If some of the children are unfamiliar with using measuring devices such as a ruler, here is another problem for them to solve. What can they use to measure the space? Does anyone hold her hands apart to show the size of the space between the block supports? Will she be able to keep her hands spread the right distance apart by the time she gets over to the block shelves? Someone else may suggest stretching a strip of paper or length of string from one support to the other. Yes, that would work. Take another photo.

What if none of the blocks on the shelf is long enough? Someone may suggest moving the supports into the river and closer together until they find a block long enough to reach them. Yes, that is another possibility. Let them try it and see. Another child's idea may be to put a third support in the middle of the river to hold a bridging block on either side of it to reach the supports on the river bank. That, too, will work. Then there is the creative child who solves the problem of crossing the river by having a toy helicopter air-lift the cars . . . or the child who floats the cars over on a boat. Let each small group experiment to discover its own solution. Then take a photo of each trial.

Another Block Problem

Another interesting block problem involves running toy cars down a block ramp and seeing how far each one can travel. Can anyone make the cars travel farther without giving them a shove? Through trial and error someone will discover that raising the ramp at one end increases the speed of the cars, which in turn makes them travel a longer distance. Someone else may discover that the size of the cars also matters. Do bigger, heavier cars go farther than little, lighter cars? Have them try it and see. You can jot down all their solutions to these problems on newsprint, even the ones that don't work, to be talked about afterward. Also take photos here of the various methods tried. Have children dictate to you what each photo represents. How many budding engineers have you discovered?

Keep your eyes peeled for problems with concrete materials that children may run into on their own both inside and outside the classroom in their normal day of work and play. What about the girl who tries to force her doll buggy through the concrete tunnel on the playground that is obviously (to you) too small? Or the boys who are having trouble moving a truck tire from one side of

Figure 7.9 Scientific Problem Solving

1. What is the problem?
2. What will you do to solve it?
3. What do you think will happen?
4. What really happens?
5. What is your conclusion?

the playground to the other by dragging it? It is not up to you to suggest a better solution, but to observe and record how the children themselves solve these problems, and then talk about how they did it afterward. The questions you will want to find answers to can be outlined as a "scientific method for problem solving" (see Figure 7.9).

How can this girl make the scale balance?

If You Have Not Checked This Item: Some Helpful Ideas

■ Play Simple Guessing Games in Small Groups

Bring in a balance scale with an empty bowl at each end of the scale and a container full of plastic blocks. The problem is to put the right number of the plastic blocks in each empty bowl of the scale until it balances. Not as easy as it looks because the blocks are of different sizes. Putting one block in each bowl will only make it balance if the blocks are the same size. Some of the deeper thinkers may conceptualize how to do it, but they will probably only be successful by trial-and-error. Have children guess about how to do it before they actually try it. Give everyone a chance.

■ Play Simple Problem-Solving Games in Small Groups

Put out a number of hair curlers of different sizes and a purse. Can anyone find a way to carry all the curlers in this one purse? (Make sure the only way all of the curlers will fit inside

Figure 7.10   Guessing
Books

Magic Thinks Big (Cooper, 2004)
If You Give a Cat a Cupcake (Numeroff, 2008)
If I Had a Dragon (Ellery & Ellery,, 2006)
If Mom Had Three Arms (Orloff, 2006)

this purse is if the children put the little curlers inside the big ones.) Does anyone solve this problem? Have them talk about it first.

■ Read a Book

In **Magic Thinks Big** (Cooper, 2004), a very large cat sits in front of an open door in his home. Should he go in or go out or stay where he is? In his mind he uses intuitive reasoning to make conjectures about what will happen in each case. Have children guess, then turn the page to find out what Magic does. Record their guesses and why they made them.

If You Give a Cat a Cupcake (Numeroff, 2008) is another favorite book in the author's series about what will happen "If You Give . . ." an animal something. In this case, if you give a cat a cupcake he'll want . . . Have your children guess what will happen next. Write it down. Children will need to use their classification skills (e.g., What goes with cupcakes? Sprinkles. What happens with sprinkles? He spills some.) Here is more practice in intuitive reasoning.

In the book **If I Had a Dragon** (Ellery & Ellery, 2006), Morton tells the story about his little brother who is no fun to play with, but if he'd only turn into a dragon, then maybe they could: Go for walks? Play basketball? Go for a swim? Play hide and seek? Go to a movie? Whistle? Ask your listeners what they think will happen after each of Morton's conjectures, before you turn the page to see what really happens. Again, record it.

If Mom Had Three Arms (Orloff, 2006) is a little boy's imagination turned loose in a "what-if" counting story. The boy imagines in rhyme what his mother would do with 3 through 20 arms on every other page in this book. Afterward have your listeners make up a new story about what their own mother might do with extra arms. Be sure to record it. (See Figure 7.10.)

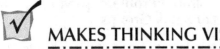

MAKES THINKING VISIBLE

Is there any way to *see* what children are thinking? We can always ask them to explain what they think about something. But this doesn't really help us to understand their thought process. If we could somehow see their thoughts, then we would know if they were on the right track. We would know what they need to do next, and what we need to do next. That's the main problem with thinking. It is invisible.

Salmon (2010) has come up with a good solution to this problem. She suggests that children document their ideas as they think through issues, problems, or topics. She believes that one of the best ways to document their thinking is by using different media. She suggests using video and transcribed conversations accompanied by photographs and children's work. When children speak, write, draw, build, or dramatize their ideas, they are making their thinking visible, according to Salmon. True, we say, but only if their artifacts are accompanied by their actual words.

If children are made aware of their own thinking, it can certainly be a boon to their cognitive development. They and their teachers can then see what they understand and what they don't understand. They could be encouraged to think further about the problem confronting them and about how to solve it. If this thinking were made visible to them and their teacher, it would help them to know what the next step should be. It would also give the teacher another observation clue as to their cognitive development.

Document Panels

Some children mount their "visible thinking" (photo captions) on a document panel for all to see. Such panels are often made by teachers as an observation tool to illustrate and inform others of the outcome of a project or of the learning taking place. They usually contain photographs, children's artwork, dictations, and transcriptions of teachers' observations.

A true panel of "visible thinking" would be somewhat different. It would contain only the children's words. It would document their thinking with photos, artifacts, and dictations by the children to go with every piece of evidence. Teachers would take a series of photos of children pursuing an activity and afterwards record what each child has to say about the photos while they are still on the camera. Teachers would ask a series of questions about each photo:

- What's happening in this photo?
- Why is it happening?
- Who thought of doing this?
- What is your idea about it?

After the photos are printed, the children's transcribed answers can accompany each one. These can then be mounted on a document panel. Children can examine the documentation, listen to the captions read aloud, and make new comments or additions. A series of printed photos like this with a child-dictated caption under each could then serve as documentation for the visible thinking that went on.

Dramatic Play Documentation

Observant teachers have long noted that in dramatic play children think aloud on their feet. They take on pretend roles and act them out as they see fit. Much of the drama in dramatic play is, in fact, in the dialog. What children have to say to one another reveals how they think about the situation. Isbell and Raines (2007) tell us how in dramatic play children develop the ability to think on their feet.

Without realizing it we have the perfect opportunity to see and hear visible thinking in action. All we need to do is to observe and record these pretend scenarios. Use a hand-held recorder, smartphone, or camera to record the actions and dialog involved. Take many photos of the action to be printed, along with transcribed dialog to accompany each photo. Figure 7.11 is the running record of a brief scenario. Two girls, Shana and Nina, are getting ready to go to a pretend birthday party. They are arguing over what presents to take.

The dialog in this scenario shows Shana's visible thinking about birthday presents. Also that she is a quick thinker on her feet. When she can't answer the question about why girlfriends don't give flowers, she quickly substitutes another idea ("They give jewelry") and even offers a creative response to Nina's refusal. To document the visible thinking the teacher takes several photos of the two girls and their argument. She prints them and asks Shana to dictate a caption about what is happening in the photos. The photos and her replies are placed in Shana's portfolio for evidence of her cognitive development.

"This is me telling Nina not to take her flower to Rose's birthday. Girls don't give flowers."

Figure 7.11   Dramatic
Play Documentation

Shana: What is that flower for?

Nina: It is Rose's birthday present.

Shana: A flower can't be a present.

Nina: My sister got flowers for her birthday.

Shana: But they were from her boyfriend.

Nina: Well, this flower is from Rose's girlfriend.

Shana: It's not the same.

Nina: Why not?

Shana: Girlfriends don't give flowers.

Nina: Why not?

Shana: They give jewelry. You could give her that necklace.

Nina: It's mine!

Shana: When you take it off it won't be yours.

Nina gets up and leaves.

OBSERVING, RECORDING, AND INTERPRETING COGNITIVE DEVELOPMENT

Using a Checklist

Sheila, the girl who was observed on the Child Development Checklist and found to have all items marked on this section of the checklist, is shown in Figure 7.12. When the classroom staff reviewed Sheila's entire checklist, they were not surprised to see her results in cognitive development. Sheila had already seemed to them to be a bright child with exceptional language and art skills, but she seemed to have difficulty gaining access to group play. She preferred to play by herself, although often parallel to others. In fact, one of the staff members predicted that every one of the items for Sheila under Cognitive Development would be checked (see Figure 7.12).

CHILD DEVELOPMENT CHECKLIST

Name _____Sheila_____   Observer _____Connie_____

Item	Evidence	Dates
8. Cognitive Development		
__X__ Sorts objects by shape, color, size	Knows colors, draws circles, squares, knows size	10/23
__X__ Places objects in a sequence or series	Lines up dolls from littlest to biggest	10/23
__X__ Recognizes, creates patterns	Draws color patterns, rainbows	10/23
__X__ Counts by rote to 20	counts to 20 & beyond	10/23
__X__ Displays 1-to-1 correspondence	counts children in class with accuracy	10/23
__X__ Problem-solves with concrete objects	when no hats were available, made paper hat	10/23

Figure 7.12   Cognitive Observation for Sheila

It is important for staff members to look at the total picture when they observe and record a child's development and to confer with the others about the results. Not every child will accomplish every item in a section, although a girl like Sheila actually does it.

LEARNING ACTIVITIES

1. Use the Child Development Checklist's Cognitive Development section as a screening tool to observe all the children in your classroom. For which of your children did you check most of the items? How did these children do on other areas of the checklist, for example, in small-motor development? Record the results.

2. Fill a sorting table with collections of various items. Have a small group of children sort and classify the items any way they want. Ask each how they sorted their items and why. See if they could sort them any different way. Record the results.

3. Read a pattern book; have a pattern search in the classroom; then put out painting supplies or colored table blocks to see if children can make their own patterns. Does their work show visible thinking? Ask them about it. Record the results.

4. Have a child who needs counting practice play with the balance scale and count how many table blocks she uses on each side to make it balance. If the numbers are different in each of the balance containers, can she tell why? Record the results.

5. Have one of the children set the table for lunch. Then get out a container of napkins, ask the child to get out the number of napkins he will need, and place one at each place. Can he do it accurately? Record the results.

6. Do a problem-solving project with the children using the five scientific problem-solving steps in Figure 7.9. Record how each of the steps was followed and what the conclusion was.

7. Make a document panel of the problem-solving project the class completed. Use captioned photos, drawings, or children's work to illustrate each of the five steps.

SUGGESTED READINGS

Blake, S. (2009). Engage, investigate, and report: Enhancing the curriculum with scientific inquiry. *Young Children, 64*(6), 49–53.

Galinsky, E. (2010). *Mind in the making.* Washington, DC: NAEYC.

Jung, M., Kloosterman, P., & McMullen, M. B. (2007). Young children's intuition for solving problems in mathematics. *Young Children, 62*(5), 50–57.

Komara, C., & Herron, J. (2012). Implementing formative mathematics assessments in prekindergarten. *Childhood Education, 88*(3), 162–168.

Pawlina, S., & Stanford, C. (2011). Preschoolers grow their brains: Shifting mindsets for greater resiliency and better problem solving. *Young Children, 66*(5), 30–35.

Ritchhart, R., & Perkins, D. (2008). Making thinking visible. *Educational Leadership, 65*(5), 57–61.

Salmon, A. (2010). Engaging children in thinking routines. *Childhood Education, 86*(3), 132–137.

Stoll, J., Hamilton, A., Oxley, A. M., & Brent, R. (2012). Young thinkers in motion: Problem solving and physics in preschool. *Young Children, 67*(2), 20–26.

CHILDREN'S BOOKS

Alborough, J. (2006). *Hit the ball, Duck.* La Jolla, CA: Kane/Miller.

Angelou, M. (1994). *My painted house, my friendly chicken, and me.* New York: Crown.*

Aston, E. H. (2008). *The moon over star.* New York: Dial.*

Chocolate, D. (1996). *Kente colors.* New York: Walker.*

Cooper, E. (2004). *Magic thinks big.* New York: Greenwillow.

Cronin, D. (2006). *Click, clack, splish, splash.* New York: Atheneum.

Dillon, L., & Dillon, D. (2007). *Mother Goose: Numbers on the loose.* Orlando, FL: Harcourt.

DiPucchio, K. (2012). *Crafty Chloe.* New York: Atheneum.

Ellery, T., & Ellery, A. (2006). *If I had a dragon.* New York: Simon & Schuster.

Guback, G. (1994). *Luka's quilt.* New York: Greenwillow.*

Joosse, B. M. (2008). *Grandma calls me beautiful.* San Francisco, CA: Chronicle.*

Joosse, B. M. (2005). *Papa, do you love me?* San Francisco, CA: Chronicle.*

Joosse, B. M. (1991). *Mama, do you love me?* San Francisco, CA: Chronicle.*

Kimmel, E. A. (2009). *The three little tamales.* Tarrytown, NY: Marshall Cavendish.*

Krebs, L. (2003). *We all went on safari.* Cambridge, MA: Barefoot Books.*

Kroll, V. (1995). *Hats off to hair!* Cambridge, MA: Charlesbridge.*

Litwin, E., (2012). *Pete the Cat and his four groovy buttons.* New York: Harper.

Martin, B. (2011). *Ten little caterpillars.* New York: Beach Lane Books.

McKissack, P. C. (2008). *Stitchin' and pullin'.* New York: Random House.*

Milbourne, A. (2006). *On the moon.* London, England: Usborne.

Numeroff, L. (2008). *If you give a cat a cupcake.* New York: HarperCollins.

Stickland, P. (2009). *Ten terrible dinosaurs.* New York: Penguin.

Olson, K. C. (2004). *Construction countdown.* New York: Henry Holt.

Orloff, K. (2006). *If Mom had three arms.* New York: Sterling Publishing.

Ulmer, W. (2010). *Zero, zilch, nada: Counting to none.* Ann Arbor, MI: Sleeping Bear Press.

Wells, R. (2007). *Max counts his chickens.* New York: Viking.

---

* Multicultural

WEB SITES

AAA Math
www.aaamath.com

Fun Brain
www.funbrain.com

Mind in the Making
www.mindinthemaking.org

National Council of Teachers of Mathematics
www.nctm.org

Odyssey of the Mind (problem solving)
www.odysseyofthemind.com

Project Construct (hands-on problem solving)
www.projectconstruct.org

Project Zero (visual thinking)
www.pz.harvard.edu

Spoken Language

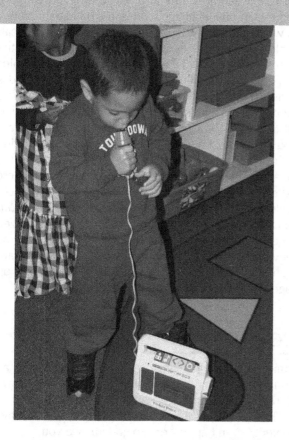

In this chapter you will learn to observe if children can:

_____ Listen but not speak

_____ Give single-word, short phrase responses

_____ Take part in conversations

_____ Speak in expanded sentences

_____ Ask questions

_____ Tell a story

_____ Be observed by using recordings and checklists

 **DEVELOPING SPOKEN LANGUAGE**

Spoken language is one of the important skills that make us human beings. We assume, without much thought, that our children will learn to speak the native tongue before they enter public school.

Language acquisition cannot be all that difficult, we decide, otherwise how could a little child do it? After all, the child does not have to be taught; language acquisition just seems to happen. It is nothing to get excited about, we think, unless it does not happen on schedule.

As a matter of fact, the acquisition of a native language is one of the greatest developmental accomplishments and mysteries we may ever encounter involving the young child. It is a great accomplishment because the child starts from scratch with no spoken language at birth and acquires an entire native tongue by age 6; sometimes the child acquires more than one language if he is in a bilingual family.

We may not show concern while all goes well, but we should learn all we can about the kinds of things that help or hinder the acquisition process to smooth the way. The years from age 3 to 5 are especially crucial in this process. Three-year-olds may acquire 900 to 1,000 words, but by age 4 their language development explodes to about 4,000 to 6,000 words, as they teach themselves the rules for putting words together to speak in complex sentences. At age 5 their vocabularies may expand to 5,000 to 8,000 words (Seefeldt & Wasik, 2006). During these years, children are often in an early childhood program; thus, the language environment you provide can have a significant effect on their progress.

Kalmar (2008) wants it to be a talk-rich environment—an accepting place where teachers encourage young children to talk, and they model the use of stress, pitch, and dialect to help children develop and refine their language skills. To support your children's language development, you should know at the outset how accomplished they already are as speakers. A good way to start is to use an observation screening device such as the six Child Development Checklist items under the Spoken Language section to assess all your children at the beginning of the year. Then follow up with written or recorded language samples of each child's speech.

STAGES OF LANGUAGE ACQUISITION

Language acquisition begins at birth. A child's first language is crying and cooing, an infant's first communication sounds. Mothers, fathers, and caregivers soon learn what such sounds mean and can respond properly. Crying in its many forms may mean "I'm hungry," "I'm wet," "I'm sleepy," "I'm uncomfortable," or "Don't leave me." Cooing may mean "I'm content," "I'm happy," or "So good to see you."

Adults' responses to these first communication sounds are important because infants see that their vocalizations have had an effect on those around them. They will then make the same sound when they want that same effect. Adults should talk to youngsters each time they respond to their sounds. "I hear you crying, Lori, and it sounds to me like you're hungry." As adults use the same words over and over, infants continue their own similar communication sounds. By the time they are toddlers, youngsters will be saying "hungie" when they want something to eat, because they have heard that word used by adults in association with feeding.

Infants and toddlers continue their sound-making because it is fun for them. Certain sounds give them great pleasure, especially when adults respond with a similar sound of their own. This playing around with sounds is the *manipulation* stage of exploratory learning. Children apply the same "3 Ms" in learning to speak as they do in learning to play with blocks, paint, use the computer, and in every new learning situation they experience. Just as they did with cognitive concepts, they are constructing their own language.

Next comes a "one-word" stage, where toddlers use only one word to express several things. Often the first word is "mama," and the youngster will use it to mean: "Where are you, Mama?" or "Mama, pick me up," or "Mama, I'm glad to see you!" or "Don't leave me, Mama!" The happy or anxious sound of the word conveys as much meaning as the word itself.

As toddlers acquire more names of objects and action words, they say these single words over and over, not necessarily because they are demanding something, but because they are in the *mastery stage* of language acquisition. Repetition is the name of the game. Next, they begin putting words together into short phrases that stand for sentences: "Mommy, hungie." ("Mommy, I'm hungry.) "Go car." ("I want to go in the car.") "All done now." ("I'm all finished eating.") They often put their own meaning into such phrases: "Jeremy TV," which the adult has to figure out. ("Jeremy turned on the TV when he wasn't supposed to!") This compressed form of speech is often called "telegraphic speech" because only important words are used, as in a telegram.

All children everywhere acquire the language they hear spoken in their homes in this manner during their early childhood years. If they hear a second language spoken consistently in the home, they will acquire this language, as well.

An explosion occurs in a child's speaking vocabulary around the end of the second year or the beginning of the third year; 30 to 50 new words a month may be added if the child hears talking around her. (Even the TV counts.) By age 3, she may know almost 500 words (McDevitt & Ormrod, 2004). The early stages of language acquisition are listed in Figure 8.1 as Jackman (2012) describes them.

Stages of Preschool Language Production

By the time children enter preschool around the age of 3, most have progressed beyond telegraphic speech to expanded sentences. However, you may not discover exactly where each youngster stands at the outset because another set of circumstances has come into play. When young children who are still at the beginning stages of language learning leave the comfortable home environment where they are

Figure 8.1 Stages of Early Language Acquisition

Crying
Cooing
Babbling
One-word usage
Telegraphic speech
Multiword speech

Figure 8.2   Stages of Preschool Language Production

Source: Based on Ramsey, P. G., *Teaching and Learning in a Diverse World,* pp. 157–158, Teachers College Press, 1987.

Preproduction

When children first enter a strange, new language environment they often respond by being silent. Children who are learning English as a second language often concentrate on what is being said rather than trying to say anything.

Transition to production

When children have become more comfortable, they often begin speaking single-word answers to questions.

Early production

Children may respond to questions and activities in short phrases. They may be able to engage in simple conversations and even do chants and singing.

Expansion of production

Children may speak in expanded sentences, ask questions, tell stories, do role playing, and carry on extensive conversations.

used to the people around them and come into the strange, new environment of the preschool, they may stop speaking altogether at first.

Preschool teachers and assistants must understand that young speakers, no matter what their language and how fluent they are at home, may progress through several stages of language production before they become fluent speakers in the classroom. Although these stages are often applied to second-language acquisition, they can be used by teachers to help all children aged 3 to 5 adjust to the new situation and progress in their language development (see Figure 8.2).

Some children are fluent speakers from the start and have no need to progress through these stages. Others are fluent at home but silent at preschool until they become acclimated to the new situation. How long this takes depends on each child's development. Non-English-speaking children (known as *dual language learners*) may take longer to progress through the stages as they acquire a new language.

LISTENS BUT DOES NOT SPEAK

Preproduction Stage

For many English-speaking children, this first checklist item refers more to the child's emotional adjustment to the classroom than to his or her speaking abilities. As previously noted, a child must feel at ease in the strangeness of the classroom environment to speak at all. The so-called nonverbal child is frequently one who lacks confidence to speak outside the confines of the home. The child may have a shy nature or may come from a family that uses little verbal communication; or the child

New children may need to adjust to the preschool before speaking.

may have a physical disability, such as a hearing impairment, that has interfered with language development.

Spend time assessing a nonverbal child using the entire Child Development Checklist. The areas of self-esteem, emotional development, and social play are especially important. Does the child have trouble separating from his parents when he comes to the center? Can he do things for himself with any confidence? Does he seem happy? Does he play by himself or with others?

Set up a meeting with his parents and discuss the checklist results with them. If the results point toward some type of impairment, the parents will want to have the child tested further by a specialist. If the parents indicate that the child talks fluently at home, then the nonverbal child may be demonstrating his feelings of insecurity in a strange new environment rather than a language or hearing problem. Figure 8.3 lists checklist items under the stages of language production.

Figure 8.3 Checklist Items of Preschool Language Production

Preproduction
_____Listens but does not speak
Transition to production
_____Gives single-word answers
Early production
_____Gives short-phrase responses
_____Takes part in conversations
Expansion of production
_____Speaks in expanded sentences
_____Asks questions
_____Tells a story

Your principal task with the shy or uncommunicative child will be to help her feel comfortable in the classroom. Using pressure to get her to talk before she is at ease may well produce the opposite results. You and your coworkers will need to take special pains to accept the child as she is and to try to make her welcome in the classroom. You can invite her to join appropriate activities, but if she refuses, you need to honor her reluctance. It often takes a great deal of patience and forbearance on the part of an early childhood classroom staff to allow the shy child to become at ease in her own good time.

If the nonverbal child seems to feel comfortable with one other child, you may be able to have that child involve her with the others. On the other hand, sometimes the only solution is to leave the nonverbal child alone. If your environment is a warm and happy one, she eventually should want to participate.

Dual Language Learners

A similar approach may help dual language learners. By pairing two children together, one English-speaking and one Spanish-speaking, for example, the partners can facilitate each other's learning. Alanis (2011) tells us that in order for children to develop their native language and to acquire a second language, they need to hear language in rich meaningful contexts that help them connect what they are learning with their experiences.

They need opportunities to hear and practice their language production in both languages. Being paired with child who is strong in English can help a partner who speaks Spanish. The partners can serve as language models and supports for one another in the classroom.

For children learning English as a second language, it was once believed that their parents should learn English and use it with them at home, rather than their native language. That is no longer true. Research has shown that the bilingual children who do best in school are those who have had a strong grounding in their home language (Tabors, 2008). In fact, young children are capable of learning more than one language at once.

Today we are coming to recognize the value of home languages that are different from English and are finally beginning to promote rather than discourage their use by children and their parents. The National Association for the Education of Young Children (2005) position statement that responds to linguistic and cultural differences in early childhood education includes some of the following recommendations:

- Recognize that all children are cognitively, linguistically and emotionally connected to the language and culture of their home.
- Acknowledge that children can demonstrate their knowledge and capabilities in many ways.
- Understand that without comprehensible input, second-language learning can be difficult.
- Actively involve parents and families in the early learning program and setting.

Figure 8.4 Helping
Dual Language
Speakers

- Pair child with strong English speaker
- Provide many opportunities to hear and speak English
- Support child's speaking
- Do not correct child's speaking
- Support child's home language

- Recognize that children can and will acquire the use of English even when their home language is used and respected.
- Support and preserve home language usage. (pp. 4–12)

If Spanish is the first or second language for many of the children in your program, be sure to provide opportunities for all the children to be exposed to the language in a natural manner. Have a Spanish hour when nothing but Spanish is spoken. Read books and sing songs in Spanish. Do number games and dramatic play in Spanish. Children love to hear and say new words. Have their favorite chants and songs translated into Spanish. If you do not speak Spanish, invite a speaker from a nearby high school, college, or the children's families. Strategies to help dual language speakers learn English are listed in Figure 8.4.

But what if your program includes numbers of children who speak many different languages? Inner-city early childhood programs are becoming more language-diverse than ever these days. How can you accommodate such diversity? Ramsey (1987) described a program attended by children of foreign students representing 15 different languages. The program rose to the occasion by requesting the parents to help them make a book with simple sentences in all 15 languages that the teachers often needed, such as "Your mother will be here soon" or "Do you need to go to the bathroom?" The parents and their children then enjoyed coaching the teachers. This activity also gave the foreign families, who were daily experiencing their lack of expertise in English, the opportunity to be the experts.

Provide a Stress-Free Environment

The environment must be stress free. For many children, speaking among a group of peers is a new and untried experience. To help them feel at ease about speaking, you need to help them feel at ease about themselves by accepting them as they are. Show you accept them with smiles, hugs, and words of welcome and encouragement. Show you are happy to see them every day and want them to participate. Take time when they leave to say you were happy to have them in the class and look forward to seeing them tomorrow.

Ongoing brain research places great emphasis on the importance of caring adults in an emotionally supportive environment during the early childhood years. In addition, as a language facilitator, you need to accept everyone's language, no matter how poorly pronounced or how ungrammatical it is, and whether it is English, a dialect of English, or another language altogether. Language is a very personal thing. It reflects not only the different children's stages of development, but also their families' language.

You must be especially careful not to correct a child's language. Telling him he is saying a word wrong or using the wrong word is a personal put-down for himself and his family. He will learn the correct form himself when the time is right by hearing you say the word and by practicing it with his peers. Nonverbal children watch closely and listen carefully to how you deal with other speakers in the classroom.

You and your coworkers can serve as good language models for everyone, helping and supporting them in classroom activities, but taking care not to correct their speech. Modern linguists now realize that it is pointless for adults to try to correct a preschooler's speech by making him repeat words according to an adult standard that he is not ready to use. Correcting, in fact, is a negative response that tends to reinforce the unwanted behavior and make the child think there is something wrong with him personally. Instead of improving a child's language, correcting often makes the child avoid speaking at all in the presence of the corrector.

Occasionally a young child who has been pronouncing words normally will slip back into baby talk or stop talking altogether. She may also display other behaviors such as thumb sucking and wetting. Because this tends to be an indication of stress or an emotional upset, you will want to talk with the parents about the pressures in her life that may be affecting her adversely, causing the temporary language regression. Is there a new baby in the family? A new father or mother? A death or a divorce? Someone in the hospital? Someone out of work? A move? Young children feel these emotional upheavals in their families as severely as adults. Sometimes the first indication of such stress for a child is her slipping back to earlier speech patterns.

But because they are in a group of other child speakers, most young children will quickly revert to the speech patterns and word pronunciations they hear around them once the stress is relieved. Their brains are programmed to do such copying at this stage of their lives. Even non-English-speaking children will soon join the mainstream of language with continued exposure to mainstream speakers. The common mispronunciations of preschoolers should be overlooked rather than corrected. As soon as the development of their vocal apparatus allows them to, they will be pronouncing English words just like everyone else.

You can keep your classroom as free as possible from stressful situations for the young child if you are sensitive to her needs. She should not be put on the spot and forced to perform verbally, creatively, or in any other way. Offer her opportunities and encouragement, but do not force the shy, unsure, or bilingual child to speak.

Listening to the Teacher Speak

Listening is also an important function for all the children in the classroom. Jalongo (2008) defined it as: "Listening is the process of taking in information through the sense of hearing and making meaning from what was heard" (p. 12). Kalmar (2008) explains that from frequent interactions with their teacher, children begin to notice and understand complex sentence structure and multiple meanings of some words.

By listening to teachers talk for a variety of purposes, children construct meaning and build conceptual frameworks.

In order to hear what is being said, children need to *attend*, that is, to pay attention to the words. In order to understand what the words are saying, children need to *interpret*, that is, to assign meaning to them. It is up to you, then, to make your words clear, to make them interesting, and to repeat them—on the spot, and again later. *Repetition* in words and in actions is an important key to young children's learning. *Keep it brief, make it clear, and say it often* should be your motto.

If You Have Not Checked This Item: Some Helpful Ideas

■ Use a Prop for Security

Many young children feel more secure when they have something in their hands, especially something soft and cuddly with the quality of a security blanket. You might want to keep several stuffed animals for children to choose from and hold when feeling out of sorts, or when first coming to the classroom and not yet feeling comfortable. Your "nonverbal child" may even end up talking to her animal. It may be the beginning of her verbal integration into the classroom.

■ Use a Puppet

Almost every child likes the idea of putting a puppet on his hand. Have a box or hat-tree of various kinds of puppets and let the nonverbal child choose a different one every day if he wants. Preschool children tend to play with puppets as if the puppets were a part of themselves rather than a separate toy like a doll. Because puppets

Shy children may sometimes talk through a puppet.

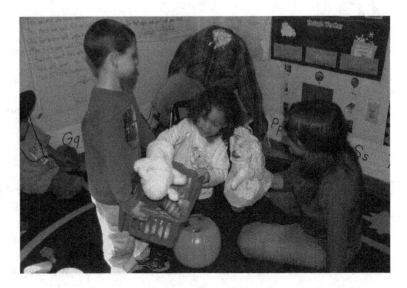

Figure 8.5 Books to
Promote Speaking Aloud

> *Say What?* (DiTerlizzi, 2011)
> *Oliver Has Something to Say!* (Edwards, 2007)
> *Pass It On!* (Sadler, 2012)
> *I Know a Librarian Who Chewed on a Word* (Knowlton, 2012)
> *SHOUT! Shout It Out!* (Fleming, 2011)
> *Fire! Fire! Said Mrs. McGuire* (Martin, 2006)

have mouths, children often first experiment by trying to bite someone with the puppet—in fun, of course. Later the youngsters get the idea of having the puppet speak with their mouth, perhaps in a whisper or in a different tone from their own voice. Shy children are often more willing to have a puppet speak for them than they are to speak for themselves. You might find yourself able to talk with a shy child's puppet through a puppet you put on your own hand.

■ Read a Book

Oliver Has Something to Say! (Edwards, 2007) is the story of Oliver, who doesn't talk because everybody in his family talks for him. When he enters preschool and the teacher asks him what he wants to play with, nobody is there to answer for him, so he finally speaks up—and keeps on speaking up at school, at home, and everywhere. Have children guess out loud what word the librarian chewed on in *I Know a Librarian Who Chewed on a Word* (Knowlton, 2012). Other books to promote speaking aloud are listed in Figure 8.5.

✓ GIVES SINGLE-WORD ANSWERS

Transition to Production

As you observe nonverbal children in the class, you may decide when the time is right to go around the class at circle time to find out who will respond to a simple question that can be answered with one word. (Have you ever seen a live cow? Tell me "yes" or "no.") If the nonverbal child does respond, then you can try asking other one-word questions to a small group that includes the nonverbal child or bilingual child.

Playing question-and-answer games with several children may help the nonverbal or bilingual child feel confident enough to try her own skill at answering. "What is Alex wearing on his feet today?" or "What kind of juice are we having for our snack?" These games should be fun and not a test of right or wrong answers. Accept any answers the children give without a fuss. Follow up by repeating what the child said, for instance: "Sneakers. Yes, Alex is wearing sneakers on his feet today."

Play follow-the-leader language games with a few children at a time, including the nonverbal children, having them march around the room behind you and name out loud any item you touch. The nonverbal or bilingual child will hear what the others say and may eventually join in. If children like this game, do it every day, touching more than one item at a time. Children love challenges, so think of other variants of this game you can play with them. How about a "Guess-What-I-Touched" game? Have the children cover their eyes while you go over to a shelf and touch something. Then they must try to guess what it was.

Have a Spanish speaker (or other language speaker) play the same simple games with the children, a small group at a time. Everyone can learn to name the items in Spanish as well as English. Once the nonverbal children join in the answering, you know they will soon be on their way to speaking more fully.

✓ GIVES SHORT-PHRASE RESPONSES

Early Production

As young children become more used to the classroom, they will begin to respond to your questions and comments in short phrases. When second-language speakers pick up enough English from the other children around them they, too, will respond in short phrases and incomplete sentences. When your English speakers learn enough of the second language you have introduced into the classroom, they should be able to repeat short phrases in that language, as well.

Some of the children mentioned earlier may already be fluent in English, but hesitant in speaking in the classroom because they are away from the comfort of their homes. When their comfort level in preschool is high enough, they will join in talking with the others, first with short phrases, then sentences.

Second-language speakers will pick up English quickly if this is the language spoken around them. They learn it not by being drilled with new words, but by hearing the language spoken around them and trying it out as they join the other children in games and activities. They, too, may be hesitant at first in using these new words. You must accept any responses they give to your questions and comments, whether in English, their home language, or in gestures.

They may not pronounce the English words the same as the other children do at first, but they should see by your actions that you accept whatever they say. You can repeat their response to see if you understood them, if this seems appropriate. This gives them yet another chance to hear English responses without being corrected by the teacher. Be sure language is spoken throughout the classroom throughout the day, not in children's shouting or noisy roughhousing, but in busy voices engaged in stimulating activities. You, as a language facilitator, can help children develop their early production of language by using some of the strategies shown in Figure 8.6.

These strategies are natural responses to children's speech that you may already be using. Obviously, you will be listening closely to what a beginning speaker is

Figure 8.6 Strategies to Foster Language Production

> *Expansion:* Repeat what child has said but add words to it
>
> *Extension:* Respond to child's statement but add more information
>
> *Repetition:* Repeat what child says or your response
>
> *Parallel talk:* Describe child's actions aloud as you see them
>
> *Self-talk:* Describe aloud what you are doing
>
> *Vertical structuring:* Ask questions after child speaks to encourage continued talking
>
> *Fill-in:* Take a pause in your speaking so child must fill in words

saying. You may add to it or repeat what was said, validating what the child has told you and encouraging her to continue. If you don't understand the child's speech in the first place, it is better for you to keep listening and try to pick up a word here and there than to keep asking the child: "What did you say?" Repeat the word you heard as an encouragement for the child to continue speaking.

As you serve as a linguistic model for the children, be sure you use simple sentences and speak slowly and clearly enough for children to understand what you are saying. You may also need to vary your tone of voice to emphasize key words. As you get used to the various children's speech and they get used to yours, their early productions should expand naturally. But whatever you do, have fun doing it. Children need to know that your conversations with them are for pleasure, not perfection.

Word Play

Just as they play with blocks, toys, and each other, children also play with words. Youngsters make up nonsense words, repeat word sounds, mix up words, say things backwards, make up chants, and repeat rhyming words. Most people pay little attention to this activity, as it seems so inconsequential. What we have not seemed to realize is that through this playful activity, children are once more at work creating their own knowledge. This time the content is language rather than cognitive concepts, and this time the child is manipulating the medium (words) with his voice. Once again, he is structuring his experiences by finding out what words do and what he can do with them. Play is once more the vehicle because of the pleasure it gives him.

All children play with words, especially in the early stages of language development, but of course there are great individual differences in the amount of language play you will witness among your children. We do know that children who are involved in rhyming activities at an early age carry over this interest in poetry into adult life, and that children who have had early experience with nursery rhymes are more successful later in reading than children who have not. It behooves us, then, to observe children's language play and provide encouragement and support for all youngsters to become more involved with chanting and finger play rhymes. Opitz (2002) found that children appear to hear rhyming words and words that begin the same first. Then they show the ability to hear, blend, and isolate individual sounds in words.

Although mothers often promote language play with their infants by playing word and action games with them such as pattycake and peekaboo, much language play is solitary. Children carry on monologues in which they manipulate sounds, patterns, and meanings of words. These three areas have, in fact, been identified by specialists as common types of word play.

Infants from 6 to 18 months often "talk" to themselves before going to sleep, repeating rhythmic and rhyming sounds. The infants sound almost as if they are really talking, only with nonsense words. With older children, **sound play** contains more meaningful words, consonants, and blends. The children often repeat these words in nonsensical fashion: "Ham, bam, lamb, sam, wham, wham, wham."

Pattern play is a common form of play that involves manipulating the structure of the language. The child begins with a pattern and then substitutes a new word each time he says it: "Bobby go out; Mommy go out; Daddy go out; doggie go out" or "Bite it; write it; light it; sight it; night it; fight it."

Meaning play is not as common among younger children, but it is really more interesting. Here the child interchanges real with nonsensical meanings or makes up words or meanings. An interesting example is children doing water play with floating and sinking objects and telling the objects to "sink-up," meaning "float" or "sink-down."

Piaget (1976) described much of the talk of 3- to 5-year-olds as egocentric. It is as if much of their speaking is not directed to anyone in particular, but rather produced for their own pleasure. Some children go around muttering to themselves most of the day, especially when they are involved in an interesting activity. The muttering seems to disappear by the time they enter kindergarten, but it may become inner speech instead. Vygotsky (1962), on the other hand, believed that egocentric speech was an "ingrowth stage" linking external social speech and internal thought. As egocentric speech turns inward, it becomes a child's most important tool for structuring thought.

Are any of the children in your class engaged in word play? They will be if you sponsor or promote it. Do finger plays and body action chants with the children during circle time or for transitions between activities. Read children books with stories that rhyme. Soon they may be making up their own. Figure 8.7 contains some of these rhyming stories.

Figure 8.7 Books Containing Rhyming Stories

Oliver Who Would Not Sleep! (Bergman, 2007)
Boogie Monster (Bissett, 2011)
Llama Llama Home with Mama (Dewdney, 2011)
Dinosaurs Love Underpants (Freedman, 2010)
Where's My T-R-U-C-K? (Beaumont, 2011)
If All the Animals Came Inside (Pinder, 2012)
Goodnight, Goodnight, Construction Site (Rinker, 2011)
Moose on the Loose (Wargin, 2009)

✓ TAKES PART IN CONVERSATIONS

Early Production

Some children still in the early stage of classroom language production may be able to engage in simple conversations with other children or with you. As soon as they are able to converse with ease, their speaking ability will show even greater improvement from practice with their peers, some of whom may speak at a bit higher level. Children improve in speaking most rapidly when in the presence of speakers whose abilities are a bit higher than their own.

For this reason, it is important to have mixed-age groups in preschool programs. The younger children learn language skills from the older ones. The older children have an excellent opportunity to practice their skills with someone a bit younger. Older children seem to be able to adapt their language level intuitively to less-mature speakers, thus enabling younger children to improve their speech.

Just as the infant is predisposed to acquire his own language in a particular manner, he also seems to bring with him in life a preprogrammed way to extract and learn the rules of conversation naturally. Researchers have noted that infants as young as 10 weeks are beginning to learn behaviors necessary for later conversation. For instance, to converse, speakers must listen to what someone says, speak one at a time, and then pause for the other speaker to have a turn.

Another interesting finding is that mothers seem to treat their baby's gestures, cries, coos, smiles, and babbling as meaningful contributions to a real conversation. An infant's arm may reach out toward her rattle. The mother responds by picking up and giving the rattle to the child, at the same time conducting the following conservation: "Oh, you want your rattle. Here it is. Here's your rattle." Baby takes the rattle and shakes it. Mother replies. "Yes, your rattle. Your nice rattle." Baby pauses to hear mother say this, shakes the rattle, and smiles. Then the baby pauses to hear the mother again respond. "Oh, you like your rattle. Shake your rattle." The baby shakes the rattle, and pauses once more for the mother's response. The mother smiles and nods her head in approval. "Shake, shake, shake," and so forth. Thus the rules for conversation are learned long before the child can speak.

We may wonder who is reinforcing whom? The mother starts the conversation, but the baby listens and replies with her physical response, which makes the mother say the next thing, and the baby responds again. It takes two to have a conversation. Children learn this from infancy, unless there is no one to talk to or no one who will listen. Parents who do not take time to talk to their infants during this preverbal period of development make a great mistake. We need to address children in their native language from the moment they are born if we want to motivate them to become fluent speakers themselves.

The Rules of Conversation

Conversation seems like such a natural activity that you may not realize it has its own unwritten "rules." The only way inexperienced children learn to take part in

Figure 8.8   Rules of
Conversation

- Look at the speaker while she is talking.
- Listen to what the speaker is saying.
- Respond to the speaker at the appropriate time.
- Send a clear message.
- Stick to the topic.
- Pause and give the speaker a turn while you listen.
- Try not to interrupt but wait for your turn.

conversations is by becoming involved with a more experienced speaker. Once they learn the basic rules their opportunities for speaking increase dramatically. Some of the unwritten rules can include those in Figure 8.8.

Sounds simple, doesn't it? But participating in an adult conversation of any length may not be as simple as it sounds, you often find. Too many adults dominate conversations without giving others a chance to respond. They may not look at you when they are talking, or they may not stick to the topic. But once you are aware of these unwritten rules, you should be able to hone your own conversational skills to help children develop theirs.

Teacher–Child Conversation

You have undoubtedly heard that one of the best things teachers of preschoolers can do is read to their children. This is true. But an even greater contribution to their language development is to converse with children, to listen and respond to them in conversational speech. Because many mothers intuitively treat preverbal youngsters as real contributors to conversations, the youngsters eventually become such. You can do the same with children in your classroom. Remember, however, the conversations you initiate with the children should be natural and not contrived.

Take time to have a personal conversation with each child in the class at least once during the day. Do not "talk down" to children, but instead treat them as equal partners in the conversation. Talk about things that are personally meaningful to the child, such as some activity he is engaged in at the moment. Keep track of whom you talk to. If you miss any of the children, start with them the next day. If they do not respond to your conversation, fill in for them as best you can. But always leave room for the child to do his part when he is ready. And remember to take turns. If children forget, remind them that speakers take turns with one another when they are conversing.

Research with preschool children at home and in school recognizes the fact that oral language is the foundation of early literacy. The skills needed to carry on informal conversations with friends and relatives become important in children's early reading and writing. Dickinson and Tabors (2002) found that opportunities to hear and use a variety of new and interesting words in conversations with adults were especially important to children in their study.

Take time to have a daily conversation with every child.

These researchers also found that *extended discourse* was an important contributor to children's language development. Teachers and parents both extended conversations with their children by adding information to what the children said and waiting for them to respond. Explanations and narratives during mealtime were another source of extended discourse. Children themselves also engaged in their own extended conversations in fantasy talk during toy play. Some ways for you to model and extend your conversation can include the ideas in Figure 8.9.

At the same time, you need to be careful not to dominate the conversation, something easy to do when the child stops speaking. Children did better on the researchers' language assessment used in the earlier study when teachers talked *less*

Figure 8.9 Strategies for Extending Teacher–Child Conversations

- Repeating the child's last words and adding your own comment
- Giving information about a past experience
- Giving reasons for what you have said
- Comparing two things you are talking about
- Talking about how you feel
- Wondering about how the child feels
- Wondering about what the child thinks about the topic
- Giving the topic an imagination twist (What would happen if . . .)
- Adding a question (which gives the child another turn)

during free play. This may reflect the fact that children need more time to put their ideas into words without adult engagement, and that *teachers may need more time to listen.*

Telephone Conversations

Children see adults using mobile phones constantly. They hear them talking into the phones. They see them holding the phones to their ears and not talking. Are they listening? Yes. Sometimes their parents hold the phone up to their children's ears to hear someone talking to them—maybe grandma. Of course they want to be involved in this interesting activity. Be sure to have at least two toy phones available. It takes two to hold a conversation, remember.

But as you observe children using the mobile phones in the dramatic play center, they seem to be using only one phone and only making up a one-sided conversation in their pretend play. If you want them to become involved in a real phone conversation, you need to enter into their play. Pick up one of the phones and say something like: "Hello, is this Sandra? I'm calling Sandra. Are you there?" Then motion to Sandra to pick up the other phone and answer you. Talk and listen to Sandra reply as long as you can keep her attention.

Make pretend calls like this to every child in the class as the days go by. Keep a list of whom you talk to and how they answer you so you don't miss anyone. Perhaps the nonverbal child or the bilingual child will actually answer you. Phone conversations like this are an excellent way to promote children's speaking. Be prepared to have a child make a pretend call to you, as well. Children are such copycats. If they realize it is a good way to get the teacher's attention, some are sure to try it. Books to read to encourage children to make phone calls include those in Figure 8.10.

Hold a pretend phone conversation with each child every day or so.

Figure 8.10 Books to Encourage Phone Conversations

I'm Calling Molly (Kurtz, 1990)

Ruby's Beauty Shop (Wells, 2002)

Hello! Is This Grandma? (Whybrow, 2008)

Max's Bunny Business (Wells, 2008)

Small-Group Conversations

Spend time every day in conversations with small groups of children. One of the best times is at snack or lunch. Be sure an adult sits at each of the children's tables and helps carry on a conversation. Talk normally about anything that interests you or the children. You do not have to be the "teacher" who is teaching them the names of the fruits on the juice can. Instead, relax and enjoy your snack or meal with the children. Say the kinds of things you would at your own meal table at home. "Whew, isn't it hot today? I think summer is coming early." "What's that you say, Jamal, you like summertime best of all?" "Me too. I love to swim and picnic." "You like to do that too, Marisa?" "Yes, you are lucky to live next to the park." Children who do not take part in this group conversation nevertheless listen to and learn from it.

Burman (2009) notes some of the benefits of small group conversations:

- More children have a chance to participate.
- Children can expand on their ideas.
- Provides links between children's conversations and experiences.
- Creates a safe place for children unsure of large group conversations. (p. 53)

Child–Child Conversations

The classroom environment itself largely determines the nature of children's oral language experience. Teachers set the stage for child–child conversations by the way they arrange the learning centers. How many children should each center serve? The number of chairs or activities available helps to determine the number of children who will choose that learning center during free play.

The block center and dramatic play center will be the largest with props and materials enough for six or eight. Their role-playing activities often encourage several groups of children to engage in talking with one another. More intimate conversations can occur in the art area if you place two easels next to each other or one basket of crayons on a table set up for four; in the computer center, with two chairs at the keyboard; in the manipulative center, with one puzzle and two chairs at a small table; in the book center, with two beanbag chairs next to one another or a couch with two pillows; in the science/discovery center, with two baskets of seashells to sort and count; or at a small water table, with two eggbeaters.

Read books full of children's conversations to encourage the children to speak. All of Child's popular Charlie and Lola books are written entirely in conversations between older brother Charlie and younger sister Lola, and sometimes include Lola's friend, Lotta, or Charlie's friend, Morten. Figure 8.11 lists some. Children enjoy participating in these humorous conversations by taking character roles and reenacting these stories.

Observing and Recording Conversations

Important child development data can be obtained by observing and recording children's conversations. If you are involved in the conversation have one of your

Figure 8.11 Charlie and Lola Books

> *I Will Never Not Ever Eat a Tomato* (2000)
> *I Am Not Sleepy and I Will Not Go to Bed* (2001)
> *I Am Too Absolutely Small for School* (2004)
> *I Will Be Especially Very Careful* (2009)
> *We Are Extremely Very Good Recyclers* (2009)
> *But Excuse Me That Is My Book* (2005)

assistants take notes on what is being said, take photos, and better yet, record or video the conversation on your smartphone. Burman (2009) explains that when conversations are documented they become more tangible. Scribing children's words, for example, makes their thinking more visible. Later you can return to their words and take time to think about them, interpreting their meaning with the help of the staff and the children's families.

When conversations take place on science topics, field trips, or other projects children are involved with, such documentation can be preserved and mounted on document panels for all to see and reread aloud.

SPEAKS IN EXPANDED SENTENCES

Expansion of Production

Young children ages 3, 4, and 5 are just at the age when their speaking develops most rapidly. From the simple phrases they spoke earlier, now they are suddenly able to expand the subjects and predicates of their sentences into longer, more complex thoughts. How did this expanded language come about? Linguists are searching for answers by starting with infants and audiotaping their utterances, videotaping their interactions with their caregivers, and comparing infants' development with deaf children, children from other cultures, and children from a variety of backgrounds.

We know that soon after an infant walks, he talks. We also know that all human infants are predisposed to acquire their native language. Their brains are wired to sort and store the information that will later be used in producing speech. Human infants give their attention to human voices, listening and responding, at first in babbles, but as soon as possible in word sounds. Then sometime between 1½ and 2 years of age the infants realize that everything has a name. Immediately their vocabulary starts expanding as they begin to absorb the words for everything they see and touch.

This is the crucial time for meaningful adult intervention. The parent or caregiver can name objects and actions. The children listen and try to imitate. The caregivers will listen to the children and respond; all this interaction takes place in the natural give-and-take manner of parents playing with their children.

This is also the crucial time for an enriched physical environment and the child's freedom to explore it. To learn names for things, the youngsters need to see them, feel them, hear them, and try them out. They learn words by interacting with the things that are represented by words in their environment. The more things the child interacts with, the more words the child will have the occasion to learn, as long as support, encouragement, and good language models are also at hand. Young children induce the meanings on the basis of hearing the words used in life experiences.

By around age 2, children are able to use the proper word order consistently in their primitive sentences. As they suddenly blossom into pretend play at this time, a parallel expansion seems to occur in their language. Their sentences grow longer and more complex, and their vocabularies increase. Once they have absorbed the basic rules for forming sentences, they are on their way, for they will no longer need to rely exclusively on imitating the language around them. Instead, they will be able to produce sentences they have never heard. For most children, this mastery has occurred by age 4. Obviously, it is important for children to be involved with competent speakers of the native language. If youngsters do not hear the language used or do not engage with someone in speaking it during these crucial years, they may have difficulty acquiring it.

You need to know which children in your class are speaking in the expanded sentences that most 3-, 4-, and 5-year-old children should be able to use. Some who are not speaking in sentences may be shy or ill-at-ease children who have the ability but not the confidence to speak in the classroom, as mentioned previously. Others may come from homes where language is not used so extensively. Still others may come from homes where English is not spoken. For these and all of your children, you will want to provide rich language opportunities that allow the youngsters to hear sentences spoken and to respond.

How will you do it? Give them fascinating things to talk about. Look around you: the classroom, the neighborhood, the community. Make a list of possible topics to explore with the children. Ask the children to add their own ideas to the list. What would they like to find out about these topics? Write down questions, too. Your list might start out something like this:

Bridges: the bridge across the river; how it was built

Dolphins: dolphins in the downtown aquarium being mammals and not fish

Guinea pigs: no guinea pigs running around outside like squirrels

If You Have Not Checked This Item: Some Helpful Ideas

■ Provide Dramatic Play Opportunities

Children's imaginative play is one of the best preschool activities to motivate and promote language growth in young children. Youngsters take on roles in which they must produce dialog. Even the shy, nonverbal, or bilingual child will learn by listening to the others. Be sure to schedule enough time for children to become involved in this pretending type of play. Take a role yourself to help the shy child join the others. Once he is involved, you should withdraw.

■ Go on Field Trips

Children need many real experiences with their world to process and use information in thinking and speaking. Give the youngsters many new things to think and talk about by going on field trips. Have one adult take three children down to the corner store to buy something. Take a small group on a walk around the block to see how many different sounds they can hear. Be sure to take an audio recorder along to play back and discuss later.

Go on a field trip to a tree every week in the spring or fall to see how it changes. You may want to take along a camera and recorder to record the experience and to motivate talk about it back in the classroom. Be sure to use new vocabulary words to label the new things and ideas the children have experienced. Also label them in a second language if this is appropriate. Then use them over and over with the children.

ASKS QUESTIONS

Expansion of Production

This language skill is another good indication that your children's command of language is developing normally. Most children are able to ask questions as adults do by about age 4. Before that, they go through a predictable sequence in learning to ask questions, just as they do in other areas of development.

Children usually do not learn to ask questions until they have learned to answer them when you ask them something. Between 1½ and 2 years of age, when they are putting a few words together to form primitive sentences, they also ask their first questions, if caregivers have been asking them questions first. The word order of these first questions is the same as a statement but with a rising intonation at the end: "Jamie drink milk?" meaning "May Jamie have a drink of milk?"

Next, they begin to learn the use of the "wh" words at the beginning of questions, words like *what, where*, and *who*: "Where Mama going?" or "Where going?" This type of question becomes quite popular because the adult generally responds, and suddenly the child realizes he has stumbled onto another way of controlling an adult: asking a question that the adult will answer. This is not always true with mere statements. Because he delights in adults' attention and their responses to the things that he originates, he will often burst into a period of questioning. It is not only that he wants to know the answer, but also that he wants an adult's attention.

The next stage in learning to ask questions comes as he expands his sentences to include auxiliary verbs such as *can* and *will*. These questions, though, are often expressed in inverted order; for example, "Where Daddy will go?" instead of "Where will Daddy go?"

The final stage is the expanded question in proper word order, which most children are able to ask at around 3 or 4 years: "Can I go with you?" "What are you doing?" "Why doesn't the light go on?"

If you discover through your observation that certain children have not yet attained this level, what will you do? Will you sit down with them and teach them how to ask a question correctly? You know the answer is "no." Young children do not develop language skills by being taught formally. How do they learn? They learn language just as they learn to develop their perceptual skills: They teach themselves word order by hearing the language forms spoken around them and by practicing language themselves when their physical and mental development has progressed to the point at which they can do so.

Linguistic Scaffolding

As teachers of preschool children, you realize your support of their speaking efforts is most important, especially because young children learn language mainly through imitation. *Linguistic scaffolding* is the direct support teachers give to help children build conversations. It may include the use of questioning, expansion, and repetition.

In other words, to keep a conversation going, teachers often insert a question. Questions are often used to clarify something the child has said, to check on the child's knowledge, or to gain information. Even young children understand when the teacher is asking a question: by the rising intonation of her words at the end of a sentence, along with her facial expression encouraging the child to respond. As pre-school children develop more complex language, they also imitate this kind of questioning to gain information.

If You Have Not Checked This Item: Some Helpful Ideas

■ Ask Questions Yourself

When you understand that children do not ask questions until they have learned to answer them, you will include your own asking of questions in your activities with the children. Circle time is a good time for everyone to hear the English word order of questions and to answer the inquiries if so inclined. Even the children who are not at the point of answering questions in front of a group will learn by listening.

■ Ask Children to Help You Gather Answers to Questions

You can ask a child to ask three or four other children for some information you need. For example, if you are planning a field trip, you might ask several children to go around asking others if their mothers would like to come along. This may not be the most accurate way to gather this information, but it is excellent practice in questioning skills, and you can always check the accuracy of the information with the parents later.

Figure 8.12 Good Question Books

> ***How Do You Wokka-Wokka?*** (Bluemle, 2009)
> ***Where's My T-R-U-C-K?*** (Beaumont, 2011)
> ***Mama, Do You Love Me?*** (Joosse, 1991)
> ***Papa, Do You Love Me?*** (Joosse, 2005)
> ***Where's the Dinosaur?*** (Moseley, 2011)
> ***How Do Dinosaurs Go to School?*** (Yolen, 2007)
> ***How Do Dinosaurs Say I Love You?*** (Yolen, 2009)

■ Read a Book

Books with a question in their title are intriguing to young children. They want to hear the story so they will know how the question is answered. You can involve them in answering the questions themselves. Some good questioning books are listed in Figure 8.12.

CAN TELL A STORY

Expansion of Production

Children whose speaking has become fluent in all the other checklist items are often competent and confident enough to tell full-blown stories about themselves or those around them to individuals, to small groups, and sometimes to the total group. Not every child will be able or willing to perform such a linguistic feat, but some are. Before children can tell such stories, though, they must first have experienced hearing many stories told and read to them. If the reading and telling of stories holds a prominent place in your program, and if your book center shelves are stocked with some of the fine books mentioned in this text, you should be able to help develop some child storytellers.

Are you a storyteller? If you want your children to participate in storytelling, they need an adult model to imitate. Don't believe you are too shy to tell stories. Anyone can do it. After all, what is a story? An anecdote, an experience, an adventure, a fable, a tale. Not every story comes from a book. Did you tell the children what happened to you on the way home from school yesterday? That's a story. Did you tell them what your pet cat did when the neighbor's dog got into the yard? That's another story. All of life that is happening around you and the children can be woven into story after story.

What happened when the children went on a field trip to the pet store, or museum, or zoo? What about the little kitten in the cow barn at the farm you all visited? How did that pesky squirrel finally reach the birdseed you put up so high in your bird feeder? All these incidents make fine oral stories. Keep your senses alert for such daily storytelling possibilities, and you will soon have a long list.

Can your children tell any stories they have heard from their grandparents or others? You might invite a family member to come in and tell such a story to the group. If the relative speaks a language different from English, ask someone to come along who will translate. Encourage the telling of stories in languages other than English.

Decontextualized Talk

Curenton (2006) notes how important oral storytelling is for young children: Storytelling prepares children for school because it allows them to use a sophisticated form of communication—*decontextualized talk*—that is not bound by the immediate context. This talk is about objects, feelings, and ideas experienced in the past or expected in the future. Contextualized talk is only about the present. Decontextualized talk promotes higher-level thinking such as planning and reminiscing. It sets the foundation for children's school achievement.

You might begin by telling the children some interesting anecdotes at circle time, and they should quickly respond with stories of their own. Maybe something about the new baby, or their pet iguana, or the trick their brother played on them last night, or the trip they are going to take during the summer. When other children see how interested you are about such stories, they will want to contribute, too.

You may want to write down the stories children tell about the field trip they went on or an incident from their lives. Use a big pad of newsprint so everyone can see what you write as the child dictates. Be sure to reread this story aloud over and over in the days to follow. Remember how important repetition is for children's early learning. Children can dictate stories into a recorder, too, and play them back whenever they want. Storytelling in preschool used to be exclusively up to the teacher. No longer. Children are now being asked to tell their own stories and retell the stories you have read to them.

Retelling Stories from Picture Books

Some teachers base children's storytelling on favorite picture books they have read to the children over and over. These need to be stories that are memorable to the children. Choose books with some of the characteristics in Figure 8.13.

Stories with folktale-like plots, where a number of incidents happen in a certain order, are especially good choices. As you read these books to the children, be sure

Figure 8.13 Characteristics in Books for Storytelling

- Plot incidents that happen in an easily remembered order
- One or two interesting characters who speak
- Attention-getting words, phrases, or incidents that are repeated

Figure 8.14   Humorous Books for Oral Storytelling

> *Snip Snap! What's That?* (Berman, 2005)
> *Stuck in the Mud* (Clarke, 2007)
> *Drat That Fat Cat!* (Thomson, 2003)
> *Oliver Who Would Not Sleep!* (Bergman, 2007)
> *Not Inside This House!* (Lewis, 2011)

Ask a child to tell the story aloud to a small group.

to pause after each incident and ask, "What happens next?" When you come to the repeated words or phrases, have the children join in saying them aloud. At some point you can ask who would like to tell the story out loud. Figure 8.14 lists some good books to use.

An exciting and funny book to begin with might be **Snip Snap! What's That?** about three children and an alligator who invades their house. Every day have a different child retell the story. Accept whatever they say, even if they leave out important parts. Eventually some of the tellers will want to tell their story to the whole class. Not only will they be demonstrating their skill of using spoken language but also they will be making stories and books memorable for everyone.

Oral storytelling by children is important in many ways. Berkowitz (2011) explains that oral storytelling encourages a heightened and more sophisticated level of engagement among preschoolers through its invitation for role-playing and performance. When children get caught up in the fun of making humorous stories like this come alive by telling them aloud, they will want to reenact them over and over—and talk, talk, talk.

OBSERVING, RECORDING, AND INTERPRETING SPOKEN LANGUAGE

Recording children's spoken language on audio or video is just as important as assessing their language by using the Child Development Checklist. Teachers need to *hear* how children's language is developing over time in order to support them in

CHILD DEVELOPMENT CHECKLIST

Name _____ Sheila _____   Observer _____ Connie _____

Item	Evidence	Dates
8. Spoken Language		
_√_ Listens but does not speak	She is beyond this level	10/22
_√_ Gives single-word short phrase responses	She is beyond this level	10/22
_____ Takes part in conversations	Speaks to others but does not converse	10/22
_X_ Speaks in expanded sentences	"She ate my orange so I can't finish my pumpkin"	10/22
_X_ Asks questions	yes	10/22
_X_ Can tell a story	She tells long anecdotes to teachers, not children	10/22

Figure 8.15   Spoken Language Checklist Observation for Sheila

their learning. Recording their oral storytelling, for example, can serve as the basis for planning new curriculum activities for individuals and the entire class. Berkowitz (2011) explains more fully that documenting children's development over time by recording it allows educators and families to follow and mark interesting milestones in the way a child processes, represents, and communicates his thinking and understanding of life experiences.

On the other hand, using the Child Development Checklist and recording evidence for each of the items checked focuses on specific areas of language development. The language checklist results for Sheila were much like the teachers in her classroom had predicted (see Figure 8.15). Every item was checked except "Takes part in conversations." Although Sheila spoke to other children, it was rarely in the form of conversation, but more often a command or a complaint. Because Sheila showed evidence of "Speaks in expanded sentences," the staff members believed Sheila eventually would join in with other children in classroom activities, including conversation. In fact, Sheila's language skill could be used to help her become involved with the others. The teachers made plans for Sheila to tell several other children, one at a time, how to use one of the computer programs the class had recently acquired that she had learned to use on her own.

LEARNING ACTIVITIES

1. Use the Child Development Checklist Spoken Language section as a screening tool to observe all the children in your classroom. Which children listen but do not speak? How do these children fare in the other spoken language areas? Record the results.

2. Choose a child who seems to be having difficulty with spoken language and observe him or her on three different days doing a running record of language activities. Compare the results with the checklist results. How do you interpret the evidence you have collected? Are any pieces of evidence still missing about this child's language performance? Record the results.

3. Choose a child whom you have screened as needing help in taking part in conversations. Have an informal conversation with this child on a topic of his or her interest. If the child can relax and converse with you, ask another fluent speaker to join in. Record the conversation.

4. Read a story to a small group of children. Include one or two fluent speakers in the the group. Discuss the story, asking simple questions about the characters and plot. Be sure everyone gets a chance to offer his or her opinion. Ask open-ended questions such as "What would you do?" Record this conversation.

5. Play a game with several children called "How would you find out?" Ask the children how they would find out about different things. For instance: what child knows how to skip; what someone's favorite color is; what someone's favorite food is. Ask them to find out and record the questions and answers. Afterwards play it back for you and the group.

6. After you have re-read a favorite story to a small group, ask who is able to tell that story, first to you, then to the others. Another time talk about fairy stories. Tell one yourself. Ask who would like to tell a "Once upon a time" story. Record the stories.

SUGGESTED READINGS

Blank, J. (2012). Fostering language and literacy learning: Strategies to support the many ways children communicate. *Dimensions of Early Childhood, 40*(1), 3–11.

Cheatham, G. A., & Ro, Y. E. (2010). Young English learners' interlanguage as a context for language and early literacy development. *Young Children, 64*(4), 18–23.

Chen, J. J., & Shire, S. H. (2011). Strategic teaching: Fostering communication skills in diverse young learners. *Young Children, 66*(2), 20–27.

Jalongo, M. R. (2011). *Early childhood language arts* (5th ed.).Upper Saddle River, NJ: Pearson.

Meier, D. R. (Ed.). (2009). *Here's the story: Using narrative to promote young children's language and literacy learning.* New York: Teachers College Press.

Parnell, W., & Bartlett, J. (2012). Documentation: How smartphones and tablets are changing documentation in preschool and primary classrooms. *Young Children, 67*(3), 50–57.

Roskos, K. A., Tabors, R. O., & Lenhart, L. A. (2009). *Oral language and early literacy in preschool.* Newark, DE: International Reading Association.

Woodard, C., Haskins, G., Schaefer, G., & Smolen, L. (2004). Let's talk: A different approach to oral language development. *Young Children, 59*(4), 92–95.

CHILDREN'S BOOKS

Beaumont, K. (2011). *Where's my T-R-U-C-K?* New York: Dial.

Bergman, M. (2007). *Oliver who would not sleep!* New York: Alfred A. Levine.

Bergman, M. (2005). *Snip snap! What's that?* New York: Greenwillow.

Bissett, J. (2011). *Boogie monster.* Seattle, WA: Compendium.

Bluemle, E. (2009). *How do you wokka-wokka?* Somerville, MA: Candlewick.

Child, L. (2005). *But excuse me that is my book.* New York: Dial.

Child, L. (2001). *I am not sleepy and I will not go to bed.* Cambridge, MA: Candlewick.

Child, L. (2004). *I am too absolutely small for school.* Cambridge, MA: Candlewick.*

Child, L. (2009). *I will be especially very careful.* New York: Dial.*

Child, L. (2000). *I will never not ever eat a tomato.* Cambridge, MA: Candlewick.

Child, L. (2009). *We are extremely very good recyclers.* New York: Dial.

Clarke, J. (2007). *Stuck in the mud.* New York: Walker.

Dewdney, A. (2011). *Llama llama home with mama.* New York: Viking.

DiTerlizzi, A. (2011). *Say what?* New York: Beach Lane Books.

Edwards, P. (2007). *Oliver has something to say!* Montreal, Quebec: Lobster Press.

Fleming, D. (2011). *SHOUT! Shout it out!* New York: Henry Holt.

Freedman, C. (2010). *Dinosaurs love underpants.* New York: Aladdin.

Joosse, B. M. (1991). *Mama, do you love me?* San Francisco: Chronicle Books.*

Joosse, B. M. (2005). *Papa, do you love me?* San Francisco: Chronicle Books.*

Knowlton, L. L. (2012). *I know a librarian who chewed on a word.* Gretna, LA: Pelican Publishing.*

Kurtz, J. (1990). *I'm calling Molly.* Morton Grove, IL: Whitman.*

Lewis, K. (2011). *Not inside this house!* New York: Orchard Books.

Martin, B. (2006). *Fire! Fire! Said Mrs. McGuire.* Orlando, FL: Harcourt.

Moseley, K. (2011). *Where's the dinosaur?* New York: Sterling Books.

Pinder, E. (2012). *If all the animals came inside.* New York: Little, Brown.

Rinker, S. D. (2011). *Goodnight, goodnight, construction site.* San Francisco, CA: Chronicle.

Sadler, M. (2012). *Pass it on!* Maplewood, NJ: Blue Apple Books.

Thomson, P. (2003). *Drat that fat cat!* New York: Arthur A. Levine.

Wargin, K. J. (2009). *Moose on the loose.* Chelsea, MI: Sleeping Bear Press.

Wells, R. (2008). *Max's bunny business.* New York: Puffin.

Wells, R. (2002). *Ruby's beauty shop.* New York: Puffin.

Whybrow, I. (2008). *Hello! Is this Grandma?* Wilton, CT: Tiger Tales.

Yolen, J. (2007). *How do dinosaurs go to school?* New York: Blue Sky Press.

Yolen, J. (2009). *How do dinosaurs say I love you?* New York: Blue Sky Press.

WEB SITES

International Reading Association
www.reading.org

Ladybug
www.ladybugmagickids.com

The Literacy Project
www.google.com/literacy

National Association for Bilingual Education
www.nabe.org

National Association for the Education of Young Children
www.naeyc.org

Read Write Think
www.readwritethink.org

Teaching Strategies
www.teachingstrategies.org

---

*Multicultural

Emergent Writing and Reading Skills

✓ DEVELOPING EARLY LITERACY SKILLS

Educators aware of the latest research in young children's development of early literacy understand that helping children learn to write and read needs to come before kindergarten and first grade. Today's research shows more clearly how writing and reading can emerge naturally in children under the right conditions. It shows how children make sense of their world through playful exploration, and how children's brains take in this information and extract rules from it to support their early literacy skills.

In addition, scientifically based reading research (SBRR) has pinpointed oral language, vocabulary development, phonological awareness, alphabet knowledge, and print awareness as specific areas needing attention in preschool (Christie, Enz, & Vukelich, 2011). Such research has changed our minds forever about the way children develop and how we can best support their growth.

We now know that writing and reading are outgrowths of the same communication urge that drives children to express themselves orally and even pictorially. We also know that given the proper tools and support, all children everywhere go through the same sequence of stages in teaching themselves to write and to read. It is true that learning to write and to read are as much a natural part of a child's development as learning to talk. Child development specialists are finally coming to realize that "learning to write is largely an act of discovery," as one specialist puts it (Temple, Nathan, & Burns, 1993, p. 2).

The term used currently to describe children's early natural development of writing and reading skills is **emergent literacy**. As researchers began to observe and report literacy activities of preschool children, they found children were able to perform all kinds of literacy behaviors: making up stories, scribbling letters to friends, writing their names, creating print-like words, and more. Today we realize that literacy is a process that begins at birth and proceeds through a sequence of developmental stages much like motor development.

Thus, writing and reading join speaking, thinking, emotions, social, and motor skills as other aspects of development that children can arrive at by playfully experimenting with the materials in their environment. This does not mean, however, that writing and reading development occurs naturally without adult support. Children need regular and active interactions with print and oral and written language.

Many youngsters come from families with few toys, let alone books for reading or the tools for writing. Furthermore, most parents are unaware that their children can develop these skills naturally. Children need their parents' support to progress in this natural development. They need the tools to write with, the print materials in their environment, and encouragement to try them out on their own. In addition, children need to practice emergent writing and emergent reading skills over time, just as they do running or speaking.

Without tools to write with at home, preschoolers can do little more than make marks on steamy windows or scratches in the dirt. Without books to look at, preschoolers have little interest in reading. Without parents' modeling their own reading and writing, children have no reason to think this is something they should do. Without parental expectations that they should experiment with writing and reading on their own, children may never try it.

On the other hand, this does not mean teachers should sit down with preschool children and formally teach them how to write and read, any more than they should formally teach them how to walk and talk. Cognitive psychologists worry that

Figure 9.1 Goals for Preschool
Children

- Enjoy listening to and discussing storybooks
- Understand that print carries a message
- Engage in reading and writing attempts
- Identify labels and signs in their environment
- Participate in rhyming games
- Identify some letters and make some letter-sound matches
- Use known letters to represent written language

preschool teachers, who are in a critical position for nurturing the "roots of literacy" in young children, may not know how to do it.

Teachers unfamiliar with current research about emergent literacy may try to impose skill-oriented tasks on their children such as copying and tracing standard print or memorizing all the letters of the alphabet. Instead, we should be filling the children's environment with examples of written language and books; we should serve as models by doing a great deal of writing and reading ourselves in the presence of the children; and we should provide them with the tools and encouragement to attempt writing and reading on their own.

All early childhood professionals need to become aware of this research and its implications for supporting young children's emergent literacy. The International Reading Association (IRA) and the National Association for the Education of Young Children (NAEYC) have thus adopted a joint position statement describing developmentally appropriate practices for young children learning to read and write in preschool through third grade. The goals for preschool children include those in Figure 9.1.

Although the natural development of writing and reading occurs simultaneously in children, this chapter discusses writing first and then reading because many children emerge into reading from the writing they do. Do any of your children pretend to write, perhaps at the easel, by scribbling letterlike symbols? Do any of them insist on writing their own name on their art products? Assess all the children in your classroom by using the first three items of the Emergent Writing and Reading Checklist. Then set up a writing table or a writing area complete with a variety of writing tools, and watch what happens.

PRETENDS TO WRITE WITH DRAWINGS AND SCRIBBLES

Young children's first natural attempts to write are usually scribbles. Isn't this drawing, you may wonder? Initial scribbling is also done at the outset in art, you may point out. True, children do not at first distinguish between drawing and writing scribbles. At an easel, they may be scribbling a picture or scribbling their own idea of writing, or both together. But if easel painting is new to them, they are probably doing neither painting nor writing. Instead, they may be just trying out the brush and paint; in other words, manipulating the medium, the first stage of the "3 Ms" playful exploration process.

You can ask them what they are doing, but often they are just playing around with the painting tools without any particular product in mind. Both drawing and writing are a fascinating process for young children when they start. They are not planning to produce a picture or a written message. This tends to be an adult's objective. Preschool children may be just learning to control the brush and paint—quite a lengthy process for some children who have had no practice at home with painting or writing tools. Remember that self-directed exploratory learning takes time for preschool children. Give them plenty of time and encouragement to experiment.

At the flat surface of a writing table, the same process is at work, but the tools seem to make a difference. Children recognize that pens and pencils are used for writing. Crayons and felt markers may be used for drawing or for writing. Children often combine the two in their initial attempts. Once again, they may be manipulating the medium, but some will be experimenting with early writing that includes pictures.

At first children do not distinguish between drawing and writing because both convey meaning. Nevertheless, it is important for preschool children to continue drawing their stories or drawing daily happenings in their journals because drawing promotes the first writing, and this writing becomes the first reading that children themselves do. Although young children may perceive the difference between drawing and writing, until about age 7 they may still draw when asked to write.

Children's early attempts at writing vary greatly according to what discoveries they have made about the writing they see done around them at home, in school, on television, in stores, and in restaurants. In dramatic play, they may make a scribble on a pad while "taking an order" at the pretend restaurant. In the classroom Writing Center, they may cover a page with swirls, lines, and circles that start in the middle and go around the outside. The lines may include a head with arms and legs protruding or an oval with "rabbit ears" as they write a letter to a friend about their pet. On the sign-up sheet for a turn at the computer, they may print one wiggly letterlike symbol that represents their name, or they may make another head with arms and legs to represent themselves. Kindra writes/draws in her journal about "fruit people." (See Artifact 9.1.) Letters and one number along the side tell her story.

We should look for the logic that children employ as they write, according to Shagoury (2009). She explains that the best way to gain insight into these processes is to pull up a chair alongside children, watch them as they work, and ask them questions based on their drawing and writing.

Ferreiro and Teberosky (1982), in their now-classic book *Literacy Before Schooling,* tell us that in children's own first spontaneously produced graphic representations, drawing and writing are undifferentiated. Gradually some lines begin to look like drawings, while others evolve toward writing.

Although drawing and writing both represent things symbolically, the two are quite different. Drawing maintains a similarity to the object it represents, whereas writing does not. Writing is an entirely different system having its own rules, whereas

Kindra draws "fruit people" and writes about them at the side.

drawing does not. Young children are unaware of the difference initially and thus use both pictures and scribbles interchangeably to convey their thoughts.

As children make new discoveries about print through their own explorations and their involvement with picture books, they construct their own ideas about writing. At some point, children seem to recognize that writing is different from drawing, and their scribbles take a somewhat different form. Children as young as 3 years may

This teacher observes and talks to the girl about what she is writing.

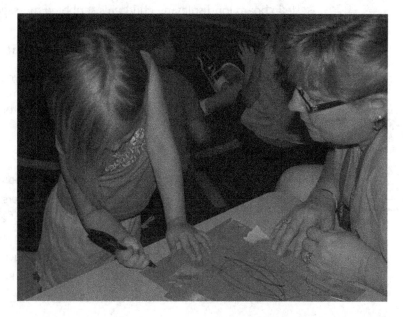

recognize the difference between writing scribbles and drawing scribbles. In fact, some children do drawing scribbles on one part of an easel paper and writing scribbles that "tell about the picture" on another part.

The two kinds of scribbles often look completely different. Writing scribbles may be smaller and done in a horizontal linear manner across the top or bottom of the page, something like a line of writing. But not always. Individual differences in writing scribbles vary greatly, with some squeezed together at one side of the drawing and others just a circle or line in a corner. The children who make such writing scribbles seem to understand that writing is something that can be read, and they sometimes pretend to read their scribbled writing, or they may ask you to read it. This is one of the first steps in the natural acquisition of writing.

If You Have Not Checked This Item: Some Helpful Ideas

■ Set Up a Writing Center

If your goal is to encourage children to explore writing on their own, then you must provide a setting for this to occur. A Writing Center can be just as exciting for children as a Block Center. Most programs put a table in their Writing Center with writing supplies on a nearby shelf. Some centers report that a more enticing piece of equipment is a real child-size writing desk, perhaps the roll-top variety or the type used in children's bedrooms. Drawers can be filled with the tools of writing shown in Figure 9.2.

Or keep these items in plastic containers on nearby shelves. Another desk or table can hold a computer. A stand-up chalkboard or small individual boards encourage scribbling and writing with chalk, as well. On the wall should be a bulletin board for displaying children's scribbled messages.

■ Fill the Room with Environmental Print

What written symbols and signs do you notice in your home environment or on the way to the classroom? You will likely see books, magazines, newspapers, catalogs, phone books, ads on TV, posters, cereal boxes, food containers, T-shirts, letters,

Figure 9.2 Writing Center Tools

Writing pads	Tape	Pencils
Tablets	Rulers	Pens
Paper	Rubber stamps	Chalk
Envelopes	Paper clips	Chalk board
Cards	Paper punchers	Crayons
Stickers	Markers	Scissors

Figure 9.3   Books to Promote Writing

Click, Clack, Moo: Cows That Type (Cronin, 2000)

I'll Save You Bobo! (Rosenthal & Rosenthal, 2012)

A Letter to Amy (Keats, 1968)

The Little Red Pen (Stevens, 2011)

Patches Lost and Found (Kroll, 2001)

Rocket Writes a Story (Hills, 2012)

Wallace's Lists (Bottner, 2004)

computer keys, computer programs, street signs, traffic signs, gas station signs, fast-food restaurant logos, store signs, billboards, all kinds of advertising, and on and on. This is what we mean by **environmental print**. All these symbols and signs can be featured in the classroom as well. Each of the learning centers can have its own signs and labels. Put out old magazines and catalogs and have children cut out pictures of favorite signs to be pasted in a sign scrapbook.

■ Read a Book

A fascinating picture book about the tools of writing is *The Little Red Pen* (Stevens, 2011), in which the tools are alive and talking. Children love the story based on the traditional Little Red Hen, with the pen acting as the leader and the stapler, scissors, pencil, eraser, pushpin, and highlighter refusing to help her. But when the pen accidentally falls in the wastebasket they all come to her rescue. Children can reenact the story by taking on all the roles. It's hilarious. Other good writing storybooks include those in Figure 9.3. Books like these are not just for reading. They are lead-ins to exciting activities you can have ready for the children to try: writing messages, typing a message, writing a letter, making signs, making lists—all in scribbles or drawings if necessary.

 ## MAKES HORIZONTAL LINES OF WRITING SCRIBBLES

Once children's scribbles have become horizontal lines instead of circular or aimless meanderings, they are indicating they understand writing is something different from drawing. Still, their first scribbled lines do not resemble letters or words at all. Temple et al. (1993) noted how different learning to write actually is from what logic tells us it ought to be.

You would think that learning to write is nothing more than learning to make letters and then to combine them into words. However, researchers have found that young children learn to write through a process that is just the opposite. Rather than learning to write by mastering the parts (letters), children first attend to the whole (sentences), and much later to the parts.

Figure 9.4   Linear Scribble
Writing

Young children, in fact, seem to have extracted through their own observations only the broad general features of the writing system: that it is arranged in rows across a page and that it consists of a series of loops, tall sticks, and connected lines that are repeated. (See Figure 9.4.) Only later will children differentiate the finer features of the system: separate words and finally, letters.

Where have they acquired even this much knowledge of written language so early in life? Look around you. They, like all of us, are surrounded by written material in newspapers and magazines, in television advertising, on the labels on food products, on soft-drink bottles, in letters in the mail, in the stories read to them, on store signs, on greeting cards, on car bumper stickers, and on T-shirts. The printed word is everywhere. This is the writing referred to previously as *environmental print*.

Some families, of course, encourage their children to print their names at an early age, and may even take time to write out the creative stories that their young children tell them. Some children have older brothers or sisters who bring written material home from school. Some children come from homes with computers. These children see family members engaged in writing or reading and try to become involved themselves. Observe to discover which of your children do pretend writing—this first step in the writing process—which ones have progressed beyond this beginning, and which have not yet started.

As young children create their own knowledge about writing, they will be extracting certain information from the writing around them that Marie Clay, the New Zealand literacy specialist, calls principles and concepts:

Principles and Concepts of Writing Extracted by Young Children

1. *Recurring principle:* Writing uses the same shapes again and again.

2. *Generative principle:* Writing consists of a limited number of letters from which you can generate a limitless amount of writing.

3. *Sign concept:* Print stands for something besides itself, but does not look like the object it stands for.

4. *Flexibility principle:* The same letter form may be written in different ways, but the direction the letter faces is the same.

5. *Page-arrangement principle:* English is usually written in lines of print from left to right and top to bottom on a page.

(Adapted from Clay, 1991; Davidson, 1996; Temple et al., 1993)

Can you tell which of these principles the child who scribbled in Figure 9.4 extracted? As children repeat lines of loops, sticks, crosses, or circles across the page in their imitation of writing, children are exhibiting the recurring principle of writing: that writing consists of the same moves repeated over and over. Horizontal lines of scribbles like this are not always produced from left to right or top to bottom. Children sometimes start at the bottom or the middle of the page, and they may even write one line from the left and one from the right.

At the same time, youngsters are also displaying the *mastery* stage of "3 Ms" exploratory play. They will fill pages with lines of scribbled "writing" like this, and it gives them great satisfaction. After playing around with this new skill during the manipulation stage, children now repeat this scribbled writing over and over to master it. At the easel or at the writing table or desk, you will see certain children hard at work filling their papers with these horizontal writing lines, just as if they were writing a letter or a story.

Be sure it is the children who are in charge of this natural emergence of literacy. You should not be the one to set goals for their writing. Instead, observe where each child stands in her own developmental sequence, put out new materials to keep her interested, and comment favorably about what she is doing. "Latoya, you have certainly worked hard this morning filling so many pages with writing. Would you like to put it up on the Writing Center bulletin board?"

If some children show no interest in becoming involved with emergent writing activities like this, do not pressure them to try. You can invite them to experiment with using markers or chalk or whatever materials you put out daily. Voluntary and not enforced participation in writing activities should be the rule in your program. Some children need to develop better eye–hand coordination before they engage in flat surface writing. They might learn more from painting at the easel or playing with the utensils you have put out at the water or sand tables instead.

If the youngsters can build a tall block tower without its toppling over, can drive a nail straight into a piece of wood, or can use a pair of scissors with ease, their eye–hand coordination is probably developed enough for them to use a writing implement. But they may use it for drawing instead of writing.

Dual Language Learners

What about dual language learners, you may wonder? Some of them have difficulty speaking English. How are they to learn to write English? Research shows us this is not a problem according to Shagoury (2009). She tells us that dual language learners can write before orally mastering a second language. They write before they can read and use drawing to explore their ideas and thinking. In fact, children who learn literacy in their first language do not need to relearn these skills; they simply transfer the skill to their second language. Be sure you involve them in all the writing activities first-language children are accomplishing.

If You Have Not Checked This Item: Some Helpful Ideas

■ Put Out a Variety of Writing Materials

Most children will not try to become involved in writing if there is no sign of writing in their environment. If you do not have a special Writing Center, set up a writing table or desk with different implements, and you may soon have a group of budding writers (see Figure 9.2).

For paper, it is best to use unlined sheets. Children will be placing their scribbles all over the page at first, and lined paper may inhibit this free-form exploration of how writing works. For them to progress to horizontal scribbles, they need blank sheets of paper. Use typing paper or stationery, as well as tablets and pads of different sizes and colors.

For writing tools, you will want to include a variety and change them every week or so. We sometimes think of pencils first, but research with beginning writers shows that pencils are the most difficult of all writing implements for young children to manipulate effectively. It is not necessary to have only the large primary-size pencils. Some preschoolers have great difficulty handling these thick pencils and prefer to use regular pencils if they use any.

Children themselves often choose colored felt-tip markers as their favorites. You should also include colored chalk and a small chalkboard, and a few pencils, in addition to the markers. Put out a variety of writing tools, and children will find out on their own what works best for them.

Children often choose felt-tip markers as their favorites.

■ **Use Sand or Salt Trays or Finger Painting**

Put out small trays of sand or salt in your writing area so children can practice "writing" with their fingers. It is easy to "erase" this writing simply by shaking the tray. Finger painting on tabletops or paper also gives the children practice doing "mock writing" (pretend writing) with their fingers.

■ **Be a Writing Model Yourself**

Do a lot of writing in the presence of the children. If they see writing is important to you, they will want to do it, too. If you are doing checklist recording or running records in their presence, children will often want to use your pen and paper to do some pretend writing themselves, as mentioned earlier. Don't give up your writing tools; instead, be sure you have a well-equipped Writing Center from which they can get their own recording notebook. Or tie a pencil to a clipboard like the one you use, so the children can "observe and record," too. Serving as a writing model like this will almost always stimulate certain of your children to try their own hand at writing.

MAKES SOME LETTERS, PRINTS NAME OR INITIAL

Just as the 1-year-old begins to say wordlike sounds that parents recognize as words, the preschooler begins to write wordlike forms by making letterlike scribbles. When adults see this, they often point it out: "Oh, Hilary, you made an *l* in your writing, see!" "There, you did it again. Do you know that you have an *l* in your name?" Many children have been taught to print the letters of their names. This is different. Scribbles evolve more as cursive writing. But as the child realizes that her scribbles are being recognized by adults as real letters, she tries to make real letters by printing them.

Although adults often intervene at this point, children still learn alphabet letters on their own by being surrounded by letters and hearing them used. This is the way it should be. The youngsters' own names are often the first source. Children may learn to say the letters in their names soon after they recognize their name sign on their cubby. Many children are then able to identify those particular letters wherever they see them. In fact, they tend to include the first and last letters of their names to a significant degree when writing, says McNair (2007).

Alphabet Letters

Reciting or chanting the ABCs is not the same as writing them. Just as children can chant the numbers from 1 to 10, but do not understand what any of the numbers means, preschoolers often chant the alphabet without the slightest idea of what they are saying. Children's television programs can help children learn the letter names, and some youngsters may have learned letters from this technique. Watching television, however, is a passive method, not for use in preschool programs.

Other children may have learned alphabet letters from a computer at home or in the classroom. A number of software programs feature alphabet games for children 2 to 6 years of age. Using the computer keyboard also helps children learn alphabet letters. In many ways, computer programs are superior to television as a learning tool because they are interactive and involve children in their own learning. Computers in the preschool should not be used in formal lessons. Rather, children should be free to use a classroom computer during free-choice time the same way they use blocks or dolls or the water table.

Also be sure to have alphabet games on the shelves of your manipulative area; alphabet letters mounted on the wall at children's eye level; alphabet books in the book area; and wooden, plastic, sandpaper, or magnetic alphabet letters available for the children to play with. Play alphabet games with the youngsters, but do not teach the alphabet formally. You will find that if you have filled the children's environment with letters, children will teach themselves the alphabet letters they need to know. Formal teaching, even of the alphabet, is not appropriate during the preschool years because this is not how young children learn.

Computer alphabet programs are good introductory programs.

Printing Letters

As children begin to print letters, their first attempts are usually flawed. Youngsters make the same mistakes in writing letters that they do in recognizing letters; that is, they often overlook the letter's distinguishing features. Development of children's written language, just as their other aspects of development, progresses from the general to the specific. Until they are able to perceive the finer distinctions in letters, they will have difficulty making letters that are accurate in all the details.

Let the children practice on their own. Pointing out errors is not really productive, just as it was not in their development of spoken language. In time, their errors will become less frequent as the children refine their perception of individual letters and gain control over their writing tools.

One of the children's problems in printing letters correctly has to do with the letters' orientation in space. Children are often able to get the features of the letters accurate, but not the orientation. Children reverse some letters, and some they even write upside down. Occasionally

Allie has printed her name backward on her picture of fruit.

their letters are facing the right direction, but just as often their printing may be a complete mirror image of the real thing.

Part of the answer may lie in the fact that children have already learned that an object's orientation—that is, the direction it faces—makes no difference in identifying the object. For instance, a cup is a cup no matter whether the handle is pointing toward a person or away from her. A flashlight may be lying horizontally or standing on end, but it is still a flashlight. Objects, in other words, do not change their identity because they face a different direction.

But letters do. Letters made with the same features are completely different, depending on the direction they face and whether their vertical lines are at the top or bottom. If children's brains have not extracted these orientation rules for distinguishing letters, they are sure to have trouble identifying and printing such letters as *d, b, p,* and *q*. All four of these letters are made with the same curved and straight lines. Yet it may take some years for children to get their orientation straight. Children often reverse letters even into the elementary grades.

One of the problems in children's playing with three-dimensional alphabet letters is the fact that they can be reversed or turned upside down. If you have such letters in your writing area, be sure to have real alphabet letters mounted on the nearby wall *at children's eye level* so that the youngsters can easily see the letter's proper orientation. Magnetic letters are better than letter blocks or plastic letters in this respect. At least the magnetic letters cannot be turned over when placed on a metal backing.

With practice and maturity, children resolve these problems themselves unless they have a learning impairment. It is not up to you to correct them. They are progressing as they should through the fascinating task of creating their own knowledge about letters and words. Your best strategy as a teacher is to fill the environment with words, letters, and occasions to write, as well as to encourage and accept the children's own attempts at writing.

If You Have Not Checked This Item: Some Helpful Ideas

■ Have Children Sign Up for Turns

Children can use their mock writing to sign up for turns to use the computer, to play with blocks, to paint at the easel, or to ride a wheeled vehicle. Put small clipboards or sign-up sheets at the entrances to your activity areas, next to the computer or easels, or wherever children need to take turns in the classroom. Tie a pencil to the clipboards and tell the children to put their names under each other's. Have them cross off their names after they have finished their turns, so that the next person can have a turn. Some children can already print their name or initials. If other children say they cannot write their names, tell them to try. Tell them to use their personal script just as they do at the writing table. They will remember which personal scribble is theirs when it is time for their turn. It is important that children understand that you consider their scribbles as real writing; they will continue in their developmental sequence on their own.

■ Make Alphabet Letters Personal

Children always learn in a more meaningful way if the subject is somehow connected to them. Help children recognize the first letter in their own first name by playing games with it. You can have letter cards on yarn necklaces that the youngsters can wear. Let the children find their own letters. Then let the youngsters see if they can find any other child with a letter like theirs. Be sure to have enough similar letters, and make them big enough so everyone can see them easily.

■ Have Alphabet Cards

Let children play with alphabet cards having a picture of an object on them. That will allow youngsters to see the letter in the proper orientation. The object on the card will also give them a clue to the name of the letter. Some educators feel that it is best to have cards showing both upper- and lowercase letters. Then children will see that each letter can be written in two different ways. They feel it is not helpful for children to use only capital letters because they will need to write in lowercase in the elementary grades.

■ Use Computer Alphabet Games

Computer alphabet programs are good introductory programs for young children. However, most of today's programs are operated with a mouse, which does not give the child an opportunity to use the keyboard to bring up an alphabet graphic on the screen like some of the older programs. Of the many alphabet programs on the

Arthur's Preschool	*Dr. Seuss's ABCs*
Caillou Alphabet	*Dr. Seuss Preschool*
Chicka Chicka Boom Boom	*Garfield It's All About Letters*
Curious George Pre-K ABCs	*Reader Rabbit Preschool*

Figure 9.5   Computer Alphabet Book Programs

market, here are some popular CD-ROMs that can be ordered online from Amazon. com (Figure 9.5).

Children's books about Arthur, Curious George, and Dr. Seuss's characters should also be available. Character dolls for Arthur, Curious George, and the Cat in the Hat, along with their books, can be purchased in most large bookstores for reenacting the stories.

■ Read an Appropriate Alphabet Book

There are many good alphabet books on the market, but you need to review any you plan to use with your children to see if they are age appropriate. Some alphabet books are for very young children. Looking at the simplicity of the words and pictures may help you determine the age level. If there are pictures of children in the book, are the children in the book the age of yours?

Some alphabet books are too sophisticated for young children. These books often display the talent of the artist rather than help children recognize letters. Other alphabet books are confusing to young children because of the unfamiliar objects used as illustrations. On the other hand, a few of the new books may make your children laugh as they search for the object being illustrated by the letter. You may want to consider the criteria in Figure 9.6 when choosing alphabet books.

A favorite of every preschooler who hears it is **Chicka Chicka Boom Boom** (Martin & Archambault, 1989). The letters themselves tell the tale as they scramble up a coconut tree, and then all come tumbling down when it gets too crowded at the top. Children really learn their letter names as they repeat them in the rollicking rhyme. Other favorites include books where Z goes first and mixes up everything. (See Figure 9.7.)

These books are more effective if read to one or two children at a time rather than a group. The children need to sit close to the teacher to identify the objects

Figure 9.6   Alphabet Book Criteria

- One large letter to a page
- Colorful objects that children recognize
- A fast-paced story or theme that rhymes
- Where letters are the characters
- A new twist (Z comes first)
- A lead-in to hands-on activities

Figure 9.7 Alphabet
Books

A Isn't for Fox; An Isn't Alphabet (Ulmer, 2008)
Alpha Oops! The Day Z Went First (Kontis, 2006)
Chicka Chicka Boom Boom (Martin & Archambault, 1989)
LMNO Peas (Baker, 2010)
Z Goes Home (Agee, 2003)
Z is for Moose (Bingham, 2012)

being named and see the shapes of the letters. Have the books on your bookshelves so children can look at them on their own or in the Writing Center where children are teaching themselves to make letters.

■ Serve Alphabet Soup

Serve alphabet soup for lunch and see if the children can find and identify any of the letters.

■ Have Fun with Pretzels

Have pretzels for a snack and see what letters your children can make by breaking off pieces before eating the pretzels. This idea comes from watching what children invent on their own.

OBSERVING AND ASSESSING WRITING SKILLS WITH CHECKLIST AND RUBRIC

Observing children's writing skills is easily done through unobtrusive observation. Give children numerous opportunities to write in the writing center and throughout the classroom. Collect and date samples for children's portfolios and also for your assessment of their accomplishments. It is best to use a checklist of skills like the one shown here or one of your own making. The checklist in Figure 9.8 lists a natural

Figure 9.8 Writing
Skills Checklist

_____Pretends to write with drawings and scribbles
_____Makes horizontal lines of scribble writing
_____Includes mock letters in scribble lines
_____Makes printed letters here and there, some
      reversed
_____Prints letters of first name, some reversed
_____Prints first name, letters in order
_____Prints other words

Figure 9.9 Name-
Writing Rubric

1—Writes name as a scribble
2—Prints name as first letter of first name
3—Prints all the letters of first name, may be backwards
4—Prints first name accurately

emergence of writing skills, not something you have taught the children. They may follow this progression or may skip some, depending on how much previous practice they have had. This should be an informal evaluation on your part and not a test.

An additional way to assess young children's writing skills is through using rubrics.

Rubrics are like a checklist written as a scale from lowest to highest. They can be useful if you need to focus on a specific kind of writing. Figure 9.9 looks at children's writing of their names.

Using this rubric as an example, you can make your own rubrics on other specific aspects of writing skills.

Once you know where children stand in their development of writing skills, you can provide more opportunities for them to write: letters, messages, invitations, cards, signs, or stories using the letters they have learned or just plain scribbles if they have not progressed to letters.

HOLDS BOOK RIGHT-SIDE UP; TURNS PAGES RIGHT TO LEFT

Children need many early experiences with books before they finally learn to read independently. It is especially important for you to make sure they have all kinds of book experiences both in the classroom and in the home. Many programs purchase paperback duplicates of books in the classroom for a home lending library. Children sign out for a book each day and return it in the morning. This also gives families the chance to read to their children the same books the youngsters are using in the classroom.

Young children need to have their favorites read again and again for them to develop a strong affinity for books and reading. McVicker (2007) emphasizes that reading aloud to children and extending books through interactions and activities hold huge educational benefits for young children, not to mention intensifying their joy.

In the classroom, it is essential for an adult to read to a small group *on a daily basis*. As every major research study on reading has found: The single most important activity for building these understandings and skills essential for reading success appears to be *reading aloud to children*.

In addition to group reading, staff members should look for opportunities to read books to individuals during the day. Before and after each reading, talk to the children about the story. Ask questions, have children talk about the pictures, and

It is essential for an adult to read to a small group daily.

discuss their favorite actions. Research has found that the talk surrounding the storybook reading gives it power, helping children to bridge what is in the story and their own lives.

Finally, books need to be available in an enticing Book Center—full of book posters, puppets, book character dolls, and stuffed animals—where children can look at the books on their own and play with book extension activities.

Book-Handling Skills

Surely, a preschool child will know how to hold a book, which side is up, and which way to turn the pages, you may think. Not necessarily. The youngest children or those with no previous book-handling experience may not know how to hold a book or turn the pages. Let them watch the way you hold a book and turn the pages. Can they do the same?

Observe how each of the children handles books. If you see a child who does not hold the book right-side up, you don't need to correct him. Instead, ask him to pick out a book he would like you to read for him. Then you might then ask him how you should hold the book. If he still does not have a clue, then say you'd like to look at the pictures together with him. Can he help you hold the book so that both of you can see the pictures? If he gives you the book upside down, ask him: Can you see the pictures if I hold it this way? Be sure to follow up with this child and books in the days to come.

Take special care to observe which children come into the Book Center and which ones do not. Invite children who do not show an interest in books to choose a book for you to read to them alone. Most children enjoy having the teacher pay special attention to them. Remember that one of your important tasks is to bring together children and books in happy and satisfying ways.

This means that you and your coworkers must serve as good book-reading models. Note in your daily plans who will be the book readers for a particular day. Ask the readers to choose books they especially like. Have them plan a book extension activity to use after they have read each book. For instance, for some of the books discussed in this text they might do the following:

- *Captain Cheech* (Marin, 2008): Have children line up two sets of chairs, one for the school bus and one for the boat, and reenact the story as you read it a second time.
- *If You Decide to Go to the Moon* (McNulty, 2005): Have each child go around the room and choose an item he or she would take to the moon, and then tell why.
- *Shoe-la-la!* (Beaumont, 2011): Have children trace around their shoes, cut out the tracings, color, and decorate them. (Help with the cutting if necessary.)

Children need such hands-on experience with books—the more the better. We need to find all sorts of ways to get books off the shelves and into children's hands.

If You Have Not Checked This Item: Some Helpful Ideas

■ Use Big Books

Although they are more often used in elementary school to teach whole-class reading, a few big books fill a useful role in preschool programs. They can help young children understand how a book works, for instance. Use big books when reading to the total group. Put the big book on an easel so children can see the pictures and text, and you can turn the pages easily. At the same time, have one or two small copies of the same book that the younger listeners can hold. Have them turn the page when you do. Some big books available from Scholastic (1-800-724-6527) are listed in Figure 9.10.

■ Put Books in Every Learning Center of the Classroom

Sometimes we categorize things so distinctly that we overlook other possibilities. That seems to be especially true with our use of picture books in the classroom. We usually keep them on the shelves of the Book Center, and they seldom find their way

Figure 9.10 Big Books from Scholastic

How Do Dinosaurs Get Well Soon?
If You Give a Mouse a Cookie
Is Your Mama a Llama?
Tar Beach
The Very Hungry Caterpillar

Figure 9.11   Books on
CDs from Scholastic

> *Chicka Chicka Boom Boom*
> *Click Clack Moo: Cows That Type*
> *Diary of a Worm*
> *Giraffes Can't Dance*
> *Miss Mary Mack*

into other areas of the classroom. If we want children to become involved with books in a hands-on way, we need to consider keeping some books in the other curriculum areas. Perhaps a plastic baggie hanging from a shelf in each area can contain a picture book suitable for that area. Or a book can be clipped to a large kitchen clip hanging from a string attached to the wall. An adult can read the book to children playing in the area, and children can look at it on their own.

For instance, put *Mike and the Bike* in the Large-Motor Center, *Max Counts His Chickens* in the Manipulative/Math Center, *Tar Beach* in the Block Center, *Diary of a Worm* in the Writing Center, *My Crayons Talk* in the Art Center, *Planting a Rainbow* in the Science Center, *My Family Plays Music* in the Music Center, and *Violet the Pilot* in the Dramatic Play Center. Don't forget to change them often.

■ Have Books on CDs to Teach Page Turning

For beginners to get used to how a book works, you may want to have them listen to a book on a CD in your Listening Center with one of the staff on hand to help them turn the pages. Books on CDs from Scholastic are listed in Figure 9.11.

*Have books on CDs to teach
page turning.*

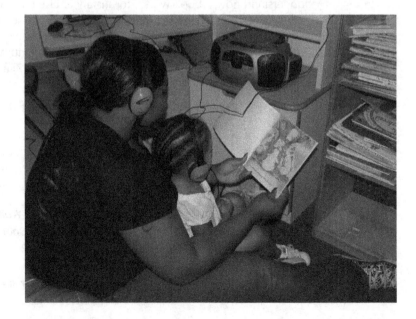

PRETENDS TO READ USING PICTURES TO TELL STORY

As children become more familiar with picture books, they begin looking through them on their own, at first flipping through and missing some of the pages, but later turning each page separately and looking at it intently. As certain books become their favorites, they go through them again and again. They will also ask an adult to read them over and over.

Now it's their turn to read. Children who have handled books and enjoyed hearing them read aloud take just as much pleasure in pretending to read these books themselves, especially to an adult reader. Because young children do not at first understand it is the words that tell the story, they re-create their stories aloud mainly from the pictures or sometimes from memory if they have heard the story repeated many times. Their story may not even include all the pictures in the book at first, but rather the ones that make the biggest impression on them.

Children may also include some real words from the story if they remember them from hearing the story repeated. Other extraneous information may also find its way into their story, especially if the adult reader has discussed the illustrations with them. Thus the story they are pretending to read often comes out quite different from the book version. But children read it along in their own way, turning the pages and saying words just as if they appear that way in the book.

If it is the children's first attempt to retell what is in a book, they may do what is called "picture-naming"; they merely point to a picture on a page and tell what it is, rather than telling the story in a narrative sequence. They still believe it is the pictures and not the words that tell the story. They have not yet developed what is called a sense of story.

It is not up to you as a teacher to correct the child's pretend reading of a story. Instead, you should accept it just as you do his pretend writing with pictures and scribbles. This emergent reading is an early stage of a child's learning to read, a wonderful display of his interest and attention to the way a book works and how a story goes. Whether it is accurate is beside the point. Your role is to thank the child for his reading and invite him to do more of it.

You will find that the more reading you do for individual children and small groups, the more you can expect the children to do "pretend reading" for you. If none of the children in your program has offered to do such pretend reading, it may mean that you have never asked them to do it. Or it may mean they are not that familiar with the books because the stories have not been repeated enough. Remember the "3 Ms"—manipulation, mastery, and meaning—and be sure to reread favorite books over and over to help children master the stories.

Favorite Books

Children need to see and hear real books read by a live person sitting close to them and talking about the story afterward. They need to do follow-up extension activities

Figure 9.12   Criteria for Favorite Books

- Is written about an experience children can relate to
- Has an interesting-looking character with a funny name
- Has simple illustrations in bright primary colors
- Has a brief text with a line or two on a page
- Uses repetition, rhyming words, or distinctive expressions
- Has an exciting or funny story line or cumulative incidents

of their favorite books by using puppets or doll characters or reenacting the story as a character themselves (Beaty & Pratt, 2015). How will you know which books are their favorites? Listen to the children when you have finished reading. Does anyone say "Read it again, teacher"? That will give you a clue. Figure 9.12 lists criteria for favorite books.

Not Inside This House! (Lewis, 2011) could easily become everyone's favorite. Its little boy character has a name bigger than he is: Livingstone Magellan Columbus Crouse, who brings his treasures into the house—much to his mother's great displeasure. A bug, a mouse, a pig, a moose, a whale—what next? Its rhyming leads listeners to wonderful vocabulary words: ruckus, circus, gloom, doom, notion, commotion, and finally leads his mother to reconsider her ban "not inside this house!"

Scaffolded Reading

Next time a child asks you to read a story, have him choose a favorite tale, one he has heard before. After you have finished, tell him it is now his turn, that he should tell the story to you. He can turn the pages if he wants and "read" the story to you. Make it fun, so that he will want to repeat the activity again and again. This means, of course, that you will need to spend much more reading time on a one-to-one basis with individuals rather than reading to a whole group. Most teachers find this very rewarding, and so do children.

At first the child may "read" along with you as you "scaffold" the child's reading. In other words, you do much of the reading of a familiar book but encourage the child to join in whenever he can. In time the child will take over more and more of the reading. After a child has participated a number of times in a scaffolded reading experience with a particular book, he will often attempt to retell the story independently (Strickland & Schickedanz, 2009).

The story may not be verbatim, but most children use some words from the book. They tend to tell the story in their own language, at their own developmental level, with the same articulation they use when they speak. If they speak a dialect, they will retell the story in this dialect. If they are learning English as a second language, they will retell the story the way they speak English rather than the way the story is written in the book. The more times the child hears the story, the more accurate her retelling will become.

*You need to spend time
scaffolding reading with a child.*

Dual Language Readers

Dual language readers, like dual language writers, can emerge into reading by discovering how it works. Shagoury (2009) tell us that young dual language learners figure out the way the written language works in the first and second language. Once they learn literacy in their home language, they do not need to relearn these skills in school. But it is helpful if you have bilingual books in your reading center and read to these children in both languages. Figure 9.13 lists some bilingual paperback books from Scholastic.

SHOWS AWARENESS THAT PRINT IN BOOKS TELLS THE STORY

The next developmental step in emergent reading skills involves print awareness. If you are reading to children on a one-to-one basis, they already may have indicated something about their print awareness or lack of it. At first children believe that the

Figure 9.13   Bilingual
Books from Scholastic

Goldilocks and the Three Bears

Little Red Riding Hood

The Three Little Pigs

Carlos and the Squash Plant

Fiesta

Margaret and Margarita

Figure 9.14 Children's Thought Sequence About Text and Pictures

1. The text and pictures are not differentiated.
2. The picture, not the text, tells the story.
3. The text must be a label for the picture.
4. The text must provide cues for the pictures.
5. The text tells the story.

pictures in the book tell the story as previously mentioned. They may not pay any attention to the text. Even when they do, they may not understand that it is the print and not the pictures that the reader is reading.

Some children are so unaware of the purpose of print that they may cover it unintentionally with their hands if they are holding the book. Others may understand that the reader needs to read the print, but they may also think the reader still needs the pictures to know what the words say.

Researchers have discovered a sequence most children go through in sorting out print from pictures in a picture book. (See Figure 9.14.)

As children pretend to read you their favorite stories, some of them use the same narrative style and almost the exact words as the book itself. Are they really reading? If you cover the print as they read, you will discover that most have memorized the words after hearing the book read many times. But eventually these same children, without being taught, will come to notice the print and realize that the print, not the pictures, tells the story in the book. Certain kinds of books help children to make this cognitive leap recognizing that print tells the story. One is the "song storybook."

Song Storybooks

Song storybooks are picture books whose stories are written in the words of a familiar children's song with a line of text on each page. Because children already know the song by heart, they may be able to follow the words along if you run your finger under them as you read. They will be delighted to see that the pictures in the book illustrate the familiar song. In addition to following along or chiming in as you read the words, have them sing the words with you from time to time. Song storybooks with songs children love to sing (and read, and act out) include those in Figure 9.15. How many of these songs do your children already know?

When they see the words of the song in a line of print, they will be able to "read" them, that is, recite them from memory. Little by little they come to realize that it is the print—those words printed on the page—that tell the story, not the pictures.

You can determine who these children are by asking them where you should look in the book for certain lines or certain words. By now, some of these youngsters may try to match the telling of the story with the print in the books, and some may even want to know what particular print says. In the final stage prior to reading, they will actually begin to read the words. This is how literacy finally emerges naturally—when interested adults bring experimenting children together with appropriate books.

Figure 9.15   Song
Storybooks

I Love You a Bushel & a Peck (Wells & Loesser, 2005)
If You're Happy and You Know It (Warhola, 2007)
Itsy Bitsy Spider (Toms, 2009)
On Top of Spaghetti (Johnson, 2006)
Over the Rainbow (Collins, 2009) CD included
She'll Be Coming 'Round the Mountain (Emmett & Allwright, 2006)
Sunshine on My Shoulders (Denver, 2003) CD included

Not all children in preschool will arrive at this stage. Individual development, personal interests, and home background have a great deal to do with children's accomplishments. Your role is to fill your program with exciting books, extension activities, opportunities for reading, and time for children to explore to their heart's content. Then reading to individual children and listening to them read to you may be one of the most satisfying activities any of you engage in.

If You Have Not Checked This Item: Some Helpful Ideas

■ Read Predictable Books

The book's structure also influences the accuracy of the child's story retelling. Research has found that the best beginning books for helping children learn to read are **predictable books**, those that contain selections with repetitive structures that enable children to anticipate the next word, line, or episode. If children are familiar with a story and can anticipate what comes next, they will have a much easier time retelling the story themselves.

If the child is familiar with the book you are reading and is familiar with books in general, she can follow the story more easily if she knows what's coming. If the book is written in rhyme, it is also easier for the child to remember the story line and to recall what comes next. The following books contain **rhyming** and **repetition**, important qualities of most predictable books. Even very young children remember rhymes and love the books that contain them. Several recent books are favorites because of their rhyming and repetition. (See Figure 9.16.)

Through listening to stories like these read over and over, young children begin to develop a *story schema,* or sense of story: a mental model of the basic elements of a story. From this mental model, children develop expectations for the setting, the characters, the order of incidents, and how the story will end.

■ Play a Rhyme Game

The awareness of word sounds is another important area that young children must recognize in their development of reading skills. We call it **phonological awareness**.

Figure 9.16 Predictable Books in Rhyme

> *Boogie Monster* (Bissett, 2011)
>
> *Dinosaurs Love Underpants* (Freedman & Cort, 2010)
>
> *If All the Animals Came Inside* (Pinder, 2012)
>
> *Llama Llama Home with Mama* (Dewdney, 2011)
>
> *Not Inside This House* (Lewis, 2011)
>
> *Where's My T-R-U-C-K?* (Beaumont, 2011)

Rhyme recognition is a part of it. Alliteration recognition, the awareness of words that start the same, is another part. Researchers have found that young children appear to hear rhyming words and words that begin the same first. Perhaps that is what draws them to predictable books. Can your children find words that rhyme with the animal names in these stories? Have them fill up several "animal rhyme baskets" with word-cards from the stories you read. Print each rhyming word a child finds on a card and have that child put it in the animal's basket. Which animal gets the most cards?

■ Retell the Stories

Do you read daily to individuals in your class? It will be evident by the number of children who are able to retell the stories from your books. Children who are not as familiar with books and reading may still agree to tell you the story, but theirs may be a story created by them as they look at the pictures. Your acceptance of any story they tell is important. As they progress in their experience with stories and books, their retelling will become more accurate. Eventually with a highly predictable book, some children will memorize the words, and then their retelling may be perfect.

■ Make Newsprint Stories

Bring a newsprint pad into the book area and have children dictate stories to you that you write on the pad. Can they read them back? Another day paste an interesting picture on the newsprint and have children dictate a story about the people or animals in the picture. Mount these stories around the room and read them with individuals from time to time.

■ Read Books with Large-Font Print

Other types of picture books that help children understand that the print tells the story are books with large-font type. More and more recent books have some or all the words in large font. *If All the Animals Came Inside* has a number of large-font words on every other page describing sounds and actions (e.g., *crash, bash)*. Did your children notice them?

Figure 9.17 Reading
Skills Checklist

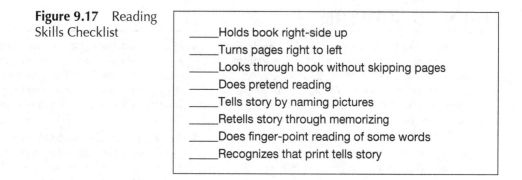

_____Holds book right-side up

_____Turns pages right to left

_____Looks through book without skipping pages

_____Does pretend reading

_____Tells story by naming pictures

_____Retells story through memorizing

_____Does finger-point reading of some words

_____Recognizes that print tells story

OBSERVING AND ASSESSING READING SKILLS WITH CHECKLIST AND RUBRIC

Although young children develop emergent reading skills at the same time and in much the same manner that they develop writing skills, we realize that we need to observe and record their accomplishments separately. As you and the staff read to the children and listen to the children's "reading" to you, be sure to observe how individuals respond, as well as what they are doing in the reading center. Figure 9.17, the Reading Skills Checklist, should be used over a period of time with the checkmarks dated. Be sure it is an informal assessment and not a test.

Not all of the children will accomplish all of the skills—especially 3-year-olds who have had little experience with books. Others may skip some of the skills, and a few may go on to actual reading. You may want to zero in on particular skills for certain children. This is where rubrics can be most helpful. Any of the skills can be converted into a simple rubric just like the book-handling skill in Figure 9.18.

You can observe individual children using such rubrics to keep track of their progress. Be sure to date them and include them in the children's portfolios. Rubrics work best with individuals who may need special help. Try to find topics of special interest to such children and provide them with books on the topics. They may need time to hear books on CDs in your Listening Center along with a staff member who will help them turn the pages at the right time.

Figure 9.18 Book-
Handling Rubric

1-----Holds book right-side up

2-----Starts with first page

3-----Turns pages right to left

4-----Goes through book without skipping pages

LEARNING ACTIVITIES

1. Use the Child Development Checklist section on emergent literacy skills as a screening tool to observe all the children in your classroom. Compare the children who have checks at the higher levels of the writing skills with their results in spoken language. Can you draw any conclusions?

2. Set up a writing area with paper and writing tools and make a running record of how children use it on three different days. If any make horizontal lines of writing scribbles, compare them with the writing scribbles of others. What does this show you about emergent writing?

3. Have children print or scribble their names on their art or writing projects. Make a card for each child with the letters he or she can write. Have them be "letter detectives" to find other objects in the class that start with those letters. Write the names of those objects on their cards.

4. Have a child select a favorite book for you to read. Have the child hold the book and turn the pages as you read. Do this with each of the children one by one. What do you learn about their reading skills? What activities would you provide for them?

5. Read a predictable book to an individual child. Go through the book a second time, reading all but the rhyming or repeated words. Have the child tell them. Go through the book a third time asking the child to say as many words as he can, or tell you the story if he can.

6. Read a predictable book to an individual child and stop when you come to a rhyming word. Ask the child to point to the word in the book. Continue reading but stop from time to time and have the child point to the words. Can the child "read/tell" the story to you, stop as you did, and have you point to the words?

SUGGESTED READINGS

Beaty, J. J. (2013). *Fifty early childhood literacy strategies.* Upper Saddle River, NJ: Pearson.

Gillanders, C., & Castro, D. C. (2011). Storybook reading for young dual language learners. *Young Children, 66*(1), 91–95.

Jalongo, M. R. (2011). *Early childhood language arts* (5th ed.). Upper Saddle River, NJ: Pearson.

Jalongo, M. R., & Ribblett, D. M. (1997). Using song picture books to support emergent literacy. *Young Children, 74*(1), 15–28.

Santos, R. M., Fettig, A., & Shaffer, L. (2012). Helping families connect early literacy with social-emotional development. *Young Children, 67*(2), 88–93.

Shagoury, R. (2009). Language to language: Nurturing writing development in multilingual classrooms. *Young Children, 64*(2), 52–57.

Yopp, H. K., & Yopp, R. H. (2009). Phonological awareness is child's play! *Young Children, 64*(1), 12–21.

CHILDREN'S BOOKS

Agee, J. (2003). *Z goes home.* New York: Hyperion Books.

Baker, K. (2010). *LMNO peas.* New York: Beach Lane Books.

Beaumont, K. (2011). *Shoe-la-la!* New York: Scholastic Press.*

Beaumont, K. (2011). *Where's my T-R-U-C-K?* New York: Dial Books.

Bingham, K. (2012). *Z is for moose.* New York: Greenwillow Books.

Bissett, J. (2011). *Boogie monster.* Seattle, WA: Compendium.

Bottner, B. (2004). *Wallace's lists*. New York: Katherine Tegin Books.

Breen, S. (2008). *Violet the pilot*. New York: Dial.

Collins, J. (2009). *Over the rainbow*. New York: Imagine Books. (CD included)

Cronin, D. (2000). *Click, clack, moo: Cows that type*. New York: Simon & Schuster.

Cronin, D. (2003). *Diary of a worm*. New York: Joanna Cotler Books.

Denver, J. (2003). *Sunshine on my shoulders*. Nevada City, CA: Dawn Publications. (CD included)

Dewdney, A. (2011). *Llama llama home with mama*. New York: Viking.

Ehlert, L. (1988). *Planting a rainbow*. Orlando, FL: Harcourt.

Emmett, J., & Allwright, D. (2006). *She'll be coming 'round the mountain*. New York: Atheneum.

Freedman, C., & Cort, B. (2010). *Dinosaurs love underpants*. New York: Aladdin.

Hills, T. (2012). *Rocket writes a story*. New York: Schwartz & Wade Books.

Hubbard, P. (1996). *My crayons talk*. New York: Henry Holt.

Johnson, P. B. (2006). *On top of spaghetti*. New York: Scholastic.

Keats, E. J. (1968). *A letter to Amy*. New York: Harper.*

Kontis, A. (2006). *Alpha oops! The day Z went first*. Cambridge, MA: Candlewick Press.

Kroll, S. (2001). *Patches lost and found*. Delray Beach, FL: Winslow Press.

Lewis, K. (2011). *Not inside this house!* New York: Orchard Books.

Marin, C. (2008). *Captain Cheech*. New York: Harper/Collins.*

Martin, B., & Archambault, J. (1989). *Chicka chicka boom boom*. New York: Simon & Schuster.

McNulty, F. (2005). *If you decide to go to the moon*. New York: Scholastic.

Pinder, E. (2012). *If all the animals came inside*. New York: Little, Brown.

Ringgold, F. (1991). *Tar Beach*. New York: Crown.*

Rosenthal, E., & Rosenthal, M. (2012). *I'll save you Bobo!* New York: Simon & Schuster.

Stevens, J. (2011). *The little red pen*. Boston: Harcourt Children's Books.

Toms, K. (2009). *Itsy bitsy spider*. Hertforshire, England: Make Believe Ideas.

Ulmer, W. (2008). *A isn't for fox; An isn't alphabet*. Chelsea, MI: Sleeping Bear Press.

Ward, M. (2008). *Mike and the bike*. Salt Lake City, UT: Cookie Jar Press. (CD included)

Warhola, J. (2007). *If you're happy and you know it*. New York: Orchard.

Wells, R., & Loesser, F. (2005). *I love you! A bushel & a peck*. New York: HarperCollins.

Wells, R. (2008). *Max counts his chickens*. New York: Dial.

Yolen, J. (2007). *How do dinosaurs go to school?* New York: Blue Sky Press.*

WEB SITES

Children's Book Council
www.cbcbooks.org

International Reading Association
www.reading.org

Ladybug
www.ladybugmagickids.com

Read Write Think
www.readwritethink.org

Reading Is Fundamental
www.rif.org

Reading Rockets
www.readingrockets.org

*Multicultural

CHAPTER 10

Art, Music, and Dance Skills

In this chapter you will learn to observe if children can:

_____ Make basic scribble shapes

_____ Draw a person as a sun-face with arms and legs

_____ Make pictorial drawings

_____ Move arms and hands in rhythm to a beat

_____ Play rhythm instruments

_____ Sing with group or by him/herself

_____ Move body to represent people, animals, feelings

_____ Dance with others to music

_____ Be observed through their products or by photos, audiotapes, videos, or checklist

CREATIVITY IN YOUNG CHILDEN

What is creativity? For young children it is a method of doing things in new and different ways. To create, a person brings into existence a new form, things that are original or unique. Creative people do not imitate; they do not follow the crowd. In a word, they are non-conformists.

Who are they? Artists, inventors, poets, writers, actors, musicians, dancers, interior decorators, chefs, architects, clothing designers, to name a few—and young children. They are all people who follow their own bent and use their ingenuity to design something new. Young children are naturally creative because everything they do, make, or say is completely new to them. They explore, experiment, put things together, take things apart, and manipulate things in ways no adult would ever think of, because the youngsters don't know the difference.

Too often creativity is not included in discussions of the major aspects of children's development—emotional, social, physical, cognitive, and language. Yet it is as notable a drive in the development of the young human being as thinking or speaking. The unfolding of a young child's creative urge is a joy to behold for early childhood teachers. To help foster and not suppress such development is just as important as it is for speaking, writing, and thinking skills. Yet somehow we equate creativity with special talent that not everyone displays; therefore we downplay or ignore the development of creativity as more of a frill than a necessity for getting along in life.

In downplaying or ignoring creativity, we deprive young children of a basic aspect of their expressional capacities. Every child has the potential to become an artist, a musician, a writer, a dancer, or an inventor, if his interests carry him in that direction and if her teachers support rather than control her urge. The fact that few people become artists is evidence of society's low priority for creativity and high priority for conformity. Fox and Schirrmacher (2012) make it clear that all children are creative, but this potential remains dormant without practice. Creativity requires exercise to grow. Anyone can develop it.

Children come into the world with a fresh point of view: their own.

Children come into the world uninhibited and with an entirely fresh point of view: their own. They continue to follow its bent until they learn how society expects them to behave. Only youngsters with strong enough psyches or strong enough outside support to resist society's inhibitions become the artists or creators whom we value as adults.

Could the children in your classroom become such creative adults? If their natural-born creativity is supported and valued by the adults around them, and if it has an opportunity to blossom and grow, children have the chance to escape the smothering pressure to conform and can enrich their own lives and those of others with the products of their talent.

This chapter on creative development deals in art with representational drawing, not only because such art is an important part of most early childhood programs, but also because many early childhood teachers need help in restructuring their art programs. Too many activities in such programs suppress rather than support creativity. Long ago De la Roche (1996) complained about all the snowflakes, shamrocks, and turkeys young children made being the same. After all, snowflakes themselves are not the same.

This chapter could just as well deal with the development of science skills, which also depend on children's natural exploratory bent. Yet science at the preschool level has somehow escaped the controlled approach that many teachers take with art. It seems good for children to explore plants and animals in all sorts of creative ways. But somehow many teachers seem to feel that drawings should be done only in the manner prescribed by adults, because "adults know better."

Observing Creativity

First of all, we need to take ourselves as observers in hand. What are we looking for in children's development of creativity? Because we tend to see what we look for, we need to make sure the art activities we offer to the children are open-ended. Children need to be in control of the way they create art. It is this process that is most important to them, not the product. This is where creativity starts. This is where we need to focus our observations.

This chapter looks at a natural developmental sequence in drawing skills that appears in all children in the same order. Even visually impaired children exhibit the beginning steps of the sequence until the youngsters' lack of visual feedback discourages them from continuing. You will note this sequence is similar to the steps children take in developing physical skills, cognitive skills, and especially writing skills with early scribbling.

It is obvious that the brain is programmed to accomplish all kinds of development in this order—from the general to the specific—as youngsters have the opportunity and materials to interact with their environment in a playful manner (manipulating, mastering, and creating meaning), thus discovering what it and they are able to do. The same creativity emerges naturally in all aspects of art, from making collages to modeling clay, but this chapter will focus on the emergence of representational drawing skills as an example.

Right Brain versus Left Brain

The two hemispheres of the brain control different functions in human beings. The right hemisphere or right brain plays a dominant role in holistic thinking, visual-spatial skills, intuition, emotions, art, and creativity. The left hemisphere or left brain predominates in rational, linear, analytical, and sequential thinking; language, reading, writing, and math skills. Babies appear to be born with a slight right-hemisphere advantage. As language skills develop, the left hemisphere catches up. By age 4, communication between the two hemispheres has greatly improved (Sprenger, 2008).

Nevertheless, in most people the left hemisphere eventually tends to dominate the right, perhaps because of its focus on literacy and math skills during the school years. In early childhood, the right brain is dominant. Thus it is the preschool years that offer young children the opportunity to develop creative skills that can last for a lifetime during this early right-brain dominance. It is just as important for you (who may be left-brain–dominant) to be aware of this right-brain dominance in young children, and become more aware of the processes children use than the end product of their efforts. Young children can teach all of us a great deal about creativity if we will open our minds to them and encourage this originality.

DEVELOPING ART SKILLS
MAKES BASIC SHAPES

During their first year of life, children really do not draw. If they have access to a crayon, they are more apt to put it in their mouths than to put a mark on paper. Around the age of 13 months children's first scribbling begins. The first marks they make are usually random. These marks have more to do with movement, in fact, than with art. The toddler is often surprised to find that a crayon, a pencil, or a paintbrush will make marks. Youngsters are often captivated by watching the lines that their movements can make on a surface. The surface is not always paper, much to their caregiver's dismay. Children will mark on walls, tabletops, or anything else that will take a mark.

This first stage of art skill development is purely mechanical and manipulative. The child is gaining control over the art tool, whether it is a crayon, paintbrush, pencil, felt-tip marker, or chalk. The child makes random marks without using eye control. Visually impaired children make the same kind of random marks in the dirt. Writing scribbles also begin like this but eventually veer off in a different direction.

Older children in your program who have had no access to art materials (or those who have been suppressed in their attempts at home) still go through these same stages (Figure 10.1). However, their progression through the stages occurs more rapidly. It takes older children far less time to learn how to handle art materials through spontaneous exploratory play.

You will note that in all these early art experiences, young children are once again teaching themselves through playful exploration of the medium with the "3 Ms" of manipulation, mastery, and meaning. The end results that appear on their papers are not art products, not paintings as such, but the footprints of the process of emerging art skills.

From about 2 years of age on through 3 and 4, and sometimes later depending on the child, an individual will mark on paper in a scribbling manner. At first the scribbles may be endless lines done in a rhythmic, manipulative manner. Eventually the child will use eye control as well as hand/arm movement to make her scribbles and direct their placement on the paper. One scribble often is placed on top of another until the paper is a hodgepodge of lines and circles. Painters may cover their painted scribbles with layers and layers of paint before they are finished.

1. *SCRIBBLE*
   UNCONTROLLED
   Marks made on paper for enjoyment. Child has little control
   of eye and hand movement. No pattern. 
   CONTROLLED
   Control of eye and hand. Repeated design. 
   NAMED SCRIBBLE
   Child tells you what s/he has drawn. May not be
   recognizable to adult.

2. *SHAPE AND DESIGN*
   Child makes shapes such as circles, squares, ovals, triangles.

   Child's muscle control is increasing and s/he is able to place
   shapes and designs wherever s/he wants.

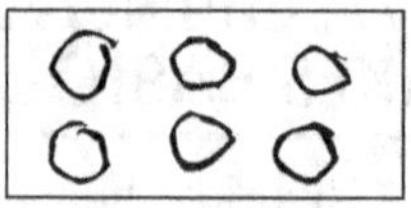

3. *MANDALA*
   Child usually divides circle or square with lines.

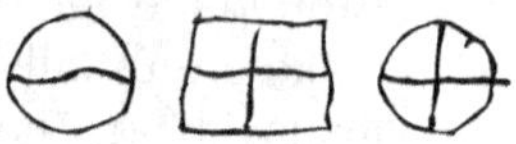

4. *RADIALS*
   Lines that radiate from a single point. Can be
   part of a mandala.

5. *SUNS*
   Formed from oval, square, or circle with short
   lines extending from the shape. The extending
   lines take many variations.

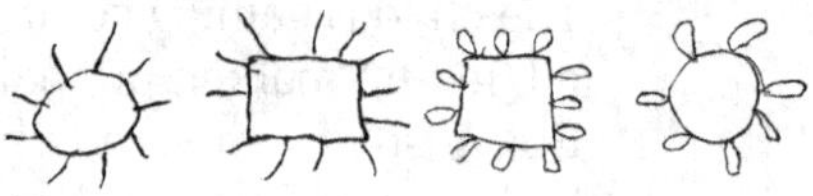

6. *HUMANS*
   Child uses SUN design and develops a face by adding
   human features. . . a "sun face."

   Child elongates several lines of the SUN design to create
   arms and legs.

7. *PICTORIALS*
   Child combines ALL stages to make recognizable design
   or objects.

Figure 10.1   Stages of Art Development

Painters may cover their scribbles with layers of paint.

The result of this effort has little meaning to the child at first, for he is not trying to create something, but merely experimenting by moving colors around on a paper. The process, not the product, is important to him. Adults, however, think of art mainly in terms of creating a product. Their response to scribbling is often either to dismiss it as unimportant and worthless, or to ask children to tell them what they have drawn. Once children learn that adults expect this sort of information, the youngsters often begin naming their scribbles. This behavior does not mean that they really had something in mind when they began moving the brush around on the paper. Our comments, instead, should focus on their efforts in the process of drawing, not on the "imperfect" products they first create. "I see that you used three different colors in your painting today, Ross."

Children work hard at scribbling. Only they know when a scribbled "drawing" is finished—actually, the *process* is finished. Some youngsters go over and over the lines they have made, almost as if they are practicing the way to make a straight or curved line. We understand these children have progressed to the "mastery" stage of exploratory art. Their early products seem to show a greater proportion of vertical lines, especially in easel paintings. But many children are able to make multiple horizontal, diagonal, and curved lines as well. Back and forth the youngsters work, sometimes changing their hand direction when they get tired and sometimes even changing hands. Whereas 2-year-olds place one scribble on top of another, 3- and 4-year-olds frequently put a single scribble on one paper (Kellogg, 1970).

Rhoda Kellogg, the art specialist who collected and analyzed thousands of children's drawings from around the world, identified 20 scribbles that children make. Not all children make all 20 scribbles that they are capable of producing. Individuals tend to concentrate on a few favorites and repeat them in many variations. The fact that all children everywhere produce some of the same 20 scribbles spontaneously—

and no others—seems to indicate that this early form of art must be genetic in the human species.

Kellogg considers these scribbles to be "the building blocks of art." The individual's scribble "vocabulary" most easily can be read in his finger painting. He will draw his "designs" with one or more fingers, and then "erase" them before starting over. Because they do not pile up one on top of the other as with opaque paint, it is easier to see which of the 20 basic scribbles he favors.

As children's physical and mental development progresses and they are able to control the brush and paint more easily, their scribbles begin to take on the configuration of shapes. Kellogg has identified six basic shapes in children's early art: rectangle (including square), oval (including circle), triangle, Greek cross (+), diagonal cross (×), and odd shape (a catchall). These shapes do not necessarily appear separately, but rather are mixed up with other scribbles or with one another.

If children have had the freedom to experiment with art as toddlers, they usually begin to make basic shapes spontaneously by age 3. Children's perceptual and memory skills help them to form, store, and retrieve concepts about shapes quite early if they have had appropriate experiences. The particular shapes a child favors seem to evolve from his own scribbles. Attempts at making ovals and circles usually appear early. This form seems innately appealing to young humans everywhere, perhaps because of their preferred attention to the oval human face.

Circular movements in their scribbling eventually lead them to form an oval. The youngsters often repeat it, going around and around over the same shape. Visual discrimination of the shape and muscle control of the brush or crayon finally allows them to form the shape by itself instead of intertwined within a mass of scribbles. Memory comes into play as well, allowing the children to retrieve the oval from their repertoire of marks and to repeat it another day.

In this manner, the child's capacity to draw shapes seems to emerge from his capacity to control the lines he makes in his scribbling. In other words, he makes one of the basic shapes because he remembers it from creating it spontaneously in his scribbling, not because he is copying the shape from his environment. As he experiments, he stumbles onto new ways to make new shapes. But certain ones seem more appealing, and individual children return to them again and again.

Three- and 4-year-olds first create rectangles by drawing a set of parallel vertical lines, later adding horizontal lines at the top and bottom rather than drawing a continuous line for a perimeter. Thus we see why it is important to give them many opportunities and much time to practice. The children are teaching themselves to draw, just as they taught themselves to build with blocks, walk, talk, speak, write, and read.

Scribbles are much more than they seem. Researchers have found that people assimilate more information from visual stimuli than through any other sense. Observers of art perceive colors, spaces, lines, patterns, sounds, sights, messages, memories, and textures. The observers are the children themselves and you.

If You Have Not Checked This Item: Some Helpful Ideas

■ Provide Controllable Materials

Beginners will not be able to progress much beyond scribbling unless they can control the materials. Be sure to provide fat, kindergarten-size crayons for children to grip well. Children can use thin crayons, too, but sometimes beginners bear down so hard they break them. Mix your tempera paints with just enough water to make them creamy but not drippy. Add cornstarch or flour to thicken them if they are too thin. Buy short, stubby easel paintbrushes that young children can manipulate easily. Wrap ends of colored chalk with masking tape to help gripping and to control smearing.

■ Be Nondirective

Allow children to explore and experiment with paint and chalk, finger paint and crayons, and felt-tip markers and pencils completely on their own. Put the materials out for their use during free play, or have materials invitingly placed on low shelves near art tables for the youngsters' own selection.

■ Provide Materials Children Can Use on Their Own

Easels always should be available. They are one of the best motivators for spontaneous drawing that you can have available. Children soon find out that all they need for painting is to put on a painting smock and go to the easel. There is no need to get out paints, for they are already mixed and waiting. There is no need to ask for help or direction from the teacher.

Remember that children are still in the exploratory stage and should not be expected to paint a picture. If they want your comments, you can talk to them about the colors, lines, and shapes they have created. They may want the paper displayed on the wall. If not, label it with their names and dates and add it to their portfolios.

DRAWS A PERSON AS A SUN-FACE WITH ARMS AND LEGS

The next step in the sequence of children's self-taught art skills involves combining two of the shapes they have made. Kellogg has observed and written a great deal about this behavior. The Greek cross (+) and the diagonal cross (×) are favorite shapes. These are often combined inside an oval or rectangle to make what is sometimes called a "mandala." Mandalas don't necessarily stand alone on a sheet of paper but are often embedded in groups of scribbles.

From mandalas to suns to humans is the natural progression that much of children's spontaneous art follows. Watch for this development in the children in your program. Talk to parents about the spontaneous way art skills develop in children if youngsters have freedom to explore on their own. Both you and the parents may want to save children's scribbling and early shape drawings to see if you can identify the sequence of their development. Be sure to date the art.

Pictorial drawing eventually evolves out of particular combinations of shapes. One of the first representations to occur in children's art is the human form. This representation seems to evolve naturally from the child's first experiments with an oval shape combined with a cross inside it (the mandala), which then leads to an oval with lines radiating from its rim (the sun), which finally evolves into an oval with two lines for arms, two for legs, and small circles inside the large head/body oval for eyes (the sun-face human).

It looks like the sun he has been drawing, only with two side "rays" for arms, two longer bottom "rays" for legs, and sometimes short top "rays" for hair. All children everywhere seem to draw their first humans in this spontaneous manner. They are known in the art world as "tadpole" people because of the resemblance. Here we are calling them "sun-face humans."

To adults unfamiliar with the child's sequence of development, these are strange humans indeed: all head and no body, with arms and legs attached to the head. Surely children age 3 and 4 can see that a person's arms and legs are attached to the body and not the head, you may say. Adult concepts about art, however, have little in common with what is happening with the beginning child artist.

All along adults have looked at the products of children's art (the drawings or paintings) as the most important thing, when to the young child, the process is more important. Children are not drawing a picture at first, but developing a skill. Their efforts progress through an observable sequence of development from general to specific, from holistic to detailed drawings in a spontaneous progression.

This 4-year-old artist paints sun-face children playing on a playground.

Production of a human is the transition to pictorial drawing for most young children. The method they apply is the same one they used for making shapes and symbols. They draw *what they know how to make,* and *not what they see.* Out of their practice with mandalas and suns comes this sun-face human with a few of the "sun's rays" for arms and legs. They do not draw stick figures until later, and then only by copying what adults or older children are drawing.

It is not surprising that children's first humans are all face. We remember that even infants attend to this image most frequently. The human brain seems programmed to take in details about faces. This, after all, is the most important part of the human being.

As children first create their sun-face humans, they do not always repeat their drawings exactly. All children make armless humans at one time or another, even though the youngsters may have drawn arm lines earlier. This behavior does not indicate the children are regressing or are cognitively immature. It may appear only because the proportion of two parallel legs to a head is more appealing alone than with arms sticking out at the sides. Children rarely draw legless humans. The behavior may result from the brain's tendency to overgeneralize in early categories. Later details will be more discriminating.

As children have more practice drawing their early people, they often add hair or hats, hands or fingers, feet or toes. The additions may be lines, circles, or scribbles. Children may identify their persons as being themselves or someone else. The actual size of the person named in the drawing is usually not considered by young children. Instead, they often draw the most important person in the picture as the biggest.

Eventually children will add a body to their head drawings. They often do this by drawing two extremely long legs and putting a horizontal line part way up between them. You may remember that this is the common method they used earlier to draw rectangles. Youngsters often will draw a belly button in the middle of the body. By this time they frequently are drawing other pictorial representations, as well. These representations, as you will note, are also based on the children's previous experience, showing once again how development proceeds in a continuous sequence from the general to the specific, as long as children have the freedom to experiment naturally.

Once children have discovered the way to draw a person, they will often begin drawing animals as well. Youngsters' first animals are hard to distinguish from humans. It is obvious the animals are based on the same practiced form: a head with eyes, nose, and mouth; a body with arms sticking out from the sides and legs coming out the bottom. Often the animal is facing front like a person and seems to be standing on two legs. We know the drawing is an animal instead of a person because of the two ears sticking up straight from the top of the head. Sometimes these are pointed like cat ears or circular like mouse ears.

Eventually the young artist will find a way to make his animal horizontal with an elongated body parallel to the bottom of the paper, four legs in a row from the bottom of the body, a head at one end, and often a tail at the other end. The features of the face are still positioned in a frontal pose and not a profile, even though the animal is positioned with its side showing. Most animal head profiles do not appear in children's drawings until around age 5 or later.

In fact, many children do not draw animals until they go to kindergarten. This behavior—or lack of it—may be due to their progress in their own developmental sequence, but drawing animals also reflects the kindergarten curriculum. Often kindergarten teachers give children outline animals to copy that may, in fact, short-circuit the youngsters' spontaneous development.

If You Have Not Checked This Item: Some Helpful Ideas

■ Draw with Chalk

Colored chalk is very appealing to children if they can grip it and control its tendency to smear. Wrap the upper end with foil or masking tape to make gripping easier. Soft, thick chalk is best. The regular size breaks too easily with the pressure some children apply. Chalk should be used dry at first for children to become used to its properties. Then you can wet either the paper or the chalk for a richer effect. Use either a water-sugar solution (four parts warm water to one part sugar) or use liquid starch, and apply it to the paper for children to draw on with dry chalk. Or use the liquid as a dip for children to wet the chalk but draw on a dry surface. Many children like the rhythm of dipping and drawing. Dry chalk marks on wet paper can also be smeared around to create different effects. Draw on brown paper grocery bags for still a different effect.

■ Draw with Felt-Tip Pens

Water-soluble felt-tip pens are always favorites with children. They seem able to control them more easily than paintbrushes or crayons. The pens' thick size and smooth marking ability make them especially well suited to preschool art. Some marking pens have brush-tip rather than felt-tip points. These have the spreading capacity of watercolor paint. It is not necessary or even desirable to give each child an entire set of pens of all colors. Give the youngsters only a few colors at a time until they express the need for more.

■ Keep Art Activities Spontaneous

Do not use pictures, figure drawings, or models for your children to copy. This is not how spontaneous art develops. Even children who have reached the pictorial stage do not need to copy. You will find that they draw what they know rather than what they see.

■ Read a Book

Current children's art picture books reflect the ideas presented in this chapter about children's creativity. Carle's **The Artist Who Painted a Blue Horse** shows a large animal on each double-spread page: blue horse, red crocodile, orange elephant,

Figure 10.2   Art
Picture Books

> ***The Artist Who Painted a Blue Horse*** (Carle, 2011)
> ***Willow*** (Brennan-Nelson & Brennan, 2008)
> ***I'm the Best Artist in the Ocean*** (Sherry, 2008)
> ***Art & Max*** (Wiesner, 2010)

black polar bear, and more. Ask your children why they think the artist used these colors. Wiesner's ***Art & Max*** has a small stand-up lizard painting a big stand-up lizard not on an easel but on himself with unexpected consequences. In ***Willow*** a little girl's responses teach her scowling art teacher to let down her hair and paint. ***I'm the Best Artist in the Ocean*** is all about drawing by a giant squid on the side of a whale. (See Figure 10.2.)

■ Talk with Children About Their Art Through Your Observations

Instead of trying to elicit stories about children's artwork or making evaluative comments, teachers should first observe several aspects of the work and then, when it seems appropriate, talk with the child about these aspects. Such aspects could include its medium, shapes, colors, design, scenes, or purpose. The teacher could mention to the child artist what she sees in the drawing/painting and hope that the child might respond.

For example, she might say: "Ricardo, it looks to me as if you started your painting with a lot of red paint and then covered part of it with yellow. Then you have a row of figures down at the bottom in still a different color. What do you like about it?" It is then up to the child to respond or not in any way he chooses. There is no right answer for what to say to children when they show you their artwork. Describing the lines or shapes will draw children back into their composition, helping them to reflect on what they have created.

MAKES PICTORIAL DRAWINGS

The first trees are also transitional drawings based on the human figures children have taught themselves to draw. Some look like armless humans with two long legs for the trunk and a circular head for the treetop, which often contains small circles or dots that may be leaves, but look more like fruit. The trees are not drawn to size. They may be similar in height to the humans in the picture or even smaller.

As children have practice and freedom to draw, more details evolve on trees. The tops of some trees resemble the sun with the rays as branches and balls at the ends of the branches as leaves. Other children make branches coming out from the trunk like arms on a human. The first flowers are also based on a familiar model: a sun with a stem.

The 5-year-old artist who painted this picture says: "I like to eat apples."

Children who are able to draw representational objects with crayons or felt-tip markers may not be able to do this same level of drawing with a paintbrush and paint if they have not used paint before. It is important to realize children must go through the same developmental stages of manipulation, mastery, and meaning with each new medium they encounter.

A few of the children in your classroom may begin doing pictorial drawings at age 3 and a few more at age 4. Do not expect all youngsters to do so. Let them progress through their own sequences of development at their own individual rates. Those who do draw pictorially will be using the previously discussed repertoire of figures they have developed. Their drawings will be representations, not reproductions, for the young child draws what he knows, not what he sees.

This principle is especially apparent in children's spontaneous drawings at age 6, when many youngsters go through a stage of so-called X-ray drawings that show both the inside and outside of objects at the same time. The children's drawings depict things as the youngsters know them, rather than just what they can see. People are shown inside houses without walls as in a cutaway drawing, for example.

The children in your classroom probably will not have reached this stage, nor will many have developed a baseline in their drawings much before age 5. Objects are still free-floating on their art papers just as their first spontaneous letters are. This different perspective used by young children is sometimes used by adult artists as well.

Children also interpret their pictorial drawings differently than adults. Youngsters often do not start out to draw a particular thing. Instead they describe their art more by the way it turns out than by what they had in mind. The way it turns out may have more to do with the materials they are using than anything else. Runny paint in easel drawings may remind the youngsters of smoke, rain, or fire, for instance, so they draw a picture of rain or a fire.

On the other hand, some children purposefully draw a picture of the post office that the class visited on a field trip. The picture will look, of course, just like the building shape they have learned to do spontaneously, and not at all like the post office itself. Children first draw buildings by combining mostly rectangular shapes in various ways and not by looking at buildings. The drawing often has a door in the middle and at least two square windows above it. Roofs may be flat or pointed and often have a chimney with smoke coming out. The drawing catches the essence of the building, not the reality. Some 4-year-olds also draw cars and trucks, as well as boats and planes. Often it is hard to tell the difference between early cars and trucks.

Once children have a repertoire of figures that the adults around them seem to accept, they will begin to put the figures together into scenes. The size and color of their objects will not be realistic. The more important the object or person, the larger the child will make it. Colors will have little relation to the object being depicted. They depend more on the particular brush the child happens to pick up, or a color the child happens to favor at the moment. Objects will be free-floating, as mentioned, and not anchored to a baseline. But the effect will be balanced and pleasing, nevertheless.

Children who verbalize about their art may tell you things about their drawings that have little to do with what your eyes seem to show you. The youngsters must be speaking about an inner vision of their world, you decide. You are right, of course. And from inner visions come creative ideas. Let's support this beginning urge toward creativity in all children by giving it the freedom to grow spontaneously.

If You Have Not Checked This Item: Some Helpful Ideas

■ Add New Art Activities

Your children may want to try drawing with liquid glue from a plastic squeeze bottle. They may want to draw with a pencil or other marker first and then follow the lines with glue. Or they can try the glue without guidelines. Because glue is transparent when it dries, you may want to add food coloring to the bottles. This liquid glue is a much more free-flowing medium; children will need to play with it for a while to see how it works and how to control it just as they did the first time they used paint. They will need to squeeze and move the bottle at the same time, a trick of coordination that may be difficult for some. Don't expect pictorial designs from glue drawing.

■ Encourage Children to Draw About Field Trips

Not all your children can or want to draw pictorially. But for those who do, you can suggest they draw a picture about a trip you have taken together. Children find it satisfying to be able to represent things they know about. They can tell about the things in words, have you write down their words, or record their words on a recorder. But it is also good to make a drawing or build a block structure about new things they have encountered. Their products help you as a teacher to find out what is important to them and how they conceptualize the new ideas they have gained.

■ Encourage Children to "Document" Their Science Projects by Drawing Pictures

In addition to use in their journals, children's drawings can also be used to document their science projects. They can draw whatever it is they are doing for their projects in either single pictures or a series of pictures or panels. For example, children who are planting seeds can draw pictures of the soil, the seeds, and the plants in their stages of growth. Have them explain what the pictures show while you print the words they say at the bottom of the picture. They may even want to create their own picture books of their projects. In the Reggio Emilia schools in Italy and the United States, art is used as a language to reinforce the art concepts children are learning.

Althouse, Johnson, and Mitchell (2003) explain how document panels display a child's work with great care and attention to both the content and aesthetic aspects. The documentation describes in the child's own words the images, ideas, and processes represented by the art work. They believe such panels are important because they show the processes of the art experience from beginning to end.

DEVELOPING MUSIC SKILLS

Most young children love music and respond readily to its sounds and rhythms. Music in the preschool classroom makes them feel happy. Whether it comes from recordings, CDs, instruments, or singing voices, its sounds and rhythms give the whole atmosphere a feeling of release and the excitement of something different happening. It is the essence of creativity.

What's even more exciting to learn is what Shore (2005) tells us: that a wide variety of research and anecdotal evidence suggests that music can do more than change our moods; it can actually change our brains. Music is the most direct route to thinking, according to Snyder (1997), because it requires neither words nor symbols to be perceived. She describes how Frank Wilson, a neuroscientist who registered brain scans of children performing certain tasks, reports that when the children read words, the language center of the brain lights up. But when they read music, the whole brain lights up like a Christmas tree!

Music can help young children synthesize experiences, transition into new activities, calm down during naptime, build self-esteem, and improve performance in language and math (Shore & Strasser, 2006). When children sing, they develop the rhythmic patterns of language and recognize the sounds of rhyming words. It taps into the right hemisphere of the brain, which operates both music and memory functions. It connects the right hemisphere with the left hemisphere, which operates speaking and reading. The steady beat of singing develops pathways in the brain that seem to be essential for learning, especially related to reading (Snyder, 1997). Hap Palmer (2001) has even used singing to teach young children to read.

In addition to the significance of music in the lives of the most children, it takes on special meaning for children with disabilities. Gould, Kaplan, and Wilson (2012) tell us: that children with disabilities are not necessarily disabled in music. Thus we can capitalize on their interest or talent, perhaps allowing them to be leaders among their peers.

With all of these advantages to its credit, music surely should be considered an important part of the early childhood curriculum. Unfortunately, this often is not the case. Too many teachers do not realize the importance of music in child development. Too many teachers may feel awkward and inadequate engaging in musical activities with children. Society seems to support them when it considers music and art education to be frills rather than necessities. Now that you know its importance, it is up to you as a teacher of young children to include music as an important curriculum component. It is also up to you to overcome any reluctance you may feel about using music with your children. Let's start with rhythm first, in which you and all the children can become easily and happily involved.

✓ MOVES ARMS AND HANDS IN RHYTHM TO A BEAT

Preschool children's acquisition of musical skills crosses several areas of development, including physical, cognitive, language, and creative. But because music itself involves both rhythm and sound (tempo and tone), we will look first at young children's development of rhythm.

All humans are rhythmical beings, whether or not we recognize the fact. Rhythm, in fact, is the essence of our life: witness the beating of our heart and the breathing of our lungs. It is not so surprising to find, therefore, that even infants can make rhythmical responses with their arms, hands, legs, and feet. These claps, kicks, or wavings seem to be triggered by internal stimuli and not by external sounds or motions.

Freeman (2012) tells us that exposure to different beats is important for a child's musical foundation. But even more important for teachers of preschool children is the neuroscience research that indicates steady beat does affect attention behavior. Geist, Geist, and Kuznik (2012) found that children have the potential to be more engaged when listening to steady beats than when listening to verbal-only instructions. How would you apply this finding in your classroom? Would playing background music with a steady beat help your children learn to listen more carefully? Try including recorded music with steady beats in your curriculum.

One of the simplest ways for preschool children to develop rhythm is by clapping. Most have participated in hand-clapping activities from infancy. They have imitated their mother doing pat-a-cake and imitated others around them who applaud a performance by clapping. Now, in this item, they are observed performing a musical activity with their hands: moving their arms and hands to a beat. This

Clapping is one of the simplest ways for children to develop rhythm.

can mean clapping with their hands or beating out a rhythm with sticks, blocks, or percussion instruments held in the hands. Simple. You can do this, too.

Rhythm is a natural part of all of us. Our heart goes on beating whether or not we think about it. Our fingers may tap out a rhythm automatically, but can preschool children clap their hands in rhythm to a beat created outside their body? They can if their physical skills have developed normally and they have had practice clapping in rhythm

As they develop physically, arm control occurs before hand control, and hand control occurs before finger control. A second sequence of development begins with control of one arm/hand independently of the other (as in waving). Next comes the simultaneous use of both arms/hands (as in clapping), and finally comes alternate movements of two arms/hands (as in drumming).

Although clapping ability appears early in a child's development, the ability to clap with control comes later. Two-year-olds, for instance, enjoy clapping, but usually cannot clap in a pattern without a great deal of help and practice. The concept of clapping in rhythm or clapping out the syllables of a name is beyond most of them. Three, 4-, and 5-year-old children also may have some difficulty following a clapping pattern. Yet most of them can learn to clap the syllables of their names and enjoy repeating the activity because it is personal.

Once they have reached this maturity, children need to have practice to follow external rhythms. When you sing songs or play CDs in your classroom, give children practice clapping to the rhythm. Or use familiar folk songs to practice clapping to different beats.

Focusing on a child's name is the surest way to interest a young egocentric child in almost any activity. At circle time or small-group time you can introduce "name clapping," clapping out the syllables in each child's name as the children say the name aloud. Make the activity more interesting by adding other words, such as "hello" or "my name is." Now the children can chant and clap: "Hel-lo-Chris-to-pher," "My-name-is-Sar-ah." As the children become more adept, add their last names to this clapping activity. "My-name-is-Mel-is-sa-Brad-ley."

✓ PLAYS RHYTHM INSTRUMENTS

Moving the two arms/hands alternately in a vertical motion, such as beating on a drum, indicates a more mature development of a child's arm/hand control than does clapping. Young children enjoy beating on drums, pans, wooden blocks, and almost anything that will make a noise. For beaters they can use their hands (fingers, palms, knuckles, fists), drumsticks, mallets, ladles, or anything else they can pound with. Fill your classroom music center with drums and beaters.

The developmental sequence of drumming with the hands follows that of clapping. But children will have more success in beating a drum in a particular rhythm if they first have had many clapping experiences. When your children demonstrate that they can clap in rhythm, it is time to introduce the drum.

Instruments used in preschool programs fall into the same categories of those used by professionals (see Figure 10.3).

Rhythm instruments such as the drum need to be taken seriously in the preschool: that is, a drum is not a toy, but a real instrument and should be treated as such. Perhaps because teachers do not understand that rhythm instruments are serious instruments used in real bands, they allow children to treat these instruments as toys. Instead, each instrument should be introduced to children separately, with the teacher showing them how to use it properly and limiting their using it improperly. In this way the children get the most from the experience; they learn how to use the instrument, to appreciate the sound it makes, and to practice the physical skills the instrument affords them.

Figure 10.3 Rhythm Instruments

Sound Makers	Melody Instruments	Harmony Instruments
Tone blocks	Xylophones	Autoharp
Coconut shells	Marimbas	Guitar
Bells	Tone bells	Harmonica
Triangles	Tonette	Ukelele
Gongs	Flutophone	Banjo
Cymbals	Ocarina	Mandolin
Tambourines		Accordion
Rattles		Piano
Maracas		Electric keyboard
Drums		

Unfortunately, rhythm instruments are often used in "rhythm bands" with all the instruments played at once as the children march around to music. The youngsters, of course, may have fun with such an activity, but it adds little to their enjoyment of music, their skill development, or their appreciation for the instruments they hold (whose name they often don't know). Instead, children tend to bang as loud as they can all at once, creating a cacophony of sound—noise—which drowns out the sounds of the individual instruments, the music, and the rhythm they are supposed to be following.

Drums

Drums come in all sizes and shapes. Some are intended to be played with the hands; some are played with two drumsticks, and some are played with one. Toy catalogs often feature cultural drums and shakers, such as the double-headed frame drum from Peru, single-headed frame drum from Java, talking drum from Africa, Chinese tom-tom, Caribbean bongo, Chinese gong, seed pod shaker from Zimbabwe, shek-ere from Ghana, juju nut arm shaker from Ghana, rain dance rattle from Guatemala, and wooden frog guiro from Thailand.

Commercial drums are usually wooden or plastic with a skin or plastic head over one or both ends. Have several drums and drumsticks available in the music center. Take time to introduce their use to a few children at a time rather than merely putting them on a shelf. Talk to them about each drum and how to use it. Let them try each one. Put on music and let them try to keep a beat with their drum. They can use drumsticks or their hands. Pass the drums around until everyone has a chance. Keep this activity going for several days with different music.

If You Have Not Checked This Item: Some Helpful Ideas

■ Send Drum Messages

Children enjoy sending drumbeat messages. If they have learned to clap out names by syllables, they will be able to send drum messages the same way. Let them try sending their names ("My-name-is-Ri-car-do") with drumbeats. Can the other children guess what they are saying?

■ Make Drums

Various types of drums can be made, depending on the material. Use large cans, ice cream containers, oatmeal boxes, round plastic containers, coffee cans, margarine tubs, or wooden or metal buckets for the body of the drum. Children can decorate the container and drum on its head. But for a realistic drumhead, you can use animal parchments (from music stores), goatskin, heavy plastic, or canvas. Remove one or both ends of the can or container. Cut one or two circular head pieces larger than the container opening. Punch holes around the edge of the drumhead material about 2 inches apart. Soak the parchment or goatskin in water for half an hour. Place the

Figure 10.4   Instrument
Books

> ***The Banza*** (Wolkstein, 1981)
> ***Boom Boom Go Away!*** (Geringer, 2010)
> ***Do You Do a Didgeridoo?*** (Page, 2008)
> ***Drum Chavi Drum*** (Dole, 2003)
> ***Jazz on a Saturday Night*** (Dillon, 2007)
> ***My Family Plays Music*** (Cox, 2003)

drum head material on either end of the drum body and lace tightly together with cord or rawhide laces.

To make drumsticks, glue small rubber balls to the ends of sticks such as pencils or wooden dowels. Wrap cloth around the ends of wooden ladles, or insert sticks into spools and wrap cloth around the spools.

■ Read a Book

Books about drumming can serve as lead-ins to drumming activities (see Figure 10.4). ***Drum, Chavi, Drum*** (Dole, 2003) tells the story of the Hispanic girl Chavi who gets to play the conga drum in the Miami Calle Ocho festival even when girls don't play drums. In ***Jazz on a Saturday Night*** (Dillon & Dillon, 2007), the great jazz musicians of a bygone era play again on the pages of this book and in the CD that accompanies it.

Sometimes all it takes to get children involved in music is reading a story about an instrument and making their own instrument. Read them ***The Banza*** (Wolkstein, 1981) the Haitian folktale about the little goat Cabree who saves his life with his magic banjo. To make a rubberbanjo, have children bring in empty shoe boxes. Cut a large oval heart-shaped hole in the cover, tape the cover to the box, cut four notches in either end, and stretch four long rubber bands across it lengthwise. Children can paint their banzas in wild Caribbean colors like those in the book. Older books like this one can often be back-ordered from bookstores or from Amazon.com.

Another great instrument book is ***Do You Do a Didgeridoo?*** (Page, 2008), which includes a CD-ROM, about a mysterious customer who demands—in rhyme—that Mr. Music Man find him this unusual Australian folk instrument. The children can make their own didgeridoos from a very long cardboard wrapping paper roll. Press both ends nearly closed with tape. Paint the instrument in brilliant bands of color and then try blowing a "low wa-hoo." Can they do it?

SINGS WITH GROUP OR BY HIM/HERSELF

Children who are not speaking in the classroom or who are speaking only one or two words can sing. Strangely enough, singing, which is controlled mainly by the right hemisphere of the brain, can occur even when speaking, which is controlled mainly by the left hemisphere, is limited. In addition, children who do not speak English can sing songs in English. They may not understand the words, but they can sing them along with the other children. Even shy, nonverbal children often join in singing before they have the courage to speak in the classroom. What about you? Do you have the courage to sing to the children?

You may be surprised to learn that singing, not only by the children, but also by the teacher, is an important ingredient in children's literacy development. K. Matthews (2012) discusses **orality**, the practice of tuning our ears to spoken or sung linguistic patterns, inflections, and contents of language. She feels that children who do not have that experiential learning of hearing rich, full oral language and song will have problems with literacy. Orality needs to come before literacy. In other words, singing supports the brain development necessary for literacy. If you don't sing with the children, who will?

With this information in mind, you should be filling your program with songs and chants. Children who get caught up in the joy of music will join in. Other children may hesitate at first, but may soon find the musical activities you provide to be so contagious they cannot resist. Do not force any child to participate. Invite everyone. Get up and march around the room singing and having such a good time yourself, no one will want to be left out.

To teach children songs, you need to repeat them over and over on a daily basis with everyone joining in. Sing morning greeting songs, transition songs, finger plays at circle time, singing games in the large motor area; songs for seasonal holidays, songs for rainy days, sunny days, snowy days; songs about animals, and especially, songs about the children themselves. Use nursery rhyme favorites of your own and make up words to familiar tunes, using the children's names whenever possible, and you will soon create an interested group of young singers.

CDs are fine for occasional use, but give your children a language boost by helping them sing their own words to songs and chants. You need not be a good singer yourself. The children will never know the difference. If you cannot sing, then chant with the children in unison or in a monotone and clap your hands. For example:

(Tune: "Are You Sleeping?")
Where is Carmela?   *Very nice to see you,*
Where is Carmela?   *Very nice to see you,*
Here she is! Here she is!   *Come and play; come and play.*

Other tunes you can use with your own words include

"Row, Row, Row Your Boat"
"This Old Man"
"Here We Go 'Round the Mulberry Bush"
"On Top of Spaghetti"

Learn folk songs from different cultures through CDs, songbooks, Web sites, the children themselves, and their family members. Invite family members to visit the class and sing songs in their home language. English-speaking children can sing along, too, just as dual language children can sing songs with English words. All it takes is repetition. Sing the songs over and over. Children are geared to enjoy such repetition. Remember the mastery stage of exploratory play?

Still another opportunity for singing is singing games. They ask for children to listen to the words of the song and then follow the actions called for. You may need to play a CD at first so that children can hear the directions. After repeating the singing game many times, children will be able to sing and act out the song without the CD.

If You Have Not Checked This Item: Some Helpful Ideas

■ Have a TV Show

Have a few volunteers put on a pretend TV show for the others in the class. They can sing, drum, or play another instrument. Use your video recorder. Then ask for volunteers in the audience to perform. If you have a karaoke machine, you should have plenty of volunteers. Play back the song and ask others to join in. Or read the hottest book around: *So You Want to be a Rock Star* (Vernick, 2012). Your class will quickly learn to play an air guitar, wear the coolest clothes, sign autographs for tons of fans, and sing a cool theme song—LOUD. The book suggests that rock stars should make up their own songs by singing their name over and over!

■ Sing Questions and Answers

Sing questions to a group of children and have them sing back an answer. For example, sing: "How are you feeling today?" They can sing the answer: "We're feeling fine!"

■ Sing Directions

Sing short direction songs and have others join in. For example, sing:

(Tune: *The Farmer in the Dell*)
It's time to pick up blocks,   *It's time to pick up trucks . . . etc.*
It's time to pick up blocks,   *It's time to go to lunch . . . etc.*
Come on everyone,   *It's time to go outside . . . etc.*
It's time to pick up blocks.   *It's time to say goodbye . . . etc.*

(Tune: *Are You Sleeping?*)
Are you hungry?
Are you hungry?   *Time to go home . . . etc.*
Time to eat,   *Are you ready? etc.*
Time to eat,   *Put your coat on . . . etc.*
Come and take a seat now,
Come and take a seat now,
Sit right down, sit right down.

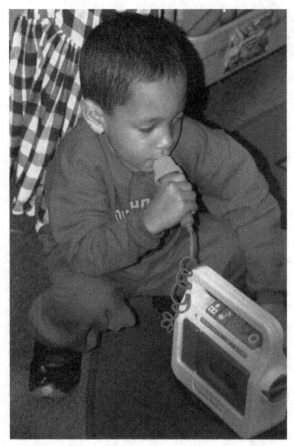

Put on a TV show using your karaoke machine.

■　Read a Book

Dooby Dooby Moo (Cronin, 2006) has Farmer Brown's animals acting up again. This time they decide to enter the talent show at the county fair. The cows sing "Dooby, dooby, moo." ("Twinkle Twinkle Little Star.") The sheep sing "Fa, la, la, la, baa." ("Home on the Range."). Duck sings "Quack, quack, quaaaak" ("Born to Be Wild.") You can have an animal talent show with your children pretending to be singing animals. Have some fun. Go a little wild.

In ***Take Me Out of the Bathtub and Other Silly Dilly Songs*** (Katz, 2001), 14 wonderfully wacky songs appear on every other page to familiar tunes such as "Take Me Out to the Ballgame," "I've Been Working on the Railroad," and "Row, Row, Row Your Boat," with illustrations as wild as the words. Your children will love singing them. (See Figure 10.5.)

Transition Songs

Transitions in preschool classrooms are the periods between activities. Children must move from what they are engaged in to something new. Not all children are able to move smoothly. Even when teachers tell children it's time to put away their materials and get ready for what's coming in five minutes, they still have difficulty making the change. New children may not know what's expected of them. Children with disabilities find it especially difficult. S. E. Matthews (2012) tells us that children with autism, for instance, often have a hard time coping with changes, even when the change seems as minor as a shift from circle time to art. Other children may not want to give up what they are doing because they haven't finished.

Transition songs can help. When transition songs become a part of the daily routines, they are signals to the children of what will happen and what to do. Before

Figure 10.5　Singing Books

Dooby Dooby Moo (Cronin, 2006)
So You Want to Be a Rock Star (Vernick, 2012)
Take Me Out of the Bathtub (Katz, 2001)
ZooZical (Sierra, 2011)

deciding what songs to use and when to use them, you must first look over your program to make sure the time periods are long enough for the completion of the scheduled activities. Step back and use your observation skills to see how the children are involved in the activities.

Did they choose their own activities or were they assigned? Are they familiar with how they can move to a new activity by using necklaces, cards, or sign-up sheets? Then introduce the children to a transition song for each activity period. Use the same song over and over for the particular transition. Make it a simple, catchy song with words that tell children what to do.

As you did with direction songs, sing transition songs to familiar tunes with words made up to suit the circumstance. S. E. Matthews points out that when teachers consistently sing songs with children during transitions, children are less likely to be confused or anxious. Singing offers stability to the daily routine and helps ensure that transitions run smoothly. Several Web sites listed at the end of the chapter are sources for songs.

✓ DEVELOPING DANCE SKILLS

Most young children love to move. They will make attempts to imitate any rhythmic activity around them. Young children also will follow their own internal rhythms with moving and singing on their own. If we want children to continue these movements, the next move is ours. Adults who notice young children moving rhythmically must compliment them, encourage them to continue their movements, and call others' attention to the children's accomplishments.

Children very quickly pick up on the values of adults around them. If the adults show interest in children's dancing, the youngsters will continue to dance. On the other hand, if adults disregard the action or reprimand children for moving around so much, the children will stop. You need to provide the stimulus in your program for young children to move rhythmically. That means you must schedule such activities early in the life of your classroom. Be creative yourself and think of the curriculum areas that might include dance.

✓ MOVE BODY TO REPRESENT PEOPLE, ANIMALS, FEELINGS

An entire class of preschool children can gain tremendously from creative movement activities if the activities are led by a sensitive teacher and held in a creative environment. The teacher can use a drum, tom-tom, tambourine, or simply hand-clapping for the beat, but she must be sensitive enough to pick up the pulse or rhythm of the group instead of imposing her own rhythm on them. CDs can be used, as well, but again, the teacher needs to rely on the group rhythm, which is usually different—often slower—than that of a CD. The environment should be attractive, orderly, and comfortable. If a gymnasium is used, it should be uncluttered. If the preschool classroom is large enough, clear a space for expansive movements. Preschoolers need to be able to run, leap, and gallop.

The teacher should be the leader—a sensitive and creative leader. If a child does not want to participate, don't make her. You can take her hand and swing it gently to the music. The teacher should be prepared, as well, with a series of simple movement activities for the children to try. Children do not like to be told: "Do whatever you want to do," or "Move any way you want to the music." This only leads to confusion.

Instead, you should lead the children into creative movement activities through the stimulus of a steady, rhythmic beat. They need to master the basic locomotor movements of walking, running, crawling, leaping, and galloping to music or to a beat. Start by beating the tom-tom slowly and having children walk across the floor to the beat. Then increase the tempo of the beat and have them come back across the floor a bit faster. Try other movements, at first slowly and then faster.

They also should master some of the nonlocomotor movements such as swinging, swaying, rocking, bending, and stretching. Not all at once. Try one movement at a time. Continue using a drum or tap on a tambourine to set the beat for movement. Have seated children tap their feet to the beat. Then have them sway or rock or bend while still seated. Change the beat, making it faster or slower, louder or softer. Then have them stand up and make the same movements as you change the beat. Whatever you do with rhythm, make it fun and do not expect perfection from these developing children.

You can also do a follow-the-leader activity in a line where you as leader set the pace. You can march, tramp, slide along, trip along on tiptoes, or walk in cadence, calling out a beat (e.g., "one-two buckle your shoe, three-four shut the door," etc.). Play a recording with a strong beat and have the children move around the room keeping time. You may want to wind down your session with a slower recording. Choose an appropriate tune for a "monster shuffle" or a "dinosaur clump." Children are usually happily exhausted after such a creative movement session. Creative movement like this calls on children to use more than their large muscles. They must also use their imaginations.

The short attention span of preschoolers makes it necessary to keep the sessions short (10–15 minutes) and include a variety of movements and dance activities. Young children like activities that take place on the floor, so be sure to include "snake" and "worm" dances where children can wriggle and crawl. Four-year-olds especially love to run. You will want to include a "jet plane zoom" or a "race car rally" in which children can run to music or a beat.

Because children love making animal movements, some teachers focus on those for their creative movement activities. The book **Move!** (Jenkins, 2006) shows all kinds of animals making two of their typical moves on every other page with a gigantic word giving the names of the movements: swing, walk, dive, swim, leap, slither, climb, fly, run, dance, float, slide, and waddle. Children can look at the pages, then get up and try to make the movement.

In **Boogie Monster** (Bissett, 2011) the monster has all the animals and even a robot making their moves. He asks the readers if they can spin like helicopters, sit down and pedal as if they're riding a bike, or dance with no knees like a penguin. In

Figure 10.6   Dance
Books

> *Ballerina Dreams* (Thomson, 2007)
> *Boogie Monster* (Bissett, 2011)
> *Dancing Feet* (Craig, 2010)
> *Giraffes Can't Dance* (Andreae, 1999)
> *Josephine Wants to Dance* (French, 2007)
> *The Jellybeans and the Big Dance* (Numeroff &
> Evans, 2007)
> *Move* (Jenkins, 2006)

Dancing Feet (Craig, 2010) the reader is asked on every three pages to guess what animal is making each of the foot sounds. Afterwards they can get up and make the dancing feet sounds. These and other books (see Figure 10.6) can serve as lead-ins to creative movement activities.

DANCES WITH OTHERS TO MUSIC

Children who love creative movement should do well with dancing. Dow (2010) talks about dance having a powerful impact in children's daily lives because it is both a physical activity and a vehicle for self-expression. It offers the rich experience of exploring and creating, with the added benefits of lively movement.

With preschool children dancing should never be formal. Let them move with other children to the beat of the music. Bring in CDs with all kinds of music: rock and roll, waltz, polka, jazz, rap, bluegrass, folk music, marching band music, Native American music, classical music, ballet. Put on a CD and let children move to the sound of the music. Read a musical story, if you have one about a particular type of music, as a lead-in.

For instance, in *Ballerina Dreams* (Thomson, 2007), a true story, five little girls have always wanted to do ballet dancing just like other little girls (one is 3, one 4, two 5, and one 7). They come together in a physical therapy class because each of them has a muscle disorder from cerebral palsy that makes movements difficult. The girls wear leg braces, use a cane or a walker, but all are finally able to perform ballet pieces from the *Nutcracker Suite* and *Swan Lake* at a recital. Help any of your children who have disabilities to perform the music you play.

In *Josephine Wants to Dance* (French, 2007), Josephine is a kangaroo in Australia who wants more than anything to dance a ballet. Her little brother Joey tells her that kangaroos don't dance, they hop. But when the prima ballerina twists her ankle, Josephine is ready. She leaps through the open theater window and onto the stage. She has learned the role and can jump higher than any dancer the director has ever seen. So they make her a tutu and ballet shoes and she dances the ballet to claps and cheers from everyone.

These boys are dancing to rock and roll music.

In ***The Jellybeans and the Big Dance*** (Numeroff & Evans, 2007), Emily and three other little animal characters attend a dance class. Emily calls them "the dancing Jellybeans" and persuades them to choose a bug they like. Then they perform in style, dressed as their favorite bugs. If you are looking at insects in science, what a great way to make them come alive.

For children who may have trouble dancing, read them ***Giraffes Can't Dance*** (Andreae, 1999) about Gerald the tall giraffe who wants to join the other animals in the annual Jungle Dance. When he enters the ring to dance they all make fun of him for his clumsy movements. But a little cricket tells Gerald that sometimes when you're different you need a different song. So Gerald tries swaying to the grass and bending to the trees, and soon he is dancing. For children who are not ready or interested in dancing, have them sway in their seats to the background music you play while reading this book. Many children enjoy reenacting this story with all of the jungle animals doing their dances.

OBSERVING AND ASSESSING ART, MUSIC, AND DANCE SKILLS WITH CHILDREN'S PRODUCTS, PHOTOS, AUDIO, VIDEO, AND CHECKLISTS

A simple checklist can be used as an observation tool for observing children in the classroom as well as observing their art products, photos, and videos. Figure 10.7 shows a Drawing Skills Checklist that can be used for individuals or as a screening tool for the entire class.

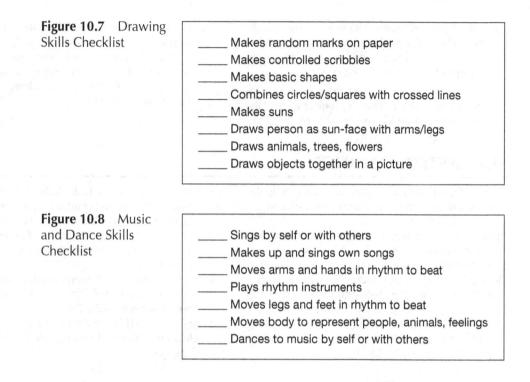

Figure 10.7 Drawing Skills Checklist

_____ Makes random marks on paper
_____ Makes controlled scribbles
_____ Makes basic shapes
_____ Combines circles/squares with crossed lines
_____ Makes suns
_____ Draws person as sun-face with arms/legs
_____ Draws animals, trees, flowers
_____ Draws objects together in a picture

Figure 10.8 Music and Dance Skills Checklist

_____ Sings by self or with others
_____ Makes up and sings own songs
_____ Moves arms and hands in rhythm to beat
_____ Plays rhythm instruments
_____ Moves legs and feet in rhythm to beat
_____ Moves body to represent people, animals, feelings
_____ Dances to music by self or with others

A similar observation checklist can help you determine how each of the children is developing music and dance skills. (See Figure 10.8.) The checklist can also be used as you listen to children on CDs or observe them on videos. If checklists like this work for you, you may want to create your own with items appropriate to your own program. Remember, observation checklists like this are informal assessment tools, not tests.

For individual children you can make a learning prescription as you did for other skills areas listing their strengths, areas needing strengthening, and activities to help. Such assessments can be kept in children's portfolios, used in staff planning, or shared with parents. Art, music, and dance are as important in children's growth as are each of the other development skills, especially as we learn their significance in children's developing brains.

LEARNING ACTIVITIES

1. Use the Drawing Skills checklist as a screening tool to observe all the children in your classroom. For children with checks at the higher levels in the sequence of art skill development, compare their scores in cognitive development, especially in "Sorts objects by shape/color/ size." What conclusions can you draw from this comparison?

2. Based on your screening survey, choose one or two children who have not shown much interest or development in art and try to involve them in an art activity. Use one of the other checklist areas in which they have shown interest and skills as the basis for the art activity. Record the results.

3. Set up your art area so children can use it with-out adult help or direction. Make a running record of what happened in this area before you changed the setup and afterward.

4. Choose a child who needs help in moving to rhythm. Involve the child using one or more of the rhythm ideas from this chapter. Discuss the results.

5. Observe and record which of the children join in the singing activities. For children who are reluctant to join in, read them song storybooks with a small group and have the group sing along. Or have a "puppet singalong." Does this help them get involved?

SUGGESTED READINGS

Bentley, D. F. (2011). Reflecting on ways to help the reluctant artist communicate. *Young Children, 66*(2), 42–46.

Browne, M., Kampman, J., & Abbey, N. (2012). The power of observation with toddlers: An investigation of music. *Exchange, 34*(1), 57–59.

Greata, J. (2006). *An introduction to music in early childhood education.* Belmont, CA: Cengage.

Izumi-Taylor, S., Morris, V. G., Meredith, C. D., & Hicks, C. (2012). Music and movement for young children's healthy development. *Dimensions of Early Learning, 40*(2), 33–39.

Kemple, K. M., Batey, J. J., & Hartle, L. C. (2004). Music play: Creating centers for musical play and exploration. *Young Children, 59*(4), 30–37.

Koster, J. B. (2012). *Growing artists: Teaching the arts to young children.* Wadsworth/Cengage: Belmont, CA.

Loomis, K., Lewis, C., & Blumenthal, R. (2007). Children learn to think and create through art. *Young Children, 62*(5), 79–98.

Mayesky, M. (2012). *Creative activities for young children* (10th ed.). Belmont, CA: Wadsworth/ Cengage.

CHILDREN'S BOOKS

Andreae, G. (1999). *Giraffes can't dance.* New York: Orchard.

Bissett, J. (2011). *Boogie monster.* Seattle, WA: Compendium.

Carle, E. (2011). *The artist who painted a blue horse.* New York: Philomel.

Cox, J. (2003). *My family plays music.* New York: Holiday House.*

Craig, L. (2010). *Dancing feet.* New York: Knopf.

Cronin, D. (2006). *Dooby dooby moo.* New York: Atheneum.

Dillon, L., & Dillon, D. (2007). *Jazz on a Saturday night.* New York: The Blue Sky Press.*

Dole, M. L. (2003). *Drum, Chavi, drum.* San Francisco, CA: Children's Book Press.*

French, J. (2007). *Josephine wants to dance.* New York: Abrams.

Geringer, L. (2010). *Boom boom go away!* New York: Atheneum.

Jenkins, S. (2006). *Move!* Boston: Houghton Mifflin.

Katz, A. (2001). *Take me out of the bathtub and other silly dilly songs.* New York: McElderry.

Nelson, D. B. (2008). *Willow.* Ann Arbor, MI: Sleeping Bear Press.

Numeroff, L., & Evans, N. (2007). *The Jellybeans and the big dance.* New York: Abrams.

Page, N. (2008). *Do you do a didgeridoo?* Hertfordshire, England: Make Believe Ideas.*

Sherry, K. (2008). *I'm the best artist in the ocean.* New York: Dial.

Sierra, J. (2011). *ZooZical.* New York: Knopf.

Thompson, L. (2007). *Ballerina dreams.* New York: Feiwel and Friends.*

Vernick, A. (2012). *So you want to be a rock star.* New York: Walker.

Wiesner, D. (2010). *Art & Max.* Boston: Clarion Books.

Wolkstein, D. (1981). *The banza.* New York: Dial.

*Multicultural

WEB SITES

Arts Education Partnership
www.aep-arts.org

Best Children's Music
www.bestchildrensmusic.org

Children's Music Network
www.cmnonline.org

The Children's Music Web
www.childrensmusic.org

Global Children's Art Gallery
www.naturalchild.com

Hap Palmer's Music and Movement
www.happalmer.com

National Art Education Association
www.naec-reston.org

National Association of Music Education
www.menc.org

National Dance Association
www.aahperd.org/nda

National Dance Education Organization
www.ndeo.org

Transition songs:
www.preschoolexpress.com,
www.songsforteaching.com,
www.preschoolrainbow.org

CHAPTER 11

Dramatic Play Skills

In this chapter you will learn to observe if children can:

____ Do pretend play by themselves

____ Assign roles or take assigned roles

____ Use particular props to do pretend play

____ Take on characteristics and actions related to role

____ Use language for creating and sustaining the plot

____ Enact exciting or danger-packed themes

____ Be observed through running records or checklists

DEVELOPING DRAMATIC PLAY SKILLS

An important aspect of creativity in young children is their development of imagination. For young children, imagination is the ability to pretend or make believe, to take a role other than their own, to create fanciful situations, or to act out a fantasy of their making. Imagining is a function of the right hemisphere of the brain, and as we know, young children are right-brain dominated. Thus, most young children seem to engage in a great deal of imagining before the age of 7.

One of the most important types of this imagining in early childhood programs is *dramatic play*, a spontaneous informal drama in which, as Isenberg and Jalongo (2010) tell us, young children spontaneously take on a role or behavior of someone else or use make-believe to act out familiar events. There is no audience and the teacher acts as an observer or facilitator.

Dramatic play is a type of activity that many adults fail to see as significant in the development of the child, because they do not do it themselves. But early childhood professionals have come to recognize children's imagining as one of the most effective means for promoting development of intellectual skills, social skills, language, and most especially, creativity (Isenberg & Jalongo, 2010).

One of the basic tools for creating is imagining, the ability to see a picture in your mind's eye. This ability allows you to tap into memories of the past and reform them as possibilities for the present or future. Children's make-believe relies heavily on this capacity to draw on such internal images and to create new ones. The Singers, who have done extensive research and writing on children's imaginative play, believe that imagining is essential to the development of intellectual and language skills, as well. Children remember ideas and words they have actually experienced because the youngsters can associate the ideas with pictures in their minds (Singer & Singer, 1977). This association reveals why children need to have many real experiences. Otherwise, they have few images stored in their brains to draw on.

A child must utilize previous experiences in new and different ways. She extracts the essence of a familiar experience such as getting ready for bed and applies it creatively to a pretend activity such as putting to bed her doll, who doesn't want to go. Or she may take the role of the doll herself as well as that of the frustrated mother, who is losing her patience with the stubborn doll.

The child experiments with the situation, playing it this way one time and that way another. If a peer joins in, there is another point of view to reckon with. If the original player strays too far from her role, she may lose it to a player with more definite ideas on how a mother should act. Or she may switch to a different role herself and try on yet another set of characteristics. She learns to recall fragments of past experiences and combine them in novel ways, adding original dialogue, fresh nuances to her characterizations, and new directions to her plots. No playwright ever had better practice.

In addition to being her own creative playwright, she is also the actor, the director, the audience for other actors, and an interacter with others, whether she plays her role or steps out of it to make "aside" comments on progress of the spontaneous play. Just as with every other aspect of her development, she is developing her own creativity when she has the freedom and time to participate in dramatic play.

Figure 11.1 Common
Dramatic Play Themes

- Family and home
- Doctors and hospitals
- Community helpers
- Transportation
- Shopping
- School
- Escape and rescue
- Superheroes

This time the knowledge children create is about real life and the other actors in it: how they behave, how they respond to stressful situations, how they carry out their work roles, how they speak, and how they interact with one another. Adult observers of dramatic play find that most of the make-believe play of children centers around the social problems of the adults with whom children have close contacts. Common themes include the family and home; doctors and hospitals; community helpers, transportation, shopping, school; and dramatizations of escape, rescue, and superheroes. (See Figure 11.1.)

Playing at life is not the inconsequential activity many adults seem to think it is. Children who have had extensive practice with dramatic play are often the ones who are most successful in life as adults. Children who have not been allowed or encouraged to engage in such play may be at a disadvantage as adults, for they have missed an important grounding in social, intellectual, and creative skills.

This chapter will look at dramatic play in relation to the development of creativity in young children. For you to discover where the children in your classroom are in the sequence of their development, assess each child using the six items of the Child Development Checklist as you observe children pretending in the dramatic play area, at the water table, in the block area, with science materials, at the painting easels, or on the playground.

You will find young children pretend about everything they do, both alone and with others. Tap into this rich vein of creativity in young children, and you may see life and the world from a completely new and fresh perspective: the *what-if* point of view. This *what-if* perspective is the true magic of childhood, the belief that children can make life anything they want it to be.

Adults know from the hard facts of reality that life cannot be changed so easily— or can it? What if we also believed we could really make life anything we wanted it to be? Does believing make it so? Children act as if this idea were true. Is there a way we can help them develop into adults who will actually be able to make their adult lives come out the way they want them to? Is there a way we can preserve the child in ourselves so we can do the same? Take a hard observer's look at the developmental sequences in imaginative play that follow to see what you need to do to keep this spark alive in children and to rekindle its essence in your own life.

This boy says he is a command module pilot taking off in a spaceship.

Observing Children in Dramatic Play

The importance of dramatic play for children's development of thinking, speaking, forming relationships, seeing things from another's perspective, and learning social and prosocial skills puts it at the top of the list of daily curriculum activities. But there is another aspect of dramatic play that is sometimes overlooked. Teachers who observe children in dramatic play find it is one of the best methods for learning about the development of children's thinking. Roskos and Christie (2001) point out that it provides a lens through which adults can witness children's knowledge. It can make visible children's thinking.

If teachers view dramatic play not just as an activity, but as an expression of children's thinking, they can begin to see what children understand about their world. Hatcher and Petty (2004) ask you to put on your "X-ray vision" to examine what dramatic play reveals about children's concept development. As you observe children's development of dramatic play skills, look for the links between play and concept development.

DOES PRETEND PLAY BY HIM/HERSELF

This checklist item describes one of the earliest of the imaginative play behaviors in young children. Incredibly enough, it appears as early as 1 year. By 18 months, infants may go through the imaginary routine of feeding themselves with an empty spoon and cup, and even saying "Yummy!" The Singers (1977) believe this tendency to play or to replay past events through imagery is one of the basic capacities of the human brain. At first the pretend actions involve only the child himself; later they may involve toys, dolls, and eventually people. The youngsters do not take a role in this play. They are themselves. The child is showing an observer she has developed the concept of "you take care of a baby by rocking it."

By 2 years of age, most children spend a great deal of time at home or in a toddler program replaying fragments of everyday experience, if given the chance. Pieces of familiar routines are repeated with little change or little effort to expand them into a longer sequence. The toddler will put the baby to bed by putting the doll in the cradle, covering it, and saying, "Night-night." Then the toddler will pick up the doll and begin the routine all over again. Once a particular routine is established with a 2-year-old, it seems to become quite rigid, almost like a ritual.

Words are not all that important in the pretending of 2-year-olds, however. The youngsters use them sparingly, mainly to accompany actions or for sound effects. Once these youngsters get an idea for pretend play, they try to put it into action immediately. They do not set the stage with words, or search for appropriate props. Props may be used, though, if they are available. Two-year-olds use props realistically, for the most part. Dishes are used realistically for eating, and not as a pretend steering wheel. Because these youngsters are also impulsive in their behavior, props can influence the type of pretend play they engage in. A toy broom can inspire them to sweep, for instance, even though they had no previous plans for cleaning.

The first imaginative play of youngsters mainly concerns chores and routines, such as eating, going to bed, caring for the baby, talking on the phone, turning on television, shopping, visiting grandma, driving the car, and getting gas for the car. Two-year-olds are very serious about it and take offense if adults make fun of their sometimes comical modes of pretending. Keep track of these play routines for each of your younger children from time to time and note what new concepts they have learned over time.

Doll play is also a frequent activity for both boys and girls of this age. Dolls are usually undressed, laid in a box or bed, and covered completely over with a piece of cloth in a very ritualized routine. These children are not pretending to be mother or anyone other than themselves because they have not yet developed a perspective-taking concept, that is, the ability to see something from another point of view.

The play of 2-year-olds is frequently solitary and rarely involves more than one other player. They and their age-mates have not yet developed the social skills for coming together in a common endeavor. When two children this age play together, one usually imitates the other. However, others will join in if they see one child doing something, and sometimes a wild melee ensues. The pretend play of children this young is brief at best, and it may disintegrate suddenly into running and squealing if other children are around.

Young 3-year-olds who have not done much imaginative play may start in this manner in your classroom: pretending by playing a familiar home-centered routine, but not taking on a role themselves. They may eventually expand their early single actions into a string of actions composing an episode. For example, they may put the baby doll to bed, get out the dishes, set the table, pick up the baby, and sit down to eat.

On the other hand, some more mature 3- and even 4-year-olds may perform solitary pretend play with little cars, people, or miniature animals. They seem perfectly happy playing out an imaginary scenario by themselves. You can sometimes tap into this play by talking to them about what you see them doing with their props.

As they become more experienced players by interacting with others around them, they are often assigned a role by a more mature player. Whether they can actually play this role depends on their perspective-taking ability: whether they can see things from a different perspective than their own. Some children merely watch what the others are doing. Some continue with their own pretend actions, but with little recognition of a role as such. Others imitate their play partners and little by little learn how to play a pretend role. Observe and record what new concepts the children have learned.

As with stages of social play, children seem to progress from watching others to solitary imaginative play, to parallel play, and eventually to group play. As an observer, you may see this progression more easily with children who play with pretend objects such as dolls, figures of people and animals, or cars and trucks. They may be playing in the block area, house area, manipulative area, or sand table. In the dramatic play area itself, where children are playing roles in a spontaneous drama, it is sometimes difficult to recognize who has a role or who is playing the same theme in the same space but in a parallel manner. (See Figure 11.2.)

If You Have Not Checked This Item: Some Helpful Ideas

■ Have Appropriate Props Available

Knowing that the youngest children pretend mainly about familiar household routines, you should have eating, cleaning, and sleeping props available in your dramatic play center. Put out all kinds of baby dolls and their beds as well. Be sure your block center contains little cars and figures of people and animals.

Figure 11.2   Children's Pretend Play by Years

> 1 year—engages in single acts of symbolic play (no props)
>
> 2 years—replays fragments of everyday experiences (may use props; mostly solitary play)
>
> 3 years—often needs particular props for play with group; will take roles assigned by more mature player
>
> 4 years—assigns roles; takes assigned roles; often the leader (parallel or group play)
>
> 5 years—mostly group play; more complex scenarios; more language

■ Read a Book

Oliver Who Would Not Sleep (Bergman, 2007) does his pretending at night in this rhyming story of how he blasts off in his toy rocketship and flies all the way to Mars and back. Talk with your listening group about how each of them pretends at night when they are in bed.

I'm a Truck Driver (London, 2010) shows a little boy driving different large vehicles on every two pages: power shovel, cement truck, crane, bulldozer, steam roller, street sweeper, fire truck, garbage truck, snowplow, tow truck, combine, and tractor-trailer. Put out little vehicle toys in the block center after reading this book.

ASSIGNS ROLES OR TAKES ASSIGNED ROLES

Three-year-olds usually find it is more fun when several children play together. You will have checked on this previously in your observations concerning social play. This item signals the beginning of peer play for most children. Pretend episodes usually do not last long in the beginning among 3-year-olds because most children of this age are not yet flexible when it comes to differences of opinion. This inflexibility sometimes shows up when it comes to who will play what role. Other 3s seldom get involved because they do not know how to play.

Leong and Bodrova (2012) are concerned about how many of today's young preschool children simply do not know how to play. This has happened, they feel, because of massive changes in the culture of childhood—such as the disappearance of multiage neighborhood play groups and the increase in time children spend in adult-directed activities after school. In the past younger children learned play skills from older children. Even in preschools many classes are age-segregated, so that young 3s have no older 4s to learn from. How is it in your classroom?

Three-year-olds who do know how to play often try to control dramatic play by assigning the roles. The dominant child takes the role he or she wants and assigns the others, who may not agree. Most children of this age want their own role. As their creativity blossoms through this type of play, their solutions to role assignment problems are often highly creative and something an adult would not have thought of. Listen to your children to see how they resolve such role assignment problems.

The role of mother is a favorite one for girls of this age. What would you do when all four girls playing together want to be the mother and no one will give in? After a few minutes of discussion—or rather argument—when it became clear that Janie (who spoke up first about being the mother) would not change, nor would the other three, a different solution needed to be found. The girls accepted the fact that the household could have only one mother, but they could not accept that they would have to be sisters or babies or grandmothers. Suddenly one of the girls said, "We'll all be other mothers who are visiting Janie this morning," and they were.

The dominant child may assign a role to another child, who may not agree.

Here is a typical role assignment situation played by 3-year-olds Sherry and Ann in a preschool and recorded in a running record:

Sherry is in the play grocery store holding a box of cereal. She hands box to child playing role of cashier. Walks back to grocery shelves. Picks up box and puts it in grocery cart. "Here's our groceries, Mother," she says to Ann, standing nearby. Picks up bag of groceries and carries it to play house. Walks back to grocery store. "I'm gonna be mother," she says loudly to herself. "Mother, it's time to go home," she says to Ann. Ann gives no response but pays for the groceries. "There are no more groceries. We have to leave now," says Sherry. Still gets no response from Ann. "I'm the mother and you're the grandmother. I'm not a little kid," she says to Ann. No response. They walk to house together. She puts her bag down and helps Ann with hers. "We have to unload everything now." They start to unpack all the groceries. "Oh, no, daughter," she says to Ann, "When it's cleanup time we have to pick all this up." Both girls laugh.

Because Ann was originally the director of this play episode and Sherry had evidently agreed to the role of daughter by taking it, it is interesting to see what strategies Sherry now uses to get out of an unwanted role. First she states loudly but to herself that she is going to be the mother. Because she receives no response, she retains her daughter role at first, but then states outright to Ann that she is the mother and Ann can be the grandmother. Sherry still gets no response. Silence does not signify consent among young children. Silence may only mean that the challenged child does not want to engage in an argument, not that she agrees to give up her role. Sherry tries calling Ann "daughter," but Ann refuses to get involved verbally, so the role problem is still unresolved before cleanup time ends the play.

Another imaginative play episode shows older 3- and 4-year-olds engaged in the type of role assignment problem being discussed here in another running record:

Katy is playing by herself with plastic blocks, making guns; she walks into other room.

K: *"Lisa, would you play with me? I'm tired of playing by myself."*

They walk into other room to slide and climbing area.

K: *"I am Wonder Woman."*

L: *"So am I."*

K: *"No, there is only one Wonder Woman. You are Robin."*

L: *"Robin needs a Batman because Batman and Robin are friends."*

All this takes place under slides and climber. Lisa shoots block gun that Katy has given her. Katy falls on floor.

L (to teacher):   *"We're playing Superfriends and Wonder Woman keeps falling down."*
                   Katy opens eyes, gets up and says:

K: *"Let's get out our Batmobile and go help the world." She runs to other room and back making noises like a car.*

L: *"Wonder Woman is died. She fell out of the car." She falls down.*

K: *"It's only a game. Wake up, Lisa. You be Wonder Woman. I'll be . . ."*

L: *"Let's play house now."*

Katy begins sliding down slide.

K: *"We have a lot of Superfriends to do." (She says this while sliding.) "Robin is coming after you!" (She shouts to Lisa, running from slide and into other room.) Lisa has gone into housekeeping area and says to Katy:*

L: *"Katy, here is your doll's dress." (Lost yesterday.) John joins the girls.*

L: *"I'm Wonder Woman."*

K: *"I'm Robin."*

J: *"I'm Batman. Where is the Batmobile?"*

K: *"It's in here."*

They run into the other room and Katy points under the slide platform, telling John what the Batmobile can do. Then they all run into the other room and back again.

K: *"John, we are not playing Superfriends any more."*

This typical pretending episode illustrates perfectly the kind of role assignment and switching so characteristic of children this age. It is obvious from the children's easy agreements that they have played together before and therefore accept certain conditions. Katy is the director here and assigns the roles. She takes the role of

Figure 11.3 Strategies
to Avoid Conflict

- Ignoring
- Distracting
- Reasoning
- Negotiating
- Cooperating
- Compromising

Wonder Woman and assigns Lisa the role of Robin. Lisa really does not agree (we soon see), but she accepts her assignment. She probably has gone through this with Katy before and knows that if she plays along without making a fuss, her turn will come. It comes quite soon, in fact, when she notes that Katy seems to have abandoned the Wonder Woman role by suddenly getting out the Batmobile and "going to help the world."

Here Lisa announces that she is Wonder Woman and has fallen out of the car and died. Katy agrees to Lisa's new role by saying: "It's only a game. Wake up, Lisa. You be Wonder Woman." When John joins the game and takes the role of Batman, the girls do not object at first. But obviously they know how to get rid of unwanted players by announcing: "John, we are not playing Superfriends any more."

(The teacher later told the observer that she allows superhero play as long as it does not get out of bounds. She does not allow gun play and did not realize that was happening or she would have intervened.)

Observe to discover what other creative ploys your children use to get peers to take role assignments or to get out of assigned roles they don't want and into ones they really want. Some are listed in Figure 11.3.

If your children are engaged in this kind of dramatic play, you will probably be checking this item. If you leave it blank, it may mean that the child is not playing because he has not reached this level of group imaginative play. This may be the case because children who play together like this soon come to an understanding about role assignments.

If You Have Not Checked This Item: Some Helpful Ideas

■ Scaffolding Dramatic Play

It is not up to you to force a child into group play. Such play should be totally spontaneous. But you might help a shy child become involved with a group by taking a role yourself and inviting the child to take a role and come along with you into the play group. Other ways the teacher can help scaffold pretending are listed in Figure 11.4.

On the other hand, teachers need to restrain themselves from entering pretend play too vigorously. After all, this is the children's spontaneous creation and should remain so. Teachers can use scaffolding, that is, support, in many ways to get

Figure 11.4 Teacher
Scaffolding Strategies

- Ask what child player is doing (e.g., cooking)
- Pick up phone and call child player
- Ask nonplayer to help someone in scenario
- Insert new idea with new prop
- Take role and model how to play it

onlookers involved or to keep the play going on an even keel, but then they should extract themselves unobtrusively as players.

■ Timing the Play

Van Hoorn, Nourot, Scales, and Alward (2003) emphasize that timing is everything when entering and exiting children's play. When teachers enter and exit children's play or shift from one strategy to another, timing is crucial. Teachers need to observe play long enough to see if any intervention is called for or if the children are best served by the teacher in a less directive role.

■ Planning

Leong and Bodrova (2012) suggest that planning with the children ahead of time can resolve many later problems. You can ask the children what they want to play, what they want to be, what props they need, and who will use the props. Planning prior to the children going to the dramatic play center can help to prevent potential conflicts. Planning allows children to discuss what might happen if there are two people who want to be truck drivers and only one truck.

NEEDS PARTICULAR PROPS TO DO PRETEND PLAY

Pioneer play researcher Sara Smilansky (1968) discusses three types of pretending that occur in dramatic play. (See Figure 11.5.)

Teachers can support children's pretend play by providing representational props, toys, and dress-up clothes. The youngest children doing pretend play may need more realistic props.

Figure 11.5 Types of
Pretending to Observe

1. Pretending with regard to a role
2. Pretending with regard to an object (prop)
3. Pretending with regard to an action

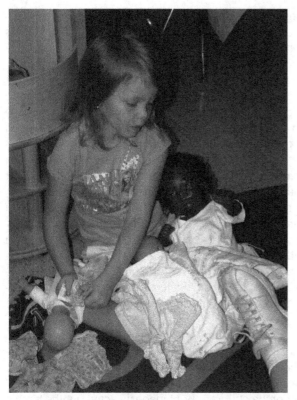

Some children cannot proceed with play until they find the right prop.

If you have bilingual children, be sure to label the props in both languages. Burton and Edwards (2006) tell us about Luis, Jose, and Sophie who are pretending to go to the subway station. The props are labeled with text and pictures of a train, ticket, money, and a caution sign in both languages, so each child knows each object in his or her language. Even though they speak different languages, they are able to recreate what happens at the subway station.

If 3-year-olds have had a chance to pretend when they were 2, they gradually develop new skills and interests in their imaginative play. Three-year-olds begin to think a bit about the pretending they are about to do, rather than acting on a sudden impulse. This forethought often leads them to preplan the play by finding or gathering certain realistic props. In fact, some 3-year-olds cannot proceed with play until they find the right prop.

The rigidity many 3-year-olds express in their ritualistic manner of pretending thus often carries over in their insistence on particular props to play. Three-year-olds may believe they need a particular hat, costume, doll, or steering wheel to carry out a role. Many times the object is the basis for the play, but not so much on impulse as with 2-year-olds. Three-year-olds very much enjoy dressing up and playing a role, and they have a much broader concept of how to do it.

Props may very well serve the children as an instrument for getting out of themselves. Because 3-year-olds are still strongly self-centered, they may need a prop to break away from their own point of view. Just as shy children can lose themselves in speaking through a hand puppet or from behind a mask, 3-year-olds may need the impetus of an object outside themselves to get them started in pretending to be someone else.

Family activities are a large part of 3-year-olds' pretend play in preschool programs. Doll play, hospital play, and pretending to be a community helper are common themes. Three-year-olds also enjoy driving cars and trains, flying jet planes, and being firefighters. They can carry these themes out in dramatic play, block building, table block games, clay creations, the water table, and the woodworking bench, as well as with puppets and toy telephones—anywhere and everywhere children gather.

It is up to you and your coworkers to provide the props that support pretend play in these areas. Bring in a set of jet planes and figures of people, place them in the sand table with posters of planes mounted on the wall nearby, and see what happens. Be sure to provide safety goggles to keep sand out of eyes. Some astute child is sure to point out that pilots of some kinds of planes wear goggles, and soon you may have several goggled "pilots" zooming around the classroom with their planes!

After a trip to the zoo or animal farm, bring in toy animals to the block center along with figures of people, toy trees, cars, and perhaps a little train to carry people around the block center zoo that the children may build. It is important to provide appropriate props for children to pretend with in various learning centers of the classroom after such a trip. Playing with such props is not just a matter of fun, but it helps young children to symbolize in a concrete way the more abstract ideas gained from the trip. Classroom staff can encourage children to remember what they saw on the field trip and build their own miniature trip site, or pretend to be one of the people they met at the site.

Young children learn best through concrete, hands-on activities. The props you provide for imaginative play can help them create spontaneous dramas about any topic of current interest and people of different cultures. Koster (2012) describes a variety of props such as culturally diverse props for different eating utensils, ethnic foods, unisex materials for different kinds of work, realistic clothing from other cultures, and props for different disabilities such as wheelchairs, crutches, canes, hearing aids, leg braces, and dark glasses. Educational supply houses such as Lakeshore have many of these.

For example, one morning Ricardo's grandmother visited his preschool and helped the children prepare tamales for lunch. Afterward, the teacher put out a plastic set of Mexican food in the housekeeping area for the children to pretend with. She also read them the book *Too Many Tamales* (Soto, 1993).

For days thereafter, a number of the children spontaneously acted out the tamale preparation, but with their own unique twist. Because the Mexican food set included only plastic tacos, the children invented their own tamales by using plastic egg rolls from a Chinese food set and wrapping them with paper for corn husks! Then they hid a toy ring in the wrapping for someone to try to find, just as in the storybook (Beaty & Pratt, 2015).

Not every child will be interested in pretending in this manner, just as not every child will like a particular book. Do not force youngsters to participate who show no interest. Read the story, put out the materials, and let those who want to engage in playing with them.

Object Substitution

Children go through a succession of levels in pretending with objects just as they do with roles. Beginners seem to need highly realistic objects for their pretend play: a toy telephone for a real telephone; a plastic apple for a real apple; a toy car for a real car. As they mature and become more experienced pretenders, children are able to use less representational props: a cylinder block for a telephone; a ball for an apple; a unit block for a car. This is called **object substitution**.

The most highly imaginative children are able to make an even greater leap in substitution of objects. They can pretend without any concrete object at all. They can call on an imaginary telephone grasped symbolically in their hand. An imaginary apple is held somewhat differently with their fingers curled around empty space. An imaginary car can speed along the floor with their hand directing its movements and their voice making sound effects.

Observe your children in the dramatic play area to see how they use objects in their pretending. Often children pay for their groceries with imaginary money, although they may carry a real purse. They may ride around the room on an imaginary motorcycle, but wear a real cycle helmet, or eat pretend food in the housekeeping area, but use real toy forks and spoons.

Not all children arrive at this stage of using imaginary objects rather than real ones. It is often children with more experience or better use of language who use less representational toys or imaginary ones. Does this mean a teacher should not include so many realistic props in the dramatic play or block centers? Not necessarily. Experienced players use realistic props in many ways not intended by the maker.

However, many toy companies carry the realism too far, making toys that move by themselves, make their own sounds, and have lights that go on and off. You will not find such toys in most preschools, and with good reason. Children's own imaginations are not challenged if the toy does everything and all a youngster can do is to turn it on and watch it perform. Such toys tend not to hold children's interest for more than a few days, while toys that children must interact with never lose their appeal.

Children will often choose a representational toy rather than a substitute object. Although it is important to have representational toys, having too many can discourage the development of imagination. Learning centers where imaginative play takes place should also include open-ended materials that children can use to create their own imaginary objects and settings: Styrofoam, tissue tubes, empty boxes of all sizes, pipe cleaners, feathers, plastic bottles of all sizes, cardboard cartons, and other throw-away items that seem appropriate.

There is one other interesting form of object substitution you should look for in your observations of children's pretending with objects. When children play with toy people, animals, and dolls—pretending they can move and talk—they are doing what is called **active agent** object substitution. At first, children play with toy figures as passive recipients of the play. They may feed them or dress them or ride them around in a vehicle. When the toy becomes an active agent, the child walks it around as if it were alive and also talks for it.

If you want your children to become involved in this highly imaginative play, be sure to provide appropriate materials: figures of people and animals, especially ones that can stand by themselves, as well as vehicles that can carry the figures.

If You Have Not Checked This Item: Some Helpful Ideas

■ Have a Variety of Props Available

In the large motor area, have large wooden riding trucks, wagons, and a wheelbarrow, as well as large hollow blocks and floorboards for building child-size structures. Put out a full-length mirror in the dress-up area. Include costume jewelry, scarves, handbags, wallets, belts, vests, shoes, aprons, all kinds of hats, doctor's equipment, goggles, binoculars, badges, umbrellas, and canes. An assortment of men's and women's clothes in teenage size is often easier for young children to handle than adult-size clothing.

Think of the learning centers in your classroom as areas for children's imaginative play to take place. What props can you put in the block area after a field trip to a construction site, for instance? What about construction vehicles and workers, string for wires, straws for pipes, and popsicle sticks for lumber? Think about filling other centers with such accessories: sand table, water table, woodworking area, clay table, writing center, and of course, the dramatic play area.

Or maybe you need just one prop, a rebozo, a Hispanic shawl. First read children *What Can You Do With a Rebozo?* (Tafolla, 2008). Then put out several shawls of different colors and observe if your children can do as many things with them as the book characters. Be sure to record the results with photos.

■ Take Many Field Trips

For children to become involved in spontaneous dramatic play activities, they must have firsthand knowledge about them. Ask children where they have gone with their parents. If many have gone on picnics, put out picnic props in the dramatic play area. If many children have not experienced a picnic, plan a picnic field trip to a nearby park . . . or even to the playground outside. Afterward, put out the props.

You may want to keeps these props together in a prop box for future use. Isenberg and Jalongo (2010) tell how prop boxes can contain a collection of real items that are related in some way, such as a picnic basket, plastic food, a tablecloth, and plastic ants. Using real items like this can stimulate children's imaginative play with particular concepts, situations, and roles.

Take other field trips to nearby sites of interest to the children such as barber/beauty shop, farm, fast-food restaurant, laundromat, farmer's market, flower shop, pet store, repair shop, gas station, shoe store, fire station, or doctor's clinic. Then put out dress-up props in prop boxes in the dramatic play center and miniature figures in the block area for children to pretend with.

■ Read a Book with a Character Cutout

Amazing Grace (Hoffman, 1991) is a classic book about an African-American girl who loves to pretend. She is Joan of Arc, Anansi the Spider, Pegleg Pete, Hiawatha, Mowgli, Aladdin, Doctor Grace, and finally Peter Pan in her school play. You can scan the wonderful illustrations of Grace in her costumes, print them, and cut them out as paper dolls for the children to pretend with on a smaller scale.

Isabella, Girl on the Go (Fosberry, 2012) takes imaginative Isabella around the world as an Egyptian archeologist, French artist, Chinese warrior, Mayan astronomer, British queen, and the Statue of Liberty, all in great costumes. More scanning, cutouts, and pretending with paper dolls.

Figure 11.6 Books
for Pretending

> ***Amazing Grace*** (Hoffman, 1991)
>
> ***Doctor Ted*** (Beaty, 2008)
>
> ***Friday My Radio Flyer Flew*** (Pullen, 2008)
>
> ***Isabella, Girl on the Go*** (Fosberry, 2012)
>
> ***Ladybug Girl*** (Soman & Davis, 2008)
>
> ***My Shoes Take Me Where I Want to Go*** (Richmond, 2006)
>
> ***Too Many Tamales*** (Soto, 1993)
>
> ***Violet the Pilot*** (Breen, 2008)
>
> ***What Can You Do with a Rebozo?*** (Tafolla, 2008)

My Shoes Take Me Where I Want to Go (Richmond, 2006) takes the reader through a child's fascinating imagination of using shoes to pretend to be a boy basketball player, a girl soccer star, a boy hockey player, a boy pirate, a girl scuba diver, a cowgirl, a boy mountain climber, a girl dancer, a boy president. These characters can also be scanned and cut out for paper doll play.

■ Read a Book with a Character Costume

In ***Friday My Radio Flyer Flew*** (Pullen, 2008) a boy gets his dreams off the ground in a simple story that may get your boys pretending. The boy finds an old wagon in the attic and tinkers with it till it flies! No costume needed but a pilot's hat and goggles—and a bit of imagination.

Ladybug Girl (Soman & Davis, 2008) shows little Lulu all dressed up in her ladybug costume ready to take off for another day's adventures. Sixteen other costumes she sometimes wears are illustrated on the end pages. This book should give your girls some good dramatic play ideas.

Violet the Pilot (Breen, 2008) is somewhat older than Lulu, but nonetheless creative. She is a mechanical genius and can build almost anything out of junk, even a plane that really flies. Both boys and girls should enjoy this one and get more ideas for dress-up dramatic play. (See Figure 11.6.)

TAKES ON CHARACTERISTICS AND ACTIONS RELATED TO ROLE

Four-year-olds have more experience than 3-year-olds when it comes to creating a role in their pretend play. Because they desperately want to participate in the adult world, 4-year-olds try out all sorts of adult roles: mother at work, father at work, doctor, nurse, bus driver, astronaut, waiter, fast-food cook, gas station attendant, mail carrier, firefighter, truck driver, train conductor, or crane operator. In addition, 4-year-olds play their roles with many more realistic details. They select props more carefully, dress up more elaborately, and carry out the role with more appropriate dialogue and actions.

If you listen carefully to 4-year-olds when you are observing them doing imaginative play, you will be able to learn a great deal about their understanding of the people and situations in their world. In addition, you may gain quite a respect for their use of creativity in developing their roles. Even the mundane roles of mother, father, brother, and baby are played with new twists and novel solutions to problems. Dialogue is expanded, and the players even express emotions quite eloquently where appropriate.

Language is used more than ever before to set the scene and create the mood. Because the players are beginning to make greater distinctions between real and pretend, they often make aside-like comments about things that are not real, just pretend, so that you, their peers, and even they themselves understand what is real and what is pretend. Four-year-olds are also more flexible about taking different roles. Children who would not take a bad guy's role at age 3 may play it to the hilt with great gusto at age 4. Your planning, suggestions, and support may be necessary to get the play going, but the children should be on their own.

You should observe your children carefully. Are they playing roles with greater realism than before, using expanded dialogue, showing more emotion, and almost becoming the character? If so, you should mark this item on the checklist.

If You Have Not Checked This Item: Some Helpful Ideas

■ Have Many Sets of Flannel Board or Cutout Characters

Children can use cutout characters from scanned copies of their favorite storybook characters to play with on a flannel board or as paper dolls. Make scanned copies of the characters from a favorite book and mount them on cardboard with sandpaper or Velcro backing, or laminate them. Keep the characters in a manila envelope with a copy of the book. The youngsters can act out scenes from the book if they want, or they can have the characters participate in brand-new adventures.

This activity is good practice in role playing with characters the children already know. A child can play by herself or with another child. Keep more than one flannel board in the book area if you want this to be a popular activity. Personal flannel boards can be made by mounting flannel or felt to a piece of cardboard folded in two and hinged at the top so that it stands easily on a table. Some favorite storybooks from which you may want to cut out characters are listed in Figure 11.7.

■ Scaffold the Desired Behavior

Some children need to see an adult pretending to get the idea of what to do themselves. Be sure you occasionally join the children in their pretending. You need to remember that it is their play, and you should only be a visitor. Better than taking a role may be to make an appropriate comment when you see them doing imaginative

Figure 11.7 Books for Character Cutouts

The Very Fairy Princess Takes the Stage (2011, Andrews & Hamilton)

Shoe-la-la! (Beaumont, 2011)

If You Decide to Go to the Moon (McNulty, 2005)

Isabella, Girl on the Go (Fosberry, 2012)

Mike and the Bike (Ward, 2005)

Sally Jean, the Bicycle Queen (Best, 2006)

So You Want to be a Rock Star (Vernick, 2012)

play. "Oh, Reggie, I bet those animals really like those pens you are building for them." Or, "Here's a cracker for your doll, Samantha. Do you think she's hungry?"

■ Read a Book

Even Fire Fighters Hug Their Moms (Maclean, 2002) shows a 4-year-old boy playing exciting roles at home while his mom watches and tries to get in a hug. Some of his props are realistic but others are imaginary. He uses a real red helmet and boots as a fire fighter, but also a tank vacuum cleaner hose for water. As an EMT, he drives an inverted wash basket ambulance with a pot cover steering wheel. As a construction worker the front loader he drives is a living room chair with golf clubs stuck between cushions for shifting gears. What props can your listeners invent for similar roles in the classroom?

USES LANGUAGE FOR CREATING AND SUSTAINING THE PLOT

Although 2-year-olds do most of their pretending without much language, 3-, 4-, and 5-year-olds depend on language to set the scene and sustain the action. If they are playing by themselves, they often will talk to themselves about what is happening. They also will speak for the characters—all of them. If the youngsters are playing with other children, they often use a great deal of dialogue to carry out their ideas. This behavior promotes their improved use of language and dialogue with others. In addition, it provides yet another opportunity for them to express creativity in the fresh and novel way they use words.

Words direct what the children do, the way they act, who the characters are, the unfolding of the plot, and the way they resolve conflict. Children involved in pretending who do not have the language skills of the more advanced players are able to listen and eventually imitate the advanced players' use of language. Everyone involved gets excellent practice in improving speaking skills, trying out new words, and using familiar language in new ways.

For some children, a new experience is the use of language to express feelings. The characters in these spontaneous make-believe situations need to express how

Figure 11.8   Function of Language in Dramatic Play

- Imitating adult speech
- Imagining a make-believe situation (mainly dialogue)
- Directing the action

they feel about what is happening to them. Many children have trouble putting their feelings into words. Younger children prefer to "act out" rather than speak out. This type of imaginative play gives them the opportunity to learn how to express feelings.

The youngsters, in fact, are projecting their own feelings by expressing what a character feels. Even if the character is a doll, a puppet, or an inanimate figure of a person or an animal, the children have yet another opportunity to speak. Children 3 and 4 years old are often more comfortable expressing the feelings of toy people than their own. The youngsters like to take their dolls or stuffed animals to the doctor's office, to listen to these pretend people express their fears, and to comfort them. In doing so, the children sort out their own impressions about the situation and try out their own sometimes novel ideas for resolving problems. Pioneer researcher Smilansky (1968) has found three main functions of language in this sort of dramatic play. (See Figure 11.8.)

If you listen carefully to the actors in most imaginative play, you will note they carry out all three of these functions. They definitely imitate adult speech. You can practically hear yourself speaking if you are the parent or the teacher of any of these children. Children also bring imagery to life in the characterizations they express through dialogue. Finally, someone in the group, usually the self-assigned director, is forever stepping outside her role to explain what is going on.

For younger players who may not know what to say in their roles, teachers may need to help. Leong and Brodova (2012) tell us that adult scaffolding is sometimes needed to help children engage in "role speech," that is, using vocabulary, sentence structure, and intonation that fit a specific role. Teachers can first introduce children to the ways people doing different jobs talk to each other during book reading or on a field trip. Use your own judgment to see if language scaffolding is necessary with your children. If it is, try reading a book about the role where the characters speak.

Spoken Words for Internal Images

If inner imagery allows the child to pretend in the first place, then talking aloud allows her to expand the meaning of what she visualizes. She not only hears herself speaking, but she also receives feedback from others' reactions. This feedback helps her revise and refine ideas and word use. Until she arrives at the point where she can create and sustain the action of pretend situations through language, she will miss the value of using her imagination in this manner. Eventually she must use mainly language and not just imagining in thinking. Thus imaginative play serves as a sort of transitional activity for the preschool child to learn spoken words for her internal images.

Alexander (2005) describes a realistic role-play between two girls who are making plans for a shopping expedition. Emily picks up a telephone book and tells

Madison her hair looks like a mop and she needs to call the beauty shop to get her hair done before she goes shopping. She actually finds the page in the phone book with a picture of a beautician. She says the phone numbers aloud as she presses their buttons on the toy phone. Then she holds a one-sided conversation with the pretend beautician discussing the best time for an appointment. When Madison also wants an appointment, Emily holds another one-sided conversation. Madison adds: "Tell her I'll pay with a credit card and we can get there right away" (p. 30).

Alexander tells us that pretending like this helps children fit into society and function as responsible citizens. It also helps children build vocabularies and reinforce concepts. An observer analyzing the girls' conversations realizes that this scenario does indeed make their thinking visible, as previously mentioned. Concepts the girls' conversations illustrate include the following:

If your hair looks bad you need to get it done in a beauty shop.

You need to make an appointment to get your hair done.

To get an appointment you call the beauty shop.

You use the phone book to get the number.

You can pay for the service with a credit card.

It's important to be on time.

One player can learn from another how you go about making appointments. Obviously Emily learned what to do from others, but in reenacting this scenario out loud she reinforces these concepts. Had she made a mistake or omitted something, another child player, listening to the conversations, would soon correct her. Conversations like this in dramatic play also serve the important function of helping second-language learners use English.

If You Have Not Checked This Item: Some Helpful Ideas

■ Use Hand Puppets

Have a variety of hand puppets available for the children: animals, characters from books, community helpers, adults, and children figures. A puppet theater made from a cardboard carton can help motivate the children's use of puppets as play actors. You may need to put on a puppet show yourself to set the stage, so to speak, for your children's dramas.

It is not necessary to have a puppet theater in the beginning, but your more advanced pretenders may expand their repertoire of imaginative play roles if a puppet theater is available.

■ Encourage Improvisation

In improvisation children make up their own dialogue and actions. The dialogue is, of course, dependent on the language skills of the children. You can encourage it by

Using puppets in dramatic play promotes children's use of language.

proposing a scenario for anyone who wants to take part. For example, you may suggest they can pretend to be on the playground where they hear a strange noise, look up, and see a spaceship coming down and landing, with strange beings coming out of it. What will your children say to them? Then what will happen? Other scenarios for improvisation might include the following:

- How to talk to a dinosaur
- How to invite your friends to a party
- How to build a spaceship
- How to find treasure at the bottom of the sea

ENACTS EXCITING, DANGER-PACKED THEMES

Most 4-year-olds do everything in a more exuberant, out-of-bounds manner than 3-year-olds, including pretending. Four-year-olds are more noisy, active, and aware of things outside themselves. They are fascinated with matters of life and death, and they begin to use such themes more often in their imaginative play. Superheroes and other television characters show up in their pretending. Bad guys are captured. Good guys are rewarded. People get shot and killed.

Adults look askance and blame television. They think that TV-watching surely must be bad for young children. By the age of 4, some young children are viewing an average of 4 hours of television a day, at home, not in school. Surely this viewing must affect their pretending and imaginations. Research by children's play specialists, the Singers, however, resulted in findings contrary to what they had expected. They found no relationship of statistical significance between watching television and imaginary play. Pretending neither increased nor decreased as a result of watching television.

The strongest correlation the Singers found was between the amount of television watched and overt aggression in the classroom. How true, preschool teachers agree, without perhaps realizing that 4-year-olds have always exhibited aggression in their play. The real reason for the increased aggression could well be that sitting and watching television for long periods does not allow young children to discharge their pent-up energy and aggressive feelings as does normal active play; or that the aggression children see and experience in their families needs an outlet.

Superhero and War Play

Four-year-olds are extremely active and must have daily opportunities to discharge this pent-up energy. It is only natural for this energy to take the form of powerful superhero character roles from the television programs the children watch. Ask adults who were raised before the days of television what form their wildest pretending took, and you will hear tales of cowboys and Indians, cops and robbers, or war play. Such play helps children release fears and build up confidence.

The argument against allowing superhero play in the classroom talks about the television cartoons children see that show superheroes controlling others through threat, force, and violence. Many teachers describe superhero play in their classrooms as being characterized by too-rough, too-loud play that they are forced to intervene in or stop completely. What should a teacher do who has a strong belief in the value of fantasy play, but does not believe the amount of adult intervention required to keep superhero play from bursting out of bounds is worth the effort? Should superhero play be banned from the classroom entirely?

No, say many teachers. There are ways to extract important learnings from this powerful play activity that seems to have so many youngsters in its grip. When there is war and violence in our own lives, children pick up on the feelings expressed around them. They may try to act out the scenes of violence they see on television.

What can we do? Banning war play from the classroom does not work as it once did. Children's intense desire to engage in this kind of play leads them to find ways to circumvent the ban. They somehow need to express these strong feelings of fear, rage, and helplessness in nondestructive ways. Some children can be redirected to paint out their emotions with bright and dark contrasting poster paints (red-black, yellow-brown, orange-purple) on paper, poster board, cardboard cartons, or brown grocery sacks. Unroll large sheets of newsprint on the floor or on the wall for a mural and invite children to finger paint large scenes of things that have been bothering them. Finger painting allows children to paint emotionally with whole arm strokes. If they show bombs exploding and people being killed, accept what they do, and have them tell you the story about it if they can.

Some children may want to make "spider webs" with string around the tacks you place on cork boards on the wall. You can help them cut out figures of people from

Figure 11.9 Controlling
Superhero Play

- Paint out strong emotions with bright and dark colors on large sheets of newsprint
- Make spider webs with string strung around tacks on corkboards; play scenario with cutout Spiderman figures
- Throw beanbags at cardboard carton targets
- Scale down superhero play with tabletop figures
- Read books about positive superheroes
- Create new superheroes with powers that help people and animals
- Use props such as power bracelets, capes, magic wands, old cell phones painted gold

magazines or picture book scans to be laminated and played with on the webs, reenacting Spider Man adventures. Others may prefer to draw their spider webs on chalkboards with white chalk and play out superhero adventures on their webs with red-and-blue chalk figures they move around. Throwing beanbags at targets is another method for redirecting strong energy with the beanbags as superheroes and the targets as buildings.

One of the more creative suggestions is to scale down the most violent play; that is, to turn it into a tabletop activity. Most of the television characters are available commercially in a variety of sizes from dolls to matchbox-scale figures, just right for tabletop play. When children are sitting at a table, the running and crashing bodies cease to be a problem. Pretending, after all, can take place anywhere. Again, teachers must control the types of characters and their props brought into the classroom. Use of guns, swords, and other weapons should be discouraged and substitutes found. (See Figure 11.9.)

Children need to talk about the superheroes they like, what powers they have, and how they use these powers. Help them create new superheroes who have powers that solve problems without using violence. Hoffman's (2004) book for teachers, *Magic Capes, Amazing Powers: Transforming Superhero Play in the Classroom*, gives other suggestions for helping children create positive superheroes.

Prosocial Superheroes

Superhero play can be welcomed into the classroom these days if it is combined with kindness and caring. De-Souza and Radell (2011) say that the timing of its introduction is important. It is optimum when the children show signs of self-regulation and are ready to begin building social skills. They decided not to read aloud books or show pictures of superheroes so the children would not have preconceived notions of what superheroes were like. They began by asking the children what things superheroes do and how superheroes could be identified. They focused on the words *kind, caring,* and *helpful*.

The children talked about saving people, finding your pet, helping you, cleaning up toys, saving birds, and saving cats like firemen do. They all wanted to wear capes

Figure 11.10 Prosocial
Superhero Books

- ***The Amazing Adventures of Bumblebee Boy*** (Soman & Davis, 2011)
- ***Do Super Heroes Have Teddy Bears?*** (Coyle, 2012)
- ***Ladybug Girl and the Bug Squad*** (Soman & Davis, 2011)

and also use props like long sticks for wands, belts, old wristwatches (without batteries), magnifying glasses, toy cell phones, flashlights, sunglasses, goggles, binoculars, crowns, hats, and visors. These they kept in a prop box in the dramatic play center.

Children took turns playing superheroes during the free-choice period. Sometimes they remained "in character" for the rest of the day. They kept busy rescuing each other (and the teacher when she played), their stuffed animal toys, jumping off large building blocks, flying around the classroom, pushing toy fire engines around the block buildings, and holding their capes over their faces to become invisible. The teachers decided that allowing young children to explore the possibilities of heroism while feeling safe and not intimidating others is both healthy and fun. Once they got started on their own, they liked hearing stories about good superheroes. (See Figure 11.10.)

The Amazing Adventures of Bumblebee Boy (Soman & Davis, 2011) from the Ladybug Girl series is a story featuring Bumblebee Boy with his purple cape and mask and his little brother Owen, who wants to play, too. The book is a great lead-in to a discussion of turn-taking and cooperation. How would your children respond to Bumblebee Boy's dilemma?

Do Super Heroes Have Teddy Bears? (Coyle, 2012) has a question on every other page that this little boy superhero has to answer. All the action takes place around his home with his sister and teddy bear. They all tie on capes and climb a tree to save the animals below. What a space ship they build out of cartons and tape! Just what your children will want to do. Be ready.

Ladybug Girl and the Bug Squad (Soman & Davis, 2011) has the Bug Squad meeting at Lulu's (Ladybug Girl's) house, all in their superhero costumes: Lulu in red wings and boots with black polka dots, Sam as Bumblebee Boy, Marley as Dragonfly Girl, and Kiki as Butterfly Girl. Can your children use these ideas for their own superhero costumes? This book can lead in to dramatic play scenarios your children can create in their own costumes.

Group Play

Group play comes into its own when children reach age 4. When they first get together, however, it often degenerates, like superhero play, into a wild sort of activity without plot or dialogue, almost a regression from children's previous role-playing. This wildness seems to be a natural progression in their learning to get along with one another. The establishment and recognition of dominance is often dealt with in such "rough-and-tumble play." Children also develop coping skills as they focus on the sometimes aggressive actions and reactions of peers. Out of these interactions comes a sense of common group purpose that sets the stage for the more organized play to follow.

Teachers can help by redirecting the energy of wild play into the exciting, dan-ger-packed themes that 4-year-olds favor. Doctor play, always a favorite, can involve taking sick or injured patients to the hospital in an ambulance with a loud siren. One teacher found her children needed help organizing and elaborating on their ambu-lance plot. Some of the children were running around the room making loud siren noises. The teacher suggested they build an ambulance out of large hollow blocks. Now what could they do? This time, the teacher decided to scaffold the play by playing a role herself. A running record of an observation of the very active 4-year-old Jessica includes the following:

Jessica runs to climber, climbs up & sits on top. Teacher tries to involve children in dramatic play; suggests they use climber as their hospital. They are building an ambulance out of large blocks. Jessica climbs down & begins stacking blocks one on top of the other. Then sits & watches others taping paper plates colored yellow on front to use as headlights. She picks up plate & tapes it to rear of ambulance. Runs to table to get felt-tip marker. "I want the yellow marker. Lots of yellow." She gets marker. "What am I gonna write on? I want to color something. I'll color the wheels black." Jessica drops yellow marker and picks up black one. She colors in back paper plate wheel with marker. "I want to color something yellow." Teacher suggests steering wheel. She does it. She runs & climbs into block ambulance. "I'm the driver." She uses her plate as steering wheel. "I wanna be the patient." Jessica gets up and lies down in middle of ambulance. She gets carried to "hospital" by teacher & other children. She lies by the climber & pretends to be sick, moaning & groaning. Other children leave, but she stays. Then she gets up & runs to table where teacher is helping children to make doctor bags. Teacher asks her what name she wants on her bag. She answers, "I want to be a nurse, not a doctor." Teacher asks what tools a nurse uses. She answers, "Nurses help, they don't use tools. Doctors use tools." Teacher asks, "What does your mother use when you are sick?" She answers, "I don't know." Jessica takes bag & runs back to ambulance with bag on arm, smiling. She yells, "Lisa, lay down, you're the patient." Jessica sits in front seat & drives ambulance using paper plate steering wheel. She hops up again & runs to teacher, asking her to be the doctor. She jumps up & down, urging the teacher to hurry. "Hurry, we're ready," she repeats. Teacher comes & helps carry Lisa to hospital.

The teacher noted that more children participated in this particular role play than any others she had witnessed. An ambulance had gone by on the street out-side earlier in the morning, siren blaring, and the children who saw it were excited but alarmed. This event prompted their building of the block ambulance, but the teacher's own participation in the play clearly stimulated the extra number of children to become involved. The teacher's idea for extending the play by helping the children make doctor bags added immensely to the drama. The running record, however, caught 4-year-old Jessica just as she normally acted, always on the run.

Jessica's stereotypical answers about doctors is also typical of this age. Gender roles seem to become more rigid, with girls insisting on playing the mother, waitress, or teacher, while boys often want to play father, driver, policeman, or superhero.

Same-gender groups form about this time, with girls' play becoming more relaxed and verbal, and boys' play faster paced and more aggressive.

Block play, for instance, may get out of hand with 4-year-olds. It sometimes disintegrates into throwing when adults are not around, or even when they are. Try to change the violent direction of the block play by giving players a new task involving excitement or mystery: "Where is the mysterious tunnel I saw on the floor this morning, boys? What, you didn't see it? I'm surprised. I thought you had X-ray vision. I could see it right through the rug. You don't believe me? Well, maybe if you make your own tunnel, you'll be able to see the mystery tunnel, too. Jeff, you and Lorenzo know how to build tunnels. Maybe you could make a mystery tunnel at one end of the rug, and Jesse and Tyrone could make a tunnel at the other end. What will happen if the tunnels come together, I wonder?"

If you observe that individual children who are 4 years old have not started playing with exciting, danger-packed themes, it may be that they are less mature than the others. How do they compare with other 4-year-olds in motor skills, for instance? Obviously, it is not appropriate to push such children into something they are not interested in. Provide them with many opportunities to engage in play themes of their own interests. You will know what some of these are from your observations and conversations with such youngsters.

The themes that 4-year-olds use in their pretending are many of the same ones they used at age 3, only much expanded. The youngsters still enjoy playing house. Both boys and girls take roles in the housekeeping corner. Doll play now includes dressing as well as undressing, but the central action usually involves putting the doll to bed. Many girls of this age prefer playing with little girl dolls rather than baby dolls. Play with dollhouses, however, is still too detailed to hold the interest of most 4-year-olds. Even block structures are not played with as much as they will be played with at age 5. At age 4, the pretending takes place during the process of building, rather than with the finished product afterward.

Doctor play is at its peak at age 4, and it will seldom be as popular again. All kinds of themes involving community helpers are used, especially after a visit by a community helper or a field trip to a work site. Superheroes are popular, especially television characters. Monsters sometimes appear, but they are still a bit too scary for most 4-year-olds to handle.

The pretend play of older 4- and 5-year-olds is characterized by the elaborate nature of the drama, no matter whether the theme is a common one or an invented adventure. Five-year-olds add all kinds of details through their dialogue, dress-up, props, and imaginations. Their play gets so involved, in fact, that it even carries over from one day to the next. The players remember where they left off the day before and can start right in again.

There is much more talk during pretend play, as well, because 5-year-olds have a better command of the language. With their improved language skills, they clarify ideas and talk out problems. Concerns about sickness, accidents, and death are dealt with more realistically in the imaginative play of 5-year-olds. Although the youngsters like to use props, those with a high level of fantasy can pretend without props.

Five-year-olds like to build big buildings and then play inside the structures. Imaginative play is at its height just before and during this period. After children

These boys are pretending to be astronauts flying to the moon.

enter first grade and games with rules become the norm, make-believe play begins to wane. It is not at all prevalent among children much after age 7.

By about age 7, a cognitive change that allows more abstract thinking has taken place within the child. What happens to pretending? We speculate that it does not disappear at all but becomes a part of the inner self to be tapped by adults in daydreaming as well as in generating creative ideas. Adults who experienced a rich fantasy life as children may be the fortunate possessors of the skill to play around with ideas in their heads, just as they did with props and toys as children in preschool.

As you observe the children in your classroom on the checklist items, you may want to make a list of the themes the children are using in their play. What can you do to help them add more themes to this list? Put out more props? Read more stories? Help the children make more costumes? Take children on more field trips so they will have additional real experiences to draw from? All of these activities are good ideas. Try them and see how your children respond.

If You Have Not Checked This Item: Some Helpful Ideas

■ Have Big Building Supplies

Four- and 5-year-olds like to build big structures to play in. Have the youngsters use hollow wooden blocks if possible. Or bring in wooden packing crates you get from a wholesaler. Cardboard cartons, plastic milk carton carriers, scrap boards, and lumber can be used for building pretend huts, forts, houses, boats, race cars, and fire engines. Play houses also can be purchased commercially, made out of pup tents, made by covering a card table with a blanket, or by hanging sheets over lines strung in a corner of the room.

OBSERVING, RECORDING, AND INTERPRETING DRAMATIC PLAY SKILLS

Running records are one of the best recording tools for observing children in dramatic play. They give the observer the opportunity to record childen's dialogue, interactions, and use of props. Information from the running record on 3-year-old Sherry can be transferred to the checklist in Figure 11.11. This information shows Sherry as a mature player in this imaginative role. The only blank on her checklist ("Uses exciting, danger-packed themes") is more typically observed in a 4-year-old, especially a boy. Table 11.1, which describes the ages and stages of pretend play, can help you interpret your findings.

Because imaginative play is an area of strength and confidence for Sherry, her teacher should consider using a dramatic play activity to help Sherry in a checklist area that needs strengthening. For example, Sherry has shown little development in the area of written language. Perhaps she could make a sign for the grocery store or pretend to write out a grocery list of things to buy in mock writing. All children's development is interrelated. We should remember to use strengths from other areas of a child's development when we design an individual plan to strengthen a child's particular needs.

---

9. Dramatic Play Skills

Item	Evidence	Dates
_____ Does pretend play by herself	Seldom plays by herself	3/12
__X__ Assigns roles or takes assigned roles	Took role as daughter but tried to change it	3/12
__X__ Needs particular props to do pretend play	Uses real bags in grocery store	3/12
__X__ Takes on characteristics & actions related to role	Gets groceries off shelf, puts in bag, goes to cashier	3/12
__X__ Uses language for creating & sustaining plot	Talked constantly in store	3/12
_____ Enacts exciting, danger-packed themes	No	

Figure 11.11   Checklist Observation for Sherry

Table 11.1   Development of Dramatic Play Skills

Age	Child's Pretend Play Behavior
1–2	Goes through pretend routines of eating or other brief actions
2–3	Replays fragments of everyday experience (e.g., putting baby to bed) Repeats routine over and over in ritualistic manner Uses realistic props (if uses props at all)
3–4	Insists often on particular props in order to play May have imaginary playmate at home Uses family, doll play, hospital, cars, trains, planes, and firefighting themes Assigns roles or takes assigned roles May switch roles without warning
4–5	Uses exciting, danger-packed themes (e.g., superheroes, shooting, and running) Is more flexible about taking assigned roles during play Uses more rigid gender roles (e.g., girls as mother, waitress, or teacher; boys as father, doctor, or police officer)
5–6	Plays more with dollhouse, block structure Includes many more details, much dialogue Carries play over from one day to next sometimes Plays more in groups of same gender

LEARNING ACTIVITIES

1. Use the Dramatic Play section of the Child Development Checklist as a screening tool to observe all the children in your classroom. Compare the checkmarks for children who score well in the sequences of Dramatic Play with their checks in Social Competence and Language Development. What conclusions can you draw from this comparison?

2. Choose a child with high-level skills in imagination and make a running record of him or her on three different days. What new details did you learn about the child's pretending?

3. Look over the activities suggested and choose one for use with one of the children who needs help in this area. Carry out the activity you have prescribed for the child. Record the results.

4. Take a field trip with your children to a site of interest where they can see and meet people at work in a special field. Put out appropriate props in your dramatic play and/or block areas after you return and record the kinds of pretend play that take place. Is the play any different from what went on previously? If so, how do you account for this?

5. Carry out one of the book activities from this chapter with one child or a small group and see if it stimulates any pretending. How could you extend this pretending?

6. Read one of the superhero books as a lead-in to pretending activities with superheroes who help people. Have a small group at a time create their own superheroes and props. Do running records of any scenarios they enact.

SUGGESTED READINGS

Berkowitz, D. (2011). Oral storytelling: Building community through dialogue, engagement, and problem solving. *Young Children, 66*(2), 38–40.

Frost, J. L., Wortham, S. C., & Reifel, S. (2012). *Play and child development* (4th ed.). Upper Saddle River, NJ: Pearson.

Leong, D. J., & Bodrova, E. (2012). Assessing and scaffolding make-believe play. *Young Children, 67*(1), 28–34.

Miles, L. R. (2009). The general store: Reflections on children at play. *Young Children, 64*(4), 36–41.

Stephens, K. (2009), Imaginative play during childhood: Required for reaching full potential. *Exchange, 31*(2), 53–56.

CHILDREN'S BOOKS

Andrews, J., & Hamilton, E. W. (2011). *The very fairy princess takes the stage.* New York: Little, Brown.

Beaty, A. (2008). *Doctor Ted.* New York: Margaret K. McElderry Books.

Beaumont, K. (2011). *Shoe-la-la!* New York: Scholastic.*

Bergman, M. (2007). *Oliver who would not sleep.* New York: Arthur A. Levine.

Best, C. (2006). *Sally Jean, the bicycle queen.* New York: Melanie Kroupa Books.

Breen, S. (2008). *Violet the pilot.* New York: Dial.

Coyle, C. L. (2012). *Do super heroes have teddy bears?* Lanham, MD: Taylor Trade Publishers.

Fosberry, J. (2012). *Isabella, girl on the go.* Naperville, IL: Sourcebooks Jabberwocky.

Hoffman, M. (1991). *Amazing Grace.* New York: Dial.*

London, J. (2010). *I'm a truck driver.* New York: Henry Holt.

Maclean, C. K. (2002). *Even fire fighters hug their moms.* New York: Dutton.

McNulty, F. (2005). *If you decide to go to the Moon.* New York: Scholastic.

Pullen, Z. (2008). *Friday my Radio Flyer flew.* New York: Simon & Schuster.

Richmond, M. (2006). *My shoes take me where I want to go.* Minneapolis, MN: Marianne Richmond Studios.

Soman, D., & Davis, J. (2011). *The amazing adventures of Bumblebee Boy.* New York: Dial.

Soman, D., & Davis, J. (2011). *Ladybug Girl and the Bug Squad.* New York: Dial.

Soman, D., & Davis, J. (2008). *Ladybug Girl.* New York: Dial.

Soto, G. (1993). *Too many tamales.* New York: Putnam's.*

Tafolla, C. (2008). *What can you do with a rebozo?* Berkeley, CA: Tricycle Press.*

Vernick, A. (2012). *So you want to be a rock star.* New York: Walker.

Ward, M. (2005). *Mike and the bike.* Salt Lake City, UT: Cookie Jar Publishing.

WEB SITES

International Play Association
www.ipausa.org

Ladybug
www.ladybugmagickids.com

Mother Goose Programs
www.mothergooseprograms.com

NAEYC
www.naeyc.org

National Association for Bilingual Education
www.nabe.org

Strong National Museum of Play
www.museumofplay.org

*Multicultural

Sharing Observational Data with Families

In this chapter you will learn to:

____ Involve families in their children's programs

____ Use the Child Development Checklist with parents

____ Make parents partners

____ Share observation results with parents

____ Plan for the child based on checklist results

____ Have parent observation in the classroom

____ Develop collaborative portfolios

INVOLVING FAMILIES IN THEIR CHILDREN'S PROGRAMS

Early childhood programs have long recognized the importance of involving families in their children's education and development. Many preschools, Head

Starts, child care centers, prekindergartens, and kindergartens have done everything in their power to bring parents and other family members closer to their children's programs. They schedule family visits, parent conferences, family newsletters, family volunteer opportunities, and parenting workshops. Involving families in their children's programs is important. Kersey and Masterson (2009) found several strong reasons for involving families. Children whose parents are involved make friends more easily; they are more successful learners; they stay in school longer; and they are more motivated to succeed.

When parents (or primary caregivers) are closely involved with their children's preschool programs, children tend to bloom. Youngsters seem to understand that if Mom and Dad and Grandma know the teacher and the teacher knows Mom and Dad and Grandma, whatever happens in school is all right. All these significant people will be talking about the child, making sure she is on the right track, and helping her along whenever she needs help.

Nevertheless, it is not always easy or even possible to involve all parents in their children's education. Most parents work and thus find it difficult to participate or even visit their children's programs. Some parents find it uncomfortable to visit schools where they may feel out of their element. Others think it is the teaching staff's responsibility to care for their children during the school day, while they take responsibility for their children at home. Is there some way all parents can be convinced to become involved?

Focusing on the Child

A most effective approach that many preschools have adopted is to focus on the child, not on the program. Both family members and teachers want the child to succeed in school and develop to his greatest ability. Thus it is the child who should concern them first and foremost. What is he or she like? What are his interests at home and at school? What is his favorite activity? How does he get along with others? What would his parents like to see him accomplish this year?

As teachers begin to develop a closer rapport with family members, they can communicate their own strong interest in this child as an individual and their commitment to helping him grow and develop in preschool. They can describe to the parents how they start by determining where each child in their class stands in his or her development. Then they are able to plan activities to meet each child's needs.

They can talk about finding out how the child handles herself in a strange, new environment; how he deals with stressful situations; whether he plays with others; and whether he can share and take turns. They can discuss what they want to know about the child's physical development; whether he can climb, draw with crayons, cut with scissors, build with blocks, sort things that are alike, ask questions; whether he ever tries to write or if he likes to paint; and what kind of pretending he does. At the same time, they will be asking the parents what kinds of things they would like to know about their child in school.

Such discussions need to be completely informal and not overwhelming to the parents. There is no need to pursue a long list of questions or child developmental

CHILD DEVELOPMENT CHECKLIST

Name _____ Andy _____   **Observer** _____ Laura _____

Program _____ Head Start _____   **Dates** _____ 10/5, 10/7, 10/8 _____

Directions:

Put an **X** for items you see the child perform regularly. Put an **N** for items where there is no opportunity to observe. Leave all other items blank.

Item	Evidence	Dates
1. Self-Esteem		
_____ Separates from primary caregiver without difficulty	Upset when mother leaves	10/5
__X__ Develops a secure attachment with teacher	Yes	10/7
__X__ Completes a task successfully	Builds road for race car	10/5
__X__ Makes activity choices without teacher's help	Goes directly to activity area of his choice	10/5
__X__ Stands up for own rights	Will not let others take his toys; pushes, grabs, hits	10/7
__X__ Displays enthusiasm about doing things for self	Hums a tune while he plays	10/5
2. Emotional Competence		10/7
__X__ Releases stressful feelings in appropriate manner	Lets teacher hold him	
_____ Expresses anger in words rather than negative actions	Sometimes hits or pushes when angry No words	10/7
__X__ Can be calmed in frightening situations		
__X__ Shows fondness, affection, love toward others	Lets teacher hold him	10/7
__X__ Shows interest, excitement in classroom activities	Goes around trying out things	10/7
__X__ Smiles, seems happy much of the time	Always smiles & hums	10/5
3. Social Competence		
__X__ Plays by self with own toys/materials	Pretends with small cars, people	10/5
__X__ Plays parallel to others with similar toys/materials	Plays with cars next to others	10/5
_____ Plays with others in group play	Not often	10/8
_____ Gains access to ongoing play in positive manner	Does not try to gain access	10/8
_____ Makes friends with other children	Has no close friends	10/8
_____ Resolves play conflict in positive manner	Sometimes hits or pushes	10/7

Figure 12.1   Child Development Checklist

needs. Play it by ear. The idea is for the parents and family members to understand your personal concern for their child, as well as the specific activities the children will be involved with.

Such conversations with parents should also let them know that the teaching staff spends time looking at their child individually to determine where she stands developmentally, and that the staff has found that the best way to determine where the child stands is to observe her by using an observation checklist to guide them.

USING THE CHILD DEVELOPMENT CHECKLIST WITH PARENTS

When the time is right, give the parents a blank copy of the first three sections of the Child Development Checklist: Self-Esteem, Emotional Competence, and Social Competence (see Figure 12.1). The entire checklist consists of nine sections on three pages. Because this is a bit overwhelming for parents in the beginning, it is better for them to work with three sections on one page at a time. Tell them that this is what you and the teaching staff use as a guide to look at where their child is developmentally.

Do not just hand them the checklist without any explanation. It is most important that you go through the first three sections of the checklist together. Have them look at the items with you. Together you might start with the items under Self-Esteem. Because their child has already been in school for a week, you can tell them what you have been able to check off so far in this area.

Are they surprised? Did they realize how well their child was able to adjust? If this is not the case, you may have to ease their concern that their child doesn't "make activity choices without teacher's help" yet, but that he no longer clings to the parent as he did during the first days.

Tell parents you use this checklist as a guide to look at where their child stands developmentally.

Make sure that the parents understand the purpose of the Child Development Checklist: that it is not a test, but an observational guide to child development, which helps you look for the areas of strength that each child possesses and note the areas that need strengthening. No two children develop the same, nor should we expect them to. Such a checklist helps you note where each child stands and how to help each one progress in specific areas of his or her development.

Then take the next important step in involving parents/primary caregivers in their child's program: Ask them if they would like to try observing their child at home in this same way. Tell them that you realize they have been observing their child for many years. Using the checklist, they will have a chance to record what they have seen. If they agree, tell them you would like to give them a blank copy of the first three checklist sections to put somewhere handy in their house—maybe on the refrigerator door—where they can check off items they see their children performing and write down the evidence. Point out that this can be very helpful to them as they note the different items their children accomplish.

It can also help you, if they care to share any of their observations. But make sure they understand that this is not a test, and that you are not asking them to do this observing for you, but rather for them to learn more about their child in the same way you do in the classroom.

This is a big step for parents to take and a completely different type of activity than most are used to. Be sure you have established some sort of rapport with the parents before you present this idea. Make sure they understand that looking at their child by using a checklist should be interesting and fun for them, not a chore, and that it can be "for their eyes only."

They do not need to share it with you or anyone else unless they feel like it. Tell them that there is no "right" or "wrong" involved. Whatever they see, they can check off. If they feel like writing down what the child does under "evidence," so much the better. Keyser (2006) found that parents are most interested in child development information when it directly relates to what is happening with their child.

If parents agree with the idea and begin to observe and record their children's behavior at home, they will often want to share what they find with you because: (a) they will want to know what certain items mean, and (b) they will want you to know how their children are doing at home. Point out that they may not be able to check off some of the items because this checklist is designed to look at classroom activities rather than those in the home, and because children cannot be expected to accomplish every item all at once. Development occurs over time, with maturity and practice.

✓ MAKING PARENTS PARTNERS

What you are doing by giving parents the Child Development Checklist is much more important than merely involving them in observing their child more closely. You are *making them a part of the teaching team*. You are helping to *make them partners in the education of their children*. One of the reasons most parents often feel so ill at ease with teachers is because they occupy such a different role. Teachers are the professionals and they, the parents, are not. In fact, most parent involvement programs focus on helping parents learn more effective ways of working with their children (Kasting, 1994). There is nothing wrong with that focus. It does, however, imply a superior position for the teacher, and therefore an inferior role for the parent. The teacher has information to impart that the parent needs to learn. Kasting also found that parents and teachers rarely collaborate on the basis of mutual respect and shared responsibilities.

Parents who accept the role of observing their child just as the teacher does can begin to change the balance of this relationship. They can, in fact, begin to become educational partners in their own right. After all, they know more about their child than anyone else. Their influence on their child is more powerful than anyone else's. But they need to be aware of the significance of child behavior. By observing their child using the Child Development Checklist just as the teacher does, they learn what is important to look for. As they discuss this information with the teacher, they learn what these findings mean.

Parents who have become child observers get really excited about what they are discovering. After all, their child is of great importance to them. Now they are beginning to unlock the "secrets" of child development that teachers seem to know, but they do not. As they share their findings with the teacher and the teacher responds by sharing his or her observations with the parent, their relationship changes dramatically. They become true partners in education.

Arlene Kasting, coordinator of the Child Study Centre of the University of British Columbia in Vancouver, Canada, reports on the model parent involvement program using shared observations that her center has developed: Addressing the Needs of Children Through Observation and Response (ANCHOR). In this project, parents and educators together observe children's activities in the preschool classroom either on closed-circuit television or in video sequences. The parent and educator relationships are defined as partnerships.

Although this was a group observation of a classroom of children containing the parents' own children, and not a home observation of a single child as discussed here, the resulting relationships of parents and educators changed for the better. Parents were not treated as persons needing instruction by educators, but as full partners in the observation process. Their input about their child's behavior was valued as a key to understanding the child. Parents felt most respected when teachers listened attentively to their remarks and asked them to give even more details. Suddenly they, not the teachers, had become the source of information.

There is another important outcome for parents who do shared observations. They develop a trust in the program because the program has entrusted them enough to give them a professional's checklist and believe they are capable of using it. And, of course, they are. They may need your help in explaining what some of the items mean and your suggestions for looking at one section of the checklist at a time, but you should be just as happy as they are about their new role.

As they look at the checklist items and realize that the teaching staff is also using these same items to observe their child, parents are brought much closer to the

Figure 12.2   Parent Outcomes
of Shared Observations

Parents:

- Felt more respected
- Developed trust in the program
- Developed trust in themselves
- Became more secure in their decisions about their child
- Became more confident about themselves as parents
- Developed observation skills
- Learned new ideas about child development

teaching team because they feel a part of it. They may feel shy at first about sharing their filled-out checklist with you. Of course, this is not called for, but most parents want to tell you what they observed for specific items. Teachers should not ask to see the checklist they have given the parents. It is theirs (parents) to keep. This helps parents realize their observations are truly "for their eyes only," to be shared only if they want, but not handed back. This information should be extremely helpful to you when you discover how the child behaves in his home setting—which is often quite different from school behavior.

Conversing about checklist results makes family involvement a real joy for all parties concerned. You and the families will develop reciprocal trust, and you will look forward to hearing from families about their children. Benefits the parents enjoy are listed in Figure 12.2. Still, you may wonder how you will have the time to keep up such a running commentary with the many families of your children.

✓ SHARING OBSERVATION RESULTS WITH PARENTS

Communication Methods

Programs that have tried using the checklist as described report a wide number of program/family communication methods. (See Figure 12.3.) The last method listed seems the most popular. Teachers run off many copies of the checklist and send out one sheet (showing three sections) at a time to share with parents what they (teach-

Figure 12.3   Communication
Methods Between Teachers
and Parents

- Exchanging information at drop-off or pick-up times
- Phone conversations
- E-mail or Web sites
- Parent conferences or home visits
- Informal breakfast meetings before work
- Information sent home with child and returned

ers) have checked off on a particular day. Parents are free to write on the same sheet what they have observed and return it with the child the next day, if they choose to do this. Teachers are the ones who need to initiate the use of the checklist, but once parents become involved, they often reply without prompting.

All of the written communications are kept in a child's folder or portfolio along with a record of phone or e-mail messages and a summary of conference results. Once a checklist has been completed by a parent or teacher, the program can invite the parent to help interpret the results and discuss how they can be used in the program or at home.

Interpreting Checklist Results

When the teacher of one preschool class, Laura, had finished observing 4-year-old Andy on three different days for about half an hour each time using the first three sections of the Child Development Checklist, she had a much better idea of Andy's strengths as well as areas that needed strengthening. Her observation confirmed for her that Andy did not usually play with other children, but seemed to prefer doing things on his own. He seemed independent, making choices on his own, defending his rights, being enthusiastic about the things he chose to do, and smiling much of the time. She chuckled about his characteristic tuneless humming as he busily engaged himself in block building or racing little cars. She always could tell where Andy was by his humming.

Being happy and smiling were especially important clues to Laura about the overall status of any child in her class. Andy demonstrated few inappropriate behaviors, in fact, except for his quick temper when other children tried to interfere with his activities. Laura had tried to get him to express his feelings in words, but without success. Now she noted that he really did not speak all that much. Somehow she had missed that important aspect of his behavior because he seemed content, and possibly because he did vocalize—if only to hum.

Now she noted that although she could understand him if she listened closely, his speaking skills were not at the level of the other 4-year-olds. She began to wonder if this might be the reason he did not get involved in playing with the others. Because dialogue is so much a part of make-believe play, a child without verbal skills might feel out of place, she reasoned. She couldn't wait to hear from Andy's mother to see what she had observed on the same items.

Laura had a strong hunch that Andy was highly creative. Watching him build elaborate roads for his race car and talk to himself as he played alone or parallel to the others, she saw that he seemed to invent all kinds of situations for the miniature people he played with. She noted that creativity certainly did not show up in his arts skills, but she reasoned that his difficulty with small-motor skills might have caused him to avoid painting, drawing, and cutting.

In looking for areas of strength, Laura picked out his enthusiasm and good self-concept. She thought he was a bright boy who used his cognitive ability in playing by himself, rather than joining others. Areas needing strengthening so far included language; controlling his temper; and especially playing with the other children.

Sharing Checklist Results with Staff

To confirm her interpretation of the Child Development Checklist observation, Laura shared the results with the two other classroom workers. They were also surprised about how little Andy verbalized, and that they too hadn't picked up this fact previously. What had they missed about the other children, they wondered? The teacher assistants were fascinated by the details Laura had gleaned in a very short time and by the way she had interpreted Andy's inability to join in group play.

Sharing Checklist Results with Parents

Laura contacted Andy's mother and found that she, too, had completed her first three sections of the checklist. Because she worked all day, she wondered if Laura could meet her at a nearby restaurant for coffee after work in the late afternoon. Andy's grandmother would pick up Andy and take him home. When they met for this first conference, both teacher and parent were full of enthusiasm for what they had discovered. Laura confided to the mother that she always looked for a child's areas of strength first because that gave her the best picture of the youngster. Also she used the child's areas of strength to help him improve in areas where he might need strengthening.

This was the first time that the teacher, Laura, had exchanged observations with a parent. Usually she was the one who had done the observing and the parent was on the other side of the fence waiting for her pronouncement. This way was so much better, Laura decided. First of all, she did not have to explain the observation method to the mother. Also, she found herself waiting with anticipation to hear how the mother's observations compared with her own, and whether they would shed any more light on Andy's development. They did not exchange checklists, only read off their observations for each item.

The mother was a bit hesitant at first because she didn't know if she had done it right. But Laura assured her that everyone felt that way at first, even the classroom staff. She said all the items on the list were positive, so you couldn't really go wrong. If you saw the behavior, you checked the item. If you didn't see the behavior, you left the item blank. If there was no opportunity to observe, then you wrote N.

The main difference between the two checklists turned out to be Andy's play with others. At home he played with his brothers, shared and took turns, and did not express aggression. The mother had written in brief explanations under the evidence section, just as Laura had.

Andy's mother was very interested in Laura's observations. She told Laura that Andy was the youngest of three brothers and did not seem to have the language skills at age 4 that his older brothers had shown. She also noted that Andy preferred to play alone, but she had never considered that his speaking skills might be the cause.

She told how all three boys invented their own games because they had few toys at home. As a single working parent, she had all she could do to provide for their food and clothing needs. When Laura suggested that Andy might like to do water play at home in the sink with empty containers, his mother thought this was a fine idea and also a way that he might help her with the dishes (!). She was especially pleased that Laura thought Andy was bright on the basis of his little car games. She asked Laura for other ideas for making up games with household throwaway items. Laura offered to lend her a booklet full of ideas. When Laura also mentioned that the center liked to send home picture books for parents to read to their children, Andy's mother said she thought Andy would like this a lot. Laura sent home **Hot Rod Hamster** (Lord, 2010), a rhyming story of animals building cars and racing them.

PLANNING FOR THE CHILD BASED ON CHECKLIST RESULTS

Laura was delighted with the outcome of the meeting. She had never had a parent conference go so well. Andy's mother wanted to continue observing, so Laura gave her the next three sections of the checklist to use: Physical Development, Cognitive Development, and Spoken Language. Then she took out a Learning Prescription form for Andy and showed the parent how she and the staff used it to plan for a child based on checklist results. Laura noted that it was really too early to fill out a prescription for Andy based on only a few observations. But she would make a temporary one so that the mother could see how it worked. This time she and the parent filled it in with areas of strength and confidence that they had detected from their checklist observations (see Figure 12.4). Then they discussed areas needing strengthening for Andy and recorded them on the form as well.

LEARNING PRESCRIPTION

Name _____Andy_____ **Age** ___4___ **Date** _10/12_

Areas of Strength and Confidence

1. _Good self-concept; happy; helpful_

2. _____

3. _____

Areas Needing Strengthening

1. _Learn to play with others_

2. _Speak instead of hitting_

3. _____

Activities to Help

1. _Interest Andy in playing cars with a partner_

2. _Interest Andy in reading a car book with a partner_

3. _____

Figure 12.4   Learning Prescription for Andy

Andy finds friends to play cars with.

Next they considered ways to use Andy's strengths to help him improve in learning to play with others and develop better speaking skills. Laura, of course, had a better idea of what activities were available in the classroom, but she listened closely to the mother's suggestions. She told Laura that Andy did know how to play with others just as he did with his brothers, so they both agreed to list as the first activity "Interest Andy in playing cars with a partner." Talking with and helping one other child should not be so difficult for Andy in the beginning as playing with a large group.

The staff decided to try these activities for a week and then discuss the results at their planning session the following week. They had already planned to do similar observations for each of the children as time permitted and to involve their parents in observing at home.

Ongoing Observations by Parents and Staff

Parents had been introduced to the idea of observing at home when they enrolled their children for preschool at the beginning of the year. They were told it was voluntary on their part, but that many parents found it to be an interesting way to learn more about their child. Not all the parents in Andy's class agreed to observe at first. But during the first parent meeting when they heard other parents talking about how much they liked the activity, several more agreed to try it. They were impressed with how the teachers were asking them to find out important things about their child by doing the same thing the teachers did. Only parents who had trouble speaking English were still unsure of what to do. Laura suggested maybe one of their neighbors with children in the program could help them, and maybe their older children could translate the checklist for them.

When home observing really caught on among most of the parents, Laura kept several copies of the text *Observing Development of the Young Child* on hand for the parents to borrow so they could read about the items they were observing. The classroom staff of three adults took turns observing each child at three different times during a week, and soon had completed a checklist for all 18 of the children.

✓ PARENT OBSERVATION IN THE CLASSROOM

Keyser (2006) found that some teachers invite family members to observe with them in the classroom. A short observation of children building a spaceship out of blocks can offer families a chance to understand children's ability to learn many things simultaneously: teamwork, science, physics, and physical coordination. Short interactions like these can enable parents to learn important child development information.

Laura decided to try it with her parents. She invited parents one by one to observe in the classroom using their own copy of the checklist. Although those who worked all day felt they could not participate, Andy's mother got so caught up with observing her child that she arranged for time off to visit the classroom and observe once a month.

Laura decided that shared observations like this gave her the most successful family involvement program she had ever known. The parents were so pleased with what they learned about their children and the program that they wanted to continue it next year when their children attended a public school kindergarten. Laura agreed to meet with a group of the parents and school personnel to make the arrangements.

Some parents found time to do a checklist observation in the classroom.

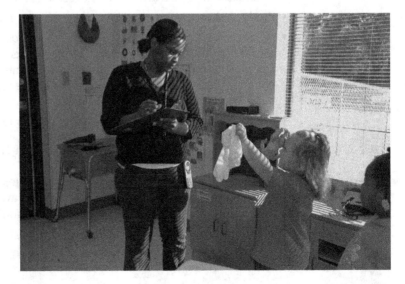

✓ DEVELOPING COLLABORATIVE PORTFOLIOS

Teachers who have initiated shared observing with parents sometimes carry this sharing one step further. They ask parents to participate in helping to create a portfolio for their children. Many early childhood educators have adopted the portfolio as one of the best methods for assessing the ongoing development of each child. A portfolio is an individual, systematic collection of documents that reflects what a child does in a classroom. It is usually assembled by both teachers and children and emphasizes both process and product in the documents collected. The missing piece in such portfolios is the parents' contributions.

Teachers of preschool children have long participated in collecting youngsters' artwork and writing scribbles. So have parents. Bringing together such a collection allows all involved to provide a more in-depth assessment of children's development. Kingore (2008) notes that portfolios are a particularly effective means of increasing productive communication among parents, a teacher, and a child through the concrete evidence the selected products provide (p. 83).

The items that go into a child's portfolio depend upon what kind of portfolio it is and how it will be used. In this text we focus on child development viewed by observation. Thus, items that illustrate a child's development in the nine areas discussed here are especially important. Such items will be used in parent conferences and teacher planning sessions. Suggestions for these items from school and home might include the following:

Appropriate Portfolio Items (Evidence of Development)

- Products representing each area of child development
- Products related to learning objectives of teachers and parents
- Products showing ongoing development over time
- A variety of products including teachers' records, parents' records, photos, artwork, writing scribbles, lists of favorite books, completed checklists, anecdotal records, communications from parents, recordings of child's speech, children's journals, children's narratives of science experiments, field trips, made-up stories
- Products that can be used for meaningful communication with parents and other professionals
- Products that can be used for making curricular decisions

Mindes (2011) finds that observational notes form the foundation of the portfolio. A collection of children's paintings, drawings, and stories shows what children know. You should also include lists of books read, transcripts of discussions with children about their work, and other products collected throughout the year.

Why Make Portfolios?

Before beginning to create a portfolio for each child, it should be clearly understood what the portfolios will be used for, thus what work samples will best illustrate this use. In the case of collaborative developmental portfolios assembled by teachers and parents who are doing checklist observations of each child, the portfolios will be used to support observational data throughout the year about the children's development in the areas of self-esteem, emotional competence, social competence, physical development, cognitive development, spoken language, emergent writing and reading skills, art, music, and dance skills, and dramatic play skills (all areas of the Child Development Checklist). They will also help the staff plan activities to help children needing special skill strengthening. Some possible items from school and home for each of these areas include those listed in Figure 12.5. The completed Child Development Checklist should also be included.

Once the collecting has started, teachers must date each piece of evidence and include who chose it and what it represents. For example, a sheet of art scribbles may represent emergent drawing or it may be emergent writing, depending on how it is done and what the child has to say about it. Take time once a week for children to go through their weekly art and select one or two items to be included. Art or other material sent from home needs to be dated and included with an explanation about it.

What Form Should a Portfolio Take?

The portfolios Jackman (2012) examined came in many shapes and sizes, such as expanding accordion-type files, file folders, cardboard boxes, scrapbooks, three-ring binders, or unused pizza boxes.

How a portfolio will be used also helps determine its size and method of material storage. Portfolios should not be too large or heavy if you intend to carry them to meetings with staff, parents, or other professionals. A large three-ring binder with transparent sheets and pockets is the choice for some collectors. An accordion file folder is used by others. Labeled dividers or index cards may also be necessary for handy data retrieval.

How Can Portfolios Be Used?

As the school year progresses, teachers need to add to each child's portfolio regularly. This can happen if portfolios are actually used in an appropriate fashion, and not just as storage containers for children's products. They should be the focus for classroom planning sessions and team meetings with parents. Whether or not parents contribute, they will want to view and discuss the contents of their child's portfolio from time to time.

Self-esteem
- Photos of child showing classroom accomplishments
- Anecdotal records about child from classroom activities
- Parents' communications about how child feels about him/herself

Emotional competence
- Teacher's records of how child handles stress, anger, joy
- Photo of books child likes to hear when under stress
- Finger painting child made to relieve stress
- Note from parent about what upsets child at home

Social competence
- Photos of child playing with others
- List of dramatic play themes child participated in
- Photo showing child playing with children in home yard

Physical development
- Photo of child on school climber
- Photo of large hollow block building child helped build
- Parent communication on child climbing stairs up and down

Cognitive development
- Pictures with colors child identified
- Computer printout of child's number game
- Photo and description of domino game child played at home

Spoken language
- Audio recording of story child tells
- List of songs child sings
- Photo and written dialogue of child on phone at home

Emergent writing and reading skills
- Page of scribbles child makes
- List of books parent has read to child
- Sign-up sheet with name child prints
- Letter child wrote to grandmother

Art, music, and dance skills
- Samples of easel painting at start and end of school
- Audio recording of child singing
- Photo of play dough creation

Dramatic play skills
- Hand puppet child made for pretending
- Video of child in dramatic play role
- Running record of child pretending with small figures
- Photo of child in pirate costume child made at home

Figure 12.5   Portfolio Items from School and Home

When you know the strengths of a child through observation, you can meet his needs.

During team meetings and parent sessions, the focus should be on what you have observed the child accomplishing and what you have interpreted her present needs to be. Activities for helping the child to accomplish these needs can be discussed and planned as the child's products and observational data are shared. Both parents and staff can contribute to such discussions in a meaningful way as they learn how children develop through the observations they have done.

Observing the development of young children is thus a teaching as well as a learning technique that should benefit all of its participants—teachers, college students, children, and families—because it outlines each aspect of child development carefully, objectively, and positively. Promoting development in young children works best when it focuses on assessing their strengths. When you know the strengths of each child in every aspect of development, you will be able to design your program to meet an individual's needs as the children in your classroom work and play together creating their own unique selves.

LEARNING ACTIVITIES

1. Discuss with members of the classroom team how parents have been involved in your program in past years and whether this method has been successful. Record in some detail what the role of the different team members has been and what they have to say about it.

2. Discuss with team members the possibility of using the Child Development Checklist with the parents for home observation of their child. Record their comments about this idea, both negative and positive. Make a list of what you believe parents could learn from such observations.

3. Discuss with team members the idea of making parents partners. Why would they want to do it? How can they do it? What would be accomplished if this happened?

4. Make a plan for sharing observation results with a parent. How will you use the Child Development Checklist? How would you expect parents to use it?

5. Based on the observation results of one child, how would you make plans for that child? How could the child's parents be involved?

6. How would you arrange for parents to observe their child in the classroom? What would be the benefits for parents, teachers, and the child?

7. Put together a portfolio for one of the children. Involve other team members, the child, and parents. What did each of them contribute? How did you organize the portfolio? How will you use it?

SUGGESTED READINGS

Beining, K. H. (2011). Family-teacher partnerships: An early childhood contract for success. *Childhood Education, 87*–95.

Garretson, S., & Thompson, J. (2012). Family literacy packs: Engaging teachers, families, and young children in quality activities to promote partnerships for learning. *Young Children, 67*(3), 104–110.

McWilliams, S., Maldonado-Mancebo, T., Szczepaniak, P. S., & Jones, J. (2011). Supporting Native Indian preschoolers and their families. *Young Children, 66*(6), 34–41.

Mitchell, S., Foulger, T. S., & Wetzel, K. (2009). Ten tips for involving families through Internet-based communication. *Young Children, 64*(5), 46–49.

Morrison, J. W., Storey, P., & Zhang, C. (2011). Accessible family involvement in early child hood programs. *Dimensions of Early Childhood, 39*(3), 21–25.

Souto-Manning, M. (2010). Family involvement: Challenges to consider, strengths to build on. *Young Children, 65*(2), 82–88.

CHILDREN'S BOOKS

Lord, C. (2010). *Hot rod hamster.* New York: Scholastic Press.

WEB SITES

Center on School, Family, and Community Partnerships
www.csos.jhu.edu

Harvard Family Research Project
www.hfrp.org/family-involvement

National Council for Community and Education Partnerships
www.edpartnerships.org

The SEDL National Center for Family and Community Connections with Schools
www.sedl.org/connections

Teachers and Families
www.teachersandfamilies.com

References

Adams, E. J. (2011). Teaching children to name their feelings. *Young Children, 66*(3), 66–67.

Ahola, D., & Kovacik, A. (2007). *Observing and understanding child development: A child study manual.* Clifton Park, NY: Delmar/Cengage.

Ainsworth, M. D. S., Bell, S. M., & Stayton, D. J. (1974). Infant-mother attachment and social development: "Socialization" as a product of reciprocal responsiveness to signals. In M. M. Richards (Ed.), *The integration of the child into the social world.* London: Cambridge University Press.

Alanis, I. (2011). Learning from each other: Bilingual pairs in dual-language classrooms. *Dimensions of Early Childhood, 39*(1), 21–27.

Alexander, N. P. (2005). "Tell her I'll pay with a credit card." *Dimensions of Early Childhood, 33*(1), 30–31.

Althouse, R., Johnson, M. H., & Mitchell, S. T. (2003). *The colors of learning: Integrating the visual arts into the early childhood curriculum.* New York: Teachers College Press.

Anderson, G. T., & Robinson, C. C. (2006). Rethinking the dynamics of young children's social play. *Dimensions of Early Childhood, 34*(1), 11–16.

Balaban, N. (2006). *Everyday goodbyes: Starting school and early care: A guide to the separation process.* New York: Teachers College Press.

Beaty, J. J. (2012). *Skills for preschool teachers* (9th ed.). Upper Saddle River, NJ: Pearson.

Beaty, J. J., & Pratt, L. (2011). *Early literacy in preschool and kindergarten* (3rd ed.). Upper Saddle River, NJ: Pearson.

Bentzen, W. R. (2005). *Seeing young children: A guide to observing and recording behavior* (5th ed.). Clifton Park, NY: Cengage.

Berkowitz, D. (2011). Oral storytelling: Building community through dialogue, engagement, and problem solving. *Young Children, 66*(2), 36–40.

Bowlby, J. (1969). *Attachment and loss: Vol. 1. Attachment.* New York: Basic Books.

Bowling, H. J., & Rogers, S. (2001). The value of healing in education. *Young Children, 56*(2), 79–81.

Burman, L. (2009). *Are you listening? Fostering conversations that help young children learn.* St. Paul, MN: Redleaf Press.

Burton, S. J., & Edwards, L. C. (2006). Creative play: Building connections with children who are learning English. *Dimensions of Early Childhood, 34*(2), 3–8.

Charlesworth, R., & Lind, K. K. (2007). *Math & science for young children* (5th ed.). Clifton Park, NY: Cengage.

Christie, J. F., Enz, B. J., & Vukelich, C. (2011). *Teaching language and literacy: Preschool through the elementary grades.* Upper Saddle River, NJ: Pearson.

Clay, M. J. (1991). *Becoming literate.* Portsmouth, NH: Heinemann.

Clements, R., & Schneider, S. L. (2006). *Movement-based learning.* Reston, VA: National Association for Sport & Physical Education.

Copley, J. B. (2000). *The young child and mathematics.* Washington, DC: National Association for the Education of Young Children.

Corsaro, W. A. (2003). *We're friends, right? Inside kids' culture.* Washington, DC: Joseph Henry Press.

Curenton, S. M. (2006). Oral storytelling: A cultural art that promotes school readiness. *Young Children, 61*(5), 78–87.

Davidson, J. I. (1996). *Emergent literacy and dramatic play in early education.* Belmont, CA: Cengage.

Deerwester, K. (2007). Teaching about feelings. *Children Our Concern, 30*(1), 7.

De la Roche, E. (1996). Snowflakes are not all the same: Developing meaningful art experiences for young children. *Young Children, 51*(2), 82–83.

De-Souza, D., & Radell, J. (2011). Superheroes: An opportunity for prosocial play. *Young Children, 66*(4), 26–31.

Dickinson, D. K., & Tabors, P. O. (2002). Fostering language and literacy in classrooms and homes. *Young Children, 57*(2), 10–18.

Dodge, D. T., Heroman, C., Charles, J., & Maioca, J. (2004). Beyond outcomes: How ongoing assessment supports children's learning and leads to meaningful curriculum. *Young Children, 59*(1), 20–28.

Ellis, S. M., Gallingane, C., & Kemple, K. M. (2006). Fiction, fables, & fairytales: Children's books can support friendships. *Dimensions of Early Childhood, 34*(3), 28–35.

Feeney, S., & Moravcik, E. (2005). Children's literature: A window to understanding self and others. *Young Children, 60*(5), 20–27.

Ferreiro, E., & Teberosky, A. (1982). *Literacy before schooling.* Portsmouth, NH: Heinemann.

Fox, J. E., & Schirrmacher, R. (2012). *Art and creative development for young children* (7th ed.). Belmont, CA: Cengage.

Freeman, R. (2012). Elements of a musical foundation for children. *Exchange, 34*(1), 46–48.

Frost, J. L., Wortham, S. C., & Reifel, S. (2012). *Play and child development* (4th ed.). Upper Saddle River, NJ: Pearson.

Gallagher, K. C. (2005). Brain research and early childhood development: A primer for developmentally appropriate practice. *Young Children, 60*(4), 12–20.

Geist, K., Geist, E. A., & Kuznik, K. (2012). The patterns of music: Young children learning mathematics through beat, rhythm, and melody. *Young Children, 67*(1), 74–79.

Gellens, S. (2005). Integrate movement to enhance children's brain development. *Dimensions of Early Childhood, 53*(3), 14–21.

Good, L. (2009). *Teaching and learning with digital photography.* Thousand Oaks, CA: Corwin Press.

Gould, E., Kaplan, R., & Wilson, T. (2012). Changing lives and developing brains. *Exhange, 34*(1), 49–51.

Gronlund, G., & James, M. (2008). *Focused observations: How to observe children for assessment and curriculum planning.* St. Paul, MN: Redleaf Press.

Hatcher, B., & Petty, K. (2004). Seeing is believing: Visible thought in dramatic play. *Young Children, 59*(6), 79–82.

Helm, J. H., Beneke, S., & Steinheimer, K. (2007). *Windows on learning: Documenting young children's work.* New York: Teachers College Press.

Hoffman, E. (2004). *Magic capes, amazing powers: Transforming superhero play in the classroom.* St. Paul, MN: Redleaf Press.

Huffman, J. M., & Fortenberry, C. (2011). Helping preschoolers prepare for writing: Developing fine motor skills. *Young Children, 66*(5), 100–103.

Hunter, R. (2000). Some thoughts about sitting still. *Young Children, 55*(3), 50.

Isbell, R. T., & Raines, S. C. (2007). *Creativity and the arts with young children.* Belmont, CA: Cengage.

Isenberg, J. P., & Jalongo, M. R. (2010). *Creative thinking and arts-based learning: Preschool through fourth grade* (5th ed.). Upper Saddle River, NJ: Pearson.

Izard, C. E. (1977). *Human emotions.* New York: Plenum.

Jackman, H. L. (2012). *Early education curriculum: A child's connection to the world.* (5th ed.). Belmont, CA: Wadsworth/Cengage.

Jalongo, M. R. (2008). *Learning to listen, listening to learn.* Washington, DC: National Association for the Education of Young Children.

Kalmar, K. (2008). Let's give children something to talk about! Oral language and preschool literacy. *Young Children, 63*(1), 88–92.

Kasting, A. (1994). Respect, responsibility and reciprocity: The 3 Rs of parent involvement. *Childhood Education, 70*(3), 146–150.

Kellogg, R. (1970). *Analyzing children's art.* Palo Alto, CA: National Press Books.

Kemple, K. M.(1991). Preschool children's peer acceptance and social interaction. *Young Children, 46*(5), 37–54.

Kersey, K. C., & Masterson, M. L. (2009). Teachers connecting with families: In the best interest of children. *Young Children, 64*(5), 34–38.

Keyser, J. (2006). *From parents to partners: Building a family-centered childhood program.* St. Paul, MN: Redleaf Press.

Kingore, B. (2008). *Developing portfolios for authentic assessment, pre-K–3.* Thousand Oaks, CA; Corwin Press.

Koster, J. B. (2012). *Growing artists: Teaching the arts to young children* (5th ed.). Belmont, CA: Wadsworth/Cengage.

Leong, D. J., & Bodrova, E. (2012). Assessing and scaffolding make-believe play. *Young Children, 67*(1), 28–34.

Lucos, L. (2007–2008). The pain of attachment—"You have to put a little wedge in there." *Childhood Education, 84*(2), 85–90.

Martin, S. (1994). *Take a look: Observation and portfolio assessment in early childhood:* Menlo Park, CA: Addison-Wesley.

Matthews, K. (2012). Singing ourselves: How to offer music to children. *Exchange, 34*(1), 52–54.

McAfee, O., & Leong, D. J. (2011). *Assessing and guiding young children's development and learning* (5th ed.). Upper Saddle River, NJ: Pearson.

McDevitt, T. M., & Ormrod, J. E. (2004). *Child development: Educating and working with children and adolescents*. Upper Saddle River, NJ: Merrill/Pearson.

McGhee, P. E. (2005). The importance of nurturing children's sense of humor. *Children Our Concern, 28*(1), 16–17.

McLean, M., Wolery, M., & Bailey, D. B. (2004). *Assessing infants and preschoolers with special needs*. Upper Saddle River, NJ: Merrill/Prentice Hall.

McNair, J. C. (2007). Say my name, say my name! Using children's names to enhance early literacy. *Young Children, 62*(5), 84–89.

McVicker, C. J. (2007). Young readers respond: The importance of child participation in emerging literacy. *Young Children, 62*(3), 18–22.

Meisels, S. J., & Atkins-Burnett, S. (2005). *Developmental screening in early childhood: A guide*. Washington, DC: NAEYC.

Mindes, G. (2011). *Assessing young children* (4th ed.). Upper Saddle River, NJ: Pearson.

Mooney, C. B. (2000). *Theories of childhood: An introduction to Dewey, Montessori, Erikson, Piaget, and Vygotsky*. St. Paul, MN: Redleaf Press.

National Association for the Education of Young Children. (2004). Where we stand on curriculum, assessment, and program evaluation. *Young Children, 59*(1), 51–53.

National Association for the Education of Young Children. (2005). *Early childhood program standards and accreditation criteria*. Washington, DC: Author.

National Association for the Education of Young Children. (2009). *NAEYC standards for early childhood professional preparation*. Washington, DC. Author.

Newman, J., & Kranowitz, C. (2012). Moving experiences that will last a lifetime. *Exchange, 34*(1), 97–99.

Nilsen, B.A. (2010). *Week by week: Plans for documenting children's development* (5th ed.). Belmont, CA: Wadsworth/Cengage.

Nissen, H., & Hawkins, C. J. (2010). Promoting emotional competence in the preschool classroom. *Childhood Education, 86*(4), 255–259.

Palmer, H. (2001). The music, movement, and learning connection. *Young Children, 56*(5), 13–17.

Parten, M. B. (1932). Social participation among preschool children. *Journal of Abnormal and Social Psychology, 27*, 243–369.

Piaget, J. (1976). *The child and reality*. New York: Penguin Books.

Pica, R. (2011). Why preschoolers need physical education. *Young Children, 66*(2), 56–57.

Puckett, M. B., Black, J. K., Wittmer, D. S., & Petersen, S. H. (2009). *The young child: Development from prebirth through age eight* (4th ed.). Upper Saddle River, NJ: Merrill/Pearson.

Ramsey, P. G. (1987). *Teaching and learning in a diverse world: Multicultural education for young children*. New York: Teachers College Press.

Ramsey, P. B. (1991). *Making friends in school: Promoting peer relationships in early childhood*. New York: Teachers College Press.

Riley, D., San Juan, R. R., Klinker, J., & Ramminger, A. (2008). *Social & emotional development: Connecting science and practice in early childhood settings*. St. Paul, MN: Redleaf Press.

Rodrigues, D., Smith-Carter, L., & Voytechi, K. (2007). Freedom from social isolation for young children with disabilities. *Childhood Education, 83*(5), 316–321.

Romero, I. (1999). Individual assessment procedures with preschool children. In E. V. Nuttall, I. Romero, & J. Kalesnik (Eds.), *Assessing and screening preschoolers' psychological and educational dimensions*. Boston: Allyn & Bacon.

Roskos, K.A., & Christie, J. F. (2001). On not pushing too hard: A few cautionary remarks about linking literacy and play. *Young Children, 56*(3), 64–66.

Rushton, S., & Juola-Rushton, A. (2011). Linking brain principles to high-quality early childhood education. *Exchange, 33*(6), 8–11.

Salmon, A. K. (2010). Tools to enhance young children's thinking. *Young Children 65*(5), 26–31.

Sanders, S. W. (2006). Physically active for life: Eight essential motor skills for all children. *Dimensions of Early Childhood, 34*(1), 3–10.

Seefeldt, C. (1998). Assessing young children. In C. Seefeldt & A. Galper (Eds.), *Continuing issues in early childhood education* (pp. 314–338). Columbus, OH: Pearson.

Seefeldt, C., & Wasik, B. A. (2006). *Early education: Three-, four-, and five-year-olds go to school*. Columbus, OH: Pearson.

Shagoury, R. E. (2009). *Raising writers: Understanding and nurturing young children's writing development*. Upper Saddle River, NJ: Pearson.

Shore, R. (2005). The magic of music. *Children Our Concern, 20*(2), 4–7.

Shore, R., & Strasser, J. (2006). Music for their minds. *Young Children, 61*(2), 62–67.

Singer, D. G., & Singer, J. L. (1977). *Partners in play: A step-by-step guide to imaginative play in children*. New York: HarperCollins.

Smilansky, S. (1968). *The effects of sociodramatic play on disadvantaged preschool children*. New York: John Wiley & Co.

Snyder, S. (1997). Developing music intelligence: Why and how. *Early Childhood Education Journal, 24*(3), 165–171.

Solter, A. (1992). Understanding tears and tantrums. *Young Children, 47*(4), 64–58.

Sprenger, M. (2008). *The developing brain: Birth to age eight*. Thousand Oaks, CA: Corwin Press.

Staley, L., & Portman, R. A. (2000). Red Rover, Red Rover, it's time to move over! *Young Children, 55*(1), 67–72.

Strickland, D. C., & Schickedanz, J. A. (2009). *Learning about print in preschool: Working with letters, words, and beginning links with phonemic awareness*. Newark, DE: International Reading Association.

Tabors, P. O. (2008). *One child, two languages*. Baltimore, MD: Brookes Publishing. (CD-ROM included)

Temple, C. A., Nathan, R. G., & Burns, N. A. (1993). *The beginnings of writing*. Boston: Allyn & Bacon.

Van Hoorn, J., Nourot, P., Scales, B., & Alward, K. (2003). *Play at the center of the curriculum* (3rd ed.). Upper Saddle River, NJ: Merrill/Pearson.

Vygoksky, L. S. (1962). *Thought and language.* Cambridge, MA: Harvard University Press.

Vygotsky, L. S. (1976). Play and its role in the mental development of the child. In J. S. Bruner, A. Jolly, & K. Sylva (Eds.), *Play: Its role in development and evolution.* New York: Basic Books.

Ward, G., & Dahlmeier, C. (2011). Rediscovering joyfulness. *Young Children, 66*(6), 94–98.

Wenner, G. (1988). *Predictive validity of three preschool developmental assessment instruments for the academic performance of kindergarten students.* State University of New York at Buffalo. (ERIC Document #331 867, EDRS)

Willis, J. (2007). Brain-based teaching strategies for improving students' memory, learning, and test-taking success. *Childhood Education, 83*(5), 310–315.

Wortham, S. C. (2012). *Assessment in early childhood education* (6th ed.). Upper Saddle River, NJ: Pearson.

Index of Children's Books

Chapter 12
Sharing Observational Data with Families

---

*Multicultural characters.

Index

Page numbers followed by "f" indicate figure; and those followed by "t" indicate table.